PLATO'S
SYMPOSIUM

PLATO'S
SYMPOSIUM

STANLEY ROSEN

SECOND EDITION

Yale University Press
New Haven and London

Set in Baskerville types.
Printed in the United States of America by
Edwards Brothers, Inc., Ann Arbor, Michigan.

Library of Congress Cataloging-in-Publication Data

Rosen, Stanley, 1929–
  Plato's Symposium.

  Bibliography: p.
  Includes index.
  1. Plato. Symposium. 2. Socrates. 3. Love.
I. Title.
B385.R6 1987   184   86–23342
ISBN 0–300–03954–9
    0–300–03762–7 (pbk. : alk. paper)

10 9 8 7 6 5 4 3 2 1

This book is dedicated to my parents

ACKNOWLEDGMENTS

Part of this book was written during my tenure as post-doctoral research fellow at the Humanities Research Institute of the University of Wisconsin in the academic year 1963–64. I want to thank the staff and visitors of the Institute for helping to make my stay there a fruitful and happy one.

I have received financial assistance toward the writing of this book from the Central Fund for Research of Pennsylvania State University, and am grateful to those concerned.

I owe much to the students of the four graduate seminars in which I first developed some of the material now included in this book.

To an anonymous reader of the Yale University Press, my thanks for a set of careful criticisms, which proved to be unusually helpful in the revision of the first version of my manuscript.

I have been especially fortunate in my editor, Mrs. Jane Isay, and want to acknowledge her loyal support and many contributions toward the improvement of the structure and content of this work.

My greatest debt is to my teacher, Leo Strauss, who taught me how to read Plato, and whose own interpretation of the *Symposium* will soon be published. In the deepest sense of the phrase, Professor Strauss is the πατὴρ τοῦ ἐμοῦ λόγου.

To the teachers, friends, and colleagues who helped me in various ways, too many to name them all, my deepest thanks.

This manuscript was completed, in its revised form, in June 1966.

STANLEY ROSEN

State College, Pennsylvania
August 21, 1967

CONTENTS

NOTE TO THE SECOND EDITION

Capital letters used as superscripts indicate notes to the revised edition. These notes begin on page 329.

PREFACE TO THE SECOND EDITION

The original edition (1968) of the following study of Plato's *Symposium* has been out of print for a number of years. Nevertheless, the book has continued to find its audience, and in response to numerous requests, author and editors have decided that a new edition is appropriate. The question naturally arises as to the form such a new edition should take. One should not disown one's children, but surely the removal of errors and the inclusion of supplementary material is allowed, as I have done here in preparing the new edition for publication.

I believe it is fair to say that this study appeared originally some twenty years too soon. When it was first submitted to Yale University Press, Platonic scholarship was dominated by the odd but largely unquestioned combination of philological historicism and analytical philosophy. On the one hand it was held that Plato must be read as a child of his time, in accord with the hermeneutical presuppositions of the *Geisteswissenschaften*. On the other hand, the actual text was disregarded by the leading English-speaking scholars, who sought to extricate from the literary ornamentation a set of arguments, to be checked for logical validity by translation into the languages of formal set theory and predicate calculus or informal natural language semantics. The philological Plato was transformed into the value of a historical function; the analytical Plato was reduced to the status of an inept predecessor of Frege, Russell, Wittgenstein, and Ryle.

The preceding observation is not intended as an exhaustive account of the style of Plato scholarship dominant in 1968. It is intended merely to remind the reader that the procedures followed in my own study, rightly or wrongly, for better or for worse, were in sharp conflict with the methodological opinions of the majority of English-speaking specialists in Plato. The same must be said for some, perhaps many, of my substantive conclusions. As a result, the book excited considerable controversy, written and unwritten, a large part of which was due to my "heterodoxy." It cannot be said that today (in 1986) the situation in Platonic scholarship is entirely different. But there are gratifying signs of change in the recent approach to Plato. These changes stem largely, but of course not entirely, from the complex of interrelated concerns jointly known as "post-modernism" and especially perhaps from the correlative and pervasive interest in hermeneutics.

One cannot help noticing that what previously passed for philological and philosophical orthodoxy is now in the process of very deep change, not to say dissolution (or deconstruction). We have reached a period in which the obscure philosophical revolution initiated in the first instance by Heidegger, himself a disciple of Nietzsche, has been disseminated throughout the more accessible strata of the *Geisteswissenschaften*. Indeed, the stain of post-modernism has infected, not merely the suburbs, but the inner precincts of professional analytical philosophy. It seems that, like it or not, we are all, if not assassins, certainly amateur deconstructors. In the language of the Academy, the epoch of post-analytical philosophy has arrived. Interestingly enough, the new state of affairs has left the dominant school of professional Plato scholars largely unaffected. But their influence is now largely confined to their own circle. Plato has once more become available (if not necessarily accessible) to his intended audience: the intelligent and imaginative reader who is trying to reconsider the opinions of his day concerning human life as a whole.

It is not necessary to reject all the views of professional Plato scholarship, nor to accept the cardinal tenets of post-modernist hermeneutics, to believe that the new interest in Plato is a good thing. In particular, I have been gratified by the attention paid to my study of the *Symposium* by recent students of literary and rhetorical theory. I allow myself the hope that, in light of the contemporary broadening of perspectives, a book that in a still more imperfect form has had its continuous audience will now be subjected to a wider scrutiny, and hence to a fruitful criticism that goes deeper than the counting of misprints or the expression of outrage at heterodoxy.

In what has been said thus far, I do not wish to give the impression that the original version of my study was either entirely unappreciated or subjected to nothing but unfair criticism. Both these inferences would be false. The book, as I have said, was controversial; this means that it enjoyed praise as well as suffering condemnation. My reservations on this score are directed to the not inconsiderable element of what can only be called ressentiment that my study brought into play. To say nothing of this issue would be to falsify the historical record and to acquiesce in the obfuscation of issues which I believe to be of independent importance. But it is not necessary to say more than this.

Let me turn instead to a brief consideration of the major criticisms addressed to the original version of my study, as well as to an indication of how I have tried to take these into account in preparing the new edition. If I am not mistaken, these criticisms were as follows: (1) too many misprints and slips on small points; (2) faulty translations engendering subjective interpretations; (3) excessive allegiance to the hermeneutics of Leo Strauss; (4) inadequate allegiance to the hermeneutics of Leo Strauss; (5) too much reading into the text of what is not there; (6) over-interpretation, that is, too much attention to what is there in the text; (7) the aforementioned radical unorthodoxy, for example, in attributing to Plato the intention to criticize Socrates' defective Eros.

This table of categories no doubt contains overlapping items, but I have decided to record them individually in order not to miss any major objections. The first criticism is well taken. I shall not attempt to mitigate the blame by citing reasons for the blemishes in the first edition. Suffice it to say that every effort has been made to remove them in the pre-

sent text. In one instance, on pages 240–44, a conflation of
distinct but adjacent Platonic passages led to a more extensive
incoherence, and it was necessary to rewrite most of the original text. The ensuing interpretation is accordingly coherent
but not substantially different. On the second point, I have
found one outright error in translation, again involving no
major issues of interpretation, and have corrected it (on page
12, covering *Symposium* 172a2–6). There are a number of
instances in which I translate literally, and hence clumsily, in
order to bring out a point of substance raised by Plato's diction. But these are not, I think, mistranslations, and they are
each explicitly identified. It should also be mentioned here
that there are a number of Greek words with a wide range
of senses, from which I have sometimes selected one that will
not be approved by every reader. But this is a difficulty intrinsic to the task of interpreting texts in foreign languages,
and not a peculiarity of my study.

The third and fourth criticisms may be taken together. I
will not conceal from the reader that I regard them as *niais-
eries*. They are of interest only as a sign of the extreme controversy engendered by the mention of the name "Leo
Strauss," let alone by his work, which, in my opinion, has
been imperfectly understood by the majority of his admirers
and detractors alike. I am happy to repeat here that my interest in Plato was first stimulated by Strauss and that I have
undoubtedly learned more than it would be possible to acknowledge in detail from his many seminars and published
works. I am myself not much interested in the question of
whether or in what degree I am a "Straussian" any more than
I am interested in whether or in what degree my critics are
"Fregeans" or "Wittgensteinians." I do not write for those
who are incapable of judging a work on its merits but who
instead engage in the hermeneutics of sloganeering. It should
be said, however, that Strauss would have objected to much
that is contained in the following pages. Likewise, I am in
considerable disagreement with Strauss's general program.
Those who are curious about this point may be asked to see

my forthcoming book, *Hermeneutics as Politics,* to be published by the Oxford University Press in the fall of 1987.

The fifth and sixth criticisms also form a natural pair, although they stimulate a somewhat different response. It would be easy but inconclusive for me to deny the validity of the first of these objections. Each reader must come to an independent decision on the basis of a close scrutiny of my interpretation together with that of Plato's text. In my view, the sixth criticism is more reasonable and certainly more interesting. It is a moot question whether the ideal of making sense of every element of a Platonic dialogue (espoused, incidentally, by Leo Strauss) is a sound one. Once more, however, the question cannot be profitably discussed in abstraction from a detailed attempt to enact the principle. There are no generally valid hermeneutical rules concerning how carefully authors may write. One should not overlook the possibility that many of those who are quick to cry "overinterpretation" have mistaken obtuseness for sobriety. If one must err, it is better to err in the direction of trying to understand too much than too little. With very few exceptions, and these on small points qualifying rather as slips, I have not been able to follow the fifth and sixth criticisms in the new edition. This is of course not to say that I am entirely justified in this restraint. But even if I had found more to excise, the principle of not disowning one's children would have forbidden wholesale revision.

The seventh criticism has only to be stated to show itself as untenable. The reason for its untenability, however, leads us into very deep waters and, in a very specific sense, into the study of the *Symposium.* Philosophy is by its nature radically unorthodox. It has nothing to do with fashionable academic schools. The distinction is well illustrated by the birth of Platonism in widely divergent schools almost immediately following Plato's death. Apparently Plato's own disciples could not agree about his teaching; hence it was necessary to invent professional philosophy. The professor, as it were, enters the stage as the philosopher is exiting, or at least disappearing behind his masks. We should all have the honesty to admit this instead of cudgeling each other with preferred methodologies. In any case, I do not offer my reading of the *Symposium* as flawless, nor as constituting the only legitimate approach. Were I writing this study today, it would take a different form in many respects. Nevertheless, the basic interpretation continues to strike me as worthy of consideration; sustained by the welcome support of some of its previous readers, I hereby reprint it, corrected and supplemented by a small number of appendices but in all essentials the same as the original.

I close this section of my preface with a general observation. For many years I accepted the judgment of my critics, although not in the same sense as that in which it was offered, on the sole point that my study was highly unorthodox. After perusing the original text with considerable care, I believe that the criticism (and so too the compliment) is unwarranted. To be sure, my study differs substantially from most other commentaries. But that in itself says little. My own sharpest criticism of the original study is that it is too cautious, too sober, yes, too close to the text. However, one cannot go beyond the text (if at all) until one has studied it minutely. At least I have done that. Those who disagree with me but cannot say the same are hereby invited to reconsider my results in their improved form and to replace them with an entirely superior interpretation. When this is done, I will be grateful and pleased. Meanwhile, I pass to more substantive considerations.

In *Götzen-Dämmerung,* Nietzsche offers a description of *great style* that is unusually helpful for the reader of the *Symposium*:

The highest feeling of power and security comes to expression in that which has *great style*. The power that needs no further proof, that disdains to please, that answers severely, that feels no testimony about itself, that lives without consciousness of the opposition to which it gives rise, that rests in itself, fatalistic, a law among laws: *that* speaks of itself as great style.[1]

When properly understood, every phrase in this description applies to the *Symposium*. Philosophy has been, if not subordinated to, then transmuted by poetry. The dialogue contains almost no trace of Socratic conversation in the usual sense (except for a brief interlude with Agathon). Instead, there is a mythical account of a youthful conversation with a woman, a stranger, a prophetess: Diotima. And even here the conversation is subordinated to Diotima's monologue. As if this were not enough, the drunken Alcibiades takes us into his bedroom to confess the attempted seduction of Socrates, a confession that plays a crucial role in his revelation of Socrates' unerotic nature. Those who insist upon being "pleased" by a Platonic dialogue have failed to assess properly the significance of these two conversations. As a youth, Socrates required an explanation of the work of Eros (206b1–6). As a mature man he is, according to Alcibiades, immune, if not to the charm of Eros, certainly to its power.

In his unjustly neglected study, *Socrates and Aristophanes*, Leo Strauss makes the following ambiguous remark on our topic:

> The only Platonic dialogue in which Aristopnanes occurs as a character or in which Socrates is presented as conversing with poets is devoted to Eros, and Socrates' doctrine is shown therein to be more profoundly erotic than Aristophanes' or any other poet's. If someone wishes, he might even say that Socrates' ascribing his doctrine to Diotima indicates that in an earlier stage of his life he did not properly appreciate Eros.[2]

---

1. *Götzen-Dämmerung, streifzüge eines Unzeitgemässen*, in *Nietzsche*, ed. K. Schlechta (Munich, 1954), par. 43.

2. *Socrates and Aristophanes* (New York, 1966), p. 173.

Surely one must wonder whether the doctrine of the mature Socrates is a doctrine of Eros, regardless of whether or
not it is more profound than that of the poets. According to
Diotima, the first step in the erotic ascent is to "head for
beautiful bodies; . . . one must love one body and generate
beautiful speeches therein" (210a4–b6). But apparently Socrates does not love bodies. It looks as though the testimony
of Alcibiades contradicts Socrates' claim to be a student of
Diotima. The assertion that it is unnecessary for the philosophical Eros to begin in accord with Diotima's instruction is
on the whole a gratuitous assumption, or one that contradicts
the general tenor of her teaching. And can we not agree that
love of the human body is an essential step in the understanding of the human soul? If Socrates is from the outset discon-
nected from human things, do not a great many puzzling
features of his behavior in the Platonic corpus become con-
siderably clearer, including the cruelty of so many of his in-
terrogations? To play with human beings is not incompatible
with wishing them well: so too humans take good care of their
toys and pet animals.

There is in Plato none of Nietzsche's nervous self-congrat-
ulation, so typical of late-modern decadence, that manifests
itself alternately as revelatory bombast and excessively refined
psychological analysis. The closest Plato comes to this is in
the speech of the drunken Alcibiades. Nietzsche, in violation
of his own canons of great style, is continually explaining
himself. In the dialogues, Plato never explains himself. Instead, he assigns to the drunken Alcibiades an explanation
of Socrates. Alcibiades is as close as Plato comes to the Dionysian intoxication of Zarathustra, just as Diotima is as close
as Plato comes to the prophetic revelations of Zarathustra. I
may be allowed the playful suggestion that the truth about
Socrates depends upon the correct integration of the testimony and in a sense of the personae, of Alcibiades and Diotima. It depends upon such an integration but is not, of
course, simply equivalent to it. The integration of Alcibiades
and Diotima would presumably be desired by neither. They

are not like sundered halves of a circular being who, as Aristophanes recounts in his speech, are driven by Eros to reunite. Perhaps there is no erotic reunion, no natural integration of opposites in a comprehensive explanation. As we shall see when we study it in detail, Aristophanes' speech tells us (if we did not already know) that erotic reunion suppresses logos; it does not produce it.

This line of reflection leads to the following suggestion: there is a radical discontinuity between Eros, an appetite of desire (ἐπιθυμία), and what are sometimes called the Platonic Ideas; the discontinuity cannot be bridged by logical discourse, but from one side one may catch glimpses of what lies on the other side. This suggestion is in fact confirmed quite directly by Socrates' great myth (attributed by him to the poet Stesichorus) in the *Phaedrus*: the "philosophical" souls catch intermittent glimpses of the hyperuranian beings, and throughout their ascent, they are silent.[3] In the *Symposium* the situation is somewhat different. Diotima tells us that the ascent toward the vision of beauty itself leads to the generation of philosophical speeches (210d4–e2) and the vision in turn to the production of true instances of virtue (211e4–212a7). She promises a μάθημα of beauty itself and a life in accordance with it, which we may fairly assume includes the production of beautiful speeches (211c1–d3). Philosophy is then in effect defined as the production of beautiful speeches about beauty. May we not infer that in the *Symposium*, as is appropriate for a conversation determined by the presence

3. See my forthcoming book, *Hermeneutics as Politics* (New York, 1987), chapter 3. David Lachterman has called my attention to *Republic* IX, 580D, in which Socrates says that each of the three parts of the soul has its particular ἐπιθυμία and ἀρχή. The ἐπιθυμίαι are those by which one learns, feels anger, and is appetitive (ἐπιθυμητικόν), respectively. But this passage is a continuation of the discussion of the tyrannical man, who is described as the erotic man par excellence (573B: τύραννος ὁ Ἔρως λέγεται; cf. 573D). It is true that, throughout this section of Book IX, Socrates associates characteristic ἐπιθυμίαι with each part of the soul. But he never associates ἔρως with any but the epithymetic part. On the other hand, the highest part of the soul is certainly associated with an ἐπιθυμία for learning, so that this is, if anything, contrary to the thesis of the *Symposium* that the desire for learning is erotic.

of poets, philosophy is defined as poetry? Or what comes to
the same thing, in the *Phaedrus*: poetry defines philosophy as
silent (and intermittent) vision.

Let us start again: πάλιν ἐξ ἀρχῆς, as Socrates would say.
What is the connection between Eros and poetry? One would
be tempted to reply that both are concerned with generating.
However, under careful scrutiny, this answer proves to be
insufficient. In the first place we need to distinguish between
the natural genesis of Eros and the artificial production of
poetry. Making children is not the same as constructing myths
or writing verses. Second, the Platonic testimony regarding
the relation between philosophical Eros and artificial or linguistic generating is ambiguous, even inconsistent, as we have
just observed. In the *Symposium,* there is an ambiguity about
the relation between love of the beautiful and love of the good
(which latter is defined in such a way as to relativize the distinction between beauty and ugliness; see my commentary on
pages 240 ff.). Furthermore, the vision of the beautiful itself
seems to have as a direct consequence, not speeches, but true
instances of virtue, or what one may fairly call a beautiful
soul. The generation of philosophical speeches is part of the
penultimate stage of the erotic ascent. But even if linguistic
generating were unambiguously associated in the *Symposium*
with the vision of beauty itself, the analogous passage in the
Phaedrus makes no reference to generating of any kind. Socrates' apparent equation there of writing with play and his
use of the sexual metaphor of sowing one's seed in the garden
of letters (276d1 ff.) could only be fully assessed once we
understand what Socrates means by *play*. Given the question
that has been raised concerning Socrates' own, possibly unerotic, or erotically defective nature, we can no longer simply
assume that his conversations, and hence his myths, are motivated by Eros. There is obviously a difference between Socrates and Plato with respect to writing. Are we to infer a
coordinate difference between the two with respect to Eros?
If the answer is yes, does this mean that the Platonic dialogues
are poems (seeds sown in the garden of letters)?

In Book X of the *Republic,* Socrates refers to a long-standing quarrel between philosophy and poetry (and on this point, one must also consider *Theaetetus* 152e1 ff., where Socrates refers to the army of those who believe that "all things are the offspring of flow and change," an army whose general is Homer). Since Socrates regularly associates himself with philosophy, it is widely assumed that the Platonic dialogues cannot be poems. But this is a non sequitur, and it flies in the face of the obvious. The *Sophist* and the *Parmenides* are as much dramas, and hence poems, as the *Symposium* and *Phaedrus.* Of course they may be poor dramas by the usual standards of theater. But that is another question, which leads to the further question *why* Plato wrote poor dramas. Why, for example, is half of the *Parmenides* devoted to the theatrically boring discussion of the one and the many? An outraged reader may be moved at this point in my exposition to interject, "But that is precisely the sign that the *Parmenides* is *not* a drama!" What then is it? Is it a treatise, like Book *Zeta* of Aristotle's *Metaphysics?* Obviously not. It is, despite our professorial expectations, a dramatic representation of young Socrates' encounter with Zeno and Parmenides. Something that looks to the professorial eye unmistakably like philosophical dialectic (or professorial shoptalk) constitutes the largest part of the dialogue. Therefore the professorial intellect concludes that the *Parmenides* is not poetry but philosophy. No thinking has been invested in coming to grips with Plato's intention. The professor has been hypnotized by the speeches within the play and therefore fails to notice, or to take seriously, that it is a play.

Let us be careful here. A drama "plays" at being real life. This fact is not altered by the content of the speeches assigned to the characters within the drama. To play at being real life, as we know from the discussion of images in dialogues like the *Sophist,* is to pretend to be what one is not. We may call the Platonic dialogues noble lies and cite Socrates' remark in the *Phaedrus* that "it is noble to strive after noble things, and to suffer whatever happens" as a consequence (274a8–b1).

This is sound procedure, but a lie remains a lie. The dialogues, like all dramatic poetry, are sophistical. It is often asserted that Plato's "official" criticism of the Sophists is unfair. This assertion is unfortunately not buttressed by reference to Plato's own "noble sophistry" (cf. *Sophist* 231b3 ff.). But to the professional philosopher, epistemology, and not the play, is the thing. To the extent that Plato is a Sophist— namely, a poet who generates changing images, not merely of eternity, but of the changing—he is to that extent himself a member of Homer's army. I say "to the extent that Plato is a Sophist," not that he is a Sophist *tout court*. As I have explained elsewhere in some detail, to the extent that the soul is sophistical, or if you prefer, a magician, and hence is continuously changing its form or perspective, so too must the philosopher be a Sophist or magician. By the same token, the need to produce changing images of eternity is that of accommodating to human perspective; it does not follow that eternity itself is an image (or nothing but an image of genesis).

Those who cannot bring themselves to entertain the thesis that Plato (no doubt intentionally) wrote poor dramas should consider the function of poetry. This function is made plain by Socrates within the dialogues. The task of poetry, as of the musical education in general, is to charm and to persuade the soul. There is no mathematical analysis of the personal soul (see *Phaedrus* 246a3–6). But even if there were, it would be useless for political as well as philosophical purposes without an antecedent musical paideia (see *Republic* III, 400d6– 10, 401a7–c9). In order to be indoctrinated in a beautiful or noble life, the soul must feed on beautiful speeches where visions of beauty itself are unavailable. Beauty reconciles us to life. But the philosopher must pay equal attention to the ugly (cf. *Sophist* 227a1 ff., *Parmenides* 130e1–3). The speeches about the one and the many, like those about the greatest genera and negation, are of course beautiful to the few persons who have acquired a specialized taste for this sort of thing; in the language of Eros, we may call them *perverts*. To the great generality of readers, and perhaps even to the perverts when they are not in the grip of their madness, such speeches are ugly. What is wanted by the cultivated Athenian, amusingly represented in the two dialogues on Eros by Phaedrus, are the speeches of Eryximachus and Lysias. To be sure, Phaedrus is temporarily charmed by the excessive (dare one say romantic, even vulgar?) erotic rhetoric of the Stesichorean myth, but this hardly testifies to the achievement of the highest poetic standards by that florid production.[4] In any case, as the direct sequel shows, the effect of the speech on Phaedrus is not to raise him up to the roof of the cosmos but to turn his thoughts to political rhetoric.

It is, then, not by chance that the many boring stretches in the Platonic dialogues are singled out by professional philosophers as alone worthy of their serious attention. Whether we evaluate this positively or negatively, nothing demonstrates so clearly the conflict between pure theoretical philosophy and human existence, or the soundness of Nietzsche's observation that art is worth more than the truth. To put this in another way, when Socrates says in the *Apology* (38a5–6) that the unexamined life is not worth living for mortals, what he means by the examined life, so far as the well-to-do young Athenians who seek his company are concerned, is his demonstration that those who believe themselves to be wise are not. The young enjoy this demonstration because it is not unpleasant (33b9 ff.). Socrates explains the significance of his public activity as follows: he has introduced no positive doctrines and was never anyone's teacher (33a5). Instead, he makes philosophy publicly acceptable, that is to say, pleasant to the young, by refuting the positive doctrines of others. We should note here that if Socrates is telling the truth in the *Apology*, then Plato was not his pupil. In this case there is no reason to assume that Plato shared Socrates' view that poetry is inferior to philosophy (if that was his view), and considerable reason to doubt it. This is of course not to say that Plato

4. Cf. Socrates' own words at *Phaedrus* 257a3–6: the "poetic" style was *forced* (ἠναγκασμένη) upon Socrates because of Phaedrus.

plainly regarded poetry as superior to philosophy, or that
Plato saw a sharp and mutually exclusive conflict between love
of the universal and love of the particular.[5] The superiority
of poetry to philosophy is closely connected to Socrates' great
interest, despite his occasional denials of the philosophical
nature of that interest, in the particularities of human experience. And yet, even this formulation is inadequate. A love
of the particular, and certainly of the unique, is an essential
ingredient of philosophical Eros. If we allow that Socrates
does not love human beings, we must still ask how one could
be a philosopher without loving Socrates. This question is
unfortunately obscured by an excessive attention to the mathematical dimension of the Platonic dialogues. Even from this
standpoint, however, what could be more unique than the
beautiful itself?

The ugly becomes pleasant, that is to say, endurable, by
being made laughable. When properly understood, this principle is even true of the ugly or professorial speeches in the
Platonic dialogues (and to understand it properly is not to
conclude that technical philosophy, properly understood, is
ugly, but rather that human beings are not computers). That,
I think, is a thesis on which Socrates and Plato agreed. But
this much is certain: by writing dialogues, Plato extended
indefinitely the audience for philosophical comedy. Alternately, he extended indefinitely the audience for the corollary
to philosophical comedy, namely, the exposition of the tragic
nature of the nonphilosophical life. This is why the *Symposium*
closes with an account of how Socrates was forcing the tragedian Agathon and the comedian Aristophanes to agree
that "he who has the τέχνη for making tragedy has it also for
making comedy" (223c6 ff.). The forcing in question is itself
as much a part of Socrates' τέχνη as it is part of the Eleatic
Stranger's τέχνη to force nonbeing to be (*Statesman* 284b7–8;

5. The first view is given an oblique defense by Seth Benardete in *The Being of
the Beautiful* (Chicago, 1984); the second is asserted explicitly by Martha Nussbaum
in the sprightly and intelligent chapter on the *Symposium* in her *The Fragility of Goodness* (Cambridge and New York, 1986).

cf. my discussion of this point in appendix A to chapter 8). The cosmos does not become orderly simply through its own nature; order is a product of technical force.

This last observation requires a brief clarification; a truly adequate discussion would fill up a volume of its own. The human being is a part of the cosmos; hence the cosmos cannot be orderly if human being is disordered. And the well-ordering of human being is a matter of τέχνη, namely, the political τέχνη. On this specific point, the Eleatic Stranger agrees with Protagoras (cf. appendix A to chapter 3, page 68). One could also argue that the *Statesman,* and in particular the myth of the reversed cosmos, makes a somewhat different point: human being, more specifically the human soul, is a cosmic interloper, or is not at home in the cosmos. This problem may also be stated as that of the bifurcation or internal disorderliness of nature. In this case, either there is no cosmos ("order") by nature, or the natural order itself produces the disorderliness of the human soul. With either of these alternatives, the human need to enforce orderliness upon itself includes, or is necessarily extended to, the need to impose its own order upon nature.

By a slight technical detour, we return to the question of the relation between Eros and poetry. It is precisely the natural discontinuity between Eros and form or order that forces us to turn to poetry. *Τέχνη* is the instrument of, not the abstraction from, desire. Needless to say, the τέχνη of poetry is not the same as that of shoemaking, nor is the forcing of poetry quite the same as the forcing by which Paul Cohen proved the independence of the continuum hypothesis from Zermelo-Fraenkel set theory. But there is a fundamental connection in all these cases. In each of them, we construct what we need. And this is also true of eternity. Nevertheless, the distinction between Plato and Kant has not been obliterated.

As I remarked previously, our need to construct images (or models) of eternity is not at all evidence that eternity is itself an image (or constructive model). The glimpses or intermittent visions of the eternal Ideas, vouchsafed for us by our

natural Eros, not only make possible but guide the redirec-
tion of erotic desire into poetry. As the root of human life,
this redirected vision is a fortiori the cause of modern science,
hence of technology, and so too of the reification of the human soul. But reification is not avoided by absorption into
the beautiful. On the contrary, it results from that absorption. The history of alienation in its various transformations
from Diderot and Rousseau to Hegel and Marx is the story
of how Eros loses its way in culture, or *Bildung*. In the twentieth century, the rediscovery of this process of alienation was
radically modified by the doctrines of Nietzsche and Freud.
I cannot do more than mention here that the consequent
return to the "liberated" Eros, which is closely connected to
the critique of Platonism or the metaphysics of presence,
apart from the fact that it is based upon an inadequate understanding of Plato, is itself the latest stage of reification. The
maxim that art is worth more than the truth depends for its
value upon its truth. And this in turn requires the regulation
or measurement of the corporeal Eros by mathematics.

One of the most striking features of Plato's portrait of Eros
is his tendency to separate it from mathematics or even, as in
the *Republic*, to give the impression that the two are in radical
opposition to one another. There is no mention of mathematics in Diotima's account of the erotic ascent. References
to τὰς ἐπιστήμας and μάθημα are closely linked to the perception of beauty (*Symposium* 210c6 ff., 211c1 ff.). Similarly,
Socrates omits any reference to mathematics in his own treatment of Eros in the *Phaedrus*. The situation in the *Republic* is
more complicated, but it may be summarized here as follows.[6]
For political reasons, Eros is brought under the control of
mathematics, as is perhaps most explicit in the regulation of
breeding by the fanciful nuptial number (VII, 546b3 ff.).
The philosophical education as described in the *Republic* is
predominantly mathematical and culminates in the description of a synoptic dialectic of pure Ideas. Nevertheless, in the

6. For details, see my article, "The Role of Eros in Plato's *Republic*," in the *Review of Metaphysics* 18 (1965), pp. 452–75.

discussion of the nature of the potential philosopher, Socrates continues to employ the central metaphor of Eros.[7] It is no doubt true that Plato regularly links mathematics to the proposed study of eternal form and, as in the *Timaeus*, to cosmic order. At the same time, it is also true that mathematical dialectic is rather praised than actually employed in the dialogues, and that the mathematical cosmology of the *Timaeus* is a "likely story" (29b–d) rather than an accomplished science.[8]

From this, two points emerge. The first is that the association of mathematics and eternity, together with the opposition of mathematics and Eros, raises a doubt concerning the erotic nature of philosophy. The second is that the absence of a genuinely mathematical science of formal structure, or the playful and mythical nature of the celebration of mathematics (entirely compatible with the excellence of mathematics and its role as an epistemic Ideal), raises the suspicion that Plato may understand mathematics itself as a poetic consequence of Eros. It is not impossible that Plato's celebration of dialectic and mathematical physics is equivalent to an invocation to *produce* the technical instruments required to preserve philosophy from poetry. If this is so, then the Platonism of the founders of modern mathematical science takes on a somewhat different light: the constructive or productive nature of mathematical theory may have its roots in the ostensible suppression of poetry by philosophy. It may be that philosophy cannot suppress poetry except by the adoption of poetic means. This does not, however, entail that poetry in the usual or Homeric sense triumphs over philosophy. It does mean that we have to rethink the usual senses of both philosophy and poetry, and thereby to arrive at a more satisfactory understanding of philosophy as an activity that includes its own version of ποίησις. And that, after all, is the plain sense of the *Republic*.

7. For references, see article in previous note.
8. For further details, see the forthcoming work cited in note 3.

The *Parmenides* is frequently interpreted as the crucial statement of Plato's quasi-mathematical ontology. Lest one be tempted to regard it as a counterexample to my way of reading Plato, it will be wise to show at some length that the dialogue is a comic drama. Once again, to do this will not compromise the function of the dialectical exercise as a regulative Ideal. The narrator is Antiphon the "horseman" (a term not associated in Plato with philosophers—see 127a1–7). Antiphon recounts from memory the complex conversation that took place long ago, first between the youthful Socrates and Zeno, then between Socrates and the old Parmenides. Echoes of the dramatic form of the *Symposium* are evident. The occasion of the conversations in the *Parmenides* is the great Panathenea. Zeno and Parmenides are visiting the home of Pythodorus, "outside the walls in the Cerameicum." Socrates, presumably a youth of sixteen or so, has come with some others to hear Zeno read his new work. The date and setting thus indicate the politically qustionable fact that deeds are entirely replaced by words. Political implications to one side, the atmosphere is that of games or rhetorical competition. The abstract content of the speeches does not alter the fact that Zeno is exhibiting his verbal skills to a group of admiring Athenians (127a–c5). Our fascination with the technical intricacies of the speeches should not prevent us from appreciating the sense in which they are examples of epideictic rhetoric—by public standards, absurd examples. Yet what is absurd to the many is, as it were, erotically irresistible to the few. Antiphon, despite his interest in horses, clings tenaciously to the memory of the speeches throughout his life (126c4–10).

Zeno's exhibition marks the first appearance of his book in Athens (127c1–5). Nevertheless, Socrates assimilates it in a single hearing. He elicits Zeno's agreement that the entire work is intended to sustain the first hypothesis of the first logos: if beings are many, they must be both like and unlike (ὅμοιά τε εἶναι καὶ ἀνόμοια), and this is impossible (127d6–e5). We may pass by the worthlessness of Zeno's reasoning, as does Socrates. He concentrates instead upon what he takes, or pretends to take, for a rhetorical deception. Zeno, according to Socrates, tries to deceive us into thinking that he says something different from Parmenides. Parmenides says that the all is one (ἐν φὴς εἶναι τὸ πᾶν) and presents his evidence "beautifully and well" (καλῶς τε καὶ εὖ). Zeno says that the many are not (ὅδε δὲ αὖ οὐ πολλά φησιν εἶναι), and he presents "an immense amount" (πάμπολλα καὶ παμμεγέθη) of evidence. Each expresses himself in such a way that the two men do not seem to be talking about the same thing, as in effect they are; hence their speeches "seem to be beyond the rest of us" (128a4–b6).

In addition to making plain that Zeno does not speak as beautifully as Parmenides, Socrates implies that Zeno pretends to be an independent thinker. Zeno responds urbanely to this rather blunt assessment. He says that Socrates, like a Spartan hunting dog, is quick to pick up the scent and to pursue what has been said. "But you have not entirely perceived the truth of the writing" (128b7–c2). This should be immediately compared with 128a1–3, where Zeno says that Socrates has "beautifully understood the entire intention of the writing." There is a fundamental distinction between the thematic content and the rhetorical intention of a writing, even of an abstract and purely theoretical writing. One can understand the argument (as it is now called) without knowing what the book is about. This point is of indispensable importance to every student of a Platonic dialogue. It is especially interesting to see the point being made in the *Parmenides,* which contains the most obscure conversation ever written by Plato. The fate of this conversation illustrates in its own way the point just made by Zeno. On the one hand, its influence upon the subsequent history of philosophy has been enormous. On the other hand, no completely satisfactory explanation of its technical content *or* of its rhetorical intention has ever been given. Some readers have discerned, correctly, in my opinion, that the lengthy exchange between Parmenides and the young Socrates is a Platonic joke. But to what purpose? Why, by any reasonable standard of humor, such a lengthy and humorless—in short, why such a *bad*—joke?

To return to the text, Zeno denies that the writing exalts itself by concealing from human beings (τοὺς ἀνθρώπους) what Socrates attributes to it. The work is a kind of defense of the Parmenidean *logos* against those who try to make a comedy (κωμῳδεῖν) of it by showing that, if the one is (ἓν ἐστι), many laughable and self-contradictory results ensue. The writing responds to those who assert "the many" (τὰ πολλά) by showing that their hypothesis suffers from still more laughable (ἔτι γελοιότερα) consequences (128c2–d6). Throughout this discussion, for a reason which will surface in a moment, Zeno refers to "the writing" (τὸ γράμμα) and not to himself. We note that "the writing" does not deny the laughable consequences of the Parmenidean hypothesis. Instead, it asserts that the consequences of the contrary hypothesis are still more laughable. Let us state the implication of Zeno's formulation as plainly as possible. The two originative hypotheses of technical philosophy (today called ontology) are, when each is taken apart, laughable. Philosophy can escape its comic nature or cease to be a joke (if it is at all) only by combining the two hypotheses in a nonlaughable or serious manner. The joke is not terminated but extended indefinitely by the sequence of attempts to produce less comprehensive hypotheses. Philosophy seeks to understand the whole. It seeks a third hypothesis that asserts, in a nonlaughable and internally consistent manner, the one and the many. This third hypothesis, in its complete and coherent articulation, is wisdom, the fulfillment of philosophical Eros. But as the two Platonic dialogues on Eros both make evident, wisdom is possible for gods only, and not for mortals (e.g., *Phaedrus* 278d3–6). Human beings at their best are capable of philosophy only. They are capable of incomplete discourse only. And incomplete discourse is laughable.

In Book VII of the *Laws*, the Athenian Stranger makes the following distinction between the serious and the playful:

I say that the serious must be treated seriously, and the
not serious not, that by nature god is worthy of a complete blessed seriousness; but human being (ἄνθρωπον),
as we said previously, has been devised as a kind of toy
of god, and this is actually the best thing about it. Every
man and woman ought to live life through in this way,
playing the noblest possible games. . . . (803c1–8)

If we are entitled to assume that philosophy is the noblest
possible game, it is nonetheless a game and not to be treated
seriously. In other words, it is to be treated playfully, exactly
as does Plato himself. Even further, the playfulness of genuine philosophy is a mark of its nobility. As human beings,
we are of course forced to consider seriously what is not worthy of seriousness, or "human affairs" (τὰ τῶν ἀνθρώπων
πράγματα), that is, what is the best way of life for the present
journey of existence (*Laws* VII, 803b1–5). This is the distinction between philosophy and politics. Philosophy is noble
play, whereas politics is enforced seriousness. Philosophy itself, we may interpolate, becomes serious when it is transformed by either or both of two hypotheses: first, the
hypothesis of philosophy as a kind of Christian theology, and
second, the ultimately political hypothesis of philosophy as a
technical instrument in the liberation of mortals from their
status as toys of the gods. As a consequence of the tacit cooperation of these two hypotheses, technique itself assumes
the ultimate seriousness previously accorded to the divine.
Finally, when its detachment from the divine is thoroughly
assimilated, technique becomes laughable. This, incidentally,
is the contemporary, post-modern situation.

In the scene from the *Parmenides* that has motivated this
reflection, Zeno rather comically (although unintentionally
so) tells us that he wrote his book as a young man, from the
love of victory or contentiousness (φιλονικία). He had not
decided whether to publish it, but it was stolen from him and
published by someone else. Hence Socrates' error: "it escaped
your attention, Socrates, that the book was not written by the

love of honor of an older man (ὑπὸ πρεσβυτέρου φιλοτιμίας),
but by a contentious young man. Nevertheless, as I said before, you have not understood it badly" (128d6–e4). Zeno
implies that there are only two motives for writing: the love
of victory and the love of honor. He also implies thereby that
the love of truth is independent of writing. We must also bear
in mind that Zeno is a philosopher of pure theory; he is
entirely silent about political or pedagogical motives for writing. His φιλονιχία is satisfied by the discursive triumph over
his fellow dialecticians; Zeno has no ἔρως for the many. Nor
does he say anything of writing as a noble game: this is a
Platonic point (made in the *Phaedrus* by Socrates). And indeed, it is Plato who employs Zeno here, as he is about to
employ Parmenides, to illustrate the comical dimension of
philosophy. This is not to deny that philosophy is noble. The
joke of the exchange between Parmenides and Socrates is
directed by Plato against himself.

We must note only two more passages from the *Parmenides*.
The first was alluded to earlier. At 130c5–d2 Parmenides, in
the course of developing Socrates' suggestion about εἴδη
(forms or Ideas), urges that to the logical, ethical, and natural
forms must be added a fourth group consisting of what might
be thought "laughable" forms, namely, those of hair, clay,
dirt, or something else of a dishonorable and paltry nature
(130c5–d2). Socrates indicates his confusion on this point. At
times he worries that the doctrine of forms must be the same
for all things. But then he runs away from this stance, "fearing that I shall fall into a sea of babble (εἴς τινα βυθὸν φλυ-
αρίας) and be destroyed" (130d3–9). Parmenides replies,
"You are still young, Socrates, and philosophy has not yet
gripped you as, in my opinion, it will when you do not dishonor any of these things" (130e1–3). Parmenides is not defending the doctrine of Ideas, but rather the need to give a
logos of everything, the laughable and the dishonorable included. The young Socrates wishes to ignore the base, although he is already hesitant on that point. The old
Parmenides believes himself to have transcended the base,

and hence the laughable, by his comprehensive hypothesis of
the whole as the one. Apparently Parmenides does not see
that an ontological or metaphysical transformation of dung
into Being is also laughable.

The second passage concludes Parmenides' criticism of the
suggestion about forms. Parmenides sounds here like the mature Socrates. He warns the young Socrates that if the criticisms they have just rehearsed lead one to deny that there
are forms of all things, "he will have nowhere to turn his
[discursive] intelligence" and thereby "he will entirely destroy
the power of conversation" (τὴν τοῦ διαλέγεσθαι δύναμιν;
135b5–c3). Parmenides gives Socrates some advice. The
young man is trying to define the forms before he exercises
(πρὶν γυμνασθῆναι). This procedure must be reversed: "you
must force yourself (ἕλκυσον δὲ σαυτὸν) to extensive exercise
in what seems to be useless and is called by the many idle
talk (ἀδολεσχίας), while you are still young. If not, the truth
will escape you" (135d3–6). Socrates then asks, "What is the
manner of the exercise?" Parmenides replies, "That which
you heard from Zeno," except that it will be applied to invisible things that are candidates for forms (135d7–e4). An
extensive discussion ensues as to the difficulty of the exercise
and whether it will be conducted by Zeno or Parmenides. The
consequence of Zeno's refusal (note that, unlike Parmenides,
Zeno laughs—see 136d4) is that Parmenides agrees to the
task:

> I am constrained to be persuaded ('Ανάγκη . . . πείθεσ-
> θαι), although I seem to myself to be affected like the
> horse in Ibycus who, as an old athlete about to compete
> in the carriage-race, trembles from experience of what
> is about to take place. The poet uses this image to de-
> scribe his own unwillingness to be forced, at his advanced
> age, into the lists of Eros (εἰς τὸν ἔρωτα ἀναγκάζεσθαι
> ἰέναι; 136e8–137a4).

And again: "Do you wish, since we are to play this laborious game (ἐπειδήπερ δοκεῖ πραγματειώδη παιδιὰν παίζειν), that I begin from myself and my own hypothesis . . . ?" (137b1–4).

The emphasis in this section is on constraint, play, and Eros. Although the exercise is to be in the manner of Zeno, we may assume that its purpose is neither contentiousness nor love of honor. It is a pedagogical modification of the Eros for truth. Since truth is divine, the exercise is necessary, in the sense that it is not play, and so is serious. But since the truth is inaccessible to human beings, the exercise is from a Platonic standpoint youthful or playful and in this sense laughable. I can now justify my earlier assertion that the *Parmenides* is a bad drama. From the standpoint of the many, it is idle talk (ἀδολεσχία), childishness, a bad joke, boring. But from the standpoint of the one, it is a noble game, and even the dramatic or rhetorical defectiveness of the final extended scene has a meaning that is serious in the sense that transcends the thematic content of the exercise. The best human beings are constrained by their Eros to engage in preparatory exercises for a triumph that will never take place. This point was well understood by Kant, who speaks in the *Critique of Pure Reason* of the inexpungable and futile nature of the metaphysical impetus. Hegel's attempt to overcome Kantian dualism by legitimating metaphysics in the form of dialectico-speculative logic is ultimately the attempt to transform erotic necessity into satisfied desire. The incomplete chatter of Eros (which Kant called *Schwärmerei*) is to be transformed into the complete logos of the wise man.

The "post-philosophical age" begins, for better or worse, with Hegel. The rejection of Hegelian wisdom is not followed by a return to erotic "babble" (φλυαρία) but by the attempt to transform philosophy entirely; in short, philosophy in the classical or Platonic sense is now to be eliminated, whether by science, art, existential pathos, or a rigorously controlled and hence entirely constructive technicism. From the original Platonic standpoint, after Hegel, we are in the age of erotic repression and what Freud calls the "polymorphous perverse." The young Socrates is thus prophetic in his fear that if he extends his suggestion about forms to include all things, he will "fall into a sea of babble" and be destroyed. This fear underlies Socratic irony, which is not simply the magnanimous dissembling of one's own superiority,[9] but the protective mask of the laughable and adolescent nature of philosophy itself. Socrates attempts to neutralize his own laughableness by making it the theme of sophisticated playfulness. The overall situation is described by Kierkegaard in a somewhat exaggerated but not misleading manner: the Hegelian system speaks endlessly, whereas irony is endlessly silent.[10]

It is striking that in the Platonic corpus, Socrates is accused of irony by three men who exhibit, each in a different way, a kind of political courage: Thrasymachus, Callicles, and Alcibiades. Thrasymachus, a teacher of political rhetoric, begins his attack on Socrates by accusing him of babbling (τίς, ἔφη, ὑμᾶς πάλαι φλυαρία ἔχει . . . *Republic* I, 336b8–c1). When Socrates excuses his own lack of ability and praises Thrasymachus' cleverness, the latter breaks into sardonic laughter and shouts: "Herakles! Here is the customary Socratic irony, and I knew it and told these people before, that you would not be willing to answer, but would be ironical" (I, 337a3 ff.). Callicles, who is preparing to run for political office, also prefaces his accusation of irony (*Gorgias* 489e1) with the abusive charge: "Look how this man does not stop babbling" (οὑτοσὶ ἀνὴρ οὐ παύσεται φλυαρῶν; 489b7). The context is that of the definition of terms; Callicles asks whether Socrates is not ashamed at his age to be "chasing after" words (i.e., playing with them: ὀνόματα θηρεύων; 489b8). This accusation is a direct consequence of Callicles' denunciation of philosophy as something that is appropriate for children but, when practiced by adults, is destructive (484c4 ff.). "It is noble to participate in philosophy for the sake of education (παιδείας χάριν), and not shameful to philosophize if one is

9. *Eth. Nic.* IV, 1124b30 and 1127b25 ff.

10. *Über den Begriff der Ironie* (Düsseldorf and Köln, 1961), p. 25. Cf. p. 90 on the two forms of Platonic irony.

a youth" (485a4–5). At Socrates' age, it is laughable, "and I am affected by those who philosophize exactly as I am by those who speak indistinctly and play like children" (τοὺς ψελλιζομένους καὶ παίζοντες; 485a6–b2). Mature philosophers are babblers and lispers, "laughable, unmanly, and deserving to be smacked" (485c1–2). An adult of this sort will never be politically respectable, a "real man," but "will flee from the center of the city and the public squares, where as the poet says, gentlemen become distinguished." Instead, he will pass his life "whispering with three or four youths in some secluded corner" (485d3–e1). Should he ever be arrested and unjustly accused of meriting the death penalty, he will be unable to defend himself (486c7 ff.).

Callicles implies that Socrates' irony conceals what will be taken for pederasty; this implication, as we shall see later in detail, is rejected by Alcibiades, who exposes Socrates' ostensibly erotic interest in beautiful youths as ironical. This is not the place to comment at length on Alcibiades' own accusation. Suffice it to say that those who are strongly motivated by the love of glory are not taken in by Socratic irony. The same point is made by Protagoras in the dialogue bearing his name. According to Protagoras, the great Sophists of the past, fearing the hatred their τέχνη engendered, concealed it with a variety of poetic, mystical, athletic, and musical masks: "I myself do not at all conform to these persons on this point. For I believe they did not accomplish what they intended. The purpose of these masks could not elude the attention of those mortals who exercise power in the cities. The many, of course, perceive as it were nothing, but sing as they are commanded" (*Protagoras* 316d3–317a6). We will learn nothing from Protagoras' speech, from Callicles' denunciation of philosophy, and hence from the link between political life and Socratic irony, if we fail to see what is plain to those with eyes, namely, that Plato understands the *seriousness* of these charges.

The allegiance of poetry and politics is in conflict with philosophy. It of course does not follow from this that poets and politicians are entirely frank; "poets tell many a lie." It is their own mastery of dissembling that enables them to penetrate the philosopher's (or the Sophist's) irony. The issue is not one of frankness, but of the conflict between poetry and philosophy, that is to say, of the poetic horizon of so-called pure or theoretical philosophy. Whereas the deeper psychological basis of this conflict is in the problematic relation between spiritedness (θυμός) and desire (ἐπιθυμία) or, more narrowly, between spiritedness and Eros,[11] the more visible form of the quarrel concerns the best life for humans. The poets warn against striving to be a god; the philosophers insist that the gods are not envious and that the divine life is an appropriate goal for human beings.[12] This is the underlying quarrel between Socrates and Aristophanes in the *Symposium*. It is also the clue to the nature of Alcibiades, who is in many ways the most complex and interesting character in the dialogue. Alcibiades, of course, was drawn to politics by his love of glory, despite his perception of the beauty of philosophy. One may say that the beautiful Alcibiades, who regularly prostituted Eros to the pursuit of glory, was immune to beauty. This immunity (at the decisive level) extended to games or to noble playfulness. Alcibiades had more serious business than this. If his own seriousness ended in tragedy, it does not immediately follow that political (and hence poetic) tragedy is lower than philosophical comedy. After all, as is implied by Socrates' final discussion, Plato's dialogues are tragedies as well as comedies.

11. Cf. the chapter on Plato by Leo Strauss in *A History of Political Philosophy*, ed. L. Strauss and J. Cropsey (Chicago, 1963).

12. *Metaphysics* A2, 982b30, 983a2 ff. David Lachterman points out that Aristotle employs poetry (κατὰ τὴν παροιμίαν) to refute the charge of the poets that the gods are envious. I take this to support my previous remarks about philosophical ποίησις.

INTRODUCTION

Some Questions of Method

I do not propose to review here the history of Platonic scholarship but simply to indicate the fundamental methodological decisions which have guided me in writing this study. The most important of these decisions has to do with the significance of the dialogue form and must be discussed in some detail. To a certain extent, I shall be repeating points which have been made by others, but it would be neither possible nor desirable to discover an altogether "new" procedure for the interpretation of a Platonic dialogue.[1] What counts is the application of sound techniques in a particular case, and the "soundness" of the techniques can be finally judged only by their results. As the dialogues themselves regularly teach us, τέχνη is under the jurisdiction of τέλος.

During the past decade or two, a growing number of scholars have recognized the central importance of Plato's use of the dialogue form. Nevertheless, it cannot be said that this recognition is uniform among contemporary students of the dialogues. Especially among English-speaking writers, the emphasis upon epistemology, logic, and linguistic analysis has directed attention away from standing dramatic form and toward the dissection of particular themes or arguments in relative independence from their context. Instead of a rigorous attention to the dramatic context of an argument as a key to Plato's intentions—and hence as an essential part of the argument itself—we are presented with speculations about the chronological order of the dialogues; the differences between one dialogue and another are taken—not as the intentional consequences of Plato's dra-

1. For a supplementary discussion of some of the themes in this preface, cf. J. Klein, *A Commentary on Plato's Meno* (Chapel Hill, 1965) and L. Strauss, *The City and Man* (Chicago, 1964).

matic art—but as conclusive evidence for the historical evolution of his thought. Thus we find an ironical, and for the most part unexamined, allegiance between historically disinterested "conceptual analysis" and assumptions derived from eighteenth- and nineteenth-century philosophies of history.

Whatever the validity of that allegiance, it must be said frankly that the Plato who emerges can scarcely be regarded as a satisfactory or philosophically interesting figure, whatever standards one uses. He seems to vacillate almost from year to year on the most important matters, is so poor a thinker as continuously to be caught up in elementary fallacies, is unable to remember his line of argument for two consecutive pages, and is subject to the most vulgar superstitions of his day. Or, alternatively, he is presented as struggling, despite the faults of his age and consequent lack of logical sophistication, to repudiate the primitive metaphysical assumptions of his youth in favor of a curiously twentieth-century amalgam of nominalism and linguistic analysis.

I do not believe that the preceding paragraph unfairly caricatures the situation it reports. But even if it were to be softened, why should we accept any version of this portrait of Plato? How rigorous is a historical scholarship that uncritically submits an ancient Greek thinker to nineteenth- and twentieth-century assumptions and techniques? What evidence is there for the view that the dialogues record the history of Plato's mental development? By what right do we disregard the central phenomenon of the dramatic context of every argument in the dialogues? What if Plato's conception of a "rational argument" is decisively different from, or broader than, our own? What are we to do in the face of Socratic and Platonic irony? Questions like these spring readily to the mind and might be multiplied. To ask them, of course, is not to suggest that we suppress all canons of conceptual or historical analysis but rather that the right ones be applied. Even if our own methods and assumptions are superior to those of Plato, must we not first ascertain what his actually were? It is one thing to ask these questions, and another to answer them. The most I can hope to do is to offer sufficient reason for doubting the procedures against which such questions are directed and thereby to warrant the reader's unbiased consideration of my own method of interpretation.

Let us begin, then, with the fact that Plato wrote dialogues rather than monologues, discourses, or treatises. This fact raises two inseparable difficulties: first, Plato says nothing in his own name, and second, whatever anyone says is relative to a specific dramatic situation. In other words, even if we knew for a fact that Plato shared the views of Socrates, Timaeus, and the Eleatic and Athenian strangers, it would still be true that these characters say different things at different times and to differing audiences. But very far from knowing that Plato agrees with his principal dramatic figures (even though they do not agree with each other), there is evidence that none of them is a spokesman for his own views. In his *Epistles* Plato explicitly renounces the writings and other public accounts of views that have been attributed to him.[2] At the same time, however, it is impossible to rest content with the literal and uninterpreted acceptance of this renunciation. If the letters are genuine expressions of Plato's thought, whether or not written by him personally, then as the author of the dialogues he must have practiced an extreme form of ironic dissimulation. But if this is so, why should we assume that the letters are not ironical? On the face of things, we seem to be in the presence of another version of the Cretan paradox.[3]

Those who deny the authenticity of the Platonic letters, in order to insist that the dialogues do express the authentic teaching of Plato, are all the more obligated to account for the fact of the dialogue form, and Plato's ensuing anonymity.[4] This fact

2. *Epistles* 2.314b7; 7.341c1 ff.

3. In "Form and Content in Plato's Philosophy," *Journal of the History of Ideas, 8* (1947), P. Merlan accepts the genuineness of the *Epistles* and infers from them and the dialogues that Plato "renounces" his views as an expression of the need for a continuous self-regeneration (cf. *Symposium* 207d–208b), and the partial nature of every expression of absolute truth. But his inference is not supported by an adequate consideration of the possible irony of the *Epistles*.

4. L. Edelstein takes this course in "Platonic Anonymity," *American Journal of Philology, 82* (1962). He assumes that the *Epistles* are spurious because they disown the dialogues, whereas Plato's associates did not. But this again fails to

goes beyond the remarks by Socrates in the *Phaedrus* which cast doubt upon the value of the written word; it is equivalent to the entire Platonic corpus. One cannot take refuge in a distinction between the "early" and "late" dialogues in this connection, since Plato never deviated from his course of anonymity. The *Sophist* is no less a dialogue than the *Euthyphro*; if anything, the introduction of "strangers" as a replacement for Socrates, together with the mixture of humor and seriousness which marks the illustrations of the diaeretic technique, complicates rather than simplifies the dramatic structure of the "later" dialogues—to say nothing of the problem posed by the *Philebus*. In general, if we reduce the dramatic structure of the dialogues to the status of an external contingency, we arbitrarily ignore their most obvious and pervasive feature.[5] Even without entering into any theoretical reflections on Platonic dialectic, it is clear that we cannot take the dialogues seriously as expressions of Plato's thought unless we take seriously the extraordinary complexity of their literary form.

The first step in the study of Plato is easy to state, even trivially obvious, and yet seldom honored: to see the dialogues in their own words, independently of presuppositions derived from modern conceptions of historical development or sound argumentative technique. As I have already suggested, what first becomes visible from such a step is not the sophistication or naïveté of Plato's logical apparatus, but his irony. Let me emphasize this. *Only by the recognition of irony as the central problem in the interpretation of Plato, do we honor the demands of rigorous and sober philosophical analysis.* For only if we successfully penetrate Plato's irony will the genuine character

---

allow for the possibility that the *Epistles* are themselves ironical; i.e., that they provide a clue for the interpreter of the dialogues which is in keeping with the style of the dialogues themselves. In general, even those who emphasize Plato's irony tend to accept the *Epistles* as straightforward, or to reject them as forgeries.

5. This is the net result of procedures like that of R. Robinson, who, in his otherwise interesting *PED*, goes so far as to suggest that Plato wrote dialogues in unconscious imitation of Socrates' use of elenchus, which amounts to the view that he did not know what he was doing.

of his arguments become accessible to our own techniques of analysis.

When we see the significance of Platonic irony, it is at once evident that the dialogues and letters do not contradict but supplement each other; and so the strongest reason for regarding the letters as spurious ceases to exist. By the same token, there is no real justification for regarding the dialogues as an irrelevant or even secondary source in the pursuit of Plato's authentic teaching. If there is any part of that teaching which altogether transcends human speech, it can no more have been communicated orally than by writing. As to what is amenable to utterance, Plato carefully says that his teaching on the highest or most serious matters "cannot be stated like the other kinds of knowledge." [6] It does not follow from this that such a teaching cannot be stated at all. The language of the Seventh Letter is in fact compatible with the crucial myth of the cave in Book Seven of the *Republic*. Both texts refer to an "instantaneous" (ἐξαίφνης) illumination in the psyche of the potential philosopher, which cannot be achieved by education alone but is a gift from nature or god.[7] Once that gift has been granted, philosophical speech, whether in the form of myth or *logos*, may occur, and under the same condition, be understood.

We may therefore agree that Plato had an "esoteric" teaching, and even that some parts of this teaching (e.g. the Idea-numbers) are referred to explicitly by his students, but never by himself, without drawing the extreme conclusion that the dialogues are merely "exoteric" documents, serving essentially secondary uses of pedagogy and propaganda. This conclusion has recently achieved a certain currency in Germany, thanks largely to the initial stimulus of the writings of H. J. Krämer.[8]

6. *Epistles* 7.341c5: ῥητὸν γὰρ οὐδαμῶς ἔστιν ὡς ἄλλα μαθήματα, and this refers to 341c1: ὧν ἐγὼ σπουδάζω.

7. *Epistles* 7.341c6 ff., *Republic* 515c6 ff. Cf. *Phaedrus* 244a5 ff.

8. H. J. Krämer, *Arete bei Platon und Aristoteles* (Heidelberg, 1959) (hereafter *ArPA*); "Retraktationen zum Problem des esoterischen Platon," in *Museum Helveticum*, *21* (1964, Fasc. 3); and "Die platonische Akademie und das Problem einer systematischen Interpretation der Philosophie Platons," *Kant-Studien*, *55* (1964) (hereafter *PlAkad*). Cf. K. Gaiser, *Platons ungeschriebene Philosophie*

Krämer is correct in saying that "the existence of an esoteric special teaching of Plato was therefore presupposed as self-evident from antiquity to the beginning of the 19th century," and he offers a detailed survey of testimonials to that effect.[9] But, as Ludwig Edelstein has pointed out, there is no statement in the writings of Plato's students and associates in the Academy to warrant the assumption that the dialogues were not a part of his genuine teaching.[10] Neither, we may add, does Krämer consider the possibility that the language of the letters may share in the irony of the dialogues. The most Krämer can be said to have shown is that Plato never speaks frankly or directly in any of his writings, and second, that in attempting to reconstruct the complete Platonic teaching, one must have recourse to sources in addition to the dialogues and letters.

Krämer's procedure, despite its many merits, has the unfortunate consequence of leading us to discount the central importance of the dialogues in favor of what must be regarded as fragmentary and conjectural secondary testimony. This testimony becomes persuasive, not as a surrogate for the dialogues, but as a commentary upon them. In the very act of making important observations about the peculiarity of Plato's literary style, Krämer commits the same error as those who disregard the tradition of esotericism altogether. That is, he fails to engage in a thorough analysis of the dialogues themselves, in their own terms, rather than in terms of hypotheses derived from external sources. As a result, he does not seem to do justice either to the explicit or implicit content of the dialogues: the peculiar mixture of frankness and reticence that constitutes Plato's style of indirect communication. A completely adequate modification of Krämer's major contentions, or for that matter of those to which he objects, can only be given in the form of a detailed interpretation of a Platonic dialogue. In these prefatory re-

---

(Stuttgart, 1963) (hereafter *Ungeschriebene*); K. Oehler, "Die entmythologisierte Platon," in *Zeitschrift für Philosophische Forschung, 19* (1965), and "Neue Fragmente zum esoterischen Platon," *Hermes, 93* (Oct. 1965).

9. Krämer, *ArPA*, pp. 18, 381, n. 2. Cf. A. S. Pease, *Cicero's De Natura Deorum* (Cambridge, Mass., 1955), n. to 1.61 and n. 8 above.

10. See n. 4 above.

marks, I limit myself to a general sketch of the approach that, in my opinion, avoids the most obvious pitfalls of the procedures employed both by Krämer and those whom he criticizes.

In order to "save the phenomena" of dialogues, letters, and the tradition of esotericism, I suggest as a working hypothesis, to be tested by the interpretation of the *Symposium* which follows, that the dialogues themselves contain both an exoteric and an esoteric teaching. It is senseless to regard them as exoteric supplements to the "true" teaching, since the dialogues, when read with care and imagination, are more comprehensive than the "true" teaching as derived from secondary reports. Both Krämer and his opponents fail to take seriously indications within the dialogues of their double structure. For example, Krämer himself collects a variety of passages in which reference is made to an unspoken teaching.[11] Some of these indicate that the formulation in the dialogue has been modified in accord with the capacities of the audience; others merely state that more could be said but will be omitted in the present context. Passages of the latter sort, when taken in themselves, do not justify the inference that the account in the dialogue is popular or secondary but only that it is incomplete. One might infer from them that the balance of the argument is not independent of the text but must be furnished by the perspicuous reader on the basis of the text itself. Similarly, with arguments accommodated to the dramatic audience: in itself, the technique is no different from that of a skilled dramatist for whom we have no evidence at all of a separate oral teaching.

My point is that there is no reason to doubt that the dialogues provide effective directions for the reconstruction of Plato's oral teachings. But even further, the attempt to reconstruct an oral teaching on the basis of documentary testimony by Plato's students is contradictory to the very passages from the letters and dialogues themselves concerning the nature of philosophy as unteachable or unsuited for writing. According to these passages, the philosopher must discover the complete or more adequate formulation of the highest themes for him-

11. Krämer, *ArPA*, p. 389; *PlAkad*, p. 74, n. 5.

self, by his own noetic activity. If this is to be taken seriously, why should Plato have informed his students privately of what they could master only by their own efforts? Is it not precisely the function of the dialogue form that it forces the reader to engage in the act of interpretation, to fill in missing links, to revise accommodated arguments, to discern the import of hints, to understand the significance of jokes?

Let me take a specific example that is especially relevant to the *Symposium*. As is well known, the dialogues are frequently called "games" or "jokes" by a Platonic character, often immediately after an especially crucial argument or obscure passage.[12] In the *Phaedrus* Socrates says that the man who possesses knowledge of the just, the beautiful, and the good "will cast his seed in the garden of letters, and write, if he ever does so, out of playfulness." [13] He will pass his life in the amusement of writing, instead of indulging in such games as banquets.[14] Are we to infer from this that the dialogues are altogether lacking in "serious" import? The specific language of the passage just cited may rather imply that Plato is playfully indicating his own superiority to the skilled speakers at the banquet in the *Symposium*, and even to Socrates. According to Socrates, written speech is an inferior imitation of speech in the psyche of the man who understands. This superior speech knows how to speak or keep silent, as the nature of the audience requires.[15] Is this not an accurate description of the dialogue form? Is Plato denying the worth of his dialogues or using the words of Socrates to praise them? In other words, the dialogue form imitates the living speech of Socrates, the man who understands, and consequently it also imitates his silence or reserve. May we not say that Plato believed himself to have surpassed his teacher through the discovery of the perfect form of writing?

To continue the same example: in the *Laws* the Athenian

12. E.g. *Phaedrus* 278b7; *Republic* 396e2 (bad men may be imitated παιδιᾶς χάριν), *Philebus* 30e6. See the listing under παιδιά and related words in F. Ast, *Lexicon Platonicum* (Darmstadt, 1956) (hereafter *LexPl*).

13. 276d1 ff.: παιδιᾶς χάριν.

14. 276d5: συμποσίοις.

15. 276a5 ff.

stranger speaks of the educational value of games and the special use of banquets.[16] Dialogues in general may be defined as educational games; the *Symposium* in particular is a game having as its principal pedagogic function the teaching of the natures and habits of man's psyche. It is true that there is only moderate drinking in the *Symposium* until the end of Alcibiades' speech (although he is himself already drunk), and that the Athenian stranger regards intoxication as the instrument by which men are tested and trained. But the intoxication of wine is replaced in the *Symposium* by the enthusiasm of Eros: wine, as it were, is replaced by ambrosia.[17] The speakers become drunk with the subject they are praising (except for Socrates), even when that praise is intended to serve purely selfish purposes.[18] If philosophy is a divine madness as well as the division and collection in accordance with kinds, then it must be a form of intoxication as well as sobriety. It is a serious weakness of Krämer's position that he omits the elements of μανία from his account of Plato's "true" and "systematic" teaching.[19] But Platonic pedagogy combines the mixture of speech and silence with that of intoxication and sobriety in a medicinal draught of rhetoric.

In sum: regardless of whether or not an oral teaching exists, the unspoken dimension of the dialogues is in fact a dimension of the dialogues and, for methodological purposes, the most important one. There is a dialectic between the speech of the characters and the silence of the author, whose subtlety alone determines the degree of complexity to which speech and silence are interwoven.[20] Within the speech of the dialogues, this web is explicitly mentioned as a kind of dissembling. I remind the reader only of Socrates' recommendation in the *Republic* that the guardians of the just city tell medicinal lies, and of Alci-

16. *Laws* 797a ff.; 650b6–7.
17. *Symposium* 203b5–6.
18. Cf. *Phaedrus* 234d2–6.
19. Krämer, *PlAkad*, p. 82.
20. Cf. the brief but excellent article by R. Hornsby, "Significant Action in the Symposium," *Classical Journal*, 52 (1956), esp. 37: "Thus we see the core of the dinner, Diotima's instruction, through four pairs of eyes."

biades' revelation in the *Symposium* of the difference between the outer and inner form of Socratic speech.[21] These are but two of the many clues that Plato practices a medicinal rhetoric or psychiatry in the literal sense of the word. His dialogues are both pedagogic and medical works, designed to lead the young toward philosophy and to mitigate the disease of ignorance or thoughtlessness. In order to fulfil this dual function, the dialogues must say different things to different readers. Those who are unable to distinguish between medicinal rhetoric and sophistry forget two things. First, the sophists say the same thing to everyone in teaching the identity between truth and persuasion. Second, medicinal rhetoric is employed by the friends of the Ideas for the sake of preserving and restoring health, and not for the sake of gaining political power.[22] It is a principle of common sense as well as of science that the physician must vary his procedures and prescriptions depending upon the nature of the patient and his ailment. Thus one may say that the use of irony by a philosophical writer is justified on scientific as well as on moral grounds.

We can now see more clearly why Plato would say that philosophy cannot be written like other forms of knowledge, and that his dialogues are about a Socrates "become beautiful and young." [23] Philosophy is a condition of the psyche and so a way of life, rather than solely a system of true propositions.[24] The mode of writing peculiar to philosophy is the dramatic portrait of individual human types confronted by a disguised Socrates. Socratic irony is beautiful and young; that is, it is noble and hopeful rather than base and pessimistic. Just as Socrates tests the nature of his interlocutors, in order to determine whether

21. *Republic* 382c6–10, 414b8; *Symposium* 221c3.

22. The most important passages for the difference between philosophical and sophistic rhetoric are to be found in the *Gorgias*, e.g. 449d8 ff., 452d5 ff., 462c7, 466b11, and 469c5 (especially important for the *Symposium*: Polus compares the rhetor to the tyrant; both can do whatever they wish). If philosophy is like medicine, rhetoric is like cooking: 464d2 ff., 500e4 ff.

23. *Epistles* 2.314b7.

24. Cf. *Euthydemus* 280a6, 281b2: σοφία or ἐπιστήμη includes the knowledge of how to act.

he may be of service to them, so Plato tests the nature of his readers. Just as Socrates is protected from unsatisfactory companions by his daimonion, so Plato is protected from unsatisfactory readers by irony. Those who cannot be cured by the inner charms of the dialogue will at least not be harmed by its exterior. The exterior of the dialogue is tinged by the beauty of youth, the interior by the beauty of maturity.

As both a drama and an exercise in dialectic, each dialogue begins with the opinions of particular individuals. Aristotle's definition of the dialectical syllogism as reasoning from opinion may also be applied to the Platonic dialogue.[25] Instead of a syllogism, however, we have a drama, and thus a rational structure which combines speech and deed, action and gesture, direct statement and indirect symbol. The opinions of the protagonists are either sick or healthy, which is to be determined by mutual consultation between doctor and patient. Just as in contemporary psychodrama the patients act out their ailments, so the Platonic dialogues show men of varying kinds acting out the consequences of the disease of ignorance. Every opinion, including those of the philosopher, is defective to one degree or another.[26] Every man, including the philosopher, is fundamentally a cave dweller, a resident of the domain of opinion. We escape only intermittently from that domain, and only by a scrupulous awareness of the nature of opinion. Mathematical knowledge, or the vision of the Ideas, is the culmination of that awareness but does not exhaust it.[27] As mathematicians or spectators of

25. *Topics* 100a18 ff. For the general significance of dialectic in both Plato and Aristotle, see P. Aubenque, *Le problème de l'être chez Aristote* (Paris, 1962), esp. pp. 251 ff., and W. Wieland, *Die aristotelische Physik* (Göttingen, 1962), esp. pp. 216 ff.

26. Krämer and his supporters believe that Plato thought himself to possess a complete system or perfect wisdom. Cf. Krämer, *PlAkad,* p. 90 and Oehler, *EntmPl,* passim. Such a view goes contrary to the spirit and explicit testimony of the dialogues. But it also over-interprets the evidence concerning the ἀρχαί of Plato's thought. Certitude with respect to principles is not the same as possession of a completed system.

27. In the paper just cited, Krämer quotes *Symposium* 211b ff. (καὶ ἅπτοιτο ἄν τοῦ τέλους) as an example of Plato's view that wisdom may be achieved. But again, an instantaneous perception of the end is not the same as a systematic λόγος. λόγος.

the Ideas, we are still rooted in the world of change, still citizens of the cave or the polis.[28]

Since it is the human condition to dwell, even as philosophers, within the domain of opinion, an accurate portrait of philosophy must reflect its context, or the manner in which it emerges in human life. In this specific sense, the dialogue is an existential portrait rather than a philosophical treatise.[29] I do not mean by this that Plato was an "existentialist" in the contemporary meaning of the term. One might as well argue that he was a "linguistic analyst" on the basis of Socrates' frequent dissections of ordinary language. Such erroneous (because partial) attempts to identify Plato's philosophical "position" arise from a failure to observe the peculiar function of the dialogue form. By portraying the emergence of philosophy from opinion, the dialogue imitates the whole of human existence, which is to say that it imitates the whole simply. The conception of philosophy that such a mimesis reflects is broader than any academic position or system that may be inferred from individual speeches within the dialogues. The dialogue is the dramatic representation of the synoptic nature of dialectic.[30] As synoptic, dialectic is not merely a quasi-mathematical measurement or division and collection according to kinds.[31] There are as many modes of "measurement" as there are distinct kinds of "phenomena." Platonic measurement, although undoubtedly influenced by mathematical procedures, "saves the phenomena" because it is not reducible to the techniques of mathematics. We in turn can save the

---

28. As the first word of the *Republic*, κατέβην, suggests, the entire dialogue takes place in the "cave." Cf. *Phaedrus* 247a8 ff.; even the divine psyches are rooted to the cosmos of genesis.

29. Cf. H. J. Gadamer, *Platos dialektische Ethik* (Leipzig, 1931), where it is said in much the same sense that the dialogues are not philosophical treatises: "Sie sind in ihrer eigenen Intention erst aufgefasst, wenn man sie als Hinführungen zu dem Existenzideal des Philosophen, dem Leben in der reinen Theorie versteht" (p. 2). Also K. Gaiser, *Protrepik und Paränese bei Platon* (Stuttgart, 1959) pp. 15, 19.

30. *Republic* 537c7: ὁ μὲν γὰρ διαλεκτικὸς συνοπτικός . . .

31. Consider esp. *Philebus* 57d ff.; there are two kinds of measuring and numbering. Cf. *Phaedrus* 265d, 276e; *Sophist* 253d; *Statesman* 283d–287a; *Philebus* 55c ff.

phenomena only by supplementing the definitions of the technique of dialectic in the dialogues by the evidence of the dialogues themselves.

The dialogues are sophisticated or artful (as distinct from "historical") imitations of the Protean nature of the human psyche. Since the psyche is both mathematician and poet, in the broadest sense of those terms, so too are the dialogues mathematical and poetic.[32] As dialectician, the psyche weaves together mathematics and poetry into a tapestry which is neither the one nor the other. No lesser technique than dialectic will suffice to unravel the pattern of the tapestry. But this does not mean that we must master every technique in order to read Plato. The technique of dialectic differs from all the others in that it alone is concerned with them all, or with the principles of all, as visible within the "pre-technical" or natural condition of the psyche. To the extent that we regard such a technique as impossible and replace it by the specialized techniques of mathematics, poetry, and the like, we deviate from Plato by subjecting the psyche to a "technical" analysis in the narrower sense of a special discipline. The psyche is then reconstituted or redefined in terms of the special discipline employed. In contemporary language, the wholeness of the *Lebenswelt* is obscured by a partial, if technically intricate, abstraction that cannot understand itself as a part because the very idea of "wholeness" is no longer accessible to it.

What I am saying here should not be mistaken for a condemnation of τέχνη, but rather of what Léon Robin has well termed *technicité*.[33] As Plato regularly shows, every technique is directed toward, and is praiseworthy in terms of, an end. The hierarchy or cosmos of ends is equivalent to the principle of coherence in human existence and is dramatically represented in the dialogues by their political structure. It must never be forgotten that, even in the most abstract discussions, the form

32. See S. H. Rosen, "The Role of Eros in Plato's *Republic,*" *Review of Metaphysics, 18* (1965) (hereafter *ErosRepub*).

33. L. Robin, ed., *Platon, Oeuvres complètes* (Paris, 1929), *4,* Part 2 (hereafter *SymBudé*) lii, n. 1.

of the dialogue as writing or publication corresponds to the political or communal nature of discourse. Similarly, the synoptic or architectonic character of dialectic corresponds to the technique of politics, or the royal art of weaving.[34] As in life, so in the dialogues; epistemic or "mathematical" investigations emerge from the horizon of opinion, or the *nomos* of the polis. (Here one may note parenthetically an important connection between Greek thought and the contemporary phenomenological conception of the Lebenswelt.) This means that the theoretical relationship between knowledge and opinion leads to practical difficulties for the interpreter of the Platonic dialogues. As citizens, we speak differently to our fellows, depending upon their political status as well as their intellectual capacities. In so doing, we practice a humble version of what I previously called "medicinal rhetoric." We do this, not from an illiberal snobbery, but in the desire to give each man his due or just portion. The immediate purpose of justice is to keep the peace, to establish a framework of general agreement within which private disagreement may safely occur.

This connection between justice and the technical function of dialectic is well illustrated by Xenophon in the *Memorabilia*. He tells us that Socrates defined "dialectic" (τὸ διαλέγεσθαι) as a "coming together to deliberate in common, sorting things according to kinds." [35] Whatever else it may be, dialectic as practiced by the Socratics has the political end of communion or general agreement, a fact which is constantly emphasized by the chief speakers in the Platonic dialogues.[36] According to Xenophon, Socrates regarded agreement as the only sound method, and called it, after Homer's description of Odysseus, "safe rhetoric." [37] In the *Theaetetus* safe rhetoric is instead called

34. *Euthydemus* 290b7, 291c4 and *Statesman* 306a1 ff.

35. *Memorabilia* 4.5.12.

36. E.g. *Symposium* 199b8–10; *Sophist* 218c1–3; *Statesman* 258d1, 260b7; *Philebus* 11d2; *Republic* 507a7.

37. *Memorabilia* 4.6.15. Cf. E. Kapp, *Greek Foundations of Traditional Logic* (New York, 1942), pp. 12–13. Kapp compares this passage from the *Memorabilia* with Aristotle, *Topics* 101a28 ff. Cf. the "safe rhetoric" of kings honored by the Muses in Hesiod, *Theogony*, 11.81 ff. This rhetoric may well be called "political music." Socrates shares the view of Hesiod that justice depends upon poetry.

"midwifery"; as Socrates says, the arguments (λόγοι) never come from himself but always from the man with whom he is conversing.[38] Whether for theoretical or practical reasons, then, Platonic irony means that every statement in a dialogue must be understood in terms of its dramatic context. Of course, we may also subject these statements to technical analysis independently of their context, and the results may well be extremely valuable. But in so doing we run the risk of misunderstanding Plato, or of understanding less than he wished to teach us. At the least, both types of analysis are advisable. To repeat the crucial point: Socrates always accommodates his speech to the opinions of his interlocutors.[39]

If, as is the case with Plato, one's aims include forcing men to think for themselves, to submit to the divine mania without publicly repudiating the divine nomos, to undergo a testing and purging of the psyche, and to protect philosophy from the rage of the nonphilosophers,[40] then the procedures of irony make perfect sense. Unfortunately they complicate enormously the task of the interpreter, especially at a time when most if not all of Plato's aims have been sacrificed in exchange for new gods. The student of Plato should recognize frankly, without any naïve repudiation of the need for accurate technical knowledge, that the metier of historical scholarship is by nature radically different from the exercise of divine madness. It may be that excessive sobriety and caution, in obedience to standards derived from another and later tradition, violate Platonic accuracy. Among many scholars the word "speculative" is a term of opprobrium. In the reading of Plato such an attitude is totally out of place. The interpreter must remember that he himself is being tested and cured by the medicinal rhetoric of Plato's dia-

38. *Theaetetus* 149a4 ff., 161b1–2.

39. Cf. *Meno* 75c8 ff. (replies to an eristic man differ from replies to friends), 75d8 (ἔστι δὲ ἴσως τὸ διαλεκτικώτερον μὴ μόνον τἀληθῆ ἀποκρίνεσθαι, ἀλλὰ καὶ δι' ἐκείνων ὧν ἂν προσομολογῇ εἰδέναι ὁ ἐρωτώμενος), and 76e7ff. (where Socrates indicates that his answers are mysteries into which one must be initiated).

40. For the danger to philosophy from the *vulgus,* cf. *Republic* 517a5 with Cicero, *Tusculan Disputations* 2.1.4. Consider also *Crito* 47b11 and c10 ff. in conjunction with *Gorgias* 499e6 ff.

lectic. Thus each interpretation is at the same time necessarily an exercise in philosophical speculation.

If we bear in mind Plato's intentions as they are explicitly mentioned within the dialogues, it then becomes possible to reconcile the long tradition of an esoteric Platonic teaching with the manifest excellence of the dialogues themselves. We need not doubt that Plato, or for that matter any philosopher, was too sensible to publish openly all of his thoughts.[41] Nor can we take seriously the argument of Schleiermacher, frequently repeated since his time, that if there were an esoteric Platonic teaching, Aristotle would have mentioned and criticized it.[42] In the first place, Aristotle does mention the "unwritten views" of Plato.[43] But more fundamentally, to those who object on moral grounds to secrecy among philosophers one must ask: why is it morally superior to reveal secrets rather than to have them? The skepticism of many contemporary scholars toward the practice of esotericism in previous epochs is not supported by an accurate knowledge of the history of Western thought prior to the Enlightenment. Philosophers like Leibniz, Hume, Rousseau, and Nietzsche were better informed; Nietzsche is especially instructive in this connection.[44]

Although Schleiermacher was the first Plato editor to deny the existence of an esoteric teaching, the decisive forces behind that denial are the great thinkers from Descartes and Hobbes to Kant and Hegel, who initiated and carried out the great rebellion against antiquity in order to free mankind from superstition and the powers of darkness.[45] A belief in the desirability

41. Even Kant practiced a certain reserve in this respect. Thus he wrote to Mendelssohn: "Zwar denke ich Vieles mit der allerklarsten Überzeugung, was ich niemals den Mut haben werde zu sagen, niemals aber werde ich etwas sagen, was ich nicht denke." Quoted in K. Löwith, *Von Hegel zu Nietzsche* (Stuttgart, 1953), p. 104.

42. F. Schleiermacher, *Introductions to the Dialogues of Plato* (Cambridge, 1836), pp. 12–13.

43. *Physics* 209b15: ἄγραφα δόγματα.

44. Cf. L. Strauss, *Persecution and the Art of Writing* (Glencoe, Ill., 1952), for an account of the problem of esotericism in its social and political context.

45. For an instructive discussion of the "disingenuousness" of pre-Enlightenment philosophers, see Kant's *Kritik der reinen Vernunft* B776 ff. The efforts by

of frank and public discussion is a relatively recent phenomenon in Western thought, and by no means one that has been universally accepted even among post-Enlightenment writers. Even Kant and Hegel recognized the need for discretion in matters of political importance or distinguished between the way in which philosophers and citizens may exemplify the truth. It remained for their successors, Marx and Kierkegaard, either to make every man a philosopher, or to subordinate philosophy to the illumination emergent from the subjective passion of the Christian individual.[46] Whatever we may believe today about the desirability of open philosophical investigation, the cause of truth is not served by misinformation about our predecessors. Entirely apart from differences in the political, social, and religious atmosphere, the use of irony is a sign of the once famous playfulness and pride of the philosophers.[47] As Paul Friedländer observes in his general volume on Plato, our knowledge of irony has been declining for the past hundred years. We are no longer in a position to appreciate what Schlegel called "double irony": "two lines of irony running parallel, without disturbing one another, one for the pit, the other for the stalls." [48]

Even those for whom the very notion of esotericism is repugnant will grant the existence of Platonic irony as a literary device.[49] In this perspective I can base my own approach to Plato upon the words of Schleiermacher himself. Schleiermacher emphasizes that a thorough analysis and outlining of the subject matter in a Platonic dialogue, sundered from the form and various "superfluities," would be misleading. In Plato's philosophy

---

the founders of modernity to free man from superstition, or to bring about a future condition in which frankness would be possible, itself made use of irony in order to cope with contemporary opinions.

46. Marx and Engels, *Die Deutsche Ideologie* (Berlin, 1960), p. 30. S. Kierkegaard, *Philosophical Fragments* (Princeton, 1962), pp. 57, 76, 81; *Concluding Unscientific Postscript* (Princeton, 1944), pp. 19–20, 33, 54, et passim.

47. Consider N. Malebranche's *Recherche de la Vérité* (Paris, Flammarion), Bk. 2, Ch. 4.

48. P. Friedländer, *Plato: An Introduction* (New York, 1964) (hereafter *Plato I*), pp. 145–46.

49. Especially valuable to the student of Platonic irony is Kierkegaard's *Über den Begriff der Ironie* (Düsseldorf, 1961).

form and subject are inseparable, and no proposition is to be rightly understood, except in its own place, and with the combinations and limitations which Plato has assigned to it.[50]

Taken in itself, this principle scarcely differs from my own canon of interpretation. It leads Schleiermacher to the following description of how Plato stimulates his readers to independent thought:

Or the real investigation is overdrawn with another, not like a veil, but, as it were, an adhesive skin, which conceals from the inattentive reader, and from him alone, the matter which is to be properly considered or discovered, while it only sharpens and clears the mind of an attentive one to perceive the inward connection.

Schleiermacher allows this to be a kind of limited esotericism: "it can only be said that immediate instruction was his only esoteric process, while writing was only his exoteric." [51]

Everything turns then upon what we mean by an attentive reader. My own understanding of the term is based upon Socrates' description of the art of writing in the *Phaedrus*:

Well, I suppose you will say this at least, that every speech must be constructed like a living being, having a body of its own, so as not to be without head or limbs, but with a middle and extremities, all written in such a way as to be appropriate relative to each other and to the whole.[52]

The unity of form and content means that attentiveness to form is also attentiveness to content. Stated another way, content may be visible as form but for that reason concealed as content. Attentive vision is therefore also recollective thinking. Hegel is right to say, apropos of the "absurdity" of attributing an esoteric teaching to Plato, that

50. Schleiermacher, *Introductions*, p. 14.
51. Ibid., pp. 17–18.
52. 264c2 ff.

when philosophers explain themselves about philosophical themes, they must explain themselves about philosophical themes, they must comply with their Ideas; they cannot keep these Ideas in their pockets.

However, he adds: "skill pertains to the communication of the idea; this remains always something esoteric, and one has thus not merely the exoteric of the philosophers." [53] What remains to be determined is the precise way in which Plato communicates his Ideas.

To summarize: philosophical psychiatry, medicinal rhetoric, and dramatic irony are all names for the complex structure of theoretical and practical principles which we know as the Platonic dialogue. It is Plato's conception of the nature of philosophy, rather than political prudence or spiritual pride alone, which determines the complexity of this structure.[54] According to the anonymous commentator whose words serve as the motto for this study, Plato and Homer share a harmony of expression which renders them accessible to everyone. But the commentator makes it clear that Plato is not accessible to all readers in the same way. Like Odysseus, Plato says one thing to the captains, and another to the troops.[55] The contemporary interpreter may disapprove of these aristocratic procedures, but that does not lessen his obligation to notice and understand them. As part of this obligation, the interpreter must be prepared to think for himself, but in obedience to the instructions of the dialogue rather than to the fashions of his own time. Only afterwards is criticism of Plato in terms of extra-Platonic principles and techniques reasonable. In emphasizing the dramatic, daimonic, or erotic dimension of Platonic dialectic, we do not slight the importance of the "mathematical" or "epistemological" themes of philosophy, but make their horizon visible.

53. G. W. F. Hegel, *Die Philosophie Platons* (Stuttgart, 1962), p. 18.

54. Cf. F. Nietzsche, *Jenseits von Gut und Böse,* in *Werke,* ed. K. Schlechta (3 vols. Munich, 1954), pars. 30, 40, 43, et passim with *Theaetetus* 180c8–d1; *Sophist* 216c6–d2; *Republic* 445c1 ff.

55. *Iliad* 2.188–206. Cf. n. 39 above.

History and Chronology

Philosophy exists today, like the circle-men of Aristophanes' myth in the *Symposium,* in two sundered halves, each seeking the other, but seldom with full consciousness of what it desires. It is tempting to name these two halves in accord with Pascal's distinction between the *esprit géométrique* and the *esprit de finesse.* The Platonic dialogue is sufficient testimony to its inventor's conviction that both "spirits" must exist in the same breast in order for philosophy to occur. Thus far I have described the division in terms of a decaying sensitivity to irony, but it may also be understood as a lapse in historical perception. As our store of historical information accumulates, we come closer and closer to resembling the walking encyclopedia covers against which Nietzsche warns in *The Use and Abuse of History.*[56] But whether history be transformed into pseudo-mathematical data or into the psychological panorama of epic poetry, when it entirely dominates man's mind the result is a depreciation of historical events themselves. When the boundary between history and philosophy disappears, or any disproportion in their relationship occurs, neither is clearly visible.

It should be unnecessary to emphasize the indispensability of philological and historical competence to the study of an ancient author. Historical tact is mandatory in order to avoid the kind of anachronism which prevents an author's best and truest thoughts from entering into genuine dialogue with contemporary procedures. The question here is rather one of the principles of interpretation. These principles depend upon scholarly tools for their successful fulfillment; they cannot be assumed as given implicitly by a "scientifically" adequate method. Neither can they be supplied by modern philosophies of history. It is a curious characteristic of modern Platonic scholarship that those who warn against excessive "speculation" in the interpretation of the dialogues as philosophical documents themselves engage in the unquestioned but highly speculative attempt to base solutions to philosophical problems upon historical hypotheses.

56. Nietzsche, *Vom Nutzen und Nachteil der Historie,* in *Werke, 1.,* pp. 232–33.

No one can object to historical investigations concerning the chronology or even contents of the dialogues, provided that these investigations are not mistaken for clues to Plato's philosophical teaching. On the contrary, a substantial clue to that teaching is Plato's manifest lack of interest in accurate historical chronology. When anachronisms occur in the dialogues, as is the case in the *Symposium,* they should not be regarded merely as evidence for the date of composition but as part of the dialectical technique of an unusually precise author.[57]

The serious problem with respect to the dialogues is to determine their internal or dramatic history, and not to find external historical coefficients for themes and characters mentioned therein. When reading the *Symposium,* for example, it is of assistance to know that Phaedrus was a student of Hippias, or that Agathon is connected with the teaching of Gorgias. On the other hand, the energy that has been expended in the effort to determine the historical existence of Diotima might have been better invested in reflection upon her dramatic significance. It is regularly taken for granted that Diotima is a thinly disguised Socrates, or even Plato. If this were true, one would have to explain with some care why Plato assigned the.highest mysteries of Eros to a woman, a stranger, and a prophetess. Similarly, it is misleading to try to understand the references to mysteries and rites as echoes of Orphic and Pythagorean practices. It is too frequently assumed, whether in a Hegelian or Comtean perspective, that Plato's conscious thought may be "reduced" to elements from his unconscious response to the historical tradition of which he is a product. As is well known, the dialogues are filled with fragments from virtually all of Plato's predecessors, and certainly he was fond of using Orphic and Pythagorean motifs. But this usage can normally be understood in terms of Plato's conscious intentions, provided that we devote enough thought to the dramatic structure of the dialogue under study. The fact that a philosopher is a citizen of his age does not prevent him from rational reflection upon the phe-

57. For a recent discussion of the date of composition of the *Symposium,* see K. J. Dover, "The Date of Plato's *Symposium,*" *Phronesis, 10* (1965).

nomena of his age, as even Hegel would have granted. But neither does it prevent him from engaging in reflections common to all ages.

Classical scholarship continues to be dominated by nineteenth-century theories concerning historical evolution, even among those whose theoretical commitments are to contemporary analytic techniques. These theories are regularly employed in order to account for variations and contradictions within the Platonic corpus. Frequently the paradigm of historical development employed is the Comtean interpretation of progress from religion through metaphysics to positive or mathematical science. This paradigm is especially useful for those who wish to discern the replacement of the Ideas by nominalistic constructions or linguistic rules. In whatever version, such historicist assumptions are essentially metaphysical, and certainly they are themselves historical anachronisms. The situation is still further confused by the combination of these metaphysical assumptions with valid stylometric and historical data concerning the probable dates of composition for the individual dialogues. But the data, though no doubt valid as far as they go, are not complete, and so they are not immune from attempts to disguise philosophical commitment as historical fact. Dialogues are judged to be early, middle, or late, even genuine or ungenuine, depending upon the critic's assessment of the merits of their content. In some cases, for example the *Republic,* the intrinsic unity of the work is ignored on the basis of hypotheses concerning the stages of its historical composition.[58]

I cannot discuss every aspect of this complex situation but must limit myself to one or two main points. To begin with, it is undoubtedly reasonable to suggest that men change their minds as they mature. I should hold it most likely that Plato

58. Cf. P. Shorey, *The Unity of Plato's Thought* (Chicago, 1904), p. 205, concerning the dissolution of the *Republic* into stages of historical development: "The *petitio principii* is the assumption that the numerous connecting links and cross-references that bind together the "parts" of the *Republic* were inserted as an afterthought. The chief and fundamental fallacy is the application to a great and complex literary masterpiece of canons of consistency and unity drawn from the inner consciousness of professional philologians."

altered the details of his views in the course of a long and fruitful life. So far as the dialogues are concerned, however, such a
commonsensical proposition is either misleading or irrelevant.
Plato was not a thinker like Kant or Bertrand Russell, who give
explicit testimony that specific differences in their written work
are to be explained as development or improvement of an essential kind. There is only one piece of evidence to support the
view that Plato passed through an evolution in the principles
of his thought, and this supports the existence of an esoteric
teaching; it does not clarify the problem of the order of the
dialogues themselves.[59]

In order to make the matter quite plain, let us assume that
we know the precise date of composition for each Platonic dialogue. We may even grant that, for the most part but not altogether, the content of the dialogues becomes more abstract and
technically difficult as Plato grows older. But all this tells us
nothing demonstrable about changes in Plato's thought. Even
worse, it distracts our attention from the possibly answerable
and genuinely Platonic question of the internal or theoretical
relationships among the dialogues.[60] Plato is moderately gen-
erous in giving us this kind of dramatic evidence; he is altogether silent about changes of opinion or historical development.
Assuming exact chronological knowledge, how could we refute

59. Krämer, *ArPA*, and others cite *Metaphysics* 1078b9 ff. here.

60. Again see Shorey, *Unity*, p. 131. Speaking of the historicist or evolutionary
method, he says: "The implicit canon of this method is that variation in literary
machinery and expression must be assumed to imply divergence or contradiction
in thought. To this I wish to oppose an interpretation based on the opposite
canon: that we are to assume contradiction or serious alteration in Plato's thought
only in default of a rational literary or psychological explanation of the variation in the form of its expression." Shorey's canon is certainly superior to that of
the evolutionists, not because the dialogues are free from contradiction, but because the aforementioned canon makes us think about these contradictions in
terms of the dialogues, and the conception of philosophy portrayed therein. Similarly with the comment of H von Arnim, *Platos Jugenddialoge und die
Entstehungszeit des Phaidros* (Berlin, 1960), p. vi: "Je nach dem Zusammenhang,
in dem er von ganz verschiedenen Seiten her an ein Problem herantritt, kann es
sich ihm in sehr verschiedener Gestalt darstellen, ohne das daraus auf eine
philosophische Meinungsänderung geschlossen werden könnte." And "Man muss
jeden Dialog, bevor man ihn mit andern vergleicht, in seinem Kernpunkt erfasst
haben."

Schleiermacher's hypothesis that every dialogue is a product of Plato's philosophical maturity, even if Schleiermacher himself was wrong about the order of composition? Given the manifest intricacy of the dialogues, together with Plato's reputation among the ancients as a stylist and master of irony, is it not reasonable to assume that the different formulations of the same questions within the different dialogues are intentional? May they not be explained on the basis of the different dramatic functions of the dialogues concerned?

Only when all else fails are we entitled to impose external hypotheses onto the dialogues. Only after we have understood each dialogue can we presume to say whether or how frequently Plato changed his views. The theory of historical evolution is unsupported by evidence from antiquity, and it ignores the very nature of the dialogue form. Those who accept it as their main principle of interpretation are inevitably prevented from considering the content of a given dialogue in its own terms; they try to assimilate that content to the artificially constructed assumption as to what Plato "must have believed" at that period of his life. Even should the hypothesis of historical evolution be correct and the stylometric evidence valid, they become relevant after the task of philosophical interpretation has been fulfilled, and not before. And finally, the significance of a given dialogue is entirely independent of its place in the development of Plato. Although scholars are widely agreed that the *Symposium* is a work of Plato's middle period, no one has ever suggested that its merits are superseded by the results of the later period. Although I shall make reference to other dialogues and to other authors, when these references are indicated within the *Symposium* by Plato himself, my concern is with the teaching of the *Symposium,* and not with idle speculation about whether Plato later repudiated or drastically modified that teaching.

The Teaching of the *Symposium*

The *Symposium* is a "middle" work, but not in a sense that is explained by its date of composition. One might say that it mediates between those dramatically early dialogues, which take their bearings by the events of everyday life, and those later dialogues, which begin almost at once with the most difficult questions. A more adequate formulation of this point would begin from the observation that the *Symposium* is about Eros, the mediator between men and gods. As we know from the *Republic*, Eros is inseparable from hybris; according to the *Phaedrus*, it may take the form of a divine madness. In the *Symposium* we are presented with a "phenomenological" account of the transformation of human hybris into the divine madness of the philosopher. Thus the most important theme of the *Symposium* is the hybris of Socrates, as well as the problem raised by his peculiarly unerotic nature. (By virtue of this theme, the *Symposium* is related to the *Apology*; the two dialogues are also similar in their rhetorical structure.) We cannot understand the *Symposium* unless we recognize the sense in which it is a criticism as well as an encomium of Socrates. The complete portrait of the philosopher's psyche emerges only when we reflect upon the difference between Socrates and Plato; to understand the difference between Socrates and the other speakers in the dialogue is only a preparation for this task.

As dedicated to the themes of Eros and hybris, the *Symposium* does not contain a complete account of Plato's teaching. Similarly the style of the dialogue is proportioned to the themes that lie at the center of its attention. This means that the teaching of the *Symposium*, once it has been understood, points toward dialogues like the *Parmenides* and *Sophist*, and its results must then be modified accordingly. In different terms, the *Symposium* portrays the "stages on life's way," or the fundamental modifications of the human psyche, as represented by the various speeches at Agathon's banquet as well as by the prologue to that banquet (which is usually ignored by commentators). This portrait is painted in pre-philosophical language, or in terms of concrete human existence. It contains the seeds of Plato's philosophical teaching, which are implanted in his account of the forms of the psyche. By virtue of that fact it is an essential part of his philosophical teaching; that is, the results of the *Parmenides* and *Sophist* are themselves incomplete unless taken together with the results of the *Symposium*.

The synoptic character of Platonic dialectic demands on our part a synoptic grasp of the Platonic corpus. It would be probably impossible, and certainly inefficient, to extricate the full range of Plato's thought from any one dialogue, however rich its content. Certainly I have not tried to do anything of the kind in this study. At best, I hope that my book may serve as a useful introduction to the reading of Plato. Although I believe that the *Symposium* provides us with an unusually good text for such an introduction, it is not the only one that might have been chosen. Every choice raises its own problems; in the case of the *Symposium*, perhaps two are outstanding. First, we are faced for the most part with long speeches rather than with conversation, and almost entirely with speeches that seem to be rhetorical exercises rather than complex philosophical statements. The remarks on method in the first section of this preface apply with special force to the student of the *Symposium*. We must not be seduced by Plato's rhetoric and playfulness from subjecting each speech to the most minute analysis. It is perfectly true that the *Symposium* is a work of art, and in a less obvious sense it is more a work of art than a philosophical treatise. But to rest content with that observation is to fall short of philosophy, and especially to fall short of the Platonic conception of the relation between art and philosophy.

Some readers may find my mode of analysis to be excessively talmudic, whereas to others it may seem too speculative. I ask them to suspend these judgments until they have finished my study, and so thought through with me the entire structure of the *Symposium*. If I have been able to make any contribution to their understanding of the dialogue, perhaps they will forgive me for what they may continue to regard as defects in methodology. I would be less than candid if I did not say that I regard my methods as justified by the nature of the subject matter. But the results must speak for themselves. The second outstanding difficulty raised by the *Symposium* is the danger that one may overstate the "poetic" or erotic dimension in

Plato's thought.[61] While reading this book one must always bear in mind that the *Symposium* exaggerates the elements of poetry, rhetoric, and even Eros. A study faithful to the emphases of the *Symposium* may seem to be guilty of a similar exaggeration. For example, I have found it necessary to deal at greater length with sexuality and pederasty in particular than with such topics as the theory of Ideas or the nature of rational discourse. This allotment of space is not an expression of the author's tastes; it is dictated by the material under analysis.

In this connection it seems desirable to close my preface by elaborating a point already mentioned briefly. Eros binds together the divine and human realms into a cosmos or whole. No technique ($\tau \acute{\epsilon} \chi \nu \eta$) is adequate to a vision of the whole which begins by sundering it in two. The erotic technique which Socrates (rightly or wrongly) claims as his own is of course equivalent to philosophy, that is, the synoptic and hence hybristic attempt to encompass the intelligible order of the whole in disregard of divine and human nomos. Eros therefore prefigures the special sciences. As a root phenomenon of human existence, it may be elicited by a careful analysis of the universal features of everyday experience (which includes, but does not consist exclusively of, ordinary language). Philosophy must study these universal features as a part of its continuing attempt to understand its own nature, and therefore its origins.

If philosophy is conceived in accord with the model of the specialized sciences, then the universal features of experience must be reduced to the status of special traits, or the subject matter of a specific technique. In that case, of course, universality is replaced by particularity; the whole is dissolved into its parts, which thereby lose even the coherence accorded to parts. Such a situation occurs in an age of unrestricted *technicism,* or a kind of pseudo-scientific destruction of the conditions for genuine science. "Science" means "knowing," and knowledge is impossible where philosophy has been replaced by methodology. A large part of the *Symposium* is dedicated to the criticism of technicism or unrestricted $\tau \acute{\epsilon} \chi \nu \eta$. It is essential that this

61. Cf. W. Jaeger, *Humanistische Reden und Vorträge* (Berlin, 1960), p. 136.

criticism not be taken for the expression of an anti-scientific attitude on Plato's part.[62] In addition to the fact that Plato regarded mathematical science as an adjunct to philosophy, one must remember that the *Symposium,* for reasons to be explained in the text, puts the case for philosophy in poetic terms. The mathematical idiom is inappropriate to a grasp of the daimonic Eros. As equivalent to the sum of techniques, or as an expression of the source of all techniques, the technique of Eros can be understood only by the application of Platonic dialectic in its most general sense.

62. Cf. *Critias* 109c6 ff.: Ἥφαιστος δὲ κοινὴν καὶ ᾿Αθηνᾶ φύσιν ἔχοντες, ἅμα μὲν ἀδελφὴν ἐκ ταὐτοῦ πατρός, ἅμα δὲ φιλοσοφίᾳ φιλοτεχνίᾳ τε ἐπὶ τὰ αὐτὰ ἐλθόντες . . .

"Plato himself, too, shortly before his death, had a dream of himself as a swan, darting from tree to tree and causing great trouble to the fowlers, who were unable to catch him. When Simmias the Socratic heard this dream, he explained that all men would endeavor to grasp Plato's meaning; none, however, would succeed, but each would interpret him according to his own views, whether in a metaphysical or physical or any other sense. This is a quality that Plato and Homer have in common: owing to the harmony of their expression they are accessible to everybody, no matter how one wishes to approach them."

—Anonymous Commentator

PLATO'S
SYMPOSIUM

CHAPTER ONE

❧ THE PROLOGUE ☙

The Return to the Origins

Toward the beginning of his essay on Plato's myths, Karl Reinhardt observes that "the conquest of myth is in Plato the reconquest of the lost land of his fathers." This process of reconquest is also a transformation of the external world into the inner domain of the psyche:

> The "soul" itself and its "self-movement" is [the myths'] origin; its self-shaping in the inner world, in order once more to permeate through that inner world an external one that has become soulless, is their end.[1]

One inference we may draw from Reinhardt's observation is that Plato, in a way reminiscent of Hegel, reconstitutes external "history" into psychic dialectic. What Reinhardt calls "reconquest" is nothing other than recollection. Provided we recognize the presence of *logos* within the dialectic of recollection, every Platonic dialogue may be called a myth.[2]

The function of myth is to transcend history in a return to the origins; one might almost say that Plato reverses the direction of Hegelian dialectic. Again, provided we do not give the term an exclusively mythical interpretation, we may speak of the eschatological function of Platonic myth. Myth re-collects the fragments of man's intermediate existence into the unity of the beginning and the end. It thereby provides man with an "instantaneous" perception of the eternal, or with the one kind

1. K. Reinhardt, "Platons Mythen," in *Vermaechtnis der Antike* (Göttingen, 1960), pp. 219, 227.
2. Cf. Klein, *Meno*, pp. 168–71.

1

of immortality that is accessible to temporal beings.[3] In the *Symposium* this dialectical process of recollection is named Eros. The theme of recollection is not explicitly discussed by Diotima because, to give only the main reason, the entire dialogue is a dramatic enactment of the recollective dimension of genesis or temporality. Whereas "recollection" in the technical sense is normally associated with the doctrine of complete and personal immortality, and is thus grounded in the mythic assertion of man's eternal nature, the *Symposium* remains almost entirely within the intermediate domain of Becoming. It is a Platonic demonstration of the degree in which a purely "immanent" analysis of the psyche can provide us with the basis for transcendence to the domain of what endures forever.[4] In dramatic terms, Aristophanes' account of the erotic striving for wholeness within Time is transformed into Diotima's account of the cessation of Eros, and so of Time, in the noetic vision of beauty.

The *Symposium* may be tentatively described as a series of recollections within a recollection. Like the *Theaetetus* and *Parmenides,* it begins with a prologue that takes place long after the recollected speeches and deeds. This suggests that there is for Plato a connection between Eros and what we now call "epistemology" and "ontology." The connection becomes explicit in Diotima's instruction, but it is present throughout the *Symposium* in the dramatic exhibition of the psyche's daimonic nature. For example, the speakers at the banquet, as intermediate between the gods they discuss and the disciples in the prologue, are themselves emblems of the daimonic. Within the

3. *Symposium* 210e2 ff.; *Parmenides* 156c1 ff. Cf. Alcmaeon, Fr. 2, in H. Diels, *Fragmente der Vorsokratiker* (Berlin, 1956): τοὺς ἀνθρώπους . . . διὰ τοῦτο ἀπόλλυσθαι, ὅτι οὐ δύνανται τὴν ἀρχὴν τῶι τέλει προσάψαι. Heidegger's etymology of λέγειν as "gathering together" is illuminating here.

4. For a similar conclusion, see J. A. Brentlinger, "The Cycle of Becoming in Plato's *Symposium,*" Ph.D. Dissertation (Yale University, 1962), pp. 2–3, 31. Attempts to read into the dialogue a defense of personal immortality are as misleading as attempts to account for the absence of such a defense in terms of Plato's historical development. For this reason rather than his own, I agree with K. J. Dover, who says, apropos of 207d1–208b6, that Plato wishes to "avoid raising the issue of the soul's survival at all": Dover, *Date,* p. 19.

speeches there are further dimensions of recollection. To mention only the most important: Aristophanes recalls the primordial dialogue between Zeus and Apollo; Socrates repeats some of his youthful conversations with Diotima, who in turn refers to an archaic banquet among the gods; Alcibiades recounts his erotic and military experiences with Socrates. Even Phaedrus, the "father of the logos" (177d5), is turned toward the past in his emphasis on the antiquity of Eros. Of the principal speakers, only Agathon, the advocate of youth and innovation, is clearly and thoroughly a partisan of the future. We may detect a similar bias in Pausanias, who wishes to change the laws governing pederasty, and in Eryximachus, the representative of unlimited technicism.

In general, then, the *Symposium* is an evocation of the past, not in a historical but in a mythical sense. As is explicitly stated by Aristophanes, the erotic desire for wholeness is a longing for our "original nature." [5] It is clear from the details of Aristophanes' speech that if this longing were to be altogether satisfied (by genuine union with one's sundered half), man would no longer be erotic. The same point emerges in Diotima's instruction: Eros is the desire of what we lack. To the extent that we grasp the eternal, we must cease to be erotic.[6] A fulfillment of Eros would lead, according to both Aristophanes and Diotima, to the disappearance or overcoming of human nature. For Aristophanes, however, man would be transformed into the circular creatures spawned by the stars, whose physical grotesqueness is matched by the psychic distortion of hybris. Mankind would be replaced by a race of monsters. To say the least, Aristophanes' conception of original nature is ambiguous and is not of something simply good or praiseworthy. The implication of Diotima's teaching is quite different in this sense. The fulfillment of Eros in permanent noetic vision would lead to the transformation of men into gods: not Homeric or personal deities, nor even versions of Aristotle's "thought thinking itself,"

---

5. 191d1–2, 192e10, 193d4–5.

6. 202d1 ff. Cf. R. Markus, "Love and the Will," in *Christian Faith and Philosophy* (London, 1960), p. 83.

but impersonal or selfless spectators of "pure beauty itself." [7]

For reasons of this kind, it would be misleading and superficial to characterize Plato's interest in the past as a mark of his political conservatism. In terms of the *Symposium*, it is Aristophanes rather than Socrates or Diotima who offers a conservative teaching. Whatever its external marks of caution, philosophy is by its nature a revolutionary activity, hence the need for caution. Plato belongs to an age in which philosophy was especially obedient to that need. In our own historically oriented time, with its devotion to open horizons as well as to sincerity and autonomy in the individual, it becomes hard to penetrate Platonic irony, and thereby to discern the radical teaching within.[8] For Plato revolution is not primarily a historical phenomenon; in mythical terms, it is directed toward the past rather than the future. "History" in the Platonic dialogues stands for the element of decay in the world of genesis; it is against this decay that conservatism is relevant as a kind of holding operation. Eros, on the other hand, is the bond or principle of accumulation and fulfillment within genesis. The praise of Eros in itself, apart from its intermediate manifestations, is ultimately praise of the daimonic "intentionality" of human existence. Plato's Eros is not a historical creature, but the daimonic "form" of temporality, and so a function or mode of the cosmic psyche.

Plato's turn toward the past is thus a turning away from history, not as a total repudiation of man's temporal existence but as an effort to recollect the origins of that existence. Despite its unhistorical character, the *Symposium* is evidence against the charge of nihilism that has been leveled against Plato by thinkers like Nietzsche and Heidegger.[9] This becomes fully evident only when we have appreciated the fact that the single most detailed criticism in the dialogue is directed against the unerotic nature of Socrates. The issue is extremely complex, and I merely

7. Cf. Aristotle, *Metaphysics* 12.9. esp. 1074b25, and *Symposium* 211e1. For Aristotle, εἶδος is itself noetic in a way that is not true for Plato.

8. Cf. Nietzsche, *Jenseits,* par. 25 for the modern view. One must also think of Rousseau in this connection.

9. Ibid., Vorrede, p. 566; M. Heidegger, *Nietzsche* (Pfullingen, 1961), 2, 282 ff.

allude to it here. Socrates himself speaks of this aspect of his nature when he tells us that it was necessary for him to be instructed by Diotima concerning the effects of Eros.[10] In other
words, his own psyche was somehow defective in this regard and
could not provide him with the relevant information. The serious meaning within this partly ironical admission will be confirmed when we study carefully the speech of Alcibiades. The
same complex situation is visible in the *Theaetetus,* where
Socrates speaks of his psychic sterility and describes the unsocia-
ble nature of the best philosophers—which extends to an unwillingness to attend banquets—and recognition of the need
"to flee this world as quickly as possible for the next." [11] It is
present in the *Phaedo,* which begins with mention of recurrent
dreams advising Socrates to "make music," and in which Socrates
describes philosophers as "preparing for nothing other than
death." [12]

The difference between the Socratic and the Platonic understanding of philosophy as a preparation for death turns upon a
difference between their psyches. This difference is represented
by the fact that Socrates wrote nothing, whereas Plato generated
the dialogues. If godhood, or the overcoming of the merely human in our nature, is a proper goal for man, it can be ap-
proached only through the active mediation of the daimonic
Eros. Such is the challenge implicit in genesis for man. The
Symposium is not a denial of life, but a statement of the structure of that challenge.

Discipleship and Communication

In the *Republic* Socrates describes the turning of the potential philosopher away from the cave of "history" and toward the
sun. The *Symposium* begins with a turning of disciples away
from the present and toward the mythical past of Socrates' philosophical existence. In the *Republic* Socrates protects us from

10. *Symposium* 201e1 et passim.
11. *Theaetetus* 150d2, 173c6 ff., 176b1.
12. *Phaedo* 60c9 ff., 64a5 ff.

the initially blinding light of the sun by taking a shorter and indirect route.[13] This route is characterized by the peculiarly erotic language of generation: the sun is an "offspring" of the good.[14] Once again, Eros mediates between the merely human and the altogether divine. Nevertheless, it is the divine toward which Socrates advises us to direct our steps. In the *Symposium* not the divine, but the daimonic Eros, is himself the initially blinding light. Further, despite the political context of the discussion in the *Republic* and the association of the erotic imagery with the good, the divine sciences of mathematics and dialectic guide us toward apprehension of the divine itself. Eros appears in human form in the *Republic* only to be criticized.[15] In the *Symposium* the decisively human phenomenon of sexuality is the key to the daimonic striving toward the divine. We must begin with men, albeit with men who have been mythically transformed into heroes.

As poetic rhetoric, the *Symposium* invites comparison with Homer even more, perhaps, than with the Sophists. It is Plato's odyssey of the psyche, in which speech predominates over deed, and the Eris of war is deepened into the Eros of philosophy. The traditional titles of the Homeric epics refer to the splendid deeds of men, to war and wandering; the title of the *Symposium* refers to men whose bodies are at rest. Whereas Homer's song is guaranteed by the divine Muses, Plato's readers are dependent upon the memories of singularly unheroic disciples. With some slight variation, Odysseus is represented in the *Symposium* by Socrates, as Plato makes explicit by a number of important references. On the other hand, there is no direct parallel to Achilles, but only a series of partial caricatures: the triumph of Agathon, the behavior of Socrates in retreat, the intoxicated general Alcibiades. The Trojan war is accordingly replaced by Socrates' invasion, assisted by Aristodemus, of the camp of sophistry, and at a deeper level, by the quarrel between philosophy and poetry.

13. Cf. *Phaedo* 99d4 ff.
14. For a more detailed discussion, cf. Rosen, *ErosRepub*.
15. Most forcefully at 573b6, 574d8, 575a3, 576b11, 579d5–8.

In sum: Homer speaks indirectly through the Muses of the semidivine heroes, whereas Plato speaks indirectly through Apollodorus and Aristodemus of the daimonic Eros. The first step in the reconstruction of Plato's speech is to grasp the relationship of distance between the characters in the prologue and those at the banquet. Aristodemus, as mediator between the two, and to that extent a caricature of Eros, must be discussed in both contexts. To begin with, the conversation upon which we are eavesdropping and in which Apollodorus repeats Aristodemus' account of the banquet, seems to have taken place at the dramatic date of 401–400; we are about fifteen years removed from the "erotic speeches." [16] But the distance is one of nature even more than history. A rapid survey of the persons at the banquet will serve to establish their objective transcendence of Apollodorus and his companions.

Of Socrates and Aristophanes nothing need be said here. The eminence of Alcibiades in 416 was perhaps at its height. Agathon is fresh from his dramatic triumph before 30,000 Hellenes. Eryximachus, as the son of Acumenus and an Aesclepiad, is a man of solid professional reputation. Phaedrus is probably of higher social standing than Pausanias; these two must be counted the least prominent of the main speakers. But they shine in the fame of their companions; in mythical terms, they, too, are minor heroes in the Socratic court. The dramatic date of the banquet adds another perspective to the scene of past glory. Athens still expects victory in the Peloponnesian war; the portrait of Alcibiades, together with Agathon's victory, place the scene just before the Sicilian expedition. But this also means that we are very close to the night of the mysterious desecration of the Hermae and profanation of the Eleusinian

16. For the evidence concerning the dramatic date, R. G. Bury, *The Symposium of Plato* (Cambridge, 1932), p. lxvi; for "erotic speeches," A. Hug, *Platons Symposion* (2d ed. Leipzig, 1884), pp. xi–xii. H. H. Bacon makes a number of very perceptive remarks on what I have called the "relationship of distance" between the prologue and the banquet, as well as on Plato's dramatic style generally: H. Bacon, "Socrates Crowned," *The Virginia Quarterly Review, 35* (1959), esp. 418–20. Cf. R. S. Brumbaugh, *Plato on the One* (New Haven, 1961), p. 29, on the function of "indirect narration."

mysteries. It can scarcely be an accident that, of our main speakers, Phaedrus, Eryximachus, and Alcibiades were all accused of taking part in these outrages.[17] The daimonic aura of the banquet is one of criminal hybris as well as of public glory, to say nothing of Socrates' ambiguous reputation.

Socrates, Agathon, and Aristophanes bring to the banquet the eloquence of philosophy, tragedy, and comedy. All the main speakers except Socrates and Aristophanes are known from sources like the *Protagoras* to have been students of the Sophists. In addition, Aristophanes is the only person named at the banquet who cannot be identified as a lover or beloved of one of the other guests.[18] The combination of verbal fluency, heterodoxy, and erotic involvement, the public events of the time, and the privacy of the banquet itself, lead us to expect speeches of unusual frankness. And yet the atmosphere of frankness is obscured by the span of time between the prologue and the banquet. If Plato had wished merely to acquaint his readers with the views presented by the several speakers, he could easily have portrayed the banquet as a contemporary event. The prologue, very far from a purely artistic ornament to the philosophical speeches, is the most evident clue to the complexity of Plato's intentions. His revelation of the erotic speeches is at the same time a concealment, or what may appropriately be called a part of the dialectic between speech and silence. In more accessible terms, we cannot understand fully the speeches at the banquet unless we grasp the role played by Apollodorus and Aristodemus. To some degree, of course, this role is to serve as signs pointing toward the mythical past. But

17. D. Macdowell, *Andokides, On the Mysteries* (Oxford, 1962), 15.21; 35.25. Cf. also Macdowell's introduction, pp. 3, 7: the rites were kept so secret that they are now unknown. "But it is clear that a most important part was the showing of certain 'sacred things' (ἱερά). Those to whom these secrets were revealed were 'initiated' (τελεῖσθαι or μυεῖσθαι), and it was believed that when they died they would enjoy everlasting bliss in the world of the dead."

18. G. K. Plochmann, "Hiccups and Hangovers in the Symposium," *Bucknell Review, 11* (1963), 6, erroneously states that "Phaedrus is paired with someone not present." There can be no doubt that in both the *Protagoras* (314c2–3) and *Symposium* he is regularly linked with Eryximachus.

signs, too, have ascertainable natures, which modify accordingly what they designate.

To begin with, Aristodemus' report is not complete. He omits altogether some speeches that he has imperfectly remembered (180c2); this suggests the possibility that he may not have remembered perfectly the speeches that he actually recounts. We are also told that he fell asleep toward the last part of the banquet, thereby missing most of Socrates' final conversation with Agathon and Aristophanes (223d1 ff.). We know only that some part of that conversation was devoted to the writing of tragedy and comedy. But at what moment did Aristodemus' drowsiness actually begin to affect his attention? Again, Apollodorus tells us that he confirmed with Socrates only some of the things recounted by Aristodemus (173b5), and the inexact nature of the report is emphasized later (178a1 ff.). The completeness of the *Symposium* as a whole includes as one aspect more than a shadow of doubt as to the completeness of its parts. Plato publishes the events of the banquet in such a way as to put the onus of responsibility upon Aristodemus. Reflection upon the prologue and upon the natures of Socrates' disciples and the accuracy of their accounts prevents us from being drawn directly up by the daimonic aura of the speeches themselves.

In terms of the initial comparison between Homer and Plato, the difference between the song of the Muses and the memorized repetitions of disciples reminds us of Socrates' criticism in the *Ion* of the understanding by *rhapsodes* of what they too have merely memorized.[19] The link between poetry and enthusiasm is a warning of the danger implicit in the apparent subsequent identification between Eros and philosophy. Certain questions immediately suggest themselves to the careful reader. What is the proper ratio between daring and caution in a philosophical exercise? If philosophy is reasonable speech, how can it be defined by the daimonic, the manic, the unspeakable? How can

19. *Ion* 533e5 ff. where the problem of "understanding" is extended to the poets as well.

one undergo erotic passion without being dissolved by it? Must we not distinguish between reason and Eros, even in the act of reasoning about Eros?[20] Finally, the device of the prologue emphasizes the imagery of initiation, revelation, and mystery within the speeches themselves. We must be purified for initiation by penetrating the significance of the prologue, by going beyond the disciples in our understanding of the speeches they recount.[21] The first word of the dialogue, "I opine" (Δοκῶ), sets the tone for the ambiguous relationship between the prologue and the banquet. The prologue is the courtyard to philosophy through which the initiate must pass in order to reach the palace of the king.[22] Similarly, if knowledge (ἐπιστήμη) is available to man it can be only through the mediation of opinion (δόξα). The reader who begins his study of the *Symposium* is in the position of the unnamed comrade to whom Apollodorus is currently repeating his account of the banquet.

The Fanaticism of Apollodorus

In beginning our ascent to the teaching of Diotima, we meet first with Apollodorus, the fanatical disciple, whose character is accordingly both good and bad.[23] Bury takes this fanaticism as a mark of Apollodorus' reliability as a witness,[24] and he is not altogether wrong to do so. A convert or disciple is, among other

20. Cf. J. Moravcsik, "Reason and Eros in the Ascent-Passage of the Symposium," unpublished lecture (hereafter *ReasonEros*), p. 7.

21. H. Wolfson, *Philo* (Cambridge, Mass., 1947), *1*, 24–25: "the term mysteries . . . referred to that kind of wisdom which some philosophers believed . . . to belong only to the gods and which had to be imparted in secret only to a chosen few. . . . In general, it may be said that the practice of keeping certain doctrines secret was common among all the schools of Greek philosophy." Cf. the discussion of esotericism in the Introduction above.

22. Maimonides, *The Guide of the Perplexed* (Chicago, 1963), Ch. 51. Cf. Bacon, *Crowned*, p. 419: "For who is the reader but the shadowy questioner to whom the whole story is told?"

23. Cf. G. D. De Vries, "Apollodore dans le 'Banquet' de Platon," *Revue des Études Grecques, 48* (1935), which easily refutes the notion of Pohlenz and Wilamowitz that the introduction to the *Symposium* is intended as a dedication to Apollodorus.

24. Bury, *Symposium*, p. xvi.

things, a man who memorizes the words of another instead of speaking his own. Apollodorus is not unprepared to repeat the erotic speeches because he has spent much time in memorizing and declaiming them. But fanaticism does not guarantee accuracy. Even if we assume that Apollodorus' account is entirely accurate, it hardly follows that he understands it properly; the dramatic significance of his nature continues to add an extra dimension to his report. Fanaticism is a degenerate form of daring, a characteristic of disciples rather than masters. It should be observed that we are indebted to Apollodorus' fanaticism for our knowledge of the speeches, which were not written down. He must be commended for his own erotic attraction to Socrates, and so to philosophy.

But fanaticism is also a characteristic of unstable natures; perhaps Apollodorus' conversion was accidental rather than essential. His extreme grief at the death of Socrates is not in harmony with the teaching of the master, nor is the abruptness of his behavior toward Glaucon and the unnamed comrade.[25] Apollodorus' philosophical credentials are tainted by excessive passion and rigidity in behavior. Thus he also stands for the difficulties that the aspiring initiate must face in turning toward philosophy. The source or cause of philosophy is also an obstacle to philosophy. As Socrates teaches in the *Republic*, no one is more easily corrupted than the young potential philosopher.[26] For example, the strongest natures are potentially the greatest criminals: Eros is a dangerous daimon; in the teaching of the *Republic*, it is the principle of tyranny.[27] As though to comment upon this danger, Plato presents in Apollodorus' speech an unmistakable echo of the beginning of the *Republic*.[28]

Apollodorus explains why he is prepared to answer questions about the banquet:[29]

25. *Phaedo* 59a; *Apology* 34a.
26. *Republic* 490e2 ff.
27. Ibid., 573b6, 574d8 ff.
28. "Apollodorus" means literally "gift of Apollo." In Aristophanes' speech, Apollo is the agent for Zeus' "gift" to man of Eros, which, as we shall see, is also understood by the comedian as a dangerous benefit.
29. Apparently Aristodemus was rather more loquacious after the banquet

11

I happened, on the day before yesterday, to be going to the city from my home in Phalerum, when one of my acquaintances, catching sight of me from behind, called out; and joking as he summoned me, said: "O Phalerian, you Apollodorus, will you not wait?" And I, stopping, waited. (172a2–6)

Socrates opens the *Republic* by telling how he "went down yesterday to the Piraeus" to observe a religious festival. On the way home with Glaucon, he is spotted by Polemarchus, who sends his slave boy to restrain them. The slave boy pulls Socrates' cloak from behind. When Polemarchus catches up with Socrates and Glaucon, he jokingly appeals to force in order to persuade them to stay for conversation, dinner, and a night festival. We see in the opening of the *Symposium* a Platonic joke on the way in which disciples imitate their masters.

But Plato's jokes generally have an ascertainably serious dramatic function. We are being asked to think about the connection between the *Symposium* and the *Republic*. Apollodorus stops of his own will, and the joke of his friend's language seems to turn upon the use of legal terminology: Apollodorus is summoned to court to testify concerning rumors about the speeches and deeds at the banquet of Agathon, and he appears voluntarily, or at least without resistance.[30] Socrates, on the other

---

than during it. Of course we cannot be sure that one of the other guests did not reveal some details of the banquet. But only Socrates, Agathon, Aristophanes and Aristodemus were present throughout. Apollodorus' expostulation at 173b1 (οὐ μὰ τὸν Δία), when asked whether Socrates was his informant, makes it clear that the latter did not communicate details to those who were not present. (When asked directly by Apollodorus to confirm certain details, Socrates did so. But this is not the same as to take the initiative in revealing the events of the banquet.) Since Agathon and Aristophanes were quite drunk toward the end of the evening, it is possible that only Aristodemus recalled, however fuzzily, the final events.

30. For disagreement concerning the nature of the joke, cf. the editions of Hug, *Symposion*, G. F. R. Rettig, *Platons Symposion* (Halle, 1876), and Bury, *Symposium* in their notes to 172a4. I agree with Hug. Bury, however, follows Rettig in deleting ᾿Απολλόδωρος from the text and construing the joke as a pretense of ignorance and contempt for the seaport: "Hey, you Phalerian!" But even if (as Stallbaum claims) the word order should present any difficulty for

hand, is restrained by physical contact and the threat of force, as well as by the will of Glaucon. The peaceful surrender of Apollodorus here is an anticipation of Socrates' voluntary acceptance of the invitation to Agathon's banquet. Socrates' appearance at the home of Cephalus, a resident alien and munitions maker, is not only constrained but unusual for him, as Cephalus notes. In addition, the ensuing conversation takes place outside the city walls, in the presence of strangers, with youths as the main interlocutors, and "between" two religious festivals. The banquet, on the other hand, is a private affair, limited to friends or acquaintances and all Athenian citizens, which occurs in the city, on the day after the official, public celebration of Agathon's victory. For these reasons, and because it is characterized by drinking, eventually even by drunkenness, we ought to expect that the banquet will move Socrates to speak more freely than in the *Republic*.[31, A]

The friend who stops Apollodorus is named Glaucon. The Glaucon of the *Symposium* is to Apollodorus as the Polemarchus of the *Republic* is to Socrates. The disciple replaces the master; a businessman replaces the leisured son of a businessman.[32] We are at a further remove from philosophy in the prologue of the *Symposium* than in that of the *Republic*. At the same time, the opening scene of both dialogues is set among men of wealth, outside the city but within the city walls, on the way from a

---

the comparison with the legal form, the words of Rettig support the interpretation that the joke is one of restraint: "Als Glaukon seiner aus der Ferne von hinten ansichtig geworden war und den eilenden nicht einholen zu können meinte, nahm er seine Zuflucht zu einer List und rief ihm, wie einem unbekannten Verbrecher oder Dieb . . ." Cf. also Hug 172a6.

31. Cf. also L. Robin, *La théorie platonicienne de l'amour* (Paris, 1908), p. 182; M. Tait, "Spirit, Gentleness, and the Philosophic Nature in the Republic," *American Philological Association, 80* (1949), 211; T. Gould, *Platonic Love* (London, 1963), p. 85; F. M. Cornford, "The Doctrine of Eros in Plato's Symposium," in *The Unwritten Philosophy* (Cambridge, 1950), pp. 70–71. For the effect of drinking on frankness, *Laws* 673 (and 640 ff.). At *Symposium* 218b, Alcibiades names the main participants at the banquet as having felt philosophical μανία. He can then speak freely before them, as he could not before the uninitiated.

32. See Bury, *Symposium*, note to 172c3 for conjectures as to Glaucon's identity.

harbor.[33] Whereas Socrates practices irony toward Polemarchus and Cephalus, Apollodorus is explicitly rude to Glaucon and the unnamed comrade in his denunciation of money making. As a consequence of his literal-mindedness, Apollodorus has forgotten the connection between wealth and leisure for philosophy. He remembers the letter, but not that "the letter killeth."

Thus the presumption at least exists that Apollodorus is not altogether fair, either to Glaucon or to the unnamed comrade. Both press him for information about the banquet even as he is denouncing them, denying their interest in philosophy. One more than suspects that Apollodorus has been deranged rather than saved by philosophical madness($\mu\alpha\nu\iota\alpha$).[34] Here again, Apollodorus' fanaticism prepares us for the subsequent revelation of Socrates' hybris, of which it is a disciple's imitation. In the *Republic* Socrates dispenses justice in response to force. In the *Symposium* hybris replaces moderation, and the status of justice becomes problematical. In the *Republic* we must infer the problem from such indirect evidence as the fact that Socrates' whole speech is a contradiction of the principle of justice: one man, one job. In the *Symposium* this ambiguity becomes explicit, both through the accusation of hybris leveled against Socrates, and, to mention only one other important point, because Diotima omits "justice" from her description of Eros' natural qualities.[35]

Apollodorus' complex nature is a paradigm of the complexity of the *Symposium*. He is both close to and far from philosophy. As a fanatic and disciple, he is one of those who give a bad name to philosophy; but he is not all bad—the power of Eros is still visible in him.[36] Nor is he so fanatical a disciple, appar-

33. Cf. Robin, *SymBudé*, p. xix and G. Krüger, *Einsicht und Leidenschaft* (Frankfurt-am-Main, 1948), pp. 77–78.

34. Bury is undoubtedly right to defend μανικός at 173d8, changed by Burnet to μαλακός; there is nothing "soft" about Apollodorus in the *Symposium*. For philosophy as a divine gift of madness, *Phaedrus* 244a3 ff.

35. *Symposium* 203c ff. Cf. H. Neumann, "Diotima's Concept of Love," *American Journal of Philology, 86* (1965), 50.

36. See Rettig, *Symposion* 173c5: "Dass Apollodorus auch heiter sein konnte, dürfte sich aus *Phädon* 59A ergeben. Der Mann hatte eben ein sehr erregbares,

ently, as to talk about his master except to those who urge him to do so (173c1–2); like Socrates in the *Republic*, he acts in accordance with necessity.[37] Glaucon, whatever his motives, is not deterred by Apollodorus' eccentricity; his forebearance before rudeness shows how eager he is to hear the erotic speeches. He is, however, strangely misinformed about the date of the banquet, although he knows its location and at least two of the guests.[38] Glaucon is not an intimate of Socrates, since he must depend upon Apollodorus, and earlier, the unknown Phoenix for his information.[39]

Apollodorus corrects Glaucon's error about the date of the banquet. Unlike the founding of the just city, and despite its dramatic occasion, it is temporally separated from the public religious observance.[40] The occasion, the victory of a tragedy,

---

auch aus den Worten unserer Stelle hervor, wo es heisst ὑπερφυῶς ὡς χαίρω." Cf. *Apology* 34a.

37. At *Republic* 328b2, Socrates gives in to Glaucon (rather than to Polemarchus): Ἀλλ' εἰ δοκεῖ . . . οὕτω χρὴ ποιεῖν At Symposium 173c1–2, Apollodorus gives in to Glaucon: εἰ οὖν δεῖ . . . ταῦτα χρὴ ποιεῖν.

38. Rettig *Symposion* 172a7, thinks that Plato indicates the special importance of Agathon, Socrates and Alcibiades by having Glaucon name them at the beginning. This may be an indication of Glaucon's special interest in beautiful young men; he inquires here about the συνουσία, which also means "sexual intercourse." Glaucon's belief that the banquet was a recent one shows that the prologue takes place after 407, when Alcibiades is back in Athens.

39. It is tempting to speculate upon the name "Phoenix, son of Philippus." Is it an allusion to the possible rebirth of the Socratic circle through the instrumentality of the publication of the dialogue? This suggestion will take on greater meaning later, when I discuss bisexuality and nonsexual generation. See M. Delcourt, *Hermaphrodite* (Paris, 1958), pp. 121 ff. The phoenix generates itself from itself, i.e. without Eros, like the androgynes in Aristophanes' speech. Note also that Philippus is the name of the παράσιτος in Xenophon's *Symposium*.

40. Krüger, *Einsicht*, pp. 19 ff. points out that "der Gott, durch den uns die Philosophie klar werden soll, ist bei den Griechen *kein offizieller, allgemein verehrter Gott*," as is Aphrodite. The praise of Eros is a mark of modernity: "Die Hervorhebung des Eros ist neu, und sie ist aufschlussreich für die geistige Luft, in der die *Philosophie* erwächst." Krüger associates erotic passion with a recognition of the self. Cf. H. Jeanmaire, *Dionysos* (Paris, 1951), p. 8: "Dionysos est le moins 'politique' des dieux grecs, au moins pour la période antérieure à l'époque des successeurs d'Alexandre . . . Dionysos est resté étranger à la religion de la famille plus encore qu'à celle de la cité . . ." See also Plutarch, *Eroticus* 756b: to ask about the gods' nature is already to deviate from piety.

raises the dominant theme of poetry. But the dialogue is not the same as a tragedy. The difference emerges within the *Symposium* in the brief dialogues between Socrates and Agathon (194a1–d8, 199b8–201c9). The first dialogue is terminated by Phaedrus, who points out that if Socrates is allowed to continue, Agathon will never make his encomium.[41] Agathon indicates his willingness to speak; Socrates is suggestively silent. He prefers dialogue to encomium, and his own speech will be a mixture of the two. Socrates will challenge the public triumph of tragedy or poetry and claim the private victory of philosophy. The erotic relationship between Socrates and Agathon is more eristic than amatory. The speeches in tragedy, however profound, owe their ultimate allegiance to the nomoi of the city. The speeches of philosophy owe their ultimate allegiance to the Ideas. Poetic speeches are encomia of men and gods; philosophical speeches praise daimons and Ideas.

The Silence of Aristodemus

The *Symposium,* like the speech of Socrates, is a mediation of poetry and philosophy; like the speech of Plato, it is a mediation between speech and silence. But the *Symposium* is also the speech of the silent Aristodemus of Cydathenaeum, perhaps the strangest character in the dialogue. Apollodorus describes his (and our) informant as a short man, accustomed to going about

---

41. The Greek emphasizes this contrast between dialogue and encomium: ἐὰν μόνον ἔχῃ ὅτῳ διαλέγηται, ἄλλως τε καὶ καλῷ. ἐγὼ δὲ ἡδέως μὲν ἀκούω Σωκράτους διαλεγομένου, ἀναγκαῖον δέ μοι ἐπιμεληθῆναι τοῦ ἐγκωμίου τῷ Ἔρωτι. For a relevant discussion of encomia, see Aristotle, *Rhetoric* 1367a28 ff. Among the helpful points which Aristotle makes, these should be cited by an interpreter of the *Symposium:* (1) one should describe a man's faults in such a way as to make them seem like virtues; (2) we must consider the audience before whom we praise, and what they regard as praiseworthy; (3) διὸ καὶ τὰ συμπτώματα καὶ τὰ ἀπὸ τύχης ὡς ἐν προαιρέσει ληπτέον . . . ; (4) praise and counsel are closely related, differing only in the turn of phrase. For some interesting remarks concerning the relation of Plato's dialogues to tragedy, see H. Kuhn, "The True Tragedy: On the relationship between Greek tragedy and Plato," *Harvard Studies in Classical Philology* (1942) esp. *52,* pp. 20–21, and *53,* pp. 53, 58.

barefoot, and as an extreme lover (ἐραστής) of Socrates (173b1–4).[42] Aristodemus' barefootedness, the mark of the Socratic disciple, contrasts sharply with the fact that his master is wearing shoes. Socrates, by nature ugly, resorts to artifice to beautify himself for the banquet, thereby emphasizing that his participation in it is voluntary.[43] Since Aristodemus was not invited to the banquet, we cannot say whether he too would have taken such preparatory measures. In any case, he appears unshod, and it seems that, like his master, he was not handsome since he is called, both here and in Xenophon, Aristodemus the short.[44] In at least two respects Aristodemus resembles the description of Eros given by Diotima later in the dialogue. Both are shoeless; both are messengers or intermediaries. Eros mediates between the human and the divine, whereas Aristodemus mediates between the speakers at the banquet and later disciples— as well as readers of the *Symposium*. In his commentary on the dialogue, Ficino interprets naked feet as symbolizing a lack of prudence or a courting of danger (just as the shoeless man is subject to frequent wounds from thorns, pebbles, and the like).[45] This makes sense here, in view of the explicit connection between Eros and hybris, and of the difference between master and disciple. The shoeless Aristodemus, although silent at the banquet, imprudently reveals its events to others. The clad Socrates, combining speech and silence in the form of irony, attributes the revelation of mysteries to a priestess.

Why was Aristodemus silent at the banquet? Probably the most obvious answer would be because he came uninvited. But he is welcomed warmly (whether or not from politeness alone) by Agathon, and is obviously accepted by the other guests.[46] Loquacity is as likely a response to the embarrassment of an uninvited guest as is silence. Since Aristodemus has recounted the

---

42. Apollodorus says at 174a1 that his words are those of Aristodemus, but this is not always so, e.g. 185c4.

43. 174a3–9.

44. *Memorabilia* 1.4.2.

45. R. Marcel, *Marsile Ficin: Commentaire sur le Banquet de Platon* (Paris, 1956), Oratio Sexta, 77v–78r.

46. E.g. by Eryximachus at 176c2.

events of the banquet to at least two others, Phoenix and Apollodorus, he cannot be taciturn by nature. A more likely and "Platonic" reason for his silence may be derived from a discussion in Xenophon's *Memorabilia*. Socrates, "learning that Aristodemus neither sacrificed to the gods nor was seen praying or using divination, but made fun of those who did so," attempts to convince him that man has been made by design, and so by intelligent gods.[47] Aristodemus' answers reveal that he is, to say the least, a man of little faith, who denies that the gods look after man or are in any need of his own service. I suggest that Aristodemus is silent at the banquet mainly because he is unwilling to praise a god. Unlike the ironical Socrates, he is defective in public piety;[48] and in mocking those who employ prophecy,[49] he denies that the gods send messengers to man. As a consequence, he must repudiate the doctrine of Eros or is not himself a genuinely erotic man. His subsequent disclosures bear out this interpretation: the man who reveals to mortals the divinely inspired speeches, or violates the mysteries, is himself an unbeliever.

Perhaps a genuinely daimonic man would never have discussed the banquet with men of a lower nature. Plato may have used Aristodemus as a symbol that the published account of the banquet cannot be understood at the literal level of Aristodemus' report. Or he may have wished to moderate the religious aspects of the speeches by allowing an atheist to communicate them. It seems safe to say that Aristodemus stands for the ambiguity of the "religious" meaning of the dialogue. The various proofs of god or gods given by Plato in the dialogues, like the

47. 1.4.2.

48. Xenophon (according to a papyrus fragment) says that Aristodemus οὔτε εὐχόμενον δῆλον ὄντα ... (1.4.2). This is the charge against which he is anxious to defend Socrates; cf. 1.1.2: θύων τε γὰρ φανερὸς ἦν ..., καὶ μαντικῇ χρώμενος οὐκ ἀφανὴς ἦν.

49. 1.4.2. This is re-emphasized at 1.4.15. See Friedländer, *Plato I*, p. 41: the demonic is the intermediate realm, "the scene of all intercourse between gods and men and, therefore, of mantic and priestly art, ritual, and magic. . . . Co-ordinate with this realm is the 'demonic man' . . ." Cf. also p. 42. The role of the intermediate in Plato's thought is discussed in Robin, *l'Amour* and more extensively in J. Souilhé, *La notion platonicienne d'intermédiaire dans la philosophie des dialogues* (Paris, 1919) (hereafter *Intermédiaire*).

revelation of Eros, can be understood only in the existential [50]
context of the "divine" life of philosophy. When such proofs
occur they are always ancillary to another theme, usually, as in
the *Laws*, to a political theme. Even the *Phaedo* is in this sense
an argument ad homines; Socrates wishes to console those who
fear not merely his death but their own. The transpolitical setting of the *Symposium* makes the situation more complex; as is
clear from the roles of Diotima and Alcibiades, the *Symposium*
is a revelation. A revelation is in one sense cryptic or mysterious,
but it is also characterized by a kind of openness or frankness.
Something is brought into the open, albeit in a mysterious manner; the revelation illustrates the dialectic between speech and
silence.[B]

One question the interpreter of Plato should keep firmly in
mind is this: why did Plato never write a dialogue about an
Olympian god? The choice of Eros rather than Aphrodite gives
an unorthodox slant to his religious encomium. Even more interesting, Eros is assimilated into the daimonic, or the intermediate realm between men and gods. The dialogue about a
god then turns out not to be about a god, but about the divine.
This fact is not easy to understand, but we may safely say that it
would be wrong to see in the Platonic Eros a philosophical justification for humanism.[51] A daimon is not a human being, not
even an idealized version of the human spirit, except in the
sense that the human spirit is itself partially divine. The highest explanation of human nature is at the same time an account
of how man transcends the merely human. This is true of Aristodemus in his love for Socrates; similarly, each of the encomiasts, despite his initially selfish motives, is raised above
himself by the erotic dimension of selfishness.

In summary, the religious character of the *Symposium* is at
least tinctured by the dubious character of Aristodemus' views
on religion. He is a lover of Socrates, but a mocker of what the

50. The word "existential" should not be confused with the contemporary
usage derived from "existentialism." For a useful portrait of the unity in Plato
between life and thought, see J. Stenzel, *Platon der Erzieher* (Leipzig, 1928), e.g.
pp. 77, 143. Still better, Krüger, *Einsicht.*

51. This is the view of W. Jaeger, *Paideia* (3 vols. New York, 1943), 2, p. 195.

Symposium calls the daimonic. A similar ambiguity exists in the nature of Apollodorus. His madness seems both to remove him from philosophy and to bring him closer to it. Perhaps he is more erotic than Aristodemus; on the other hand, the flawed character of his Eros is shown by the fact that it has brought him misery rather than *eudaimonia* (173d1–10). Philosophy, it is true, has replaced his ceaseless motion with unchangeableness, but unfortunately the resemblance between Apollodorus and the Ideas seems to end at this point.[52] The unnamed companion is more moderate but perhaps by that token less erotic.[53]

On the Way to the Banquet

We turn now to what is in effect Aristodemus' account as remembered, and so modified, by Apollodorus.[54] Most commentators have observed that Socrates is not the narrator since details of his life are presented in the dialogue, which is really an encomium to him. This opinion does justice neither to the significance of the prologue nor to the intricacy of Socrates' nature. Furthermore, there are other dialogues, of which the *Apology* is the clearest instance, in which Socrates praises himself in an autobiographical mode. In the *Symposium,* however, secrets about Socrates' nature are revealed: soberly and unthinkingly by Aristodemus, drunkenly and with real penetration by Alcibiades.[55] To put this more sharply, both Agathon and Alcibiades present what one may call the private, or more serious,

52. Cf. 173a1 ff. and 173d4: Ἀεὶ ὅμοιος εἶ, ὦ Ἀπολλόδωρε.

53. The ἑταῖρος (a word with a political flavor) requests Apollodorus at 173e4: οὐκ ἄξιον . . . νῦν ἐρίζειν. The Eris is closely connected to the discussion of Apollodorus' madness. In the *Republic* the political context makes explicit the connection between war and philosophy.

54. See 178a1 ff.

55. Friedländer, *Plato I,* p. 352, n. 8: "Ludwig von Sybel, in his edition of Plato's *Symposium* (Marburg, 1888) says (p. 102) that we hear Plato himself speak directly through Alcibiades' words. We must also realize how much of Alcibiades was in Plato." These words surely point in the right direction, although they require careful interpretation.

version of the public charges against Socrates recorded in the *Apology*: Socrates is accused and condemned of hybris.[56]

The connection between Eros and tyranny has already been noted;[57] in our effort to understand the philosophical nature, we must consider the dangerous consequences of its desire for union with the divine. Such a desire is regarded by traditional Greek wisdom as excessive and a sort of madness. It leads a man to disregard the authority of nomos, of political and religious moderation, of the basis for private and public stability. Little wonder that Socrates regularly disguises his hybris by irony; in fact, Socratic irony amounts to the difference between philosophical and unphilosophical hybris. It is thus also an expression of philosophical as distinct from political justice.[58] Philosophical hybris aspires to a height which, although beyond the reach of the many, can nevertheless be occupied simultaneously by more than one. Unphilosophical hybris, on the other hand, leads one to aspire to tyranny: to stand physically and politically beyond the few as well as the many, who are thus reduced from citizenship to slavery. In its accusation or revelation of Socrates' hybristic nature, the *Symposium* seems to confirm his innocence of political treason by showing the transpolitical end of philosophy. Unfortunately, as directed beyond the city, philosophy cannot be entirely freed from charges of treason. Nor is it altogether clear that philosophy does not aspire to political rule, however disinterested or exalted its motives. The most one can confidently say is that the *Symposium* teaches us with unusual, but not absolute, frankness the implications of Socratic irony.

This point is illustrated at the beginning of Socrates' encoun-

56. Explicitly at 175e7, 215b7, 219c5; implicitly at 216e4–5, 217e5, 221e3. Consider also Socrates' behavior at 174a9, 174e1–2, 177d6 and 199a1–2.

57. *Republic* 573b6 et passim. Cf. F. Nietzsche, *Menschliches Allzumenschliches*, in *Werke*, ed. Schlecta, *1*, par. 261: the Greek philosophers "hatten einen handfesten Glauben an sich und ihre 'Wahrheit' und warfen mit ihr alle ihre Nachbarn und Vorgänger nieder; jeder von ihnen war ein streitbarer gewalttätiger *Tyrann.*"

58. Cf. Aristotle, *Nichomachean Ethics*, 4.3.22 and 28, where the "great-souled" man is said to practice irony πρὸς τοὺς πολλούς.

ter with Aristodemus.[59] Seeing Socrates fresh from the bath and wearing shoes, "which he seldom did" (174a4), Aristodemus asks him where he might be going, "having become so beautiful." [60] Socrates has prepared himself for an erotic encounter in the physical as well as spiritual sense.[61] He conceals, or attempts to conceal, his ugliness, thereby incidentally preparing us for a theme that will be of crucial importance beginning with the speech of Agathon. As Socrates himself will eventually rephrase Agathon's premise, one must tell those truths which are beautiful.[62] The connection between Socrates' ironic artifice and hybris is shown by the fact that he has three lovers in the *Symposium,* including Agathon and Alcibiades, the two most beautiful persons at the banquet. Socrates' erotic technique amounts to "overreaching"; at the same time, it is a harmonizing of opposites, since he is silently loved by the ugly Aristodemus.

Despite his general principle of accommodation, Socrates' manners are not good in the same sense as defined by a gentleman. The "pride" (μεγαλοψυχία) of the gentleman is tempered at least by lip service to moderation and certainly by a kind of urbanity; the result of both is a regular condemnation, for prudential or aesthetic reasons, of hybristic insolence. Socrates is neither simply a gentleman (καλὸs κἀγαθόs: literally "beautiful or noble and good") nor a commoner, neither an ἀνήρ (distinguished citizen) nor quite an ἄνθρωπos (plain man).[63] His beauty is artificial, and his behavior insolent. After explaining that he

59. Consider here *Republic* 392d ff. Aristodemus' narrative is almost exclusively mimetic; only occasionally does he remind us of his presence.

60. οὕτω καλὸs γεγενημένos. Cf. *Epistles* 2.314c2 ff.

61. See Friedländer, *Plato I*, p. 53 and Stenzel, *Erzieher*, p. 275: "immer wirkt der Eros doppelt, als Trieb zur Sache und deshalb zur Gemeinschaft mit andern, zu Charis, zu eigener Freude und zu persönlichem Glück."

62. *Symposium* 198c5 ff. By comparing Socrates with a satyr and silenus, Alcibiades reminds us that Greek art also concealed or abstracted from the ugly as a general rule. In comedy this rule is regularly violated. The perfect writer must combine the beautiful and the ugly; cf. 223d1 ff.

63. At 174a7 Socrates explains that he did not attend the public ceremonies, φοβηθεὶs τὸν ὄχλον. Ὄχλos is also used by Plato to refer to the popular assembly (*Gorgias* 455a). In the *Republic* Socrates does attend the public festival.

has adorned himself so as to go beautiful to the beautiful,
Socrates asks Aristodemus if he would like to "go uninvited to
the dinner" (174a8 ff.). Aristodemus is neither beautiful nor invited, but like a smitten lover he surrenders to Socrates' hybris.
Socrates then does violence to a proverb in order to justify his
hybris; to add insult to injury, he explains the saying in a context that depreciates Aristodemus. The saying is given by Socrates as "the good go uninvited to the tables of the good." In
the Greek, there is a pun on the name of Agathon, the beautiful host of the banquet.[64] Despite the authority of the proverb,
the procedure that it recommends is actually of questionable
taste.[65] Socrates then mentions an instance of the proverb's application by Homer, which also illustrates the poet's hybris:
Homer makes Menelaus, the worse man, go uninvited to the
feast of Agamemnon, his superior. The generally low regard in
which Menelaus was held makes the tacit identification with
Aristodemus a rude comment on the nature of a faithful lover.[66]
Aristodemus' reply indicates that he has not missed the point.
But it does not seem to have upset him; perhaps he is inured
to Socratic hybris. In any case, he agrees to go, and transfers the
blame to Socrates. Socrates again replies with a quotation from
Homer: "when two go together, it is better than one for planning what we shall say." [67]

The implied comparison between Menelaus and Aristodemus
is the first instance in the *Symposium* of a frequent Platonic device: the use of quotation from, or allusion to, other works,
especially poetry, in order to make an indirect point.[68] The
sentence which Socrates adapts is uttered in the *Iliad* by Diomedes, who volunteers to spy on the Trojan camp, but who
asks for a companion:

64. For a historical and philological discussion of the proverb, see the note in
Bury, *Symposium*.

65. "Uneingeladen zum Gastmahl zu gehen galt im allgemein als unanständig."
Hug, *Symposion*, 174b1.

66. Cf. Euripides, *Andromache*, esp. 445 ff.

67. *Iliad* 10.224: Socrates' words only partially correspond to those of Homer.

68. I am here elaborating upon as yet unpublished observations of Leo Strauss
(see acknowledgments). Cf. *Symposium* 221c2 ff.

but if some other man would go along with me there would be more comfort in it, and greater confidence. When two go together, one of them at least looks forward to see what is best; a man by himself, though he be careful, still has less mind in him than two, and his wits have less weight.[69]

Among those who volunteer to accompany him, Diomedes selects "Odysseus the godlike, he whose heart and whose proud spirit are beyond all others forward in hard endeavors, and Pallas Athene loves him." There are three aspects to this Platonic joke. Socrates cannot wish unqualifiedly to compare himself to Diomedes and Aristodemus to the wily Odysseus, except perhaps to emphasize the martial character of his own role at the banquet.[70] Still, as if in recompense for his previous harshness, Socrates gives Aristodemus a promotion from the comparison with the soft fighter, Menelaus.[71] Finally, Socrates indicates that he and Aristodemus are about to enter the camp of the enemy.

The home of Agathon is compared to the camp of the Trojans. As in the *Protagoras,* where the same quotation appears, the enemy is sophistry. With the exception of Aristophanes, all the main speakers of the *Symposium* are present in the *Protagoras,* and in both dialogues Alcibiades makes an abrupt entrance.[72] We learn from the *Protagoras* that Eryximachus and Phaedrus were associated with Hippias, Pausanias and Agathon with Prodicus. Socrates notes that Pausanias seems to be in love with the beautiful Agathon; also interesting is his remark that Protagoras is much more beautiful than Alcibiades.[73] In sum,

69. 10.222–26, Lattimore translation.

70. At 10.503 ff. Diomedes pauses to think after having killed thirteen enemies, just as Socrates pauses on his way to the banquet. Socrates also quotes 222 ff. in *Protagoras* 348d1, where he is presumably the Odysseus to Protagoras' Diomedes. Cf. *Phaedrus* 261b6 ff.

71. *Iliad* 17.588.

72. *Protagoras* 316a4: Hippocrates, who takes Socrates to the gathering of the Sophists, is the son of Apollodorus.

73. Ibid., 315c2, 315d6, 309c4. Just as Alcibiades reveals the secret Socrates, so does Protagoras boldly reveal the esotericism of the Sophists who preceded him (316d3 ff.).

the *Protagoras* is a preparation for the *Symposium*: first the famous teachers are portrayed, then their students.[74] As we shall see, Aristophanes and Socrates are allied in their opposition to sophistry, but they are opposed with respect to the alternative. The substitution of Aristophanes for Protagoras is also an indication of a connection between sophistry and poetry, but this we shall discuss later.

Shortly after setting out with Aristodemus, Socrates turns his thoughts inward[75] and lags behind his disciple, who is forced to appear at Agathon's home alone and uninvited. If Aristodemus is Odysseus in this particular context, it must be in the ironical sense that his unexpected appearance is intended by Socrates to disconcert the others, and so to give him the advantage or initiative of their frustration. The incident emphasizes the fact that Socrates prepares his mind as well as his body for his appearance at the banquet. When Socrates stops to think, it is a sign that we must do the same, lest we be overwhelmed by the apparent "spontaneity" of the banquet:[76] we must guard against the wrong kind of intoxication. The connection between thought and silence must not blur for us the connection between thought and speech. Socrates' subsequent sobriety is the public form of his intensive introspection. We shall have to keep before us the question, how can Socrates' sobriety be reconciled with the divine enthusiasm of Eros? How can we reconcile thought and madness?

By pausing to think, Socrates places Aristodemus in an embarrassing situation. The demands of theory and practice do

---

74. Prodicus is generally well-regarded in the Platonic dialogues; for his famous myth of Herakles, see Xenophon, *Memorabilia* 2.1.21., and S. H. Rosen, "The Irrational Choice," *Journal of General Education*, 17 (1965). I will discuss Hippias in Chapter Two. The speeches of Pausanias and Agathon, the students of Prodicus, are marked by a concern with virtue, whereas the speeches of Phaedrus and Eryximachus, the students of Hippias, emphasize political honor and *technē*. Cf. V. Brochard, "Sur le 'Banquet' de Platon," in *Études de philosophie ancienne et de philosophie moderne* (Paris, 1954), p. 68. Dr. Drew A. Hyland, in an unpublished doctoral dissertation, "Eros and Philosophy: A Study of Plato's Symposium" (Pennsylvania State University, 1965), has drawn up a list of the parallels between the *Protagoras* and *Symposium;* Ch. 2, n. 45.

75. 174d5.

76. Cf. Klein, *Meno*, pp. 96 ff.

not always coincide: Aristodemus finds himself at the open door of Agathon's home, feeling somewhat foolish without the excuse that Socrates had promised him.[77] As Aristodemus enters the open door he encounters a slave boy, who escorts him to where the guests are about to dine.[78] Agathon responds with what is at first glance the height of urbanity:

> O Aristodemus, you've come in good time for dinner. If you're here for any other reason, put it off. I looked for you yesterday to invite you, but couldn't find you. (174e5–8)

This sophisticated beginning is betrayed by the next sentence: "but haven't you brought Socrates to us?" [79] When Aristodemus explains the situation, Agathon's language reveals how little interested he is in his uninvited guest: "you did well, but where is the man himself?"

Agathon sends a boy to look for Socrates, and then seats Aristodemus at the side of Eryximachus the physician. The boy's report that Socrates does not wish to join the banquet baffles Agathon: "What you say is extraordinary!" (175a10). Agathon is either unfamiliar with Socrates' habits or too egotistical to grasp how anyone could prefer solitary reflection to his company. The language of the slave boy indicates that Socrates has not fallen into a trance: "when he summoned Socrates, he did not wish to enter." In the face of the spontaneity or motion of the banquet, Socrates prepares himself by coming to a standstill. Motionlessness is thus linked with profound reflection; when Agathon orders the slave boy to insist that Socrates come in, Aristodemus warns: "don't move him, but let him be" (175b3). Agathon prefers motion to rest. Like many men, he feels the erotic

77. 174e1. There is also an uninvited guest in Xenophon's *Symposium*, Philippus, a γελωτοποιός or παράσιτος. But Philippus, unlike Aristodemus, is far from silent.

78. At 174e2 Rettig, *Symposion*, quotes Plutarch, *Symposium* 76: Aristodemus comes ahead into the light of the open door like the shadow cast by Socrates' body.

79. For different interpretations of Agathon's greeting cf. the notes of Hug and Bury to 174e7. I agree with Hug, up to the point of the inquiry about Socrates.

force of Socrates without understanding it. Wisdom is for him somehow physical, and thus in effect physical beauty captured in speech. The wise speech mirrors the beauty of the body, and so it ripples or glides like the shining splendor of beauty in the body itself.[80] Since motion is the defining feature of the body, it is for Agathon inseparable from beauty.

Agathon reluctantly acquiesces in Aristodemus' advice: "one must do thus, if you think so" (175b4). His willfulness is counterbalanced by softness, a combination that reappears in his behavior toward the servants. Agathon requests them to serve up a dinner of whatever dishes they choose, as though no one had commanded them. Perhaps agitated by the continued absence of Socrates, as well as by his own triumph, Agathon contradicts his intendedly liberal appearance in emphasizing that such freedom is a novelty.[81] The servants are to pretend that they are the hosts; Agathon has written a little play for the celebration of his dramatic victory. Unfortunately, the main character is absent from the first act. Agathon's great concern for Socrates is not assuaged until after dinner begins (175c3 ff.). "Agathon often ordered Socrates to be sent for, but [Aristodemus] would not allow it." Socrates' absence is as important as his presence. Plato improves his own drama at the expense of Agathon's by delaying the entrance of the hero.

The Arrival of Socrates

Not even Socrates' delay is in accord with custom. He arrives after a shorter period of meditation than usual, and in the middle of dinner. By terminating his meditation, Socrates reminds us that his presence at the banquet is voluntary; by missing half of dinner, he demonstrates his abstinence. As he enters, Aga-

80. Cf. *Phaedrus* 234d2 ff.
81. Whatever the difficulties in establishing the grammar of the text at this point (for which see Bury 175B), I believe there is no problem concerning the meaning. None of the editors seems to have thought of Agathon's agitation as a possible reason for the disjointedness of his speech. Bury and Hug both quote Teuffel's observation on "die Liberalität und Humanität des Agathon, mit welcher er selbst kokettiert . . ."

thon, again impatient, is the first to greet him: "Here, Socrates, sit down next to me in order that I may enjoy your wisdom by touching you . . ." (175c7). The sexual undertone of Agathon's language is not mere flirtation; he regards physical contact as the prelude to a contest with Socrates.[82] Agathon hopes to triumph by his superior beauty over Socratic wisdom. The touch is the necessary condition for Agathon's speech, as it is decisive for our comprehension of Diotima's teaching. Socrates does in fact sit next to Agathon; the competition is also a communion. Socrates does not succumb to Agathon's beauty, but accommodates himself to it. He enters ironically into the domain of genesis.

Socrates' abstinence toward food and sex, the conditions of bodily generation, is emphasized by his denial that wisdom can be communicated through physical contact. He thereby insults his host: as things are, it is not an honor to sit next to Agathon (175d7). Socrates' wisdom is "paltry" (he says) and "as disputable as a dream," whereas Agathon's is shining and visible, palpable enough to enchant 30,000 Hellenes (175e3 ff.).[83] Agathon immediately recognizes the insult, if not the implicit ironical distinction between psyche and body: "You are hybristic, Socrates, and in a little while I'll take you to court about wisdom, and our judge will be Dionysus." (175e7) In his charge and challenge, Agathon sets the dramatic context within which the discussion of Eros will occur: the quarrel between philosophy and poetry. His choice of judge, however, shows that he lacks a true conception of the difference between the two. In the *Phaedrus* we learn that Dionysus is associated with telestic rather than poetic madness, both of which are distinguished from erotic

---

82. We are also told that Agathon has the last seat on the right. At 177d4 Phaedrus is said to hold the first seat on the left. Cf. Bacon, *Crowned,* p. 423. Bacon sees the sexual meaning of the "touch" passage but goes on to infer from it an identity between Socrates and Dionysus, and hence his victory as the perfect poet, which is too strong. Alcibiades, not Socrates, is Dionysus.

83. Cf. *Republic* 476c4 ff. where the life of the lover of bodies is called a dream. In the *Symposium* the body is "real" or at the center of the argument, and so it conditions the "upward" dialectic in a way that is not true of the *Republic*.

madness.[84] Like the poets in the *Apology*, Agathon does not understand his own *technē*. But the consequence of his ignorance is an essential clue to Plato's intentions: Dionysus is neither Socrates nor Agathon. If it is permissible to identify him with any character in the dialogue, the only serious candidate would be Alcibiades.[85] However that may be, poetry and philosophy are both brought before the bar of mystic or religious madness.

Agathon's language prepares us for the fact that the main speaker at the banquet is not Socrates but Diotima. We cannot understand this fact by engaging in hasty identifications between Diotima and Socrates or Plato.[86] Nor does Dionysus appear in the *Symposium* or *Phaedrus* simply as the god of tragedy. In both dialogues Socrates subordinates or accommodates himself to Dionysus by recounting the speeches of a prophetess and a poet.[87] He plays a role in a mystery-drama, or assists in the revelation of the Dionysiac dimension of man's psyche. The result is in neither case simply philosophy or tragedy; it is, instead, a poetic statement of philosophical religion. Tragedy seems to mediate between the psychic and corporeal: it renders the daimonic Eros visible by connecting speeches to living bodies.[88] Philosophy supplies a further articulation to this speech, whether through myth or logos. Yet both are divine gifts: neither is presented in the Platonic dialogues as the product of man's autonomous will. Such an observation is in no way an ex-

84. *Phaedrus* 265a9 ff. Cf. n. 82 above; those who, like Bacon and Brentlinger, identify Socrates as Dionysus, fail to take into account the distinction between kinds of madness, especially important since they regard him as the embodiment of Eros also.

85. Cf. *Symposium* 212d5 ff. and my discussion below.

86. The most interesting analysis of Diotima's speech I have found is Neumann, *Diotima*. Neumann treats her teaching as distinct from that of Socrates, and reads it as a kind of sophistic, advocating the selfish interests of the lover. If he is correct (I shall return to his paper in Chapter Seven), then Diotima's conversation comes full circle to the speech of Phaedrus, with which it is complementary.

87. It is often overlooked that Socrates attributes his main speech in the *Phaedrus* to Stesichorus (244a2).

88. See especially the third and fifth of the seven reasons given in L. G. Westerink, *Prolegomena to Platonic Philosophy* (Amsterdam, 1962) to explain why Plato wrote in dialogue form.

planation of Plato's religion, nor is it an account of Diotima as a symbol of divine transcendence. I mean to emphasize again that the dramatic structure of the *Symposium* raises the question of what Plato means by "divine." To say nothing of the answer, the intricacy with which he puts the question is already apparent in Socrates' first exchange with Agathon.

After warning Socrates that he will involve him in a legal dispute concerning wisdom, Agathon urges a temporary recess for dinner. Socrates acquiesces and sits down. After dining "they performed the libations, together with the hymn to the god and the other customary things, and turned to the drink" (176a2 ff.). The word for "libation" ($\sigma\pi\acute{o}\nu\delta\eta$) also means "peace treaty" or "truce." The quarrel between Socrates and Agathon is temporarily resolved by a legal (and so religious) harmony. In the dramatic metaphor, the elements in the harmony are not citizens, but warring cities which therefore meet as the embodiment of distinct nomoi. That is, their political autonomy is subject to religious accommodation. Socrates and Aristodemus are fundamentally Hellenes among Trojans; the communion of Eros is tempered by the presence of Eris. Nor should we forget Aristophanes, who seems to be hostile to both groups. Of course, a more minute analysis will reveal that each speaker is inflected by his characteristic Eros. But the speakers are not simply autonomous; apart from the explicit erotic relationships, we must be on the look-out for unstated allegiances.

Intoxication and the Erotic Order

The next scene is introduced by Pausanias, whose name could be translated by a Socratic etymology as "allayer of sorrows." Pausanias wishes to allay the sorrows attendant upon excessive drink. He is suffering from the effects of the previous night's celebration and has need of a respite, as do those who were also present at the earlier gathering. Aristophanes supports the request for temperance, whereupon Eryximachus the physician makes an important classification of drinking capacities.[89] If we

89. Note the echo in $'A\varkappa o\acute{v}\sigma a\nu\tau a \ldots \tau\grave{o}\nu \ 'A\varkappa o\nu\mu\varepsilon\nu o\tilde{v}$. Eryximachus also has need $\acute{a}\varkappa o\tilde{v}\sigma a\iota$ from Agathon how ready he is for strong drinking.

except Alcibiades, there are three levels of endurance among the main characters: on the first level is Socrates alone; then come Pausanias, Aristophanes, and Agathon; and, on the third level, Eryximachus, Aristodemus, and Phaedrus. The question naturally arises whether there is a connection between the order of drinking capacities and the order of erotic excellence. In a passage already mentioned (page xix), the Athenian Stranger says that the purpose of symposia is to test men in a way which leads to "knowledge about the natures and habits of psyches." [90] Wine drinking moves men beyond pleasure and confidence to the height of freedom in speech and action, a license akin to philosophical hybris in that "each man thinks himself worthy to become the leader of himself and the others." [91] The heat generated by the wine softens the psyche of the drinker, making it more youthful and ductile (like heated metal), and so more capable of being molded or trained by the good legislator.[92] Thus the Stranger says that wine has been given to us, not to madden us, but rather to produce shame or modesty in the psyche, and health and strength in the body.[93]

The theme of the *Laws* is a moderate political regime, as discussed by very old men; this should warn us that its treatment of wine drinking cannot simply be applied to the *Symposium* without modification. The replacement of Dionysian madness by shame is a sufficient expression of the difference between the two dialogues. On the other hand, the very sobriety of the *Laws* serves as a helpful corrective to the intoxicated atmosphere of the *Symposium*. If nothing else, it shows us Plato's readiness to reflect soberly on "spontaneous" behavior and to attach a theoretical significance to it. Not only the *Laws* but the structure of the *Symposium* makes it evident that the speakers represent different levels or types of psyche. This has led some interpreters to find a metaphysical or abstract dialectical relation in the given order of the speeches.[94] I do not question the ultimate

90. *Laws* 650b1–7.
91. Ibid., 649a4 ff., 671b5 ff.
92. Ibid., 671b10 ff.
93. Ibid., 672d5 ff.
94. The most elaborate attempt known to me in English is M. Isenberg, *The*

necessity of such an investigation, provided it emerges from a
minute inspection of the intricacies of the *Symposium*. The criterion of alcoholic endurance is in itself insufficient for the construction of an encompassing dialectical schematism. It does,

Order of the Discourses in Plato's Symposium (Chicago, 1940). Despite its "dialectical" character, Isenberg's analysis abstracts from the dramatic structure of
the dialogue. He tries to base his schematism on the fact that four of the seven
speakers begin with a critical reference to their predecessors. This is a subtle
point, but would demand a much more exhaustive defense than Isenberg gives.
I shall only indicate one or two of the major defects of his results. According to
him, the speeches of the first four guests are on the level of Becoming, those of
Agathon, Socrates and Alcibiades on the level of Being. Thus, e.g. "the discourse of Agathon is on the level of Being and deals almost entirely with unchanging things or gods" (p. 10). As I will show in the appropriate place, this
is an altogether erroneous interpretation of Agathon, who is dedicated to perpetual innovation or complete change. More fundamentally, Isenberg thinks
that Eros can be placed "on the level of Being" (p. 34) in some parts of the
dialogue, but again, this totally distorts the nature of Eros as perpetual striving.
Similarly, Isenberg's distinction between one-, two- and three-term dialectics,
although useful and suggestive, is imposed by him with so little attention to detail and nuance as to obscure the complexity of the speeches rather than to exhibit their joints. For instance, he sees in Aristophanes "the encomiast of the
good times gone now, the extoller of cakes and ale" (p. 54). As Krüger has correctly seen, and as I will show in detail, Aristophanes' speech is a complex
tragedy and analysis of the enduring human situation, and not a banal appeal
to rural simplicity. Finally, Isenberg ends with the shocking comment that it
is "of little significance" to discuss why Plato wrote the *Symposium*, so long as
we know the order and unity of the discourses (p. 67). He assumes that we can
know or understand that order without considering the concrete structure of
the dialogue itself because he believes it possible to impose a metaphysical dialectical schematism onto the speeches, one derived from a general study of
Plato. Hence the many keen observations in his study are vitiated by the arbitrary character of his methodology.

A more plausible, but still arbitrary and misleading account of the meaning
of the order of speeches is given in Plochmann, *Hiccups*. For example, he sees
in Pausanias advice to love one particular body as well as beauty in laws and institutions, or a willingness to abide by local customs. This leaves unexplained
Pausanias' great exertions to change the local customs and laws. Plochmann's
characterizations of the speeches are in other words seriously incomplete; no
chart will do justice to what is contained within each encomium. Brentlinger,
Cycle, also contains some speculations on the overall dialectical structure of the
Symposium. Thus he sees Socrates as advocate for "self-discovery" or "a projection of the highest values of the self on to the world" (pp. 26, 27); the greater
mystery, accordingly, is that the self creates itself (p. 28). But this is the position
of Agathon! Brentlinger's interpretation of the teaching of Diotima, if correct,
would bear out Neumann's claim that she is a super-sophisticated Sophist and

however, provide us with valuable evidence of the difficulties that such a construction must face.

For example, if endurance is correlative to erotic excellence, then the speech of Eryximachus must be inferior in scope and coherence to that of Pausanias. On the other hand, one might reasonably suppose that drunkenness is the dramatic sign of intense erotic possession, in which case Socrates must be altogether unerotic. Next, according to the *Laws,* drink produces freedom of speech and act, thereby enabling the legislator to understand the nature of the affected psyche. In these terms, the *Symposium* will presumably teach us least of all about Socrates, more about Aristodemus, and most of all about Alcibiades. Finally, the ranking by endurance is ambiguous with respect to the specific erotic function of the characters. There are two lovers (Eryximachus and Aristodemus) on the lowest level, and only one (Pausanias) on the second.[95] Of course we are in no position to decide anything about the significance of the order of the speeches until after we study them. But these questions do not exhaust the interest of Eryximachus' "true speech" (176c7) about intoxication.

Eryximachus tactfully inquires after his host's health before proceeding to deliver his professional assessment of the situation. Perhaps his advice would have been different if Agathon had favored heavy drinking. It would be unsafe to concur too hastily with the opinion of most commentators that Eryxima-

---

partisan of entirely egoistic self-happiness. All these attempts at the construction of dialectical frameworks are by no means unjustifiable in principle, but in practice those cited bear out the maxim that, in Platonic study, "haste makes waste."

95. I may also note here the ambiguous erotic status of Aristophanes, who is never identified as either lover or beloved. Leo Strauss has offered the interesting suggestion that Aristophanes is the beloved of Plato. Plato is said to have kept a copy of Aristophanes' plays in his deathbed, and he published an epigram honoring the comedian:

αἱ χάριτες, τέμενός τι λαβεῖν ὅπερ οὐχὶ πεσεῖται
ζητοῦσαι, ψυχὴν εὗρον Ἀριστοφάνους

Again, I doubt that such a suggestion can be made into part of a dialectical framework for the *Symposium;* what Plato loves is not Aristophanes, but the whole range of the human psyche.

chus is merely a pompous pedant.[96] Eryximachus is not without
a heavy handed cunning or hybris of his own. That his advocacy
of sobriety does not exclude Eros is immediately brought to our
attention. Phaedrus, Eryximachus' beloved, interjects: "I am
accustomed to be persuaded by you in other things, and especially when you speak about medicine . . ." (176d5). And so
the union of technicism and self-interest (which Phaedrus represents) puts the seal on the unanimous agreement to drink for
pleasure rather than intoxication: to avoid madness for a kind
of enlightened hedonism. A capacity for wine is thus in accord
with the banqueteers' initial decision to drink for pleasure. The
increasing enthusiasm, which comes to a peak in the drunken
appearance of Alcibiades as Dionysus, is not intentional but is
a sign of the presence of Eros himself. The counterpoint between the wish for sobriety and the almost unconscious undertone of daimonism produces the fundamental rhetorical structure of each encomium. The speakers, except for Socrates, say
more than they intend to, and their words must be read on two
levels. Erotic compulsion takes the place of Socratic irony in
their speeches.

The agreement to drink for pleasure is related to the atmosphere of freedom; as Eryximachus says, "each man may drink
as much as he pleases: there is no compulsion . . ." (176e5).
The usual banquet custom has been rescinded; even the flute
girls are dismissed.[97] To rephrase an earlier formulation: the
speeches on Eros are introduced by a sober and rational effort
to win pleasure through a detachment—or freedom—from Eros.
The means suggested is more like discursive speech than ecstatic
intuition. Even the banqueteers reflect Plato's cautious approach

96. E.g. Rettig, *Symposion* 176d1: Eryximachus, "was Jedermann aus der
täglichen Erfahrung weiss, erst aus der Heilkunst erkannt zu haben *glaubt,
ὅτι χαλεπόν* . . " For a defense of Eryximachus, see L. Edelstein, "The Role
of Eryximachus in Plato's Symposium," *American Philosophical Association
Transactions and Proceedings*, 76 (1945).

97. Hug, *Symposion* 176e7–8: *"ταῖς γυναιξὶ ταῖς ἔνδον.* Der Ausdruck ziemlich
verächtlich gegen die Frauen, die nicht die Bildung der Männer haben, um sich
selbst zu unterhalten, andrerseits aber auch nicht zu den Gesellschaften der
Männer zugezogen werden."

to Eros or divine madness. If Eros is a mode of Necessity, freedom would seem to lie in a rational exposition of what has been
divinely intuited. In the *Symposium* at least, the freedom of
reason is circumscribed by the force of the divine. The spokesman for technē is wrong to deny the presence of compulsion.
This point is illustrated by the specific manner in which Eryximachus introduces the theme of Eros.

Eryximachus begins with a quotation from Euripides, the
student of Socrates and the most "enlightened" of the great
dramatists: "The speech is not mine, but that of Phaedrus . . ."
(177a3).[98] Phaedrus has been constantly complaining to Eryximachus about the failure of the poets to praise Eros, "though
he is so ancient and powerful a god" (177a8). The complaint
undoubtedly stems from Phaedrus' interest in rhetoric, rather
than from his devotion to the god. As is evident in the *Phaedrus*,
and as we shall see in his speech, he is not, despite his own
beauty, a very erotic man; even his choice of a physician as lover
is dictated by practical considerations. Why, then, is the partisan of sober Eros (in the *Phaedrus*, the non-lover) presented
here as "the father of the discussion" (177d5: πατὴρ τοῦ λόγου)?
Phaedrus is certainly lowest in the erotic ascent, whatever the
final order may be, and thus Plato exhibits one of the fundamental principles in his teaching: The highest is already visible
in the lowest or most common. Try though we may to immerse
ourselves in selfishness, in "common sense," the daimonic will
transform it. Phaedrus is the "businessman" of the group; he
takes the position of interest, profit, or utility for the beloved.[99]
As such, he is a caricature of the pursuit of freedom through rational calculation. But he too will be overcome by the compul-

98. Fr. 488 (Nauck): οὐκ ἐμὸς ὁ μῦθος ἀλλ' ἐμῆς μητρὸς πάρα . . . (See Bury's
note). The "manly" Eryximachus thus speaks through the words of a woman,
and Phaedrus is his "mother."

99. Phaedrus' poverty cannot be responsible for his views; Lysias 19.15 says of
him: πένητι γεγενημένῳ οὐ διὰ κακίαν. Macdowell, *Andokides*, p. 74 says of Lysias
19.15 and 22.14: "these references illustrate the effects of the confiscation of the
property of those denounced in 415" for having profaned the Eleusinian mysteries. The *Symposium* takes place shortly before the profanation, and so
Phaedrus is still in possession of his property. Phaedrus is closely linked with utility
and pleasure without Eros in the *Phaedrus*.

sion of Eros just as, in a broader perspective, his "progeny" are the illuminations of the highest mysteries.

Phaedrus' "utilitarianism," which in a more serious form is present in Socrates as well, is inseparable from a degree of impiety or hybris. He speaks of the various eulogies by "the useful Sophists";[100] even salt has been praised "for its utility." "But no man has dared up to the present day to hymn Eros in a worthy manner" (177c2). Eros, in other words, is far more useful than salt and even, as the reference to Prodicus' praise of Heracles implies (177b2 ff.), than moral virtue. But it takes daring to praise Eros for his utility, because this is to take a sober, calculating attitude toward the divine. To a certain extent, Phaedrus possesses that daring, or at least its practical equivalent, tactlessness.[101] He is not, however, daring enough to act alone; hence the need to be implemented by Eryximachus.[102] When Eryximachus urges the acceptance of Phaedrus' proposal, and also says that now is an appropriate time "to adorn or order the god" (κοσμῆσαι τὸν θεόν), we may take him rather literally. He advocates not simply an adornment but an ordering or regulating as well: a transformation of the myth (so far as possible) into a technical logos.

Of course, in making his proposals Eryximachus is partly, perhaps largely, moved by his erotic feeling for Phaedrus. One might say that he is attempting to demonstrate his utility to Phaedrus, and that the need to do so places him on a higher level than his beloved. From Plato's viewpoint the deeper irony

---

100. 177b2: τοὺς χρηστοὺς σοφιστάς. Χρηστός means both "useful" and "good" but is not the only word meaning "good" which Plato could have written in this passage.

101. At *Phaedrus* 229c4 ff. he does not dare to say that he disbelieves the myth of Boreas, but Socrates' reply indicates that he regards Phaedrus as one of those who indulge in the "boorish wisdom" (ἀγροίκῳ τινὶ σοφίᾳ) of rationalizing myth by physics. Such "boors" certainly possess some of the marks of a scientific enlightenment.

102. Protagoras, in the dialogue bearing his name, first exposes the timidity of the previous Sophists and his own daring, and then tells the myth of Prometheus, who steals τὴν ἔντεχνον σοφίαν σὺν πυρί from Hephaestus and Athena, and gives it to man. Protagoras preserves the link between the human and the divine in his myth, thereby revealing a limit to his daring. Eryximachus is the representative of a more daring branch of Sophistic thought.

lies in the fact that it is precisely Eros which moves us to tame Eros: sobriety is a consequence of intoxication. If this be so, we may assume that Socrates is a consequence, but not necessarily himself the embodiment, of the highest intoxication. We do not yet understand the connection between Socratic hybris and Eros. For example, Socrates hybristically speaks on behalf of the entire group: "no one, O Eryximachus, will vote against you" (177d6). He uses legal terminology in response to Eryximachus' echo of a formula employed in political meetings.[103] In a few pages of the prologue, we have found numerous instances of legal language. The *Symposium* is a trial; in the most obvious sense, the contest is between poetry and philosophy. But from that contest it is not too remote an inference to say that Socrates is himself on trial, and not merely as the authoritative witness for philosophy. Socrates boldly asserts his own competence: "I may say that I understand nothing but the erotic things" (177d7: τὰ ἐρωτικά). What, however, if the charge of hybris is well founded, and Socrates is wrong in his claim?

A part of philosophical rigor is what one may call skepticism in face of the apparent piety of Plato's portrait of Socrates.[104] In learning to read a Platonic dialogue, we must appreciate that Socrates is also a dramatic character, not just a historical figure. It is not self-evident that Plato agrees with whatever Socrates says or does, and so that he changes spokesmen after his own "development" takes him beyond the thought of his master. Nothing about Plato's relation to the Socrates of his dialogues is self-evident, except perhaps that Socrates did not write dialogues. I have already indicated that, as the student of Diotima, Socrates must be presumed to be defective by nature to one degree or another, in erotic strength. His personal sobriety, traditionally regarded as evidence of extraordinary mental power, may not be an unmixed blessing; certainly there is no prima

---

103. 177d2: "δοκεῖ γάρ μοι χρῆναι Eröffnung des bestimmten Antrags am Schlusse seines Votums, smit einer ähnlichen Formel wie in der Volksversammlung oder im Rate. Dem. IV. 17 . . . I.2 . . . Darauf spielt auch Sokrates an in seiner Antwort οὐδείς σοι—ἐναντία ψηφιεῖται—λόγον εἰπεῖν ἔπαινον . . ." Hug, *Symposion*.

104. Cf. Neumann, *Diotima*, pp. 35 ff.

facie reason to regard it as such in a dialogue devoted to the daimonic Eros.

On the whole, then, the prologue presents us with an intricate dialectic between proximity and distance, between intoxication and sobriety. It also gives us reason to suspect the allegiance of the two most important guests to the god or daimon who is being honored. Socrates, whose own nature we have found evidence to suspect, provides us with the clue about Aristophanes, "whose occupation is altogether concern with Dionysus and Aphrodite" (177e1–2). Aristophanes is identified as a devotee of the city cult-goddess, not of Eros. The result is to civilize or tame his link with Dionysus. His praise of Eros will actually be a defense of Aphrodite; Aristophanes is a spokesman for the polis, not only by his dramas but by intention. The character of Aristophanes' sobriety will become evident only when we study his speech. Meanwhile Socrates bids Phaedrus good luck and orders him to begin his speech. Through his hybris Socrates has replaced Eryximachus as master of ceremonies. Finally Apollodorus, in turning to the speeches, warns us that Aristodemus' account was not verbatim, any more than his own. "What seemed especially worthy to me of memory, of these things I shall give you the logos of each" (178a3–5). Thus Plato ends the prologue-within-a-prologue with a further twist of ironical ambiguity. The *Symposium* is the *Memorabilia* written by Apollodorus.

CHAPTER TWO

🎀 PHAEDRUS 🎀

The Student of Hippias

Phaedrus is an excellent example of Plato's tendency to give crucial roles to men of relatively insignificant gifts. To some extent, this may be explained by the principle that the higher is prefigured or reflected in the lower. In the case of Phaedrus, common and even base opinions are joined to physical beauty: the "father of the logos" stands for the opposition between body and psyche, or the two fundamental terms of the erotic dialectic.[1] As a passive homosexual, whose erotic strength may be inferred from his admiration for Lysias' praise of the nonlover and the subsequent "utility" to the beloved, Phaedrus does not directly generate children, whether of the body or psyche. On the other hand, he may properly be called "Phaedrus, blessed with beautiful children," since according to Socrates, only Simmias of Thebes has excelled him as the occasion for the generating of discourses.[2] It is not Phaedrus' erotic nature, but the visibility of Eros in his beauty, that lends him a generative capacity. Similarly, Phaedrus is not moved by a love of poetry, as has sometimes been suggested,[3] but by the lower passion for speeches or rhetoric.

The same point may be established by a brief consideration of Phaedrus' religious status. There are strong reasons, two of which have already been mentioned, for the judgment that Phaedrus is not very pious. First, he was implicated in the prof-

1. For this reason alone, Isenberg oversimplifies in attributing a "one-term dialectic" to Phaedrus (*Order*, p. 16). Phaedrus' speech is not intelligible in isolation from the speaker.

2. *Phaedrus* 261a3, 242a7 ff. Note the implied connection with the *Phaedo*.

3. E.g. in Brentlinger, *Cycle*, pp. 20–21.

anation of the Eleusinian mysteries. Second, in both the *Symposium* and the *Phaedrus* he advocates the cause of the non-lover, and thus of what may be called the pseudo-beloved; his praise of the god is thus actually a repudiation. Third, he is associated in the *Phaedrus* with those who, by means of a "boorish wisdom," reinterpret myths in terms of physics.[4] Phaedrus says that he is unfamiliar with the details of the rape of Oreithuia by Boreas, and asks Socrates: "Do you believe that the mythical story (τὸ μυθολόγημα) is true?" Socrates replies: "Well, if I should not believe, like the wise, I would not be unusual." [5] These "wise men" (σοφοί) give "sophisticated accounts" (σοφιζόμενος) of myth; that is, they are Sophists or closely related to the Sophists. There is an intimate connection between the "atheistic" physics of the pre-Socratic cosmologists and the rhetorical teaching of the professional Sophists. Although Phaedrus is not pious, and may even be an atheist in the sense that he does not believe in the traditional or mythical gods, he nevertheless attains to the divine, thanks to his love of rhetoric, as Socrates explicitly says.[6] Because of this love, Phaedrus is literally brightened or illuminated with a joy that transcends his initial selfishness: he shines in the light of the divine which he does not consciously recognize.[7]

Phaedrus represents the union, in its first or lowest form, between "demythologizing" or materialistic physics and sophistry. His sophistication is boorish because, rooted in selfishness, it interferes with a proper study of the self.[8] It interferes with that attention to the self which arises from a respect for the gods and from obedience to the Delphic oracle. Needless to say, Phaedrus is not a physicist, nor even a rhetorician, but a dilettante, a dabbler in things divine and human. He imitates his teacher, Hippias of Elis, who also concerned himself with the whole and

4. *Phaedrus* 229c4. Cf. Krüger, *Einsicht*, p. 19.
5. *Phaedrus* 229c4 ff.
6. Ibid., 242a7; θεῖός γ'εἶ περὶ τοὺς λόγους, ὦ Φαῖδρε . . .
7. Ibid., 234d1 ff.
8. Ibid., 229e2 ff.

who passed as an expert in all sciences and arts.[9] Despite Plato's frivolous portrait of Hippias, we know him to have been a man of some competence, especially in mathematics.[10] Phaedrus, like Apollodorus, is a disciple, and so a caricature of his master. The *Symposium* as a whole begins in a caricature of philosophy; the speeches at the banquet begin in a caricature of sophistry. But in the foolishness of discipleship is contained at least a shining reflection of the divine love of truth.

The disciple is an "appearance" (φαινόμενον) of his master; similarly, the dialogue begins with "opinions" (δόξαι), or with what seems to be the case. Behind the appearance of Phaedrus is the opinion of Hippias that he, Hippias, is wise in all things, and so joins practice to theory. His special competence seems to lie in "the affections of the stars and heavens," next in arithmetic and geometry, and then in the study of letters, syllables, rhythms, and harmonies.[11] He also claims to be the best rhetor and teacher of rhetoric, and thereby to have made an unbelievable amount of money.[12] His skill as a "judge and messenger of words" keeps him constantly busy as diplomat for his native polis.[13] Finally, Socrates has heard Hippias boast that he is "wisest of men in the most *technai* [arts]"; special reference is made to the fact that Hippias once went to Olympia wearing nothing on his body that was not his own work.[14]

Hippias unites physics and sophistic rhetoric and is especially interested in measurement and calculation.[15] He is much concerned with money and luxury. He says that Achilles is more

9. I am of course concerned exclusively with Plato's conception of Hippias, or his significance for the *Symposium*. For an elaborate vindication of Hippias, see E. Dupréel, *Les sophistes* (Neuchâtel, 1948).

10. Cf. the account of Hippias in *Pauly-Wissowa*, where his mathematical accomplishments and extensive scientific knowledge are described.

11. *Hippias Major* 285b8–d2; *Hippias Minor* 367e1–7; *Protagoras* 315c5.

12. *H. Minor* 364a7 ff.; *H. Major* 282d6 ff.

13. *H. Major* 281a3 ff.

14. *H. Minor* 368b2 ff.

15. Apelt has conjectured that Hippias was a student of Hippodamus, the town planner who also combined politics and mathematics. Cf. Aristotle, *Politics* 1267b22 ff.

admirable than Odysseus because honesty is preferable to deceit; yet he himself admits that he is deceitful in his praise of the ancients, as a precaution against the envy of his contemporaries.[16] He is partial to definitions of the beautiful as appropriate, useful, and beneficial.[17] He defines the appropriate as what makes things appear to be beautiful—a point which is connected to his earlier remark that Socrates may avoid all refutation if he says "what seems so to all." [18] In the *Protagoras* Hippias introduces the principle of kinship by nature rather than by kind: "for like is by nature of the same kind as like, but the nomos, tyrant of humans, does much violence against nature . . ." [19] Like Socrates, Hippias distinguishes between the few and the many in terms of the distinction between nature and convention.[20] But unlike Socrates, he condemns convention in the strongest terms by altering the famous phrase of Pindar: "nomos is king of all, both mortals and immortals . . ." [21] Hippias' textual emendation amounts to the charge that Zeus is a tyrant; in condemning nomos, he is also condemning the Olympian gods. Man's freedom lies in the repudiation of nomos for the study of nature, the source of the unwritten laws which serve as the true basis for justice.[22]

Although Hippias prides himself that, like Socrates, he never says the same things about the same subjects,[23] he regards nature as a principle of uniformity or homogeneity. Variety in speech must presumably be justified by knowledge of nature as it is homogeneously exhibited in heavenly bodies and human ac-

16. *H. Minor* 369c2 ff.; *H. Major* 282a4 ff. Cf. *Protagoras* 317a ff.

17. *H. Major* 290d5–6, 295c1 ff.

18. Ibid., 294a3, 288a3–5. Note also 297b1 ff., where Socrates observes that the discussion of the beautiful has terminated in the "unsatisfying" (but not necessarily false) result that the beautiful is a sort of father of the good, and so that the two are not the same.

19. *Protagoras* 337c7 ff. Note the context; at 336b1 Socrates says he cannot follow long speeches, a remark he repeats to Hippias in *H. Minor* 373a2 ff.

20. Cf. *Republic* 415a1 ff. The three kinds of psyche correspond to natural degrees of distance from the Ideas.

21. Fr. 169. There is a useful summary of references concerning this passage in M. Untersteiner, *The Sophists* (New York, 1954), p. 297, n. 30.

22. Cf. Xenophon, *Memorabilia* 4.4.19 ff.

23. Ibid., 4.4.6: Ἀμέλει . . . πειρῶμαι καινόν τι λέγειν ἀεί.

tivities.[24] How the rhetoric of novelty is to be reconciled with the need for agreement among those who know nature, remains a problem for Hippias, just as it does for at least some of the speakers in the *Symposium*. The principle that like is naturally akin to like means that men are diverse by nature, and not by convention. What should be the response of those who know nature to the natural basis for the conventional diversity of men? Must they not practice a kind of deceit, a kind in which we have already caught Hippias? Furthermore, if we think through the consequences of the homogeneity of nature, or of the divine and the human, we find that there is a contradiction between the physics to which it gives rise, and the world of human events. Hippias is forced to recognize this contradiction as a rhetorician, even if he does not observe it as a physicist. He thus exemplifies the contradiction in his own person.

A consistent application of the principle of the uniformity of nature seems to have the great advantage of overcoming all forms of dualism. As applied to mankind, however, it must lead eventually (barring dualistic compromise) to the suspension or suppression of all that is characteristically human. This problem, familiar to us as a consequence of Newtonian physics in the seventeenth and eighteenth centuries, appears in the Platonic dialogues as a criticism of the physics of total flux, which is regularly linked to or represented by the thought of Heraclitus.[25] In Plato's treatment such a physics is an argument for the instantaneous disappearance of the whole cosmos and so is refuted by the appearances themselves. Hippias presents us with a specifically human instance of the dangers involved in the praise of uniformity, and one that is of special importance in the *Symposium*. The bridge between the uniformity of na-

24. Cf. Dupréel, *Sophistes*, pp. 332–33: "L'être devenait multiple sans perdre sa consistance ni sa prise sur le changement et l'action . . ."

25. E.g. *Cratylus* 440a6 ff.; *Theaetetus* 152d2 ff. For a careful discussion of the sense in which one may refer to the pre-Socratic natural philosophers as "mathematical physicists," and for the failure of these pre-Socratics to distinguish between the numerical or geometrical and the living, cf. Charles Kahn, *Anaximander and the Origins of Greek Cosmology* (New York, 1960), esp. p. 97.

ture and the natural difference of kinds is the principle that "like loves like." In human terms, this may lead to a sanctioning of incest; for example, a handsome or intelligent father might be erotically attracted to his handsome or intelligent son. And in fact, Hippias denies that the prohibition against incest is sanctioned by nature, since there are those who violate it.[26]

The precise status of the prohibition against incest is ambiguous or veiled, and no less for Plato than for the Sophists, as we shall have occasion to see. It is, however, closely connected to the divine foundations of the polis, or to the basis upon which man preserves himself in the face of the nonhuman aspects of nature. In terms of Phaedrus' speech, the cosmic Eros of pre-Socratic physics is difficult if not impossible to reconcile with the human Eros ostensibly being praised. This is the theoretical background against which Phaedrus' speech must be studied. Although Phaedrus tends to express himself in terms of rhetoric and poetry, the significance of what he says (as distinct from what he himself may understand by it) will emerge only if we bear in mind the complex views of Hippias. These views are also part of the background for the speeches of Pausanias and especially of Eryximachus, Phaedrus' lover,[27] who will enunciate the principle that like loves like.

In sum: Phaedrus introduces, in the crudest theoretical terms, the union between what we may call "process physics" and sophistic rhetoric. He thereby also anticipates the problem of poetry, or novel speech, which is to be developed in different ways by Aristophanes and Agathon. Finally, he introduces one of the most pervasive dramatic metaphors in the *Symposium*: the significance of pederastic or nongenerating Eros. The dilemma raised by the speech of Phaedrus may be summarized in this question: Can there be genesis, and so a cosmos, or literally order and beauty, without generation? The cosmic problem of the relationship between the heavens and human beings appears within the specifically human horizon as the problem of the relationship between psyche and body. Is it possible to

26. Xenophon, *Memorabilia* 4.4.20.
27. *Protagoras* 315c2–5, where he is also associated with Hippias.

praise psychic activity in essentially corporeal terms? Within Phaedrus' speech, these questions will be articulated by means of a dialectic between the love of material possessions and the love of honor.[28] And the dramatic link between Phaedrus and Eryximachus—or selfishness and medicine—suggests the ultimate anthropocentrism of the subsequent theoretical attempt to reconcile physics and sophistry.[29]

Genesis and Generation

The first words of Phaedrus' speech are: "A great god is Eros, wonderful among men and gods, for many reasons, and not the least with respect to his genesis" (178a7 ff.). The wonderful thing about Eros is that no one, whether in prose or poetry, tells of his having been born of parents: he has a genesis but not a generation. The distinction, although initially puzzling, is by no means unreasonable. If Eros is the god of sexual love, then he cannot be the cause of his own origin. At the same time, although emphasizing Eros' great antiquity and consequent honor,[30] Phaedrus does not elevate him to the status of an eternal or unchanging principle. As neither eternal nor generated, must not Eros possess some intermediate status? Phaedrus draws our attention to this difficulty without resolving it for us. Nor could he do so without taking a radically heterodox stand, since the difficulty is implicit in traditional Greek religion.

Phaedrus' caution is sufficiently clear from his emphasis upon

28. See n. 1 above.

29. Robin describes Phaedrus as "préoccupé de sa santé, attentif à son hygiène, plein de foi dans les théoriciens de la médecine et aussi bien de la rhétorique ou de la mythologie, curieux de savoir mais dépourvu de jugement, superficiel dans ces curiosités et naif dans l'expression de ces sentiments, admirateur fervent des réputations dûment cataloguées et consacrées." (SymBudé, p. xxxvii). This is undoubtedly on the right track, but exaggerated and oversimplified.

30. The second sentence of Phaedrus' speech is unusually ambiguous, as is suggested by the fact that the best mss. give three different readings. J. Burnet, *Early Greek Philosophy* (London, 1899) (hereafter *EGP*), and Bury, *Symposium*, follow W in printing τὸ γὰρ ἐν τοῖς πρεσβύτατον εἶναι τὸν θεὸν τίμιον. B reads πρεσβύτατον . . . τῶν θεῶν and T πρεσβυτάτοις . . . τῶν θεῶν.

antiquity; he seems to accept Aristotle's version of the traditional view that the most honorable is the oldest.[31] Similarly, he quotes Hesiod, the "official" theologian, in support of Eros' ungenerated nature:

"Hesiod says that first Chaos came to be (γενέσθαι)
and next
broad-bosomed Earth, always steadfast seat of all,
and Eros." (178b3–7)

But Phaedrus' language, however cautious, is by no means simple. To begin with, the distinction between genesis and generation is itself quite shrewd. Next, Phaedrus does not argue from the nature of the cosmos or the god, but from what has been written about Eros by "private or public" men.[32] His words suggest that whatever we know about the gods is derived from books, and thus open to question. This is true especially because of the ambiguity, even inconsistency, of these written accounts.[33] After all, the fact that no writer makes mention of Eros' parents may be a sign of human ignorance rather than a divine truth. Phaedrus' quotation from Hesiod is itself an example of what I earlier called demythologizing, or, if that is too strong, a highly selective use of scriptural texts.

Phaedrus carefully directs our attention to the obscure status of the first gods or principles in traditional Greek thought. They are not eternal, and their origin is inexplicable. For example, the passage in Hesiod does not say that Eros and Earth were generated from Chaos; it posits a temporal, but not a causal sequence of genesis. Whatever may have been the intentions of the oldest mythmakers, their words certainly justify a distinction between pre-erotic genesis and erotic generation. But this means that Eros is not the oldest god, or else that the gods are preceded by cosmic principles; and the connection between

31. *Metaphysics* 983b6 ff.

32. Hug, *Symposion* 178b3: ". . . Der Dichter ist immer nach eher eine öffentliche Person als der Prosaiker, da seine Productionen durch das Theater, Chöre u.s.w. umfassendere und schnellere Verbreitung finden als auf dem mühsamen Wege der Abschrift."

33. For conflicting reports on Eros' parents, see Bury, *Symposium* 178b2.

principles and gods is open to interpretation. Since gods and men, in the view of Phaedrus, descend from Eros, there is a disjunction between sexual beings and the Earth, which provides their "steadfast seat";[34] it is the Earth, rather than Eros, that is steadfast. The descendants of Eros must share in the unstable or intermediate nature of their ultimate ancestor. But why is Earth more steadfast than Eros? The difference can be made intelligible in terms of the appetitive nature of Eros. The off-spring of Eros strive for the steadfast; the Earth, as pre-erotic, has no such desire. Within the language of myth the ultimate transiency of Earth is not incompatible with its being steadfast —for as long as it endures. Eros, however, is the principle of unstable desire; as the principle, its own status differs from what it generates, as well as from what is represented by "Earth."

Even as he introduces and quotes it, then, the passage from Hesiod immediately raises some of the most important themes in the *Symposium*. But the quotation is in all likelihood inaccurate. Let me now cite the text of Hesiod as it was traditionally accepted:

> Indeed, Chaos first came to be, and next broad-bosomed Earth, always steadfast seat of all (the deathless ones, who hold the peaks of snowy Olympus, and murky Tartarus, in the deepest nook of wide-wayed earth) and Eros, who is most beautiful among the deathless gods, who loosens the limbs, and conquers the mind and wise counsel within the breasts of all gods and men.[35]

The lines enclosed in parentheses, although they appear in all manuscripts and are cited by authorities after Plato and Aristotle, are nowadays usually athetized by editors. One of the principal reasons for doubting their authenticity is the fact that they are not mentioned by Phaedrus in the passage under

34. According to Hesiod and Pindar, gods and men sprang from a common source. Cf. K. Kerenyi, *Prometheus* (New York, 1963), pp. 22–23. For the attribution of birth and death to the immortal gods, cf. O. Kern, *Die Religion der Griechen* (Berlin, 1963), *1*, pp. 65 ff.

35. *Theogony* 116–22.

consideration. But one cannot assume that they were unknown to Plato unless we can be sure that he did not omit them intentionally. Plato ends Phaedrus' quotation with a period after the word "Eros." Are we to assume that he did not know the balance of the line, and hence that it is spurious? Not even the most zealous editor, it seems, has taken this step.[36] Would it not be more reasonable to see whether we can understand the partial quotation in terms of Plato's dramatic intentions?

In fact both of Phaedrus' omissions from the Hesiodic passage are explicable, and by the same motive: Phaedrus omits mention of the deathless gods. More emphatically, he omits mention of the Olympian gods while pointing out to us the obscure, though generated, status of the pre-Olympians. This distinction between Olympians and pre-Olympians is crucial in subsequent speeches at the banquet. Pausanias will introduce two Aphrodites and two Eroses, the Uranian or pre-Olympian, and the Pandemotic or Olympian (180d6). By this means he will explicitly denigrate the gods of Olympus—and of political orthodoxy.[37] Phaedrus proceeds by silence or suppression. But the need to introduce two Eroses is already prefigured in his distinction between genesis and generation. In terms of his distinction, one might then identify the pre-Olympian Eros as eternal becoming, the unnamed principle for the genesis of Chaos, Earth and the Olympian or sexual Eros. Phaedrus, of course, does not himself make this identification. Given his major premise, however, it is a reasonable step to take, and it provides us with the theoretical transition from his speech to that of Pausanias.

For the first three speakers at least, the theoretical back-

36. I am indebted to Professor Fritz Solmsen for discussing the status of these lines with me, but must absolve him of any responsibility for my own interpretation. Professor Solmsen notes that Tartarus is not mentioned again in the *Theogony*. For a defense of the authenticity of lines 118–19, cf. M. Stokes, "Hesiodic and Milesian Cosmogonies, Pt. II," *Phronesis, 8* (1963) and M. L. West, *Hesiod: Theogony* (Oxford, 1966).

37. Thus Plochmann's account of Pausanias' role in the dialectic of the banquet is inadequate; he sees in him a willingness to abide by local customs and a love of beauty in nomos. *Hiccups,* p. 17.

ground is "process physics" and probably a cyclical cosmology. The latter theory may be inferred from the distinction between genesis and generation. Thus Chaos would come to be from the dissolution of order in the previous cycle of eternal becoming. This also makes sense in view of the central teaching of the dialogue that Eros is at once being born and dying. Diotima's interpretation of Eros may then be understood as an attempt to reconcile process physics with the principles of human existence. In the cosmology introduced by Phaedrus the first principles of the cosmos are discontinuously generated by pre-Olympian Eros, an eternal becoming that is neither generated nor ungenerated and that, in the form of successive cosmic cycles, is coming to be and at the same time passing away. By suppressing the deathless gods, Phaedrus uses poetry to suggest what will be developed more "scientifically" by Eryximachus; but the fundamental line of reasoning is the same. When the previous order degenerates, the result is Chaos. Out of discontinuous or random motions the Earth comes to be, but not in such a way as to allow us to speak of Chaos as its parent. The Earth is a spontaneous accumulation of the primitive chaotic elements and provides the first permanent basis for the sexual generation of living things.[38]

The fundamental divisions of Phaedrus' cosmos are not heaven, earth, and hell, but Chaos and Earth. Even Tartarus is suppressed, perhaps because, like heaven (Olympus), it suggests a boundary or natural terminus to becoming. By removing heaven and hell Phaedrus indicates that Earth will again fall into Chaos. So, then, must the gods, with one possible exception: it may be that Phaedrus believes in the divinity of genesis. This possibility is at least supported by Phaedrus' next citation, this time from Parmenides: "And Parmenides says that Genesis 'devised Eros first of all the gods.' " (178b9–11)[39] On the basis of this authority, genesis cannot itself be Eros, the prin-

38. The ἀεί in line 117 refers to the function of the Earth in each cycle; it is always the foundation of the whole.

39. See Bury's note for precedents in taking ἡ Γένεσις as the subject of μητίσατο. In the context of Phaedrus' speech, there is surely no other possibility.

ciple of sexuality, and the subject of Phaedrus' encomium. This Eros is not the first principle of the cosmos; however aged, he is not eternal.

Selfishness and Visibility

Phaedrus' is the first step in a general argument whereby the *Titanomachia* is restaged, only this time with the intended victory of the pre-Olympians. But the real motive of this argument is neither theological nor religious. Whatever may be the precise intentions of the speakers as dramatic individuals (and it is still far too soon to say), it is necessary for us to understand what Plato wishes to designate as the consequences of their related positions. This is, of course, a philosophical rather than a philological problem. The degree to which we are able to reconstruct the thought of a philosopher is controlled by the degree of our own speculative "hybris," to put the point in the terms of the *Symposium*. Hybris alone, however, may lead to an all-too-human madness; it must be balanced by caution in the form of a rigorous fidelity to the written text. Fidelity entails a perception of what has been left unsaid, but what needs to be said on the basis of the total dramatic situation. The reconstruction of Phaedrus' cosmology depends in part on his function within the *Protagoras* and *Phaedrus*, as well as in the *Symposium*. Within the *Symposium* we must recognize his affiliation with Eryximachus as well as the degree to which "the father of the logos" anticipates Diotima's teaching.

As I have already suggested, the human significance of Phaedrus' speech is developed in terms of a dialectic between body and psyche, wealth and fame, or more fundamentally, between selfishness and visibility. His cosmological interests are motivated by the desire to reduce the authority of the gods, and thus to make man the measure of his own conduct. Consequently Phaedrus mentions no gods in his speech, which is entirely about the actions of heroes or human beings. The "good" is regarded not as the pious or holy, but as what is useful to man. Still more specifically, Phaedrus conceives the good effects of Eros as utility to the beloved. He thereby prefigures, in his relatively crude selfishness, the more complex narcissism of Agathon.[40] Just as Agathon's narcissism will be overcome by his love of fame, so too will the selfishness of Phaedrus. Base desires cannot be adequately gratified without some degree of transcendence toward the noble. This is the basic stratum of the Platonic exhibition of Eros.

The utility of Eros is established by his antiquity, together with the general proposition that "as the oldest, he is the cause of our greatest goods" (178c2). What Phaedrus means by "good" may be shown in a literal, and therefore awkward, translation of his next sentence: For I cannot name a greater good (ἀγαθόν) from his earliest youth than a useful lover (ἐραστὴς χρηστὸς) and a sweetheart to the lover" (178c3–5). Phaedrus' first thought is for what benefits the beloved; his elliptical language[41] betrays the degree of his selfishness. Private reflection blends unintentionally with public speech at this point; the utility of the beloved to the lover is virtually an afterthought. Similarly, he replaces "good" by "useful," echoing his earlier phrase (as reported by Eryximachus), "the useful Sophists" (177b2).

As though suddenly aware of his slip, Phaedrus attempts to strike a more exalted tone by interpreting away the base implications of his previous sentence:

> For what men must follow who wish to live their whole
> life properly, this cannot be achieved so well by family,
> honor, wealth, or by anything else as by love. (178c5 ff.)[42]

Phaedrus' words have a curiously modern ring; certainly they deviate from the traditional Greek view. In effect Phaedrus is sanctioning the subordination of political institutions to the gratification of individual desire. Far from rectifying his earlier

---

40. Isenberg (*Order*, p. 33) makes a comparison between the speeches of Phaedrus and Agathon which is useful and perceptive, but from which the erroneous inference is drawn that the two are logical "contraries."

41. See Bury's note to εὐθὺς νέῳ ὄντι.

42. I have translated καλῶς, with some hesitation, as "properly." This follows a middle line between "nobly" and "happily." I suspect that Phaedrus has the latter meaning in mind.

expression of selfishness, Phaedrus now gives it a broader base. In so doing, he practices a kind of demagoguery.[43] He regards the polis as serving the convenience of the beloved, who is in turn conceived as standing for all men. But the advocacy of universal individualism is therefore dependent upon the polis. Thus he characterizes "living well" or "properly" as "shame for the shameful and ambition (φιλοτιμίαν) for the noble" (178d1–2).

Phaedrus imitates philosophy by placing the individual above the polis. His imitation is defective because it replaces "seeing" by "being seen"; knowledge is replaced by opinion.[44] In this respect Phaedrus again anticipates Agathon's speech, or the dependence of poetry upon the applause of its audience. What "shines forth" in Δόξα may be the genuinely splendid or noble, but the shine is dependent upon the eyes of the onlooker.[45] Thus Phaedrus himself makes visible the weakness of the nonphilosophical understanding of happiness as the appearance of honorable acts:

> And I say this of the lover, if he should be visible (κατάδηλος) doing something shameful or, suffering it, not warding it off through cowardice (ἀνανδρίαν), he would not be so pained to be seen by his father, nor by his companions, nor by anyone else as by his sweethearts. We say the same about the beloved, that he is especially ashamed when seen doing anything disgraceful by his lover. (178d4 ff.)

The more general significance of Phaedrus' speech emerges if we replace "lover" by "hero" and "beloved" by "polis"; the result is essentially the Socratic critique of Athenian statesmen: "like the poets," they strive to gratify the public in seeking their private good, instead of being concerned with the genuine

43. With the following lines, cf. *Thucydides* 3.82.8 and *Phaedrus* 227c9, where Socrates criticizes the nonlover's position as "democratic."

44. For a discussion of the relationship between vision as δόξα and as knowledge, cf. H. Boeder, *Grund und Gegenwart als Frageziel der Früh-Griechischen Philosophie* (Hague, 1962), ch. 1.

45. Cf. M. Heidegger, *Einführung in die Metaphysik* (Tübingen, 1953), pp. 78 ff.

public good.[46] In Phaedrus' words disgrace is connected with being seen, that is, in not pleasing or gratifying. Phaedrus cares little about the shameful in itself.

This concern with visibility is again emphasized in Phaedrus' erotic fantasy of a polis or army composed entirely of lovers and their sweethearts. The power of such an army would be virtually unlimited (179a2) since it is equivalent to the potential shame of lovers, who would choose frequent deaths rather than be seen in cowardly behavior by their sweethearts (179a3: ὑπὸ παιδικῶν ὀφθῆναι). In this passage Phaedrus no longer mentions the shame of the beloved. The ambition or love of fame, initially reciprocal, is now narrowed down to the case of the lovers. Power is in the hands of the beloved, not the lover. The lover, as will become explicit in the speech of Pausanias, very far from living nobly, is the slave of the beloved. The lover will come to the rescue of the beloved, having been made courageous by his desire. Nothing is said about the beloved coming to the rescue of the lover. In fact, Phaedrus comes close to telling us that the lover is not really manly or courageous, but is made to resemble the best man (ὅμοιον εἶναι τῷ ἀρίστῳ φύσει) by his passion, no matter how base (οὐδεὶς οὕτω κακὸς) he may be (179a7–8).

Eros, then, is for Phaedrus a substitute for virtue, and especially for courage. It enables inferior men to perform "great and splendid deeds." Deeds are great and splendid if they conform to the verdict of public opinion; greatness and splendidness depend upon being seen. Being seen and being loved are more important than doing or loving; passivity is more important than activity. Phaedrus debases the Homeric heroes by identifying their might (μένος) with a slavish subjection to the beloved. The martial virtue of a Hector or Diomedes is transformed into a semblance of virtue.[47] It is entirely compatible with Phaedrus' position to argue that the vulgar acts of vulgar men, so long as they look like the heroic acts of heroes, are equal to them in excellence.[48] Even more, there are no heroes

46. *Gorgias* 502c12 ff.
47. 179b1–3; cf. Homer, *Iliad* 10.482, 15.262.
48. Cf. the treatment of the ring of Gyges in Bk. 2 of the *Republic*.

but only vulgar men who look like heroes. Phaedrus substitutes the vision of the valet for that of the hero, and the result is a morality of valets. All men are selfish, but the most effective form of selfishness is to make use of the desires of others.

The Rewards of Love

In his substitution of Eros for virtue, Phaedrus tacitly appeals to the premise that Eros will gain more of virtue's benefits for more people than virtue would itself. The falseness of the premise does not alter the fact that his justification of selfishness forces him to distinguish between the higher and the lower. Pure selfishness is impossible as a political principle. Since utility is inseparable from visibility, the benefit to the beloved rests upon the presence of selflessness in the lover. Phaedrus cannot avoid offering a more serious praise of the lover than he intends. Let us turn now to the next section of his speech, which consists of three examples of loving self-sacrifice.

The first is that of Alcestis, who alone was prepared to die for her husband Admetus, as even his parents were unwilling to do. Despite his passive homosexuality, Phaedrus is prepared to place women on a par with men in discussing the strength of Eros. One commentator interprets this as an attempt by Phaedrus "to transform sexual love into a kind of pederasty." [49] A more reasonable inference would be that it shows the weakness of Phaedrus' own passion. He does not adhere to the belief in the superiority of male to female love. Phaedrus' homosexuality is, as it were, for convenience rather than as an expression of his manliness. He thus extends the range of possible benefits to himself to include women as well as men—a democratic gesture.[50] The force of his example is to cast doubt on the utility of parental or filial, as opposed to romantic, ties.[51]

49. Rettig, *Symposion* 179b5.
50. Cf. n. 43 above.
51. Cf. N. D. Fustel de Coulanges, *The Ancient City* (New York, 1956), pp. 48–51 and A. Zimmern, *The Greek Commonwealth* (New York, 1956), pp. 66–67. Euripides' *Alcestis* is also relevant to Phaedrus' use of the legend.

The suggestion is implicit that the love of parents for children is not genuinely erotic, or that sexual generation is not the most compelling consequence of the ungenerated Eros.

The generating of children neither links us to the gods nor preserves our immortality, since there are no gods and since only Genesis is immortal. If one were to act upon the principle of selfishness, the ultimate consequence would be the disappearance of mankind. We have already seen what this means from Plato's viewpoint, in terms of a physics of flux: the human phenomena cannot be saved. In human terms, despite his amiability toward women, Phaedrus is tacitly advising against generation, or denying the selflessness of parents toward their children. Thus far, Eros emerges clearly from Phaedrus' speech as selflessness, the anti-passion of the lover which corresponds to the anti-passionate selfishness of the beloved. But the lover's selflessness leads to death, the extreme form of the absence of passion. The beloved, in being preserved, dissociates himself from Eros, but so too does the lover in dying. The assertion of Eros is the negation of Eros: again, a caricature of Diotima's teaching. Similarly, Phaedrus denies the selflessness of Alcestis by having the gods give her a present (179c6: γέρας) of resurrection. Even for the lover virtuous action submits to the standard of gain. And Phaedrus conveniently places the lover's gift in the next world; this world is his domain.

Each of Phaedrus' three examples concerning the rewards of love focuses on the willingness of the lover to die for the beloved. The gods honor especially those who exhibit zeal and virtue for the sake of their love (179d1–2). Phaedrus reverses the situation of religion: men are no longer said to honor the gods. If the higher honors the lower, then the lower becomes the higher. Phaedrus' exaltation of mankind, although based upon the premise of selfishness and a special concern for the beloved, leads in fact to the demonstration of the Δόξα, or visibility of the lover. This is not Phaedrus' intention, of course; for him, those who honor the lovers are not the gods, but the beloved. For Plato, however, the beloved necessarily, if unconsciously, grants the superiority of the lover, precisely because his advantage depends upon being loved.[52] This is another reason for the emphasis upon death in Phaedrus' speech. When selfish gain, or the gratification of desire, is the sole purpose or highest good in life, then death becomes the greatest evil. To a surprising extent Plato anticipates in Phaedrus the thought of Hobbes.

I suggested earlier that Phaedrus does not admire poetry as art but rather as a kind of rhetoric. In a Platonic perspective the artist, whatever his selfish desires, transcends them in the work of art, which carries what is best in him and his hope for immortality. The rhetorician, whatever his virtues, degrades them by making persuasion, and so immediate gratification, his primary goal. Phaedrus' attitude toward art may be seen in his treatment of the poet Orpheus, his second example of the rewards of love. Orpheus was unwilling to die for his beloved but tried to preserve her and his life by "contrivance" (διαμηχανᾶσθαι), a word that will recur in important passages throughout the dialogue. This attempt to conquer death by intelligence is scornfully condemned by Phaedrus: "He was held to be a weakling, like the minstrel he was, and did not dare to die for love, like Alcestis, but contrived to go living into Hades" (179d4–7).[53] According to the original myth Orpheus is punished with death because he challenges the gods with his art. Phaedrus "puts him to death" because Orpheus challenges the dependence of the lover. If Orpheus could have stayed alive by means of contrivance, he might also have devised a way to enjoy his beloved without sacrificing himself entirely to her selfish advantage.

Phaedrus' critique of Orpheus has consequences that become fully clear only when we study the speech of Agathon, who also advocates the preservation of life through the contrivances of art. Of all the speakers in the *Symposium* Phaedrus is unique in not advocating the generation of anything, whether children of the body or of the psyche. The immediate reason for this uniqueness is that Phaedrus alone is a spokesman for the be-

52. With this point, cf. Hegel's dialectic of the master and slave.

53. Isenberg, *Order* points out that Phaedrus does not use words like νοέω or γιγνώσκω.

loved rather than the lover. One might suppose that, in appealing to the standard of martial or heroic courage, Phaedrus favors the generation of noble deeds rather than works of art or theory. But this is not his intention. The standard of honor is a camouflage for the true aim of obtaining gratification for the beloved's selfish desires. As we have seen, there is no evidence that these desires are erotic. In the same vein, Phaedrus' admiration for the courage of Achilles is not due to an aristocratic temper; it is identical with his admiration for Alcestis. In considering the last of Phaedrus' three examples, we should notice that there is an inner ascent in Phaedrus' speech. He moves from (1) the utility of the beloved (honor = public opinion) to (2) the sacrifice of the lover (nobility for the sake of a reward) to (3) the sacrifice of the beloved (albeit again for a reward). Phaedrus' speech is not internally coherent and it is not intended to be; but Plato makes it clear enough that Phaedrus is being led upward by Eros, despite himself.

Phaedrus shows a certain spiritedness in rebuking Aeschylus and at the same time tries to indicate his own courageousness by an implicit identification with Achilles:

> Aeschylus is talking nonsense when he says that Achilles is the lover of Patroclus. For Achilles was more beautiful, not only than Patroclus, but than all the other heroes; besides, he was beardless, and also much younger [than Patroclus], as Homer says. (180a4–7)

In this sentence Phaedrus again points out how the poets contradict each other; his harshness with Aeschylus, at that time the voice of traditional political morality (a not altogether deserved reputation), may be taken as an innuendo against Aristophanes. If Phaedrus is Achilles, then Eryximachus, his lover, is Patroclus. At this point, however, Phaedrus' reasoning seems to break down, or at least to contradict the interpretation thus far given:

> But in fact, the gods especially honor the virtue that springs from love; however, they especially marvel, are

delighted, and grant rewards (εὖ ποιοῦσιν), whenever the beloved loves the lover; more so than when the lover loves the beloved. For the lover is more divine than his sweetheart, since he is possessed by the god (ἔνθεος) (180a7–b4).

Has not Phaedrus deviated from his major premise by granting that the beloved will die for the lover, who is higher (more divine) than he? Let us notice exactly what Phaedrus is saying. Orpheus died a coward's death at the hands of women because he contrived to save himself as well as his beloved. Achilles died a hero's death because he was willing, indeed, dared (179e5) to avenge his lover's death, thus dying not only for but with him. His reward is honor, and he receives more than Alcestis: he is given eternal life in the isles of the blessed. Thus Phaedrus does not actually say that Achilles died for love of Patroclus (although this is of course implied by the context), but that the gods were overjoyed and honored him exceedingly because "he made such a fuss over his lover" (180a3).

The emphasis is upon the honor that redounds to Achilles, and not upon his love for Patroclus. Besides, Patroclus is already dead, having, as it were, previously died for Achilles. Despite his being "more divine," Patroclus is not translated to the happy isles, nor is mention made of honor which accrues to him. Instead, the implication is that Patroclus acted as one must when he is under the influence of necessity (in common parlance, a god). The credit, if any, must go to Eros rather than to the lover.[54] Since the beloved is not "possessed" he is free to consult his own interests.[55] The beloved wins more honor by acting in human terms rather than with divine inspiration. Again, the authority of the gods is questioned on behalf of the

54. Hug calls attention here to *Phaedrus* 231A: whoever is under the influence of a god, according to Lysias' speech, acts unwillingly, and so is less responsible morally.

55. Cf. Isenberg, *Order*, p. 16. Isenberg notes that Phaedrus has only the lover share directly in the power of Eros, "while the beloved is influenced only secondarily through the lover." But he does not draw the inference that Phaedrus represents the interests of the nonerotic beloved.

autonomy of the beloved. The very least one can say is that it is still advantageous not to be a lover.

The beloved acts not from inspiration but by calculation of his political advantages (represented by fame). He must therefore engage in contrivance, very much as did Orpheus. What Phaedrus objects to is not contrivance simply, but poetic contrivance. He objects to "reason assisted by inspiration," and consequently to generation. In rejecting inspiration Phaedrus rejects Eros' authority as well. He thus represents the vulgarization of reason into selfish calculation, the result of the sundering of reason from Eros. At the same time, Plato shows us through Phaedrus that the attempt to be consistently selfish cannot be consistently maintained. Phaedrus' speech terminates with the death of the beloved, whatever his motives, or rather, with the death of both lover and beloved. Since their relationship was nongenerating, they leave nothing behind them. Their joint demise symbolizes the disappearance of mankind altogether through the calculative adoption of a thorough-going "process physics." Man cannot be constructed from purely cosmological principles in a dialectic of motion. If these principles are in turn a man-made "theoretical construct," then they too must disappear with man: only chaos remains. It is thus dramatically appropriate that the last word of Phaedrus' speech should be "the dead."[A]

CHAPTER THREE

🦚 PAUSANIAS 🦚

The Division of Eros

Pausanias is a student of Prodicus, author of the famous "Choice of Heracles," in which virtue is praised and vice condemned.[1] It is thus appropriate that he should be the lover of Agathon, or "the good." Prodicus is mentioned several times in the Platonic dialogues, and in a relatively favorable light, if we bear in mind Plato's opinion of the Sophists. In the *Protagoras* Socrates says that Prodicus seems to be "an all-wise and divine man."[2] We may take this remark with several grains of salt, but it is not to be simply ignored. For example, Socrates was accustomed to send many young men, for whom he himself could do nothing, to other teachers, among whom Prodicus alone is named.[3] Without exaggerating the significance of such passages, it is apparent from the "Choice of Heracles" that Prodicus taught a moral doctrine which, however conventional, could only be approved by Socrates.[4]

Prodicus' shortcomings emerge when we look for the theoretical foundations of his moral doctrine. According to the extant reports, Prodicus was primarily concerned with linguistic distinctions and terminological precision.[5] In the "Choice of Heracles" virtue bases her address to the young hero on her

1. Xenophon, *Memorabilia* 2.1.21 ff. Cf. *Symposium* 177b1 ff.
2. *Protagoras* 315e7 ff. A few lines earlier, Prodicus is described as still in his bedclothes, lying down and wrapped in sheepskins (315d4–6). For the consequences of this portrait, cf. Diels, *Vorsokratiker*, 2, p. 309, Fr. A 1a. Certainly both Pausanias and Agathon are depicted as self-indulgent in the *Symposium*: as "soft" rather than "hard."
3. *Theaetetus* 151b5.
4. Cf. Rosen, *Choice*.
5. Diels, *Vorsokratiker*, 2, pp. 308 ff.

observation of his genesis and nature.[6] In a Platonic perspective it is dubious, to say the least, that a scrupulous concern for linguistic convention is an adequate basis for the cultivation of human nature. What is right by convention may not be best by nature. Even further, the greater our skill in drawing verbal distinctions, the more flexible our interpretation of what convention itself allows. To take only the crucial example, the persona of virtue condemns vice before Heracles for compelling lust "beyond necessity by all kinds of contrivance, and by using men as women." [7] Although a student of Prodicus, Pausanias intends precisely to revise convention, or to go beyond necessity by means of verbal contrivances, and thereby to make permissible (under certain circumstances) the "use of men as women." Prodicus distinguishes between two women in the form of virtue and vice. Pausanias distinguishes between two boys in the form of homosexual and bisexual Eros. This division of Eros is the basis for his distinction, not between virtue and vice, with which he is only secondarily concerned, but between the "noble" and "base" method or technique.

The general situation in Pausanias' speech is thus in a way prefigured in the teaching of Prodicus. Pausanias is moved by nature to a sophistic revision or interpretation of convention: he wishes to justify and safeguard his own erotic appetite. With this end in mind, he begins by "correcting" the speech of Phaedrus (180d1–2).[8] Phaedrus distinguished between genesis and generation, or cosmogony and theogony; this proved to be an inadequate basis for a proper articulation of human experience. Pausanias is virtually silent about cosmogony; one may say that he begins with nomos, or directs his linguistic skills toward human opinions about the gods. Despite his greater

6. Xenophon, *Memorabilia* 2.27.
7. Ibid., 2.30.
8. According to Rettig, *Symposion*, p. 13, the speeches of Phaedrus and Pausanias are linked by the fact that ". . . zwischen beiden Reden . . . kein Zwischenspiel stattfindet, was bei allen andern Reden der Fall ist." This is not quite correct. We are told by Apollodorus (180c1–3) that some other speeches followed that of Phaedrus, which Aristodemus did not remember. If anything, the "Zwischenspiel" emphasizes the relation between the two speeches.

sophistication in the domain of nomos and the superiority of his rhetorical style,[9] Pausanias' speech is not a theoretical advance upon Phaedrus in every way. This has something to do with the nature of the two men. Phaedrus' self-centeredness gives him a kind of courage whereby he attempts to deduce his own advantage directly from the nature of genesis. Pausanias, although a lover and so presumably more erotic as well as more crafty than Phaedrus, is nevertheless softer and, by comparison, a coward. Hence his attempt to provide legal rather than cosmic justification for pederasty.

The two speakers' difference in character is suggested by their opening words. Whereas Phaedrus began with "a great god," Pausanias' first words are a negative reference to himself: "Not properly does it seem to me . . ." (180c4). We have descended, so to speak, from the cosmos to man. However, Phaedrus' courage was not the result of theoretical daring, but a selfishness so complete as to lead to self-forgetfulness. As a corrupt imitation of philosophical self-forgetfulness, Phaedrus forgets to look for self-knowledge. Pausanias is too clever to aim as high as Phaedrus; that is, his own selfishness is buttressed by a clearer perception of the complexity of human affairs. Phaedrus' speech was too "simple";[10] there is not one Eros but two. "Since he is not one, it is more correct for us to decide what sort one must praise" (180c7). Pausanias knows that self-gratification depends upon the preservation of the polis. He begins, not with a moral judgment but with deliberation, or the technical condemnation of an error in calculation. In so doing, however, he himself employs faulty logic.

Pausanias distinguishes two Aphrodites. The first is Uranian or Heavenly; her father is Οὐρανός, but she has no mother, and so is in a way ungenerated. In this, she reminds us of Athena, who sprang ungenerated from the forehead of Zeus. Pausanias has transformed Phaedrus' cosmogonical reflections in such a

9. Rettig, *Symposion*, p. 13: "Die sprachliche Darstellung unserer Rede ist mit Recht schon in Alterthum bewundert worden." According to Robin, *Sym-Budé*, pp. xli–xlii, his speech imitates the style of Isocrates.

10. 179c5: ἁπλῶς. Cf. 182a8–b1 for the crucial contrast between ἁπλῶς and ποικίλος.

way as to render them politically useful, as we shall see when he turns to the "intricate" character of Athenian nomos. The second is the Olympian Aphrodite, the daughter of Zeus and Dione. Pausanias' subsequent revision of Athenian nomos is here anticipated by his implication that the higher, genuinely Athenian, Aphrodite is the Uranian rather than the Olympian. He then commits his error in logic: since there is no Aphrodite without Eros, there must be two Eroses. Pausanias disregards the possibility that the two Aphrodites might share the same Eros, in the way that one child is both son and grandson.

Pausanias, however, is seriously concerned with neither logic nor morality. He is engaged in an intricate and sophistic attempt to secure his own erotic advantage. If Pausanias were an orthodox moralist or a loyal citizen, he would praise the Olympian Aphrodite and Eros. Instead he condemns these as "Pandemic" or vulgar; Pausanias will praise the Uranian or pre-Olympian Eros, sprung from the ungenerated Aphrodite, and the god of refined pederasty. According to Gerhard Krüger, "when Pausanias distinguishes between a 'good' and a 'bad' Eros, he has then removed the divinity of Eros." [11] Krüger sees in Pausanias a defense of "formalist ethics," such that a decision on the value of the content rests with man and not with god. But it is not quite accurate to say that Pausanias distinguishes between a "good" and a "bad" Eros. Good and evil for him depend on the style of the action, whether it is done well or badly. And this is for Pausanias a pre-moral distinction.

Thus the division of Eros, although grounded in the cosmogony of Phaedrus, is in fact a pre-political basis for the distinction of proper and improper style in human actions (and not in poetry). Pausanias takes an important step toward the imposition of human categories onto nature or Eros. The right style renders a specific natural appetite correct or acceptable to public taste. On the other hand, it is a specific natural appetite which leads Pausanias to elaborate his theory of style. This elaboration contains two fundamental steps. First, Pausanias must change the existing nomos, which, whatever the actual

11. Krüger, *Einsicht*, pp. 98 ff.

practice, sanctions very harsh treatment against pederasts.[12] Second, he must succeed where Phaedrus failed; namely, he must present an interpretation of the nongenerating Eros that can support a conception of human excellence.

The Sophist as Prometheus

Whatever the degree of "individualism" or "enlightenment" each represents, Phaedrus and Pausanias both conceive of satisfaction in such a way as to be dependent upon the polis. This is enough to indicate how each falls short of philosophy, or the genuine gratification of the highest, and so private, desire. Phaedrus praises war, and Pausanias is an advocate of peace. They praise war and peace as the fundamental modalities of political existence, as consisting essentially of deeds rather than speeches. Their own speeches are means to an end, subordinate to a desired mode of action. They do not speak for the sake of the logos alone, but to an audience. For both, reality is at bottom indistinguishable from appearance. As is especially clear in the case of Pausanias, the heterogeneous character of appearance is subject to no principle of organization other than the cleverness of human speech. Pausanias' concern with proper ways of acting amounts to a definition of nomos in terms of taste rather

12. For the laws concerning pederasty in Athens, see Aeschines, *Against Timarchus* 9–12, 16–21. They are unusually strict, and death is a frequent penalty, even in some cases where intercourse does not occur. This is of course not to suggest that the law was universally invoked, or that there were not a variety of forms taken by pederasty. For a long discussion, with many useful citations, see R. B. Levinson, *In Defense of Plato* (Cambridge, Mass., 1953), ch. 5. Levinson is concerned to show (a) that pederasty was widespread, heterogeneous, and not restricted to the Athenian aristocracy; and (b) that Plato disapproved in principle of sexual intercourse between lover and beloved. The validity of both conclusions does not alter the cowardice of Pausanias in face of the ποικίλος νόμος. Neither does it justify our overlooking (as does Levinson, along with most commentators) Pausanias' desire to legitimate precisely what "reputable Athenians deplored" as "deplorable" (p. 90). Pausanias is opposed to all heterosexual relations, and in favor of carnal, effeminate pederasty: a position manifestly out of tune with the Athenian nomos. Cf. M. I. Finley, *The Ancient Greeks* (New York, 1963), p. 124; Stenzel, *Erzieher*, pp. 202–03; H. I. Marrou, *A History of Education in Antiquity* (New York, 1964), pp. 51 ff.

than divine order; in that sense, he anticipates Eryximachus' praise of technē.

In the *Symposium* the students of the Sophists are united by a taste for pederasty and the praise of technē. As the division of Eros brings out even more clearly than the distinction between genesis and generation, this union is an allegiance of war against the Olympian gods.[13] However selfish their intentions, the first three speakers can all claim to be motivated by philanthropy in advocating the use of technē for man's greater freedom. This enterprise is immediately reminiscent of the myth of Prometheus, and especially of Aeschylus' *Prometheus Bound.* In that play Prometheus, who is of a philanthropic bent,[14] regards Zeus as a recent tyrant whose rule will end as it began, by force. As a Titan or Uranian,[15] Prometheus claims to be hated by all the Olympians; but in fact, we know that this does not include Hephaestus.[16] Hephaestus explicitly approves of Prometheus' action; he emphasizes Zeus' harshness and the newness of his power (ll.18–35). If Prometheus has succeeded, Hephaestus, the god of technē, will ultimately receive more honor than Zeus. Is it too much to suspect that Hephaestus is the successor to Zeus prophesied by Prometheus?

13. Not always a consistently fought war, but always ποικίλος: e.g. Pausanias invents a Uranian Aphrodite as part of his campaign.

14. Line 11: φιλανθρώπου τρόπου. There is a "subterranean" connection throughout the *Symposium* between Eros and the gods Prometheus, Hermes, Dionysus, Hephaestus, possibly even Kronos. For the general background, see M. Delcourt, *Héphaistos ou la légende du magicien* (Paris, 1957): divinities who function as intermediaries between gods and men are characterized by binding and being bound (cf. the Platonic σύνδεσμος), magic (cf. *Symposium* 203d8), sexual (especially phallic) associations, and a variety of other characteristics (connection with ungenerated genesis, philanthropy, thievery, and "crooked counsels"). Cf. W. Otto, *Die Götter Griechenlands* (Frankfurt-am-Main, 1961), p. 35 and Kern, *Religion,* 2, 16 ff. The connection between Socrates and Apollo reinforces my view that Socrates is not to be identified with the erotic Dionysiac strand of the *Symposium,* certainly not without the most careful qualification.

15. And so as a paradigm for the Eros of the Sophists; cf. K. Reinhardt, *Aischylos* (Bern, 1949), pp. 43 ff.

16. Cf. lines 12 ff. and 120 ff. with Kern, *Religion,* 2, 10 ff; Kern finds that Hephaestus does not seem to have been a genuine Olympian. Delcourt, *Héphaistos,* is more convincing in her analysis of the magical and shamanistic "prehistory" of the Olympians, as still represented by Hephaestus.

In Aeschylus' drama technē and philanthropy are joined in a rebellion against the Olympians which is carried out not by man but by cosmic forces. The god Prometheus champions the cause of man, just as Pausanias calls upon the Uranian Eros. As Prometheus expresses it, "technē is weaker by far than necessity." [17] In practical terms, the Greek natural philosophers and Sophists were engaged not in the effort to master nature but to establish a greater zone of freedom within the horizon of necessity.[18] Even Zeus is weaker than necessity; Prometheus has seen "two tyrants cast out . . . Shall I not see the third who now rules cast out most shamefully and swiftly?" [19] The true rulers are the Moirai and the Erinyes.[20] In other words, the gods change. This means in effect that everything changes, or that change and necessity are virtually the same. Genesis is god; this is the bond that cannot be broken, even through the rejection of Zeus. "An unknown company is proved by time," Aeschylus writes in the *Suppliants*.[21] The chorus in *Prometheus* says: "Zeus rules lawlessly with new laws; what was previously mighty is now unseen." [22] As the principle of legitimation, time or Kronos, the union of heaven and earth, is king, or the god Genesis. But man cannot rest content with his worship alone. Time is made humanly bearable only through the intercession of gods like Zeus or Hephaestus.[23]

Aeschylus' version of the Prometheus myth illustrates the cosmic significance of the revolt against the Olympians. In order

17. 514 ff.

18. Even Empedocles, whose doctrines are relevant to an understanding of sophistic physics (and the speech of Eryximachus), and who calls himself θεὸς ἄμβροτος (Diels, *Vorsokratiker*, Fr. 112), warns mankind that there is a limit to what mortals may know (Fr. 2, 3). This defines the horizon within which he promises his student, whose name, incidentally, is Pausanias, power over old age, natural forces, and even the ability to bring a dead man back from Hades (*Diogenes Laertius* 8.60).

19. 957–59.

20. 515 ff.

21. 993: Cf. Pindar, *Olympian* 1.30.

22. 144 ff.

23. Cf. Krüger, *Einsicht*, p. 51: man is mastered by the end which he chooses as the fulfillment of his life, whether with respect to happiness or significance. These are the "human" gods.

to see more clearly the role of man, as conceived by the Sophists, we may turn to Plato's *Protagoras*.[24] In this dialogue, as I have indicated, we find the main speakers of the *Symposium* (with the exception of Aristophanes) placed in conjunction with their Sophist teachers. The *Protagoras* is thus one of the essential clues to Plato's understanding of the relevance of sophistry to the speeches on Eros, which is of course to say nothing about its objective or historical significance as evidence for what the Sophists themselves meant, or believed themselves to mean. According to Protagoras' version of the myth, there were once gods but no mortals. The gods made creatures inside the earth from the physical elements and assigned to Prometheus and Epimetheus the task of equipping them with suitable powers. Epimetheus, who was not very wise, obtained permission from Prometheus to do the distributing, which the latter might then review.[25] Epimetheus' little wisdom led him to exhaust the supply of adornments and powers just before reaching mankind. Upon inspecting the scene Prometheus had no recourse but to steal "the technical wisdom of fire" from Hephaestus and Athena, in order to save man from total destitution. The political technē, however, was in Zeus' hands and more carefully guarded; this Prometheus could not steal. As a result, men were unable to live peacefully with each other, and so faced destruction by either the beasts or their fellows. The share which the nonpolitical technē gives man in the divine fate is thus insufficient to preserve him. Zeus, seeing this and pitying men, sent them "shame and justice, in order that cities might be well-ordered and bonds of friendship unite them" (322c2).

Hermes, acting on Zeus' instructions, distributed these gifts

24. It is interesting that Protagoras prefers to speak mythically rather than give a frank answer to Socrates' question (can virtue be taught?). Just previously, Protagoras had explained that, although earlier wise men used disguises and veiled over their words, he himself admits his wisdom openly (316d3 ff.). Thus Socrates' "forethought" (316c5) in broaching cautiously the possibility of a conversation with Protagoras is even more appropriate than the latter admits.

25. Protagoras fails to mention it, but is this not a curious lack of "forethought" on the part of Prometheus? Or was this oversight the necessary condition for his subsequent fame, and so in fact the highest example of his forethought?

to every man. (We may interject that he thus plays the role assigned to Eros in the *Symposium;* the *Protagoras* is a more political, or less daring, dialogue.) To be human, then, is to share "in some way or another" in justice (a virtue not assigned to Eros in the *Symposium*), but this virtue is neither "by nature nor automatic." [26] In other words, the share must be cultivated or developed by practice. And this is the basis for the function of sophistry. Protagoras is not merely a spokesman for Zeus. The divine share in justice is not the same as a character which is by nature just. If justice were natural, one could not blame those who lack it, nor would one need special instruction from Protagoras and the other Sophists. The need to cultivate justice is the premise from which Protagoras infers that it can be taught. On the other hand, it can be taught only to the race which has been given the appropriate capacity by Zeus.

Protagoras and, by inference, the other Sophists are still in allegiance with the Olympians. According to the *Symposium*, the students of the Sophists have gone beyond their masters. Since Protagoras wishes to earn his living by teaching justice to Athenians, he must be discreet and even veil his words when speaking of Zeus. Nor, unlike the Prometheus of Aeschylus, does he forecast the downfall of Zeus. It is not in Protagoras' interest for Zeus' reign to be replaced by, say, that of Hephaestus.[27] Protagoras is not a physicist; his livelihood depends upon the primacy of politics. Protagoras wishes to be the "prime minister" or chief counselor under the reign of Zeus. Pausanias, however, is a consequence of the generation of Protagoras and his professional colleagues. Pausanias is not a political teacher, but a citizen who has been trained to use nomos for his private advantage. Especially within a private and nocturnal setting, he need not be so discreet toward the Olympians as was Protagoras. Pausanias thus prepares us for the link between sophistry and physics, a link which was implicit in the speech of Phaedrus, but which belongs properly to the domain of Eryximachus.[28, A]

26. 322c1: ἁμῶς, 323c5: οὐ φύσει . . . οὐδ' ἀπὸ τοῦ αὐτομάτου.

27. This is not to suggest that it is in the interest of Aeschylus, who had the gift of placing himself in the mind of barbarians as well as gods.

28. According to Hesiod, the Prometheus episode results in the creation of

The "Noble" Pederast

Having distinguished between the Uranian and Pandemic gods, Pausanias draws a further distinction between morality and what we may call "style":

> in itself, [each act] is neither noble nor shameful. . . . When a thing is done nobly and rightly, it turns out (γίγνεται) nobly; when not done rightly, shamefully. Similarly with love; Eros is not altogether noble or worthy of praise, but only he who turns us to loving nobly [i.e. in a noble way or style]. (180e4–181a6)[29]

Pausanias establishes at one stroke the possibility of noble pederasty. At the same time, he is forced to justify the generation of noble deeds, thereby correcting Phaedrus. Gratification is dependent upon approval by an audience of connoisseurs, rather than upon the *demos*. There is no reason to doubt that Pausanias would prefer refined to uncouth acts, and so, too, the approval of refined men. It is another question whether his natural desires admit of such a restriction.

The distinction introduced by Pausanias is as dangerous as it has become familiar. Its danger lies in a defective imitation of philosophy. For Plato, too, no act in itself is either good or bad; but the moral quality is derived from the end toward which the act is directed. Wisdom alone is good in itself.[30] In the *Republic* Socrates says that wisdom alone is a virtue of the psyche; the others are only "called" virtues. He goes so far as

women, a dangerous consequence for pederasts which can be neither praised nor totally condemned. By this tradition, at least, "enlightenment" is not an unmixed blessing for the partisans of the Uranian Eros.

29. I follow Bury in omitting πραττομένη at 180e5, but its retention does not alter the sense of the passage. See also Bury's references to the *Meno, Phaedrus,* and Aristotle's *Politics*. To these should be added *Euthydemus* 281d6 ff.: nothing is good but σοφία, nothing bad but ἀμαθία. Xenophon's *Symposium* (8.9) also introduces the notion of a dual Eros, but strangely enough the speaker is Socrates! Socrates says that "even Zeus, although supposed to be one, has many names." Hence it is not clear whether there are two Aphrodites; nor, we may add, whether there is really only one Zeus. Socrates' subsequent words confirm Bury's remark that the pandemic Aphrodite was regarded as *Venus Meretrix*.

30. See the previous note.

to identify moderation and justice as forms of "the demotic virtue." [31] From this, one may infer the association of wisdom and courage, the defining marks of the philosopher-kings and guardians. The wise man must have the courage to act on the basis of his wisdom, however dangerous in itself his act may be. He must never consider any act "in itself," for in itself it is unintelligible, and so neither good nor bad—but only dangerous. What is called evil in one context may be necessary in another. In the *Republic* Socrates speaks first of useful or medicinal lies, and later of the noble lie.[32] In other words, not all medicinal lies are noble. But there are times in life when we require medicine rather than nobility.

In philosophy, danger is subject to the control of wisdom. Pausanias replaces wisdom by refinement, or good taste. The pandemic Eros is "vulgar" and haphazard; accessible to everyone, it is not characterized by a discriminating technique. We find it in the meaner or ordinary sort of lover:

> These love, first of all, women no less than boys; next, they love the body more than the psyche; finally they choose the least intelligent people they can, since they look to the deed alone, and are unconcerned with whether or not it is done nobly. (181b2–6)

Pausanias does not mention the cases in which women are the lovers; they seem to be beneath his attention. Again, this is a correction of Phaedrus, who had the bad taste to praise Alcestis. The chance (ὅτι ἂν τύχῃ), and therefore indiscriminate, behavior of the vulgar erotic is rejected in the name of technique or style, and intelligence. But it is clear that intelligence is in the service of technique rather than wisdom. Technique rather than nature or custom gives man a certain degree of control over chance. Despite Pausanias' aestheticism or refined tastes, the rule of technē does not provide him with a criterion for beauty or nobility, but only for efficiency. One might expect him, per-

31. 518d9 ff., 500d7. With this paragraph, cf. Krüger, *Einsicht*, pp. 97 ff.
32. 382c6, 414b8 ff.

haps against his will, to move toward an identification of nobility and efficiency. We shall soon see this take place.

Especially in view of many mistaken contemporary opinions about Plato, it is important to see that, for philosophy, there is no such thing as noble pederasty. Even in legislating nomoi, philosophy is itself governed by wisdom. Sexual behavior cannot be settled by a simple appeal either to nature or convention, just as criteria for taste in art or refinement in manners have no valid status independent of the whole range of human affairs. In part, the conception of noble pederasty rests upon the typically Greek view that men are superior to women. We know from the *Republic* that Socrates did not share contemporary Greek opinion, and from the *Laws* that Plato opposed pederasty as unnatural.[33] The Athenian stranger does not deny that males are sexually attracted to each other, but he emphasizes that the natural end of sexual intercourse is the generation of children.[34] There are many forms of sexual pleasure offered by nature, but the pleasure attached to an act is not the criterion for its justification. One may say that there is an order of ends in nature, of which pleasure is one, but not the highest.

The Athenian stranger gives two arguments against homosexuality. The first, that homosexuality is the purposeful attempt to murder the human race,[35] is detailed in the *Symposium*. In the *Laws* the main argument is against the encouragement of sexual excess. Homosexual license is not merely biologically unnecessary, but it contributes to license in other forms. The indiscriminate indulgence in pleasure must be subordinated, not to Puritan rage but to the cultivation of political virtue. In addition to moderation, Plato is concerned here with the preservation of the family, with respect for parents and the quality of the breed. For reasons identical to those which emerge in the *Symposium* (and to which we must subsequently return), the Athenian stranger links the prohibition against

33. 836b8 ff. Cf. n. 12 above.
34. 838e6.
35. 838e7.

71

homosexuality with the prohibition against incest.[36] Awe or shame before one's parents is the center of a virtuous polis. Since the desire for pleasure is natural in a way that the desire for virtue is not,[37] an uninterpreted nature no more restricts sexual desires than it guarantees other forms of moderation in the relations between parents and children. Hence opposition to pederasty and incest must have recourse to the same technē.[38] This technē is the utilization of "a little phrase," namely, the nomos that such acts are "absolutely unsanctioned, hated by god and most shameful of shameful deeds." [39]

Plato no less than Pausanias must revise the religious and political nomos and the common tradition,[40] but the extirpation of pederasty symbolizes his purpose. He uses the political technē in order to replace the "noble" pederast by the noble citizen. Pausanias uses the technē of refinement in order to render the two forms of nobility identical. The inadequacy of Pausanias' technē begins to emerge almost as soon as he has made his distinction between noble and ignoble love. His commentary on the distinction, instead of preserving it, amounts to *a steady suppression:* the noble is transformed into the ignoble before our very eyes:

> From whatever chance [Eros] falls upon [the vulgar lovers], at random, they act, sometimes in a good way, and equally in the opposite manner. For it comes from the goddess who is much younger than [the Uranian], and who in her genesis shares in both the female and the

36. It is no accident that, in the revolutionary scheme of the *Republic,* where the abolition of the family leads to problems concerning incest, no such violent denunciation of pederasty occurs: brave warriors, for example, will be allowed to kiss beautiful youths. This is not to suggest that the *Republic* is more licentious than the *Laws,* but that the works differ radically in intent and execution.

37. *Meno* 98c10, *Phaedrus* 237d6, *Laws* 963e5.

38. For Plato, of course, "art completes nature" in a sense different from that of Pausanias or the other speakers. But even if the love of wisdom should be justifiable by nature, the fact remains that φύσις is an extremely ambiguous concept in the dialogues.

39. 838b7.

40. 838d6.

male. But the [Eros] of the Uranian does not share in
the female but only in the male, and this is the love of
boys. Next, it is older, and without any share of hybris.
Whence those who are inspired by this Eros are turned
toward the male, loving the more robust nature and the
one having more mind. . . . Thus they do not love boys
until the latter begin to develop in mind, at about the
time that the beard starts to grow. (181b6–d3)[41]

These lines show not only Pausanias' cunning, but also its
inferiority to the force of Eros within him. Although the Uranian Aphrodite has no mother, she is herself the mother[42] of the
refined and praiseworthy Eros. There is no justification for
Pausanias' claim that Uranian Eros has no share in the female;
if anything, its share would seem to be exclusively female. This
is evident in its lack of hybris: Pausanias is a passive lover.
Cleverness is his substitute for daring. One may suspect that it
is the "robustness" or "manliness" of the older boy more than
his "mind" which excites Pausanias. In any case, Pausanias began his speech by emphasizing style or refinement. He now
emphasizes the link between mind and strength in the beloved,
and the moderation, fidelity, even the surrender and so effeminacy of the Uranian lover. Perhaps a noble manliness without
hybris is not possible.

Pausanias' cleverness is directed toward his selfish advantage
rather than the support of virtue. He is neither manly nor
young, which probably means that he is not handsome. The
fundamental effeminacy of his Uranian moderation goes well
with the next step in his commentary: a guarantee of stability
to the beloved (181d4 ff.). Since fidelity and stability are normally regarded as virtues, they may prevent the beloved to whom
they are offered (Agathon) from asking why it would be desira-

41. I follow Burnet in retaining καὶ ἔστιν οὗτος ὁ τῶν παίδων ἔρως. There is no
difficulty either in the manuscripts or syntax. Bury excludes it (following Schanz)
on the ground that it anticipates and partially contradicts Pausanias' subsequent remarks. This is an example of the unfortunate habit which leads many
scholars to disregard Plato's style on behalf of their own canons of clarity.

42. Or at least the source; Pausanias does his best to blur this difficulty:
ὁ δὲ τῆς Οὐρανίας (181c2).

ble to have a life-long obligation to a lover of Pausanias' nature.
Pausanias tacitly assures his sweetheart that those who love him
for his beauty alone will desert him with the passage of youth.
He, on the other hand, is bound to Agathon by a professed love
for the psyche, which will never lose its charm, more than for
the body, which must inevitably do so. The fact that Pausanias
loves Agathon is extremely important for an understanding of
his speech. Agathon, as his own speech will show, is an exponent
of softness, delicacy, rhetoric: a perfect mate for the timid, middle-aged lover of refinement and girlish masculinity. Since Agathon is now about thirty years old, and was presumably Pausanias' beloved as a boy (cf. the reference in the *Protagoras*),
their love has lasted for perhaps fifteen years. This in itself is a
proof of Pausanias' constancy.

Pausanias next gives further evidence of the timidity that underlies his stability by defending a legal restriction upon pederasty. To prevent the seduction and desertion of young boys,

> there ought to be a law against loving boys, in order that
> much effort not be spent on what is not yet clear. For the
> end of young boys is unclear with respect to how they
> will turn out concerning vice and virtue in the psyche
> and body. (181d7–e3)

May we not sympathize with the picture of a middle-aged Pausanias, short of wind and perhaps of money, turning timidly toward and away from one beautiful boy after another, lacking
the hybris to overcome the cautious whisper of his own cunning? Again nobility has become selfishness: seduction is opposed in order to save lovers from the temptation of uncertain
expense. And then the opposition between general principle
and individual defect is transcended by an almost Hegelian
Aufhebung:

> good men, however, willingly serve as a law unto them-
> selves, and one ought to force the pandemic lovers [to
> obey this law], just as we constrain them as much as pos-
> sible from corrupting our free-born women. (181e3–
> 182a1)

Pausanias caricatures the philosophical conception of the sense in which the good are a law unto themselves.[43] For him, the independence of the good is a matter of self-protection and advantage. Unfortunately, this advantage is not guaranteed by such goodness. The virtuous pederast must be protected by the nomos of the vulgar against the violence of vulgar bisexuality.[44]

It may well be true that the interest of every lover is endangered by promiscuity and rape, but it is certainly not true that the welfare of the lover depends upon his becoming a refined pederast. In emphasizing the violence of the pandemic Eros, Pausanias is again forced to allude to women. The virtue of the free-born wife is the mainstay of the polis, and so too of boys with sufficient refinement to be of interest to Pausanias. The virtue of a wife, however, is defined not only by fidelity but also by the law. Pausanias mentions women because he wishes to legitimate his own enterprise by a condemnation of seduction. He tries to assimilate his conception of virtuous pederasty into the public nomos concerning feminine chastity. His condemnation of hybris draws its respectability from the public interpretation of heterosexual Eros. Ironically, it is at bottom the pandemic Eros that he is praising. His Uranian Eros is at best an imitation of the political love to which it pretends superiority. Pausanias advocates marriage to youths rather than to women, and the generating of noble deeds instead of children. But this is Plato's irony, not his.

The Athenian Nomos Revised

Pausanias began with a conception of nobility defined by style rather than virtue or wisdom. We have watched him move cautiously toward a redefinition of nobility in terms of his own interest. This maneuver now culminates in an explicit suggestion to change the Athenian nomos. "For whatever we do in an orderly and lawful manner, no one could justly censure" (182a4–

43. Cf. Aristotle, *Politics* 1284a11.

44. Cf. N. Machiavelli, *Il Principe e Discorsi* (Milan, 1960), Ch. 18, p. 74, esp. n. 12: "in the world, there is nothing but the *vulgus*, and there is no place for the few where the many have a place to rest."

6). Justness, fitness, order, and law are instruments employed on behalf of the timid lover. Pausanias will now have recourse to the "complicated" or "intricate" (ποικίλος) Athenian nomos[45] in a way similar to Phaedrus' use of the complicated stories about the origins of the gods. A simple law banning all pederasty would be for Pausanias a disaster. But given his personal situation, so too would a simple law legalizing pederasty in all its forms. Boys could then form attachments with whomever they pleased; handsome, wealthy, politically powerful men would have a tremendous advantage. Since Pausanias' major asset is cleverness, he needs a clever, complex law; the legal principle which he adopts is that of clever speech.

Pausanias prepares his interpretation of the complex Athenian situation as follows. First, he cites examples of foreign behavior; second, he offers a general political justification for refined or intricate pederasty. To begin:[46]

> In Elis and Boeotia . . . the law quite simply designates as noble the gratification of lovers, and no one whether young or old would call it shameful, in order, I suppose, not to have the trouble of trying to persuade the young by logos. (182b1–6)

Pausanias knows that love will not come easily to him. He welcomes those obstacles which are reflections of his own strength:

> But in Ionia and elsewhere, where they live under the barbarians, the law regards [gratification] as in many ways a disgrace. For this, philosophy and love of gymnas-

45. Let me emphasize here that Plato wishes to show how "intricate" Athenian nomos really is.

46. Burnet retains the mss. readings at 182a8–b1: ὁ δ'ἐνθάδε καὶ ἐν Λακεδαίμονι ποικίλος. Many editors follow Winckelmann in bracketing the reference to Lacedaimon. Bury summarizes the reasons as follows: Laconia was a hotbed of pederasty, and the Spartans would not be classified separately from those who do not speak wisely. I have decided to omit from the text a discussion of the Lacedaimonians in this passage. I suspect that the text is sound and that we are again in the presence of a Platonic joke. It is just the frequency of pederasty which would lead Pausanias to praise the nomos of Sparta. But there are further difficulties, and the point is not essential to the interpretation.

tics are shameful to the barbarians because of their tyrannical regime. It is no advantage to the rulers, I suppose, for great thoughts to be generated (φρονήματα μεγάλα
ἐγγίγνεσθαι) in those who are ruled, nor strong and common friendships, all of which and more Eros is wont to
produce. (182b6–c4)

According to Herodotus, the Persians learned pederasty from
the Greeks.[47] The tyranny to which Pausanias refers obviously
postdates their acceptance of this custom. Given the initial Per-
sian virtues of simplicity,[48] one might argue the reverse of Pausanias' contention. Perhaps the introduction of pederasty contributed to the luxury and corruption upon which tyranny
feeds. Pausanias' first inference is rather dubious.

He is on safe ground, however, in noting that the barbarians
dislike philosophy, which is here mentioned for the first time
in the dialogue. The link of philosophy and gymnastics to an
appreciation of beautiful boys is an obvious reference to Socrates' behavior.[49] But again there is an ambiguity. In the gym-
nasium both mind and body receive their training for the life
of a free citizen. Philosophy wishes to preserve or intensify
freedom by stripping the mind of the tyranny of nomos. Pausanias, one fears, is more anxious to strip the body by a revision,
and so restriction, of nomos. He imitates philosophy in order to
transform it into rhetoric: hybris is thereby transformed into
cunning. The rebuke of tyranny is an illusion; and, as we shall
see, it is a step in the process whereby Pausanias himself becomes a slave to Eros. Nevertheless, the passage is of special interest because it makes explicit the pervasive metaphor of the
analogy between pederasty and philosophy: both encourage generation of lofty thoughts rather than children of the flesh. As a
consequence, despite his interest in nomos, Pausanias in part
imitates the philosophical disregard of conventional divisions

47. 1.135.
48. Cf. Xenophon, *Cyropaideia* and A. R. Burn, *Persia and the Greeks* (New
York, 1962), pp. 78–80.
49. Cf. 1.2.46 and *Gorgias* 485c1 ff. for the general Greek view that youth is
the appropriate age for philosophy.

between Greek and barbarian. If the barbarian adopts pederasty and clever speech, he will be indistinguishable from the refined Greek. The imitation is only partial, however; rhetorical skill may be taught to men of all kinds, and not merely to middle-aged and timid lovers. What one may call the universal accessibility (in principle) of wisdom is incompatible with Pausanias' special physical interests.

Pausanias cannot establish specialized or private vice except through a concern with public virtue. He therefore praises pederasty as engendering friendship and community, and so as a safeguard against tyranny. Pausanias ignores the very strong tradition which associated tyranny and pederasty in Greece,[50] and confirms his thesis with a reference to the famous affair of Harmodius and Aristogeiton:

> the Eros of Aristogeiton and the friendship ($\phi\iota\lambda\iota\alpha$) of Harmodius became so strong that it dissolved [the tyrants'] rule. Thus where it was regarded as shameful to gratify lovers, this was due to the evil of the founders (of that tradition), to the greedy excess ($\pi\lambda\epsilon o\nu\epsilon\xi\iota\alpha$) of the rulers, and to the unmanliness (= cowardice) of the ruled. (182c5–d2)

Pausanias distinguishes between the Eros of the lover and the *philia* (friendship) of the beloved. He is less capable of arousing desire than affection, the more usual result of habit and fidelity. But he does not mention the fact that Hipparchus, brother of the tyrant, was himself a pederast with designs upon the beautiful Harmodius. Nor does he tell us that the Pisistratidae, despite their tyranny, were noted for a lack of greed ($\pi\lambda\epsilon o\nu\epsilon\xi\iota\alpha$). Thus Hipparchus did not attempt to force the surrender of Harmodius, but used persuasion instead, exactly as Pausanias would wish.

Pausanias' example is also defective with respect to the manliness of the famous lovers. Thucydides speaks of the episode as "an act of daring engendered by an erotic incident," and still

50. Cf. L. Strauss, *On Tyranny* (New York, 1963).

more disparagingly as "thoughtless daring . . . generated by momentary fear." [51] According to Herodotus, the result of this thoughtless fear was not to free Athens but to enrage the kinsfolk of Hipparchus and so, we may presume, to increase the load of the tyranny.[52] It almost seems from Thucydides' account that the one man to act with any degree of moderation or intelligence was Hipparchus. True, he insulted Harmodius' sister by rejecting her as a basket bearer in a particular procession, but this is scarcely the mark of greedy excess or tyrannical passion. Fear resulting from the petulance of Harmodius and the jealousy of Aristogeiton led to the apparently wasted deaths of the beloved and his two lovers. If the lover acted from daring, then he does not illustrate Pausanias' interpretation of Eros. If he acted from thoughtless passion, he did not show the cleverness of the moderate lover. If he acted from cowardice, the result was not gratification but death for himself and his beloved.[53]

In Pausanias' account, then, barbarian intolerance to pederasty rests upon their tyrannical regime, whereas Greek acceptance of pederasty simply or with no restrictions is due to laziness in the psyche of the law-givers.[54] He thus accuses the two undesirable extremes by attributing to them his own defects: unmanliness and laziness. Having established his own moderation and cleverness (which our analysis has shown to be sophistry), Pausanias turns to the "much nobler" Athenian nomoi, which are "not easy to understand." [55]

> Let us consider that it is said to be more noble to love
> openly than in secret, especially when the lovers are
> among the most noble and virtuous, even if they are ug-
> lier than others . . . . (182d5–7)

51. 6.54.1: τὸ γὰρ . . . τόλμημα δι᾽ ἐρωτικὴν ξυντυχίαν and 6.59.1: ἡ ἀλόγιστος τόλμα ἐκ τοῦ παραχρῆμα περιδεοῦς . . .

52. 6.123.

53. 1.20.2, 6.54.1: Thucydides notes in these passages that the Athenians were not well informed about the incident; but certainly Plato, and undoubtedly men like those at the banquet, could hardly have failed to know the facts as presented in Herodotus (and in Plato's case, in Thucydides).

54. 182d3.

55. 182d5. Unlike Phaedrus, Pausanias refers to νοῦς.

Pausanias begins by praising himself. His speech is an open declaration that he is a lover, and we have seen that beauty cannot
be his strong point. Thus he claims that his particular situation
is sanctioned by Athenian public opinion. The balance of this
passage should be quoted in full:

> and that the lover gets wonderful encouragement from
> everyone. It is not as though he were doing something
> shameful; success[56] is thought to be noble and failure
> shameful. And the nomos gives license to the lover to
> win praise in the doing of marvelous deeds, which if any-
> one would dare to do while pursuing any other end or
> desiring to accomplish anything but this, he would reap
> the greatest blame [of philosophy]. (182d7–183a2) [57]

Pausanias' language is very intricate. The lover cannot be en-
couraged by everyone to succeed in physical gratification; as we
shall see in a moment, fathers do not cheer on the would-be se-
ducers of their sons.[58] Pausanias therefore appeals to the base
criterion of success as a guarantee for the nobility of the intention. He tries to justify the word "everyone" by deflecting attention from the specific act to the general quality of "love of
victory", which was so pronounced among Athenians. But this
is accomplished at the price of revealing the amoral basis of his
argument, as well as by allowing a criterion which cannot restrict our approval to instances of refined or Uranian erotic
competition. He tries to cover his tracks by a reference to nomos
(here "custom" rather than "law") which, he carefully says,
gives license to the doing of marvelous deeds for the sake of
success, and not to success itself. Pausanias stresses openness,
success, wonderful deeds, or the splendid and visible accom-
paniment to the private, invisible, and scarcely splendid con-

56. ἐλόντι: "winning" or even "grasping"—the physical connotation is very
strong.

57. Schleiermacher, *Introductions*, secludes φιλοσοφίας. I am not convinced that
he is right to do so, but the point is a minor one. It may be that Pausanias
wishes to enroll philosophy as an ally, and that this is a subtle gibe against
Socrates' fondness for beautiful youths.

58. Cf. Aristophanes, *Birds* 137 ff.

clusion. He is here very close to Phaedrus, although he speaks in terms of the lover.

With this careful and yet soon transparent preparation, Pausanias speaks next with a mixture of frankness and sophistry about the lover's behavior. Again full quotation is needed:

> For if someone wanted to get hold of another's money or win [political] rule, or get hold of some other power, and if he should behave as lovers do toward their sweethearts, offering oaths and entreaties in their pleas [or needs], swearing vows, sleeping on doorsteps, desiring a submission to slavery that no slave [would accept], he would be hindered from doing such a deed by both friends and enemies. The latter would chastise him for flattery and servility (ἀνελευθερίας); the former would admonish and feel shame for him. Grace is granted to a lover for doing all this, and he is allowed by the nomos to act without shame as accomplishing an altogether noble deed. What is most marvelous [also "most frightening," "cleverest": δεινότατον], as the many say, he alone is excused by the gods when breaking a sworn oath. For they say that an aphrodisian vow is none at all. Thus the gods and men have given absolute license to the lover, as our nomos here says. (183a2–183c2)

In these words, intricacy triumphs over cleverness; Pausanias loses control over his argument. With all his skill, he has been carried away by passion.

Pausanias' argument seems to have been scattered by the fury of Eros. In the first place, the "marvelous deeds" turn out to be base and due to blinding passion. Second, far from encouraging freedom and manliness, the erotic passion drives the lover to the most abject form of slavery, and so transforms the beloved from a friend into the most powerful of tyrants. Third, whereas Pausanias began by insisting that pederasty is justified by the refinement and nobility of the manner in which it is accomplished, he now admits that the manner of the lover is shameless; the end of gratification is most noble. Pausanias has sur-

rendered his initial distinction between the Uranian and pandemic Eros: if the end legitimates any kind of behavior, then
selective refinement cannot be justified. Thus Pausanias commits the shocking error of appealing to the vulgar or many as
an authority for the most frightening of the lover's licenses—
permission to break his vows. The sphere of private desire is
thereby given absolute precedence over the public. This is undoubtedly the most revolutionary point in Pausanias' speech.

In allowing the lover to violate all nomoi and so to behave
as either a tyrant or slave, is Pausanias momentarily deranged
by passion, or does he still wish to maintain a distinction between preferable and not preferable behavior? By his previous
position, no act is good or bad in itself, but becomes so by the
way in which it is done. Pausanias would like to maintain the
moral superiority of his own tastes, sexual and otherwise, but
he cannot convert this superiority into a natural criterion for
excellence without justifying erotic desire simply. To exclude
the natural character of heterosexual love would be to end the
supply of youths, not to mention the human race. To restrict
the term "natural" to refined pederasty is to employ a nonsexual
criterion, and therefore one which might apply to heterosexual
relations as well. But can refinement as Pausanias sees it be the
natural standard of excellence? The refinement of an act derives from a conception of a way or style of life, which is in turn
dependent upon an evaluation of conflicting styles and so of
ends. The naturalness of an act thus depends upon natural ends:
there must be natural standards for goodness, which is not at
all the same as to say that specific acts must be naturally good or
bad. For Pausanias, the end becomes identical with the manner
of performance and therefore cannot serve to distinguish the
manner of a well-performed act from the act itself. The act is
absolute. But this is only a step away from permitting all acts,
or the post hoc definition of man by his acts.[59]

Pausanias is thus unmasked as a tyrant for whom "nothing is
good by nature, but my tastes are best." His timidity prevents
him from identifying the "law of nature" as the will of the

59. Cf. M. Heidegger, *Sein und Zeit* (Tübingen, 1953), pp. 47–49.

stronger.[60] Hence law is for him the more moderate principle of the will of the cleverest speaker. Since cleverness will serve to justify all tastes, Pausanias is driven by his own principle to contradict himself and justify Eros altogether. From Plato's viewpoint, his attempt to revise the Athenian nomos, so far as we have considered it, is a satire on the weaknesses of Athenian democracy.

Utility and Slavery

The difference between philosophical and sophistic virtue may be illustrated by the different ways in which each conceives of the relationship between utility and goodness. An especially pertinent example is the discussion of justice in the *Republic*. The topic arises in the first book when Socrates asks Cephalus what he regards as the "greatest good" (μέγιστον ἀγαθόν) arising from much wealth. Cephalus replies that "not the least" of the uses (χρείας) of money is the power it gives us to atone for acts of injustice.[61] In his subsequent dialogue with Polemarchus, Cephalus' heir, Socrates preserves the modification of "good" into "useful," and the fundamental question of the nature of justice is developed in utilitarian terms.[62] In the fourth book, when this question is given its definitive answer, in an exchange covering some twelve Stephanus pages, the words "utility" and "useful" have virtually disappeared.[63]

In this example the movement of the dialectic is from "useful goods" in a sense equivalent to or inseparable from an external possession or object, to "goodness" in the sense of an inner psychic condition.[64] Justice, says Socrates,

60. Cf. *Gorgias* 483d–e.

61. *Republic* 330d1–331b7.

62. 332e3 ff.; 333a10: τί δὲ δή; τὴν δικαιοσύνην πρὸς τίνος χρείαν ἢ κτῆσιν ἐν εἰρήνῃ φαίης ἂν χρήσιμον εἶναι;

63. 432–44. At 438a2–3 Socrates refers to the desire for χρηστοῦ ποτοῦ and σίτου, but immediately suppresses χρηστός in the general statement: πάντες γὰρ ἄρα τῶν ἀγαθῶν ἐπιθυμοῦσιν. However, χρηστοῦ then reappears with respect to the singular thirst.

64. Cf. also the change in meaning of οὐσία from 330d2 on; as early as 359a5, it refers to the "nature" of justice, whereas its initial use is as "material possessions."

does not concern external activity (τὴν ἔξω πρᾶξιν), but internal [activity], what is truly [one's] self and [one's] own. . . . [The just man] truly sets his house in order, becoming his own master . . .[65]

Things are useful for the sake of psychic goodness, which is an end in itself; from this end, useful things derive their own goodness. Thus there is a connection between utility and goodness, which in the last analysis is established and governed by philosophy, or the vision of the good. Socrates begins from utility and moves upward to freedom in the sense defined by philosophical goodness. To return to the *Symposium*, Pausanias begins from utility but moves downward to slavery as a consequence of his own allegiance to sophistic cleverness.

The just man rules himself because his Eros has been subordinated to, or transformed into, *philia*. As has already been observed, according to the *Symposium* itself, Eros is not just; hence the enslavement of Pausanias to Eros means enslavement simply. The situation of Pausanias is not unique to him or to the Sophists, but points to a fundamental problem in the meaning of the *Symposium* which will become clearer later in the dialogue. The proper ordering of Eros depends upon a vision of, or friendship for, the good. Although Eros is called a philosopher by Diotima,[66] it is evident from the speeches of all the other encomiasts that Eros alone is insufficient to make a man a philosopher. This problem, which can only be mentioned here, should be kept in mind as we proceed. It has become visible now because Pausanias stands for the political (and not simply moral) results of the replacement of philosophy by sophistry. Pausanias cannot master or know himself because he understands himself in terms of infinitely variable desire.[67] He "is" what he "does," and despite his cleverness, what he does depends not upon himself, but upon others.

We saw above how Pausanias was driven to justify the most

65. 443c9–d4.
66. *Symposium* 203d7.
67. Cf. T. Hobbes, *Leviathan* (Oxford, 1947), p. 56.

vulgar deeds of the lover. This vulgarity is a consequence of the intricate and self-contradictory character of the Athenian nomoi. To a considerable extent, Pausanias is correct in his assertion that public opinion, as distinct from the written statute, encourages the lover. But he is not altogether correct; as he now admits, Athenian fathers place an attendant in charge of their sons, with the explicit duty of not permitting the beloved even to speak to the lover. As fathers, Athenians recognize the dangers of "free speech" (παρρησία), toward which they are more tolerant as lovers (183c4 ff.). In this brief passage is contained the whole problem of the tension between public and private interests raised by Eros in its dual role. Pausanias avoids the issue by repeating two points made prior to his descent into slavery. Every act is noble or shameful if it is done nobly or shamefully (183d4 ff.; cf. 180e4 ff.); the bad or pandemic lover desires the body more than the psyche, which leads to his inconstancy (183d8 ff.; cf. 181c5 ff.).

Even here, however, Pausanias has modified his initial formulation. Previously, he had not explicitly said that the nobility of gratification depended upon the goodness of the lover. He now adds this qualification, but with a significant note of ambiguity. The word used to designate the goodness of the lover is χρηστός, which has the primary meaning of "useful" (cf. 177b2, 178c4). It also replaces ἀγαθοί as applied to superior lovers at 181e3, whose goodness amounts to self-restriction in seduction until the mind and body of the boy have developed sufficiently so as to ensure that attentions paid to them will not be wasted effort. Goodness is now apparently understood as a combination of efficiency and utility. Another ambiguity emerges when Pausanias says that the bad man loves the body more than the psyche. He never actually says that the good (= useful) man loves the psyche more than the body. If Pausanias were a lover of the psyche, then the body would be irrelevant in cases of noble but ugly youths. Instead, his position is this: of those boys with beautiful bodies, only those with good character are useful to "the lover of the useful ethos" (183e5: ὁ δὲ τοῦ ἤθους χρηστοῦ ὄντος ἐραστής); that is, those who are intelligent enough to be won over

85

by clever speech, and virtuous enough to remain faithful to timid lovers.

For Pausanias intelligence is a secondary, or epi-, phenomenon, of the body. Similarly, refinement is for him an epiphenomenon of cautious or efficient selfishness. His real commitment to efficiency leads him to praise vice in the act of honoring virtue. According to him the Athenian nomos tests the nature of lovers by "putting them to the torture" (184a1), thereby deciding which are to be gratified and which to be shunned. This amounts to the suggestion that the written statute, the strictness of fathers, and the strong segment of anti-pederastic public opinion, have as their true purpose the safeguarding of Pausanias' own sensual gratification. In keeping with the political satire which his persona embodies, he transforms himself by a sleight of hand into a new Athenian tyrant, ruling in the name of the Uranian Eros. In his erotic fantasy "quick surrender is thought to be shameful (184a5–6) because an interval of time is needed to test both lover and beloved. Amusingly enough, in his discussion of this test, Pausanias concentrates upon the character-defects of the beloved. It is as though the offer by the lover of money, political power, or force were themselves tests of the beloved's virtue rather than signs of the lover's vice.

Now Pausanias plays his trump card. The nomos permits (that is, does not regard as scandalous) only one reason for gratification of the lover: "slavery for the sake of virtue" (184b6–c3). Not even Pausanias quite dares to speak of "noble slavery"; he restricts himself to calling it "nonshameful" (οὐκ ἐπονείδιστος) Slavery here corresponds to the Socratic category of acts that are necessary for virtue but are neither noble nor base. Pausanias holds the office of tyrant on a purely contingent or metaphorical basis: both lover and beloved are enslaved to the real tyrant, Eros. Whereas Socrates maintains that virtue is necessary for freedom, Pausanias teaches that slavery is necessary for virtue: in order to be free, one must be a slave. Pausanias' sexual inversion, assisted by the teachings of the Sophists, leads to a parody of both the polis and philosophy. Thus he once more links pederasty to philosophy, or justifies slavery on the supposition that it will lead to "some sort of wisdom" or "any other part of virtue" (184c4–7).

It is not shameful for the beloved to wish to be a servant, provided that he is motivated by a desire for self-improvement rather than by Eros. Once more we see the connection between Pausanias and Phaedrus. Although the former substitutes culture for money as the wages of prostitution, the real motive which each attributes to the lover is the same: gratification. Pausanias' lover must already have those qualities which entitle him to enjoy the beloved. The lover does not obtain virtue from the beloved but only physical pleasure. Thus lover and beloved represent separate nomoi, "the one about pederasty and the other about philosophy and the rest of virtue," which must be compared in order to decide whether it is noble for the sweetheart to yield (184c7–d3). Since there is a division of nomos in the fanciful pederastic polis, the likelihood of strife and revolution arises. To give only the most obvious example, the youth may be persuaded by another clever speaker that sexual intercourse and the pursuit of culture are not necessarily related.

Pausanias stresses the importance of fidelity in the lover, but how can he guarantee it in the beloved, who is not motivated by sexual passion? For reasons that have already been explored, he cannot encourage this passion in the beloved. As a result, the very virtue of intelligence to which his appeal is directed may guarantee his future betrayal:

> For when lover and sweetheart come together, each with his own nomos, the one to serve justly in any way the sweetheart who has gratified him, the other to assist justly in any way the one who makes him wise and good, the one able to contribute intelligence (φρόνησιν) and the rest of virtue, the other to acquire education and all wisdom (τὴν ἄλλην σοφίαν) in which he is lacking; then, when these two nomoi come together in one place, it happens that it is noble for the sweetheart to gratify the lover, but otherwise not at all. (184d3–e4) [68]

68. This intricate statement is rich in double entendre; see Bury's note.

Pausanias must admit the separate purposes of lover and beloved; he advocates a treaty of mutual self-interest. But he cannot demonstrate why, if the lover loves virtue or a virtuous psyche, he requires the services of the body.[69] There is a disjunction between body and psyche in Pausanias' argument: he has divided man in half rather than made him whole. And at best, he has proved that the beloved ought to gratify Socrates rather than himself. Differently stated, the beloved may virtuously betray his lover when confronted by a superior teacher. But he may also be betrayed, as Pausanias now admits:

> to be deceived in this purpose is not shameful. . . . if someone were to submit to a supposedly good man, and be deceived in thinking that he will become better through the friendship (τὴν φιλίαν) of the lover, when the latter is shown to be bad and lacking virtue, nevertheless the deception is noble. (184e4 ff.)

The reasonable consequence, which Pausanias does not draw, would be for the beloved to withhold his favors until the character of the lover is adequately tested. To surrender at any point during his beautiful years would be always to run the risk of immediate betrayal. The only safe course is abstinence, or insistence that the lover reveal the virtue he claims to possess. Pederasty passes over into philosophy.

Instead of giving this reasonable advice, Pausanias assures the beloved that it is noble to be deceived in a good cause. Since he does not attribute erotic passion to the beloved, he must affirm that it would be still nobler, and more efficient, not to be deceived but to practice and therefore to gain virtue anyhow. Pausanias makes an unstated but tangible threat: if the beloved does not yield, he will never obtain the virtue in question. He must pay this price because the lover charges a salary for his lessons; the lover is a Sophist. Through Pausanias Plato criticizes Athenian democracy as susceptible to corruption by the Sophists. It is the Sophists, and not Socrates, who corrupt the young in the name of freedom and virtue. The Sophists pretend

69. Cf. Isenberg, *Order*, p. 25.

to teach virtue but identify it with persuasion, and so with nomos. Intelligence enters only instrumentally, as a tool for satisfying desire. Mind is degraded into the technē of rhetoric. In the name of the psyche, the Sophist pays homage to the body. If payment is the standard of virtue, then it is virtuous for the Sophist to deceive his client for the sake of money. But by the same logos (cf. 185a5) it is virtuous for the client to deceive his teacher, not to mention his fellow citizens. The principle of mutual interest transforms peace into war and the polis into a battleground. Justice becomes deception made noble by habit.

So much then for the Uranian Eros, which Pausanias says is "most worthy both for the polis and for private affairs" (185b6).

CHAPTER FOUR
🕸 ERYXIMACHUS 🕸

Hiccoughs and Hippocratica

On the basis of the seating order, Aristophanes should have spoken after Pausanias. The conventional arrangement is disrupted by a natural misfortune: Aristophanes is silenced by a "chance" attack of hiccoughs.[1] Perhaps because of satiety,

> he was unable to speak, but [only] to say to Eryximachus the doctor, who was seated below him: "O Eryximachus, it is just that either you bring a pause to my hiccoughs, or speak in my behalf until I can make them pause." And Eryximachus said, "but I shall do both, for I shall speak in your place, and you, when they pause, in mine." (185c6–d2) [2]

The full significance of this intermission can only be appreciated after we have studied the speeches of doctor and patient. Meanwhile, a preliminary discussion is necessary.

Aristophanes' hiccoughs have elicited a wide variety of responses from other authorities.[3] The most frequent explanation

1. The juxtaposition of conventional necessity and natural chance is expressed in the text by the opposition of δεῖν and τυχεῖν: 185c5–6. This is reinforced by the pun of Apollodorus: Παυσανίου δὲ παυσαμένου, which introduces the "medical" intermission. Pausanias pauses of his own volition; not so Aristophanes. For the pun, cf. Bury's note and Rettig, *Symposion* 180e5, 185c4.

2. The word παύω occurs five times in the brief exchange between Aristophanes and Eryximachus, echoing the pun of Apollodorus. One effect of this repetition is to call our attention to the importance of the "pause" in the series of encomia.

3. A. E. Taylor, *Plato* (New York, 1958), p. 216, demands that we refrain from assigning any theoretical significance to the episode: "The numerous persons who are unhappily without anything of the Pantagruelist in their own composition will continue, no doubt, to look for hidden meanings in this section . . ." Taylor apparently forgets the caricature of philosophy that was so

is that Plato here caricatures Aristophanes in vengeance for the comedian's portrait of Socrates in the *Clouds*.[4] No doubt such a motive is present, but this explanation fails to account for the details of the caricature, or its specific function in the *Symposium* of relating the speeches of Eryximachus, the "fighter of eructations,"[5] and Aristophanes.[6] These two speeches present what are intended as separate attacks upon the authority of philosophy. Eryximachus, as already noted, is a spokesman for "technicism."[7] Aristophanes' position is more difficult to summarize; he speaks on behalf of "political poetry," or justice. Aristophanes undoubtedly regards technicism as a bad consequence of philosophy. As I shall show later, it is Plato's opinion that poetry cannot maintain its independence, either as the "legislator for mankind" (Agathon) or as the *defensor pacis,* the bulwark of political justice. The poetic interpretation of Eros, if not subordinate to that of philosophy, finally becomes absorbed by, and so subordinate to, the claims of technicism. In this specific context the hiccoughs with which "chance" afflicts Aristophanes symbolize the inarticulateness of poetry and justice. Aristophanes is forced to yield to Eryximachus in word and deed. In both treating and speaking for him, Eryximachus disregards the "just" alternative posed by Aristophanes.

The substitution of Eryximachus for Aristophanes functions in several ways within the *Symposium*. It serves to suggest the final subordination of poetry to technicism and at the same time indicates Plato's own preference for Aristophanes, who is given

---

obviously a part of Rabelais' own Pantagruelism. More imaginative accounts may be found in Plochmann, *Hiccups,* p. 10 and Brentlinger, *Cycle,* p. 14. Brentlinger sees the "cosmological" symbolism in the disease and its cure: "violent inner motion applied to violent inner motion."

4. Cf. Bury, *Symposium,* pp. xxii–xxiii.

5. O. Apelt, *Platonische Aufsätze* (Leipzig, 1912), p. 78, n. 1, and Bury, *Symposium,* p. xxix.

6. Isenberg, *Order,* p. 60: the purpose of the   episode is to indicate that Aristophanes' speech should follow that of Eryximachus. But Isenberg does not explain why such a sequence is necessary, or why it required so elaborate a preface.

7. I almost agree with Robin's observation on Eryximachus: "La technicité le préoccupe beaucoup plus que la *cosmologie,* dont la place dans son discours est moins grande qu'on ne le dit souvent." *SymBudé,* p. lii, n. 1.

a higher position in the dialectical ascent. The interplay of nature and convention, of necessity and chance, forces us to careful reflection upon the relationship between the two speeches. The necessary triumph of the technical manipulation of nature is shown to be not necessarily a higher manifestation of Eros. Finally, the link between Eryximachus on the one hand, and Phaedrus and Pausanias on the other, is rendered ambiguous. All three defend pederasty, yet it is chance alone that brings Eryximachus into a closer conjunction with the first two speakers. Whereas Pausanias' speech is essentially a development by correction of Phaedrus' position, Eryximachus does not simply correct Pausanias. He moves into a new dimension.[8]

As human types, the three defenders of pederasty are related by their selfishness. Phaedrus began by debasing reason into a utilitarian calculus; his implicit theoretical justification was process physics. Pausanias raised the somewhat brutal calculus of Phaedrus to the level of rhetorical cleverness, grounded in a perception of nobility and so in a concern with the psyche. Eryximachus is both a descent and an ascent from Pausanias. He lowers the context of nobility from the psyche to the body, but his medical technē gives him more adequate access to a natural standard for distinguishing noble or right actions from ignoble or wrong ones.[9] Health is the standard; it remains to be seen whether its practical attractions are accompanied by theoretical adequacy in comparison to philosophy, rather than to rhetoric. In the pursuit of selfishness, Phaedrus advocated death for the lover; Pausanias introduced restrictions upon his pleas-

8. Thus it is not quite correct to say that "Eryximachos ist in der Tat mit Pausanias einig. . . . Das Neue bei Eryximachos ist die Erweiterung der ethischen Aufklärung zur aufgeklärten *Weltbetrachtung überhaupt*." Krüger, *Einsicht*, pp. 105–06. The link between the two of pederasty means that Eryximachus, like his predecessors, will argue for a fundamentally "selfish," and to that extent "enlightened" interpretation of Eros. Aristophanes sees this, and opposes it; thus his use of the dual at 189c3 in referring to Pausanias and Eryximachus. But this does not exclude the difference between the two: a difference between dualism and an unresolved monism.

9. Cf. *Regimen in Acute Diseases*, IV. 1 ff. in W. H. S. Jones, *Hippocrates* (3 vols. Cambridge, Mass., 1947), καὶ γὰρ ὁπόσα ἔργα καλῶς ἔχει ἢ ὀρθῶς, καλῶς ἕκαστα χρὴ ποιεῖν καὶ ὀρθῶς . . .

ures. Eryximachus offers life and the safeguarding of pleasure by means of the technē of medicine. His is a more efficient, even cosmic version of selfishness.

By using the word "selfishness," I do not mean to suggest that Eryximachus' position is clearly or entirely wrong. Whatever the advantages of good health and technical proficiency, these two cannot function as a philosophical standard for the arrangement of human existence. This is Plato's objection to what its admirers have called "medical humanism." [10] Such an orientation tends to become, if it is not already, a justification for living under any circumstances rather than for living well. "Well" comes to mean no longer "justly" or even "in good health" but is virtually a synonym for "being alive" as opposed to dying. Once again we come upon the complexity of Plato's conception of nature. The natural desire to survive must be subordinated to the natural hierarchy of ends, within which survival is not the highest. The overwhelming power of man's love of life makes medicine the perfect representative for the theoretical doctrine of technicism. Technicism is the most powerful consequence of Eros undisciplined by philosophy, and medicine is the most powerful techne.[11]

It is on these terms that one must approach Plato's attitude toward medicine. In the *Republic* the conflict between medicine and justice, suggested above by the words of Aristophanes and Eryximachus, is explicit.[12] Medicine is linked with legal rhetoric or sophistry (as was historically the case); an excessive

10. Cf. L. Bourgey, *Observation et Expérience chez les Médecins de la Collection Hippocratique* (Paris, 1953) (hereafter *Hippocratique*), pp. 267 ff.

11. The connection between medicine and the scientific conquest of nature is explicit in Descartes, *Discours de la méthode* (E. Gilson, ed.; Paris, 1947), pt. 6, p. 62 where he speaks of "la conservation de la santé [to be achieved by "une infinité d'artifices], laquelle est sans doute le premier bien et le fondement de tous les autres biens de cette vie; car même l'esprit dépend si fort du tempérament, et de la disposition des organes du corps que, s'il est possible de trouver quelque moyen qui rende communément les hommes plus sages et plus habiles qu'ils n'ont été jusques ici, je crois que c'est dans la médecine qu'on doit le chercher." Descartes even anticipates our future ability to exempt man "de l'affaiblissement de la viellesse." Cf. Gilson's commentary, pp. 449–50. Also Krüger, *Einsicht*, p. 111.

12. *Republic* 405–10.

dependence upon "skilled doctors and jurors" is a sign that political justice and virtue have succumbed to the disease of selfishness and fear of death.[13] Even here, in his political criticism of medicine, Socrates by no means condemns the technē altogether but provides us with a medicinal reinterpretation of the "restraint" (or "irony") of Asclepius. One must also notice that medicine is not subjected to the rule of political justice and certainly not to poetry, but to philosophy. In nonpolitical terms, the techniques of medicine, to the extent that they reveal or make known "what is," [14] are part of, or the same as, the techniques of philosophy (which is not itself, of course, merely a technē). Thus, in a much commented-on passage in the *Phaedrus*, Socrates cites "Hippocrates and true reasoning" as joint authorities for methodological remarks on the study of nature.[15] Whether Plato or Hippocrates was the first to develop the technique of *diaeresis*, both employ it in their respective attempts to understand man.[16]

On the whole we may safely leave the question of Plato's medical authorities to specialists in that domain. It is, however, not uninteresting to consider briefly some of the possible philosophical and medical antecedents for the speech of Eryximachus. The most obvious philosophical authorities for Eryximachus would seem to be Alcmaeon and Empedocles. Alcmaeon's revision of the Pythagorean theory of opposites is of special

13. Ibid., 405a6 ff. At 407e3 Adeimantus says to Socrates: πολιτικόν . . . λέγεις Ἀσκληπιόν.

14. Cf. *On Technē*, 2.5 ff. in Jones, *Hippocrates*, 2.

15. *Phaedrus* 270b–e, esp. c9 ff. For general discussion of this passage, cf. Bourgey, *Hippocratique*, pp. 90 ff.; J. H. Kühn, *System- und Methodenprobleme im Corpus Hippocraticum* (Wiesbaden, 1956), pp. 44, 65, 84 ff.; A. J. Festugière, *Contemplation et vie contemplative selon Platon* (Paris, 1950), p. 9; R. Hackforth, *Plato's Phaedrus* (Cambridge, 1952), pp. 149–50; and R. Kucharski, *Les chemins du savoir* (Paris, 1949), pp. 129 ff.

16. Cf. *Phaedrus* 270b4 (διελέσθαι φύσιν) and Kühn, *Hippocraticum*, pp. 65 ff. The transition from Phaedrus to Pausanias is a diaeresis of Eros, but E. Hoffmann radically oversimplifies in suggesting that Eryximachus again divides Eros into four (medicine, music, astronomy, religion). To give only one example, Hoffmann omits gymnastic and agriculture, also treated by Eryximachus. Hoffmann's schema overlooks the unification of the two Eroses into a double Eros. E. Hoffmann, *Über Platons Symposion* (Heidelberg, 1947), pp. 9–12.

interest here because he expresses the difference between health and disease in political terminology. Health is an *isonomia* or democratic equilibrium of conflicting "powers," whereas "disease" is the *monarchia* of one among them.[17] As Rettig has pointed out, Empedocles and Eryximachus, despite their similarity, differ in important respects. The double Eroses serve Eryximachus as cosmogonic principles instead of Empedocles' friendship and strife (φιλία and νεῖκος). Furthermore, Eryximachus does not speak of four elements, and his moral views belong to the time of the Sophists.[18] I shall return below to Empedocles' teaching; here it may be appropriate to mention that, like the Pythagoreans, he advocates a kind of Socratic reserve or irony in speaking before the uninitiated.[19] The fifth-century physicians also belonged to secret societies, and the Hippocratic texts "use language which, on a literal interpretation, do imply the existence of 'mysteries,' 'initiation,' and 'brotherhood.' "[20] We see here another reason for the choice of a doctor as the spokesman for technicism in the *Symposium*. Eryximachus and Diotima are rival prophets.[21]

So far as Eryximachus' medical theories are concerned, a recent authority has said: "the closest parallel to Eryximachus' speech of which I am aware is to be found in the Hippocratic writing *On Ancient Medicine* where πλήρωσις and κένωσις are named as the tendencies to be considered in the healthy and in the sick . . ."[22] Without questioning this judgment, it may also be noted that there are parts of the same treatise which contradict Eryximachus' position: for example, the injunction against

17. Diels, *Vorsokratiker, 1,* pp. 210 ff., Fr. A3, B4.
18. Rettig, *Symposion,* p. 16. Of the two Erotes, he says: "diese sind nicht schöpferische Kräfte wie jene, und stehen nicht selbständig da und bearbeiten den Stoff, sondern sie sind an den Stoff gebunden und stehen im Dienste des Asklepios oder anderer Wissenschaft."
19. Diels, *Vorsokratiker, 1,* pp. 276 ff., Fr. B3; cf. *Pythagoras* Fr. A8a (19), A17; *Hippasus* Fr. A4.
20. Jones, *Hippocrates,* 2, p. 336; cf. pp. 273 ff.
21. *Prognostics* 1.1 in Jones, *Hippocrates,* 2: τὸν ἰητρὸν δοκεῖ μοι ἄριστον εἶναι πρόνοιαν ἐπιτηδεύειν . . . κτλ. Cf. 1.10 ff.: to restore all men to health would be better than predicting the future.
22. Edelstein, *Eryximachus,* p. 92, n. 25.

statements about "things in the heavens and beneath the earth," and the refutation of the view that diseases are cured by a harmony of opposites.[23] On the other hand, passages may be found in a number of the other Hippocratic writings which are reminiscent of themes expressed by Eryximachus.[24] It seems clear that Eryximachus is intended to represent a generalized picture of those aspects of the Hippocratic school which Plato found especially significant for the argument of technicism. It would be fruitless and unnecessary to attempt to specify with precision his historical sources. With this in mind, we may now turn to the details of Eryximachus' speech.

The Double Eros

After Aristophanes has agreed to follow Eryximachus' recommended treatment,[25] the doctor begins his praise of Eros:

> It seems to me to be necessary, since Pausanias, having begun his speech nobly, did not adequately finish it, it is necessary that I attach an end to the speech. (185e6–186a2)

The three key terms here are "seeming" (δόξα), "necessity" (ἀνάγκη, δεῖ), and "end" (τέλος); they provide us with the skeleton of Eryximachus' encomium and serve also to indicate its ultimate defect. Eryximachus moves by way of nature or necessity from human opinion to the *telos* of cosmic health. As it seems to Eryximachus, Pausanias offers no adequate standard by which to justify the distinction between noble and base. The opposition between Uranian and Olympian gods is cosmic rather than human and must be supported by physics rather than rhetoric

23. *On Ancient Medicine* 1.20; 13; 14.1–10, in Jones, *Hippocrates, 1.*

24. In addition to those which have already been quoted, I may mention here *Breaths* 1.30 ff. (opposites cure opposites); *Euschēmosynē* 5.1 (the doctor is ἰσόθεος); *Nature of Man* 3.20 (on the homogeneity of genesis and decay) and 9.1 ff. (ὅσα πλησμονὴ τίκτει νοσήματα, κένωσις ἰῆται . . . κτλ), *Regimen One*, 2.1 ff. (to know the correct regimen, we must first know παντὸς φύσιν ἀνθρώπου): all in Jones, *Hippocrates, 1, 2, 4.*

25. See the reference to Brentlinger in n. 3 above.

or aesthetic taste. The body, not the pysche, is the standard
of *aisthēsis* (literally, "sense perception"). Hence medicine, the
technē of the body, must provide us with the interpretation of
aisthēsis, or the perception of noble and base.[26] But the identification of nobility with health means that the living body is
the paradigm by which the cosmos must be understood. The
difference between the living and the nonliving body, however,
is precisely the psyche, and in this case, the human psyche.
Eryximachus interprets the cosmos in the light of man's psychic
evaluation of health, and so he does not finally transcend δόξα.[27]
The telos of medical humanism is man made, and so as problematic as the telos of rhetorical humanism.

As we saw above, chance, in the form of Aristophanes' hiccoughs, necessitates that Eryximachus speak after Pausanias.
Within the dramatic context the detailed structure of Eryximachus' speech makes it virtually impossible to suppose that it
is a spontaneous response to the new situation created by the
disruption of the original seating order. To say the least,
Eryximachus must have been planning his remarks for some
time prior to Aristophanes' attack of hiccoughs.[28] We need not
ignore the relations between Eryximachus and the first two
speakers in observing that the telos which he adds to Pausanias' encomium is also, and perhaps more fundamentally, intended as a telos to Aristophanes. As I shall indicate in the next
chapter, the teaching in Aristophanes' speech may be found in
his comedies as well, with which Eryximachus was undoubtedly
familiar. In sum, Eryximachus revises his planned remarks to
some extent, but there is no reason to assume that Pausanias'
speech is not a satisfactory basis for what he wants to say. For
the time being, we must simply bear in mind the implicit connection with Aristophanes.

26. Cf. *Ancient Medicine* 9.10–20 in Jones, *Hippocrates, 1.*

27. Cf. Kühn, *Hippocraticum,* pp. 26–28: "Der Verfasser de prisca medicina
folgt im medizinischen Bereich den Anschauungen, die Protagoras für den
gesamten Erkenntnisbereich vertreten hatte, als er den individuellen Menschen
zum Richter über das Sein der Dinge bestellt hatte. . . ."

28. He introduced the theme at 177a1 ff. in such a way as to show that he and
Phaedrus had already given the matter some thought.

Eryximachus changes or suppresses the end of Pausanias'
speech, and so its overall significance, by introducing his own
ending. He will develop Pausanias' use of "intelligence" into
a theory of technicism; that is, he will complete Pausanias'
speech by introducing the notion of the "whole" or cosmos as
the object, guide, or fulfillment of intelligence.[29] But here
Eryximachus is faced with a problem. The distinction between
the Uranian and Olympian gods would seem to cut the whole
into two halves. Eryximachus must avoid a drastic form of
dualism while preserving the distinction between noble and
base Eros. He tries to solve this problem by replacing the two
Eroses in Pausanias' speech with a double Eros; that is, a single
principle in which opposites are harmonized:

> That there is a double Eros (τὸ μὲν γὰρ διπλοῦν εἶναι τὸν
> Ἔρωτα) seems to me a good distinction. But there is
> not only [an erotic attraction] among the psyches of men
> for beautiful men, but also among other beings for a
> multitude of things, present in the bodies of all living
> things, in what grows in the earth, and so to speak in all
> beings; and I seem to have observed from medicine, our
> technē, how great, marvelous, and all-extensive is the god,
> who directs both human and divine things. (186a2–b2)

Eryximachus here takes up the introductory themes of
Phaedrus' speech[30] as well as the Pausanian distinction between
Uranian and pandemic, but at a higher theoretical level. One
may say that he attempts to resolve the dualism in Pausanias'
speech at the Uranian level, by giving a properly "scientific"
interpretation to Uranus. This attempt is subject to personal
as well as abstract or theoretical difficulties. By referring to
"our" technē, Eryximachus prepares us for a later explicit
acknowledgment of his membership in the Asclepiad guild.[31]
But Asclepius was the son of Apollo, the god of medicine; by
his profession, Eryximachus is bound to the Olympians, whom

29. Cf. n. 15 above.
30. 178a6 ff.
31. 186e2.

his sexual tastes lead him to overthrow. We shall soon find this conflict between medicine and sexual taste repeated at a theoretical level within Eryximachus' speech. One element in this conflict has already been identified. For Eryximachus, man's completeness is a function of the cosmos as a whole. It may be that Eryximachus discerns the need to express the principles of the cosmos in such a way so as not to destroy the human dimension. In any event, loyalty to his technē has the same practical consequence: the corporealization of the cosmos proceeds in accordance with the model of man. If the cosmos is one and contains living things—including beings who distinguish between the noble and the divine—then the cosmos must in some sense be alive; the principle of the noble and divine must be cosmic. Upon these premises rests the primacy of medicine.

Despite its double nature, Eros is the force which binds the cosmos into a unity—or so Eryximachus intends; this stage was not reached with any clarity by Phaedrus or Pausanias. Thus Eros must himself be a unity; despite his acceptance of a double Eros, Eryximachus refers to the god, exactly as did Phaedrus. And he concludes his speech by referring to the "total power" of "Eros conceived as a whole" (188d5: συλλήβδην μὲν ὁ πᾶς Ἔρως). He speaks twice of the double Eros (186a2, 186b4), but not of the two Eroses mentioned by Pausanias (180d5). Eryximachus thus prefigures the teaching of Diotima (not to mention Aristophanes) with this conception of Eros. One might suspect that defects in Eryximachus' formulation will prefigure difficulties for Diotima as well. That is, the duality in Eryximachus' Eros is not peculiar to his medical physics. The problematic character of the teaching that Eros binds human and divine into a whole, may be shown in two ways. First, Diotima herself states that there are many daimons or intermediate entities, and not one alone.[32] Second, we should remember the famous passage in Plato's *Laws* which tells of the plurality of psyches in heaven.[33]

32. 203a6 ff.

33. *Laws* 896d5–e6. The uniqueness of this passage in the Platonic corpus emphasizes its importance.

According to the Athenian stranger, there are no less than two heavenly psyches, "the beneficent worker and the one whose power is opposite." If Eros is the defining or binding nature of the psyche, must there not be two Eroses as well? This seems to follow from a slightly later passage, in which the Athenian stranger speaks of the "eternal war" in heaven between the good and bad directing gods of the cosmos.[34] In the *Laws* the Athenian stranger wishes to demonstrate not only that psyche rules the cosmos, but the corollary that technē, the work of psyche, is prior to nature as understood by materialists.[35] Eryximachus' position is a curiously similar one, except that he posits one god, and so one psychic principle with dual powers. Furthermore, the technē to which he gives priority is developed into the fundamental technē of all nature; as a consequence, he might almost be described as a "vitalistic materialist." That is, psyche, or the god Eros, is corporealized by Eryximachus, just as it is made the ruling principle in the living cosmos. Life is defined in terms of the body; this is Eryximachus' attempt to synthesize monism and dualism.

In still other terms Eryximachus represents the claim of technē to terminate the war between the good and bad forces in the cosmos, and so to permit man to live in peaceful harmony with nature. Not only must we evaluate this claim, but we must finally decide upon the adequacy of Plato's own answer to the problem. One reason that I have cited the *Laws* is to remind the reader that no such decision can be made upon the basis of the *Symposium* alone. If Eros binds man to the gods, is there any force bringing harmony to the gods themselves? Or if Eros is the binding factor in psyche, whereas there are at least two cosmic psyches corresponding to the noble and base Eroses, how shall we extricate ourselves from the dilemma faced by Pausanias? If there is one Eros with a double propensity for evil

34. Ibid., 906a2 ff: μάχη ἀθάνατος. The relation between this section of the *Laws* and the speech of Eryximachus is further indicated at 889d4 ff., where the stranger says that the serious technai are medicine, farming and gymnastic, since their power has most in common with nature. At 906a2 doctors and farmers are again mentioned (as are athletic competitors at 905e7 ff.).

35. *Laws* 892b5 ff.

as well as good, what is the principle by which Eros is guided
in the proper direction?

Like and Unlike

Thus far, two sources of difficulty in Eryximachus' teaching
have emerged: the corporealization of psyche and the duality
within Eros. In terms of physics or cosmology, the problem is
one of accounting for unity in the cosmos while at the same time
saving the human phenomena. So far as these phenomena themselves are concerned, the problem is to distinguish between
nobility and baseness. In order to make such a distinction without introducing an irresolvable dualism between the human and
the divine, Eryximachus must establish a cosmic basis for
human excellence. He tries to do so by identifying the noble as
the healthy, and by rooting the distinction between noble health
and base disease in the duality of the cosmic principle of Eros.
But the medical theory to which he subscribes is in turn based
upon an understanding of health as the harmony of opposites.[36]
Unfortunately for him, if such a principle were applied to
human affairs, it would lead to the identification of health and
heterosexual love, or the harmony of male and female. There
seems to be a conflict in principle between medicine and
pederasty.

This conflict emerges directly from Eryximachus' reduction
of psyche to an epiphenomenon of body. In cosmic terms if
"unlike loves unlike" (186b6), then the harmony of opposites
must be a love between the unlike pair of body and psyche.
What the body loves must be unlike what the psyche loves;
since there are only these two ultimate components, they fulfill
the condition by loving each other. An attempt to find other
objects of love for each (for example, health in one case and
disease in the other), would result in suppression of the desired
unity or homogeneity in nature. We should have not one

36. A comparison of 186b8–d5 and 186d5–e3 will show that the principle of
πλησμονῆς and κένωσις is a general (ἐν κεφαλαίῳ) and less fundamental formulation
of the basic medical technē of producing ἔρως and ὁμόνοια between τὰ ἐναντιώτατα.

double Eros but two sundered Eroses, not ensouled body but body cut off from, and not desiring, psyche. But Eryximachus insists that "the nature of bodies is this double Eros" (186b4).[37]

> The health and sickness of the body are admittedly other and unlike, and the unlike desires and loves the unlike. Hence the erotic love of a healthy body is one thing, and that of a sick body another. (186b5–8)

That is, the unlikeness of health and sickness, corresponding to the double Eros, is the "nature" or "principle" of body; it does not correspond to a distinction between body and psyche.

If health is equivalent to heterosexuality, then Eryximachus can justify pederasty only by a defense of disease, which would lead to the perversion of his technē and a dissolution of cosmic harmony. Therefore, Eryximachus is driven to interpret the principle that unlike loves unlike apart from the principle of the harmony of opposites. That is, he simply disregards here the difference between male and female, which in the domain of human Eros correspond to body and psyche in the cosmic domain. The distinction between health and sickness is applied by Eryximachus to the male body only. He may then agree with Pausanias that "it is noble to gratify good men, shameful to gratify the licentious," by analogy with the medical care of bodies, according to which "it is right and necessary to gratify the good and healthy parts of each body" and "shameful to gratify the bad and sick parts . . ." (186b8 ff.). But even the suppression of the female does not solve Eryximachus' problems. The principle unlike loves unlike must now mean that healthy (male) bodies love other healthy (male) bodies, or in other words that like loves like. This apparently straightforward reading of "unlike loves unlike" in fact rests upon the assumption of a universe of discourse including only male bodies. If the principle thus interpreted is true by nature, then (1) there is no natural principle to overcome the disjunction between like and unlike, and (2) medicine is unnecessary in the pursuit of

37. Cf. Krüger, *Einsicht*, pp. 111–12: Eryximachus moves from visible bodies to invisible gods. This is only part of the story; cf. p. 117 in the text.

pederasty. Both consequences are of course repugnant to Eryximachus. Apart from the cosmic harmony of opposites, the
body itself falls apart into a dualism of health and sickness, with
the respective desires of each.^A

Once again, theoretical adjustments are needed. According
to Eryximachus, the skilled doctor (τεχνικός) must frustrate the
bad and sick parts of the body. More generally,

> He who discerns in these matters the noble and shameful
> love is the best doctor, who can act so as to exchange
> them, so that instead of one erotic desire the other is
> established. And he will be a good demiurge who knows
> how to engender erotic desire where it is absent but
> should be present, and how to remove it when it is pres-
> ent. (186c7–d5)

In other words, it is now admitted that like sometimes loves
unlike, or that healthy bodies by nature love sometimes healthy
and sometimes sick bodies. Implicit in this is the admission
that, as Aristophanes will make explicit, heterosexual love is as
natural as homosexuality. Eryximachus of course ignores this
implication. His point is that the doctor is needed to suppress
shameful love, whether of man for woman or of healthy for
sick men. The doctor's technē makes him a demiurge; it is he
who brings about the pederastic principle that like loves like.
This principle does not obtain by nature but ought to (186d3:
δεῖ δ' ἐγγενέσθαι). It is a moral principle and so one of human
taste rather than of medical physics. Thus the identifications
of health with nobility, sickness with shamefulness, are called
into question by the very effort to justify them.

Medical demiurgy makes the doctor like a god,[38] but a god
who acts counter to the cosmic Eros. Or more accurately: the
technē of medicine is in itself neutral with respect to the meaning of "noble" and "shameful." Eryximachus attempts to combine personal sexual taste with the principles of his technē,
and the result is a reasonably skillful obscuration of an intrinsically incoherent enterprise. The most obvious objection

38. *Euschēmosynē* 6.1: ἰητρὸς γὰρ φιλόσοφος ἰσόθεος. In Jones, *Hippocrates*, 2.

to Eryximachus' argument is no doubt that base men (including many heterosexuals) may enjoy superb physical health, whereas the noblest may be the sickliest. Again, health and beauty are not necessarily correlative; the doctor might direct the lover to a robust but hideous sweetheart. The distinction between health and sickness is not equivalent to that between beauty and ugliness, since health is compatible with a taste for either of the latter.[39] The trouble lies with a defect in Eryximachus' teleology. In his view, the order of ends ought to be implicit in the order of the physical cosmos. But by no reasonable interpretation of this order can one arrive at the estimate of pederasty as the highest form of human Eros. The crucial point lies in the nature of the physical cosmos as genesis, or in reproduction through a harmony of opposites. If pederasty is the noblest form of Eros, it can only be so by recourse to a principle higher than, and to a large extent in conflict with, the principle of the body. A serious defense of pederasty, if it is possible at all, rests upon the psyche as different from the body.

Eryximachus differs from Phaedrus, his sweetheart, not in the final defects of his theoretical position but in the greater skill and completeness with which he makes his case. Having done the best he can with the principle of unlike loves unlike, Eryximachus now moves on to the principle of the harmony of opposites:

> [The doctor] must be able to make the greatest enemies
> in the body into friends and mutual lovers. For opposites
> are the greatest enemies, as is cold to hot, bitter to sweet,
> dry to moist, and all the rest. Our ancestor Asclepius, as
> the poets say and I believe, by knowing how to produce
> love and unanimity in these, established our techně.
> (186d5 ff.)

If like attracts like, the inference that opposites are the greatest enemies is possible but not necessary. Like, for example, might be neutral with respect to unlike. But for Eryximachus the inference is necessary as a bridge to his second principle of

39. Cf. *Republic* 474d4 ff.

the harmony of opposites. In other words, the cosmos would fall apart without that harmony upon which human existence also depends. At this point, Eryximachus might wish to imply that, to the extent that heterosexual love is necessary, it is brought about by the cosmic force which the doctor's technē imitates. However, even if it were possible to conceive of male and female as opposites whose enmity is overcome by the cosmic Eros, many problems would remain. I shall mention only one: the enduring presence of the cosmos shows that the harmony of opposites is not dependent upon the doctor. Asclepius discovered medicine; he did not make the world.

The existence of the human race prior to the discovery of medicine, and the independence of cosmic genesis from medical demiurgy show that the harmony of opposites holds initially by nature, not by technē. At most the doctor may induce pederasty where none exists, or transform it into heterosexual love. But the desirability of doing either is not among the principles of medicine. In terms of Eryximachus' second principle, medicine is the ability to re-establish an original harmony of opposites in a now diseased body. In terms of the first principle, the healthy body desires and attracts other healthy bodies. I trust that we have now ample reason for agreeing that the two principles contradict each other. But there is one more step which we may take in attempting to defend Eryximachus: perhaps each individual member of the harmony of similars is in itself a harmony of opposites. By this reasoning, which Eryximachus himself does not supply, in order for male to attract male, each must first be brought by medicine into a condition of inner harmony or health.

Medicine, then, would be the primary technē because it discovers the basic principles of the cosmos. The doctor is able to produce physical health, and he does so by encouraging the good and eliminating the bad erotic desires of the body. The good desires the good and the bad desires the bad: unlike loves unlike. It is good to have a harmony of opposites, and so the good love or strive after such a harmony. But the goodness of the harmony of opposites justifies heterosexual rather than

105

pederastic love. Hence we need still another harmony: a harmony of harmonies. This seems to be as close as one can come to saving Eryximachus' position. The naturalness of the harmony of harmonies is in accord with the principle that unlike attracts unlike, understood as equivalent to like loves like. But does this not mean that a healthy (=harmonious) man may be attracted to a healthy (=harmonious) woman? And is not heterosexual harmony more in accord than homosexual harmony with the second premise that health requires the harmony of opposites? The harmony of a healthy man and woman satisfies both premises, as that between two males does not.

I have observed that Eryximachus tries to move from opinion to the telos of health by way of nature. Common to all the difficulties we have found in Eryximachus' speech is an unclear conception of nature, one which ought to but cannot be adequately explained in corporeal terms alone. The word φύσις (nature) appears just once in his whole speech, in the phrase "the nature of bodies" (186b4). But the intelligibility of the body is derived from the opinions of the psyche. The psyche discovers the technē and the telos; the psyche decides which of the bodily inclinations it will honor. Eryximachus is not a materialist in the strictest sense of the term, since for him bodies are alive or filled with the god Eros.[40] But his "pantheism" is so expressed as to guarantee the submission of the psyche to the body. We can also say that Eryximachus fails to understand the significance of the distinction—which he himself has drawn —between man and the cosmos. Man discovers medicine by imitating the cosmic procedure whereby opposites are reconciled. But this discovery enables him to alter aspects of the cosmic order. For example, he can change the natural Eros of the body or postpone its dissolution by curing disease. Man is a peculiar part of the cosmos; although he is more fragile than the whole, he can take steps to combat his fragility which are inaccessible to plants and animals.

Whether we refer to medical demiurgy as a creation or an

40. Cf. the saying attributed to Thales: ἀρχὴν δὲ τῶν πάντων ὕδωρ ὑπεστήσατο, καὶ τὸν κόσμον ἔμψυχον καὶ δαιμόνων πλήρη Diels, *Vorsokratiker, 1,* p. 68.

imitation of nature, the fact remains that man exemplifies a disjunction, even a quarrel between nature and technē. By the use of technē, man can impose his own desires onto nature. There is a duality within nature which cannot be accurately explained in merely corporeal terms. Nature stands against herself in the production of a being who is capable of altering nature.[41] The ends of man are not the same as those of nonhuman nature.[42] This is clear in the case of love. As we have seen, the praise of pederasty cannot be justified by reference to the cosmos. One may of course justify it in the neutral sense by saying that all natural impulses are acceptable; but an estimate of pederasty as noble depends on the creation of an artificial hierarchy of values. The technē of making values cannot itself be regarded as noble or base so far as the corporeal structure of the cosmos is concerned. In general: a purely technical study of nature supplies no basis for preferring the cosmos to chaos.

Soft and Hard Music

Eros, as a god, governs not simply man but his technai as well. For Eryximachus man is primarily a technical animal, and the remainder of the physician's speech is concerned with the way in which the main technai are manifestations of Eros. As the principle of harmony might lead us to suppose, music is the most important technē after medicine:

> For medicine, as I say, is altogether governed by this god, and so too gymnastic and farming. The same holds good for music, as is evident to anyone who pays the least attention, and as perhaps Heraclitus wished to say, for his words are not well spoken. He says that the one, "differing with itself, comes together with itself, like the harmony of bow and lyre." Now it is altogether senseless to

41. Of course, the modern solution to this problem is to replace nature by history; but Eryximachus is not a modern man.

42. This distinction underlies modern philosophy from Machiavelli onward. Cf. his *Il Principe*, Ch. 25 with Nietzsche, *Jenseits 1*, p. 9.

say that a harmony is disrupted, or that it can exist although derived from what is disjoined. (186e4 ff.)

There are passages in two other dialogues that will help us in understanding these words. With their aid we may distinguish three forms of process physics arranged in degrees of increasing "softness" on the basis of their attitude toward music; that is, by a greater accommodation to love, poetry, the psyche, and the peaceful resolution of difficulties in the interpretation of human existence.

The first passage occurs in Book Ten of the *Laws*.[43] The Athenian stranger is discussing the views of those for whom the cosmos is a product of the four elements, through the action of nature and chance, rather than of any mind, god, or art.[44] Technē, as derived from nature and chance, is younger than they; it is "itself perishable, and generated from perishables." There are some striking resemblances between this doctrine and the speech of Eryximachus. In both cases the physical cosmos arises from a blending of opposites, but the thinkers in the *Laws* replace Eros as the harmonizing agent by "necessity in accord with chance." [45] The consequent atheism[46] of these materialists is symbolized by their attitude toward music. Although they mention music, medicine, gymnastic, and farming in conjunction with their doctrine, the last three alone are said to be serious arts having most in common with nature.

In accordance with this view, the technai derive their "seriousness" from cooperation with or the tending of natural bodies. Those arts, including music, which produce not bodies but images, fail to share in "truth." [47] These materialistic physicists are stricter, purer, or "harder" than Eryximachus, for whom nature is equivalent to the divine Eros of bodies, and whose

43. Cf. nn. 33–35 above.
44. 889c5–6: οὐ δὲ διὰ νοῦν . . . οὐδὲ διά τινα θεὸν οὐδὲ διὰ τέχνην ἀλλά . . . φύσει καὶ τύχη.
45. τῇ τῶν ἐναντίων κράσει κατὰ τύχην ἐξ ἀνάγκης συνεκεράσθη.
46. *Laws* 889e3–4: the gods exist by the τέχνη of νόμος, and not by nature.
47. 889d1–2: ἀληθείας οὐ σφόδρα μετεχούσης.

rule is visible in music. Eryximachus' greater softness is also
clear from his failure to identify necessity and chance. The defect of this softness is obvious from his failure to draw a distinction between bodies and images. Eryximachus blurs the difference between the two because, in divinizing the body, he
blurs the difference between it and psyche. Images depend upon
mind. If truth is corporeal, then mind must be as well. For
the hard materialist, images are defective perceptions of bodies.
(Whether this is an adequate account is another matter into
which we cannot here enter. It will arise again in a slightly later
passage, when Eryximachus is forced to make an ambiguous distinction in the nature of music.) The point so far is that
Eryximachus shuns hard physics by making all arts tend bodies.
The encomiast of Eros is, so to speak, more musical than the
hard physicists. But we must not forget that his music depends
upon a lack of clarity about mind or psyche. In this sense,
Eryximachus' music is excessively soft; his apparent defense of
the psyche is at bottom a blurred materialism.

In extending the domain of Eros to music, Eryximachus corrects an obscure saying of Heraclitus.[48] This brings us to the
second related passage, in the *Sophist*, where the view of
Heraclitus is contrasted to that of Empedocles. Another stranger,
this time from Elea, tells Theatetus that Parmenides and the
others who have discussed the number and kinds of beings speak
carelessly and in myth[49] "as though we were children":

> One man says that there are three kinds of being (τρία
> τὰ ὄντα), some of which are in a way at war with each
> other; then they become friends, marry, have children,
> and proceed to raise them. Another says that there are
> two kinds, moist and dry or hot and cold, which he sets
> up in housekeeping and gives to each other in marriage.
> Among us the Eleatic tribe, taking their beginnings

48. For alternative versions of this saying, all substantially the same, cf. Diels,
Vorsokratiker, 1, p. 162 and Bury's note.
49. Cf. *Timaeus* 29c4–d3.

from Xenophanes or even earlier, relate their myths on the assumption that what are called "all things" are really one. Later, certain Muses in Ionia and Sicily realized that the safest course would be to weave both views together and to speak as if being (τὸ ὄν) is both many and one, secured by both enmity and friendship. The severer of the Muses say that in its division, it is always being brought together; while the softer Muses unstrung (relaxed) the everlastingness of this condition, and say that the whole is alternately now one and peaceful because of Aphrodite, now many and at war with itself through a certain strife.[50]

In this passage a distinction is drawn between what I call the harder and softer music of Heraclitus and Empedocles. Heraclitus' muse is harder because he advocates the more difficult doctrine of the perpetual simultaneity of opposites, and not their alternate appearance. Both men, however, differ from the materialists discussed in the *Laws* by their association with the Muses. The greater "hardness" of Heraclitus is also suggested by the fact that his harmony of opposites is related to the distinction in the *Laws* between the good and bad psyches which are perpetually at war in the heavens.[51] Eryximachus' effort to soften the hard saying of Heraclitus is a result of his relation to Empedocles. For our present purposes, Heraclitus stands between the strict materialists, and Empedocles and his soft Ionian music. The Eleatic stranger associates the softer Muse with Aphrodite rather than Eros; he does not say which kind of love, if any, is a characteristic of Heraclitus. Perhaps one of the implications of the passage in the *Sophist* is the judgment that Eryximachus has not genuinely praised the Uranian or pre-political Eros. However this may be, the more severe music of Heraclitus differs from that of Empedocles by the singing of a harmony between opposites in each moment of

50. *Sophist* 242c4 ff. Note that neither Eros nor Aphrodite figures in conjunction with the Eleatic tribe. If all is one, there can be no intermediate function or bond.

51. Cf. Heraclitus, Fr. 53 in Diels, *Vorsokratiker* Πόλεμος πάντων μὲν πατήρ ἐστι . . .

the duration of the cosmos. The cosmos endures as the continuous bringing together of what is at the same time opposed. In each moment of genesis, peace is in fact war.

Empedocles, on the other hand, conceives of a double genesis and so too a double destruction.[52] Instead of a double Eros, he speaks of love with a word that signifies "friendship"(φιλότης), and its opposite, enmity (Νεῖκος). After the elements have been united by friendship, an increase in enmity or strife leads gradually toward chaos and the gradual banishment of friendship.[53] Empedocles' cosmogony consists of four stages: (1) the complete union of friendship, (2) the complete dissolution of strife, (3) the cosmos which results from the decay of union, and (4) the cosmos which results from the process toward union.[54] Stages (3) and (4) differ in direction of flux; the result is an alternation in the rule of friendship and strife. According to Heraclitus, there is just one cosmos; its endurance as harmony, despite internal opposites or war, means that the contestants are evenly matched. For Empedocles, there are at least two cosmoi; if we take all four stages as one process, we may say that his cosmos is radically less stable, radically softer, than the cosmos of Heraclitus. There is no true harmony of opposites in Empedocles. The severity of the Heraclitean muse, although in conflict with what may perhaps be called peaceful common sense, nevertheless is more successful in holding together the disparate elements of the cosmos.

One way to express Empedocles' sundering of the cosmos is by saying that friendship is the attraction of unlikes, whereas strife is the attraction of like for like.[55] If we were to apply this dualism of principles to the discussion in the *Symposium*, pederasty would be a striving toward chaos. This result is of course unacceptable to Eryximachus, and he avoids it (whatever his reasons) by rejecting the Empedoclean dualism. In this he

52. Diels, *Vorsokratiker, 1*, p. 315, Fr. 17: (line 18) δοιὴ δὲ θνητῶν γένεσις, δοιὴ δ' ἀπόλειψις.

53. Cf. Burnet, *EGP*, pp. 248 ff.

54. Empedocles' distinction between two *cosmoi* seems to be echoed in the myth of the reversed world in Plato's *Statesman*.

55. Burnet, *EGP*, pp. 246–47; Aristotle, *Metaphysics* 985a23 ff.

is akin to Diotima; but whereas she posits three principles (the human, daimonic, and divine),[56] his "triad" is in fact a monism containing an inner articulation, or a precarious sublation of dualism. Eryximachus' music is a blurred version of the soft Sicilian kind.[57] In his reinterpretation of Heraclitus he maintains that opposites, while they are at variance (ἐκ διαφερομένων ἔτι), cannot enter into a harmony. But he does not mean by this (as is implied by Empedocles' cosmogony) that elements in a harmony cannot be opposites without a consequent deterioration of the cosmos. The technē of music brings opposites like fast and slow into agreement with each other. Like medicine, music engenders "mutual love and unanimity; and so music is erotic knowledge with respect to harmony and rhythm" (187b5–c5).

Eryximachus advocates the use of technai like medicine and music to eliminate the natural war of opposites. Even though technē takes its cue from nature, what it generates is artificial rather than natural. Nature apart from technē exhibits both harmony and strife. Eryximachus goes beyond both Heraclitus and Empedocles in suggesting that man is able to reduce strife to harmony. The defense of pederasty is one consequence of this suggestion: although by nature the love of like for like is a mark of strife, technē permits us to transform it into a harmony of love. In this sense, Eryximachus is softer than the Ionians and Sicilians. And yet one may say without contradiction that there is a peculiar hardness implicit in this soft ambition for cosmic equilibrium, a hardness which does not genuinely emerge until the strict materialists return to the arena of

56. K. Gaiser finds an unresolved dualism in the two Platonic principles of the One and the Undetermined Two: cf. *Ungeschriebene,* pp. 9 ff. But this overlooks altogether the ἰδέα as the third or exhibition of the determination of the Two by the One. Cf. S. H. Rosen, "Ideas," *Review of Metaphysics, 16* (1963) 410, n. 4. The triad of human, daimonic and divine is another instance of the nondualistic character of Plato's thought, which does not come to the fore in purely "mathematical" or "ontological" interpretations of his teaching, whether written or unwritten.

57. Cf. W. Kranz, "Platonica," *Philologus, 102* (1958) 77–79: δαίμονες as an intermediate are a feature of Ionian thought. Kranz also points out that 3 was a holy number in this tradition.

history, only this time armed with technai adequate to their ambition.

The Double Music

As the principle of harmony, music is crucial in Eryximachus' analysis of technē. But his excessive desire for harmony, as represented by his pederastic tastes, leads him to blur one theoretical distinction after another. As a result of this softness, he is forced to make distinctions where none are desirable. What began as the desire of tolerance for an ambiguous sexual taste, and was then elaborated into a doctrine of cosmological harmony, is beginning to assume the severity implicit in the attempt to define nobility by technique. And Eryximachus' hardness, because it is soft at the core, is a philosophically and humanly defective imitation of Heraclitean severity. Technicism triumphs by force, and so its victory will prove to be pyrrhic. The hardness of Eryximachus is not living or dynamic, but sclerotic. Eryximachus cannot overcome dualism, not even in his conception of music itself:

> It is not difficult to perceive the erotic in the system of harmony and rhythm itself, for the double Eros is not present there. But when we must apply rhythm and harmony to men, either by making what is called "music" (μελοποιία), or by using correctly melodies and measures already constructed, which [latter] has been named "education," then the matter is difficult, and one needs a good demiurge. (187c5–d4)

The double Eros, the distinction between nobility and baseness, was called by Eryximachus the nature of all bodies, both human and divine (186b1–4). He also said that music is erotic knowledge of harmony and rhythm (187b5). How can it then be absent from the system of harmony and rhythm? The answer would seem to lie in the fact that pure music is not a body. Here we see Eryximachus' heritage from strict materialism. His theory is necessarily a kind of *praxis*. The system of har-

113

mony, as separate from the tending of bodies, is for him neither noble nor base, and hence it is not a serious or really difficult system. Seriousness and difficulty arise only within technē understood as the tending of bodies. Since music can (but need not) be applied to bodies, it falls under the domain of Eros. Eros is a demiurge or craftsman, a tender of bodies to whom pure music is of interest only in its practical applications.

Eryximachus recognizes incorporeal reality, in the form of pure music, but he can give us no serious theoretical account of this dimension of the cosmos. Since Eros is the essence or nature of bodies, there are realities (if that is the right word) like music whose nature is not explained. If we remember the relation for Plato between music and mathematics, his implied criticism of Eryximachus becomes sharper. Mathematics is an incorporeal domain, common to body and psyche yet differing from both, and it cannot be explained as an effect of Eros. That is, number and proportion do not result from our love of them, or from the use to which we put them, but have a being of their own. Music, then, reveals a double form: as pure mathematics, its origin is not erotic—numbers are not the song of the psyche. From this observation it is an easy step to the recognition that technē altogether cannot properly be called erotic. There is a dimension of pure music in every technē; every technē is, as it were, a double music. And this in turn means that the double Eros is not isomorphic to the duality in music; Eros as a whole is at best the principle of only one half of the double music.

Eryximachus has not genuinely accounted for the whole, and it is especially instructive to see the defects of technicism as a scientific or mathematical failure. The technicist does not know how to handle incorporeal beings unless they are accessible to a corporeal psyche; but the practical result is to corporealize all of being. In religious language, if the gods are incorporeal then they do not share in the nature of the double Eros, which is hence not the highest principle in the cosmos. If the gods are corporeal, then they do not rule the incorporeal beings like the system of pure music (=mathematics), except in their corporeal applications. Success in technē is no sign of theoretical understanding of the whole, but only of the whole as it is useful to the human body. But this in turn leads to the result, unpalatable for Eryximachus, that the utility of medicine and technē generally is perspectival, and so not genuinely free from the power of rhetoric or persuasion. The best Eryximachus might hope for is the seduction of rhetoric by the enchantment of material power.

In the last analysis Eryximachus' evaluation of the powers available to man is governed by the pleasure they afford. Eryximachus is a hedonist; he is not concerned with the pursuit of power or knowledge for their own sakes:

> Once again, the same logos results. One must gratify the well-ordered men, and those who are not in order that they may become more orderly. This is the noble, the Uranian, the Eros of the Uranian muse. The Pandemic Eros is derived from the muse of many hymns, with which one must be careful in dealing when we apply it to anyone, in order that we may pluck the fruit of its pleasure without producing licentiousness. In the same way, it is very important in our art to use properly (καλῶς) desires connected with the culinary technē, to pluck the pleasure without disease. Thus in music, in medicine, and in all other things both human and divine, so far as is practicable, one must obey each Eros. For both are present. (187d4–188a1)

In this extremely interesting passage the same fate befalls Eryximachus that did Pausanias. At 182a3 ff. Pausanias forgets the distinction between Uranian and Pandemic Eros, and allows "absolute license" to the lover, or permission to practice vulgar as well as noble pederasty. Eryximachus, armed with technē, goes a step farther: the doctor, thanks to his skill, may indulge in heterosexual as well as pederastic love. Whereas Pausanias' lover becomes a slave to Eros, Eryximachus' technician is free to cull pleasure wherever he finds it. The principle of cosmological equilibrium thus transforms the distinction between noble and base Eros into a vulgar eroticism. Eryximachus is not tolerant, but indifferent to the very standard of excellence he pretends (or believes himself) to establish.

Eryximachus compares the double Eros, which here comes very close to dissolving into two Eroses, to two kinds of music. These two kinds are not analogous to mathematics and corporeal desire, but rather to the hard and soft music discussed above. The medical technē leads to a hedonistic softness in allowing its practitioners to combine the hard Uranian music of nobility with the soft Pandemic Eros of baseness. The result is a suppression or forgetting of the distinction between nobility and baseness, which is indicated when Eryximachus relates medicine to cooking. Technicism is inseparable from sophistry.[58] The cosmic order provides us with no standard for the kinds of love that are permissible; the important point is to avoid pain or disease. Morally, love is on the same level as eating. The nobility introduced by technē (rather than by nature) into human and divine behavior is equivalent to pleasure. The celebration of technē thus results in the denial that pederasty has a special or cosmic justification—one more sign of the self-contradictory character of Eryximachus' teaching, or of the unsatisfactory relation of hard and soft elements.

Eryximachus turns next to agriculture, or the study of heavenly phenomena as they bear upon the existence of terrestrial creatures. In other words, astronomy is of interest to Eryximachus only as an applied science. The two forms of Eros are now referred to as "orderly" and "hybristic." The former stands for the mathematical component of the double music of technē but is interpreted in corporeal or practical terms of "fertility and health" as well as in terms of the absence of injustice (188a1–6). The orderliness of the responsible Eros is its capacity to be used by man for the sake of pleasure. Eros in this sense of "cosmic activity" is in this passage not a god (cf. 188a3, a7, c2). In the next passage, however, the god reappears as "the Eros characterized by hybris" (ὁ μετὰ τῆς ὕβρεως Ἔρως), whose

---

58. Cf. *Gorgias* 464d2, 500e4.

mastery of the seasons brings much destruction and injustices (188a7–8). The Pandemic Eros, as juxtaposed to the Uranian, is easily identifiable as the principle of the Olympian gods, who are called "hybristic" by Eryximachus because they restrain man's pursuit of pleasure.

Eryximachus brings astronomy from the heavens down to the earth in the form of agriculture. His technē is somehow more political [59] than the erotic technē of Diotima, which moves upward from bodies and the earth toward heaven. The transformation of astronomy into agriculture makes the same point as the suppression of pure music; Eryximachus, although the representative of technicism, imitates the *Symposium* as a whole by abstracting from mathematics. In the dialogues generally, mathematics is most akin to the divine dialectic, or is the study that is most instructive for conceiving of the Ideas, the non-corporeal and divine beings. The absence of mathematics (except by implication in the young Socrates, prior to his conversion by Diotima) should lead us to suspect either that the dialectic of Diotima is not in fact the highest, or that it must be completed by some other component. To return to Eryximachus, however, he is uninterested in the "system" (187c6, 188a1) of pure music or cosmic motion. His praise of the Uranian gods is not a genuine theoretical teaching, but an imperfect derivative. Eryximachus imitates pure physics or anthropomorphizes it; not Zeus and his cohorts, but meteorological phenomena bring justice and injustice to man. Nature serves merely as the "stuff" that is refined by technē into pleasure.

After defining astronomy in terms of health and disease, or the practical problems of seasonal violence (188b1–6), Eryximachus turns to sacrifices and divination. This section of his speech replaces the discussion of gymnastics, which according to 187a1, should have followed next. The knowledge of divination or communion between gods and men has "no other purpose than the guarding and healing of Eros": "For all cases of impiety occur when someone does not gratify the orderly Eros nor honor and prefer him in every deed . . ." (188b6 ff.). The

59. Cf. Cicero, *Tusculan Disputations*, 5.10 and Strauss, *City*, pp. 13 ff.

cosmic Eros is now capitalized because Eryximachus is apparently speaking in a religious or pious vein. In fact, however, his remark is impious, since he extends the application of medicine, in the form of divination,[60] to the healing of Eros. As the substitution of divination for gymnastics indicates, Eros in the sense of cosmic deity is really a body, and therefore under the control of man. In the traditional religion sacrifice is intended to gratify the gods.[61] In the Eryximachean religion we honor the cosmos by the technical gratification of man. Medical divination thus has the task of treating "the lovers," namely gods and men.[62] The mantic doctor is himself like a god—a demiurge (188d1). He establishes friendship between gods and men by his knowledge of the human erotic that leads toward right and piety (188b6–d3). In sum: the erotic community between gods and men is subsumed under the more fundamental community between human activity and the orderly motions of the cosmos. This means that the gods, too, are subject to these motions. As Eryximachus is careful to say, impiety results from a failure to gratify the orderly (cosmic) Eros, not from a failure to gratify the gods.

Eryximachus wishes to complete or give a basis to human existence by his version of the physical cosmos. At the same time, however, he interprets the cosmos in terms of the human body. The equivalence of nature and body does not provide a secure basis for understanding or evaluating human actions, as is clear from the simple observation that it gives no justification for preferring the desires of the human to the motions of nonhuman bodies. To put the point in a relatively modern way, the preference of order or cosmos to disorder or chaos is a human taste; more generally, it is a taste of psyche. This fundamental

60. Cf. n. 21 above.

61. And this is associated with feeding; cf. Hesiod, *Theogony* 535 ff. and Aristophanes' *Birds*.

62. I follow Burnet in accepting τοὺς ἐρῶτας, the reading of W, rather than τοὺς ἔρωτας of B and T. Bury's Ἔρωτας has no manuscript authority and is certainly wrong. Ἐρῶντας seems preferable because μαντική regulates the communion of gods and men (who are thus lovers). It is they who must be supervised and treated, in order that the orderly Eros receive its due of piety.

dilemma occurs again in Eryximachus' peroration. He gives all power to "Eros as a whole" (ξυλλήβδην μὲν ὁ πᾶς Ἔρως) or the cosmos but immediately reintroduces his distinction between the good and the Pandemic Eros, or human taste. Since the pandemic component is part of Eros as a whole, disorder, disease, or bad things are as natural as good things. Eryximachus' pride in his technē triumphs over theoretical reflection, and the result is unwarranted optimism: the greatest power is attributed to the Uranian component, which "accomplishes good things with moderation and justice . . . and provides us with complete happiness. (188d4–9)

In unravelling the strands of Eryximachus' speech, we study not so much his intentions as Plato's commentary on those intentions. Plato's tacit critique of Eryximachus is that he uses elements from the severe teaching of materialistic physics for the inappropriate purpose of explaining human existence. His scientific interpretation of Eros must lead to the suppression, not merely of the divine, but of the characteristically human as well. Although not stupid, Eryximachus himself is an incoherent thinker; at least part of this incoherence arises from the conflict between his physical passions and his technical pride. This incoherence is present in every aspect of his discussion of Eros, and so in his attitude toward the gods. Eryximachus' unorthodoxy need not be equated with atheism; the consequence of that unorthodoxy is another story. Eryximachus closes his speech by raising the theme of friendship between man and the gods (thereby providing a transition to the speech of Aristophanes). He does not ask whether it is possible for friendship to exist between masters and slaves, perhaps because his conception of technē is designed to free man from servitude. Yet his speech implies that man may cease to be a slave only if the gods cease to be masters.[63]

63. This is a consequence that cannot be avoided by Aristophanes, as we shall see in the next chapter, and it symbolizes his ultimate surrender to the heirs of Eryximachus.

CHAPTER FIVE
🦢 ARISTOPHANES 🦢

The Double Logos

Eryximachus reaches the telos of his encomium by turning over to Aristophanes the task of "filling in" whatever he may unintentionally have omitted (188d9–e4). Aristophanes lost his ability to speak because he stuffed himself with food. His logos is compromised by an indulgence of the body, which makes him subordinate to Eryximachus.[1] Whereas Socrates denies that one may be "filled up" with wisdom in a corporeal sense, as Agathon implied, Aristophanes inherits just this position from Eryximachus.[2] Of course Aristophanes wishes to repudiate technicism, but he has been infected by the principle he opposes. Eryximachus' double Eros reappears in Aristophanes' speech as the double- or circle-men, who, once divided by the surgeon Apollo, will struggle in vain for reunion. Sexuality, which replaces logos as the principle of human wisdom (or as the third which binds together the two halves), is inadequate for the function it has been allotted. The replacement of the Uranian by the Olympian medicine is insufficient to heal man's divided nature.

In the *Republic,* which abstracts from the body as much as possible,[3] Socrates severely chastizes poetry and even expels it from the city in his pursuit of justice. The just or decorporealized city, we recall, is the psyche writ large.[4] In the *Symposium,* however, it is Aristophanes, not Socrates, who represents the claims of justice; not only are both comedy and tragedy

---

1. Aristophanes speaks after Eryximachus, but only through his disease, and he speaks at all only thanks to the medical technē.
2. Cf. 175c8–e1.
3. Cf. Strauss, *City,* pp. 50 ff.
4. *Republic* 368c8 ff.

present in the *Symposium,* but the home of a poet takes the symbolic place of the city. The praise of Eros is essentially the praise of the body, from which even the ascent to the "higher mysteries" must begin. It would not be wrong to say that the *Symposium* stands to the *Republic* as the body to the psyche, although such a formulation obviously requires a lengthy commentary. Suffice it to say here that there is considerable injustice in the attempt to force a conception of justice from either the psyche or body alone. Justice entails a harmony of psyche and body; for this purpose, the music of poetry as well as that of mathematics is required.

Although two poets speak in the *Symposium,* only one praises justice.[5] Aristophanes, whose business is "entirely with Dionysus and Aphrodite" (177e2), represents not pure but political poetry.[6] Unlike Agathon, Aristophanes does not praise an autonomous Eros, but one whose "philanthropy" (189d1) is a consequence of the "medical" technē of Zeus and Apollo. Aristophanes' poetic technē is in the service of the Olympian gods of the city. His "philotheism" is the same as his patriotism.[7] The city, man's highest good, depends for its existence on the generation of human beings and on belief in the Olympian gods. Here, however, a problem arises which Aristophanes, as we shall see, is incapable of solving. For what one may call fundamentally erotic reasons, the virtuous or old-fashioned city

5. Cf. 196b4–7: Agathon does not say that Eros is just, but only that he "neither does nor suffers injustice," and this is followed by the implicit identification of Eros as a benevolent tyrant (b7–c3). Although Aristophanes does not actually say that Eros is just, there can be no doubt that his whole speech is intended as a defense of political justice and peace. For the connection between Aristophanes and justice, cf. L. Strauss, *Socrates and Aristophanes* (New York, 1966) (hereafter *SocrArist*), pp. 77–78, 193, et passim.

6. For the decisively political character of Aristophanes' plays, cf. K. Reinhardt, "Aristophanes und Athen," in *Tradition und Geist* (Göttingen, 1960), p. 263: "Das Ekstatische des dionysischen Festcharakters transformiert sich ins politische . . ."

7. Cf. Aristotle, *Metaphysics* 1074a38 ff. The ancients θείως ἂν εἰρῆσθαι in making the heavenly bodies gods. But the Olympians were developed later μυθικῶς . . . πρὸς τὴν πειθὼ τῶν πολλῶν καὶ πρὸς τὴν εἰς τοὺς νόμους καὶ τὸ συμφέρον χρῆσιν. (I am indebted to Mr. Richard Kennington for calling this passage to my attention.)

falls into corruption, from which it can only be rescued by an innovating logos.[8] Although justice is more like silence than speech, its very silence makes it hard to distinguish from injustice. To borrow a phrase from one of Aristophanes' own comedies, logos would seem to be both just and unjust. The problem is to decide how, if the old logoi are just, yet can be preserved only by innovations, to permit only just innovations. If the just is the same as the old, the new is by definition unjust.

Aristophanes associates innovation and consequent injustice with physics, sophistry, and philosophy. Since the themes of his speech in the *Symposium* are easily exhibited by means of his comedies, I will preface my analysis of the speech with a brief inspection of the two comedies that are most important for the study of the *Symposium*. The results of such an inspection will serve to buttress our understanding of the use to which Plato puts Aristophanes in his own drama. Similarly, Plato's interpretation of Aristophanes casts considerable light on the comedies themselves. It is especially appropriate to begin with Aristophanes' interpretation of Socrates. It has often been said that the portrait of Socrates in the *Clouds* is grossly inaccurate.[9] Such a judgment fails to grasp the unity in physics, sophistry, and philosophy, when seen from the viewpoint of Aristophanes' conception of justice. The key premise is easily stated: rational investigation of the cosmos leads to atheism and the destruction of political stability. By replacing the gods with natural principles, investigation removes the sole criterion for distinguishing between the just and unjust logoi. The problem of the double Eros becomes the problem of the double logos.

In the *Clouds* Pheidippides, having been tutored by Socrates and the Unjust Logos, defends his right to beat his father by denying the difference between men and beasts:

> But look at the cocks and all these other animals, how they revenge themselves on their fathers. And how do

8. Similarly, in the *Republic* the just city falls into decay because of Eros and θυμός. Cf. Strauss, *SocrArist*, p. 104.

9. For a more reasonable judgment cf. W. Schmid, "Das Sokratesbild der Wolken," *Philologus*, 97 (1954), 222.

they differ from us, except that they don't write down
their decrees? (1427–29)

When Strepsiades, his father, asks: "Since you imitate the cocks
in all things, why don't you eat dung and sleep on a perch?"
Pheidippides replies: "That's not the same thing, old fellow,
nor would it seem so to Socrates" (1430–32). But he does not
retract the essential similarity between men and beasts. Logos
is not an essential differentia of the human herd. The psyche
in both beast and man is reduced to erotic epiphenomena of
the body, just as the Olympian gods are replaced by Vortex, Air,
Clouds, and other meteorological phenomena.

Aristophanes associates Socrates with the heavenly or Uranian
gods, who are depersonalized or reduced still further to natural
forces. In reducing men to beasts Pheidippides does not say that
there is a still stronger resemblance between the cocks and the
Uranians, who also beat their fathers, who do not write down
their decrees, and who eat ambrosia and sleep in heaven and
Hades.[10] The reason for this reticence is undoubtedly that
Zeus also gained power by beating his father.[11] That the Olympian gods be purified is compatible with the innovating logos of
Socrates, but not with the old or traditional logos of Aristophanes. The problem Aristophanes faces is thus already present in the tradition upon which justice rests. Since the tradition
is unreasonable or inconsistent, Aristophanes must attack the
rational investigation of the divine.

The same situation exists with respect to physics. In Aristophanes' portrait philosophy is represented by astronomy, me-
teorology, geology, together with such physical experiments as
the measurement of a flea's jump. Socrates "looks down upon"
the sun from his floating basket, and his students investigate
"the things under the earth" (224–25, 188). His gods are Chaos,
the Clouds, and the tongue (423–44): the invention of human
speech would seem to lead inevitably to the corporealization of
the divine. Thus the Socratic Ideas are replaced by Clouds

10. Hesiod, *Theogony* 138, 155, 170 ff. (the castration of Uranus by Kronos),
460 ff. (Kronos swallows his children, since Gaia and Uranus had warned him
that he would be beaten by his son).
11. Ibid., 490 ff.

(289: ἀθανάτας ἰδέας), which appear as mortal women who, says Socrates, "become any form that they wish" (348). Yet the same objections may be made against the traditional Olympian gods who also are physical, have human form, are generated out of women, and can change their forms. The Aristophanean Socrates gives a series of examples which show that the Clouds assume a physical representation of the nature of the person who looks at them (352). The Ideas combine physics and sophistry; they are also the principles of rhetoric which teach the Unjust and the Just Logos, or how to make the worse appear the better. As the consequence of this daring or hybristic teaching,[12] the existence of Zeus is denied, the young become licentious, and the Unjust Logos triumphs. But is this not the same accusation that Socrates directs against the traditional religious mythology in the *Republic*?

Interestingly enough, the strongest part of Aristophanes' attack upon the new teaching concerns not theory but Eros in its practical manifestations. The justice and temperance of "the old education," overthrown by the new philosophy, is represented by the virtue of boys (961 ff.). Pederasty is associated with rational physics throughout the play. References to astronomical investigation are frequently accompanied by jokes concerning the anus (171 ff., 193–94, 294–96), and the final defeat of the Just Logos occurs when it is forced to admit that the majority of Athenians are εὐρύπρωκτοι or homosexual (1100 ff.). Finally, Strepsiades is forced by Socrates to take off his cloak, since "it is customary for those who enter the phrontisterion to be naked" (497–98).[13] The gods of Homer and Hesiod do at least seem to be free of the vice of pederasty, although it might be argued by an innovator that Hesiod makes clear the connection between women and evil in the story of Pandora.[14] In general Plato and

12. At 375 Strepsiades calls Socrates ὦ πάντα σὺ τολμῶν. Cf. 457, 1506: "why did you teach hybris toward the gods?"

13. At 727 ff. Socrates trains Strepsiades to find cheating thoughts by making him lie on a couch beneath a bug-infested coverlet: a physical representation of Socratic irony.

14. *Theogony* 570 ff. Zeus makes Pandora because Prometheus stole fire, the principle of technē, and gave it to man.

Aristophanes are agreed upon the symbolic meaning of pederasty, or the revolt against the fundamental law of genesis. The
problem is how to contain the hybris of the body by justice, or
how to transform it into the just hybris of the psyche.

From a Platonic perspective Aristophanes makes a fatal error
in his formulation of the problem. In his mistrust of logos, he
attempts to subordinate the hybris of the psyche to the nomos
of the body. Despite his recognition of the dangers of pederasty,
it seems as though Aristophanes forgets the duality of Eros, or
the fact that logos is needed in order to keep pederasty in check.
In his own way he becomes subject to the inconsistencies of
Eryximachus' teaching. For example: although sexuality is in
principle the domain of human preservation and contentment,
it must not be allowed to follow its natural bent toward hybris.
Logos, because it is lacking in implicit virtue or morality, is too
dangerous to be made the supervisory principle. Aristophanes
must therefore find a way either to restrict Eros through the
body or to turn Eros against itself. If I am not mistaken, this
need accounts for Aristophanean obscenity (and perhaps for
that of later moralists like Rabelais and Swift as well). We must
note that, in the *Clouds,* the sexual Eros is not praised but criticized. The central character, Strepsiades, is a simple country-
man whose troubles stem from marriage to an aristocratic but
licentious townswoman (41 ff.). He should not have desired to
rise above himself; he should have resisted the upward and un-
settling force of Eros. Thus the Unjust Logos, in praising vice,
observes that even Zeus is conquered by Eros (1080). Similarly
the Chorus identifies Strepsiades as an *erastēs* or "lover of evil
things" (1458 ff.; cf. 1304–05).

When Aristophanes employs sexual obscenity in the *Clouds,*
it is generally in a negative caricature of pederasty, the most dangerous form of Eros. What we may call his positive obscenity
usually refers to the bodily processes. In the *Clouds* Aristophanes advocates a "downward" rather than an "upward" Eros.
There is a double Eros, part of which is assigned the function
of keeping the other in check. Sexual Eros raises man up or beyond himself; Aristophanes uses vulgarity to celebrate the inno-

cence and so the virtue of the humblest bodily satisfactions, which are guardians of piety. Thus throughout the first part of the play, when Socrates or his student explain an aspect of the cosmos in astronomical or meteorological language, Strepsiades counters with an example taken from the acts of eating, defecation, and the like.[15] Aristophanes' hiccoughs in the *Symposium* are a discreet and ironical reference by Plato to the importance in the *Clouds* of breaking wind. That is, Aristophanes advocates the sublimation of the sexual Eros in eating and the associated activities, but not in thinking.

Neither incorrect morals nor rational investigation can safely be subject to rational analysis; therefore Aristophanes ridicules them. Obscenity is the corporeal language by which Aristophanes hopes to replace the need for clever speech. But this hope cannot be fulfilled. In a society already so corrupt as to require the purgation by obscenity, constant innovation in obscene language is required to attract and enchant the citizens. Just as Aristophanes himself is silenced by a surfeit of food, so too may a corrupt society be silenced by a surfeit of obscenity. Such silence, however, is not equivalent to a return to traditional virtue but rather, to employ a modern term, to nihilism. The silence which Aristophanes recommends is rustic rather than urban. Strepsiades remains free from corruption only so long as he avoids the complexities of city life. The relative ease with which he is corrupted is an indication of the fragility of the traditional nomos. Strepsiades is saved from complete destruction by a faulty memory, which prevents him from mastering the lessons of Socrates (785, 855), and by an unexplained or unthinking revulsion against Pheidippides' avowed intention to beat his mother (1437 ff.). Strepsiades is capable of intermittent cleverness but not of continuous reasoning. He lacks the philosophical gift of recollection, hence he is also incapable of following a rational defense of traditional ways.

No explanation, for example, can justify Strepsiades' horror against incest; if it could be put into words, it too might be defeated by sophistry. Man is evidently saved by corporeal silence

15. E.g. 188, 294–96, 408 ff., 636 ff,

rather than by psychic speech. Thus the Chorus warns: "Perhaps, perhaps, he will wish that his son were voiceless" (1320: ἄφωνον). The voice generates logoi, which are both just and unjust. Even further, the Unjust Logos correctly predicts that it will destroy the Just Logos, which it virtually admits is stronger, by using the wisdom of "the discovery of new thoughts" (893–6: γνώμας καινάς). The unjust is as much a logos as the just; in other words, justice and logos are not the same thing. Aristophanes is perfectly well aware of the tension between theory and practice. The highest allegiance of theory is to logos rather than to justice. But it is precisely at this point that Aristophanes' argument breaks down, just as it will in the *Symposium*. If Strepsiades remains silent, and if he does not force his son to become articulate, he will still be unable to preserve himself from the corruption of the city. The *Clouds* ends with the destruction of the phrontisterion; it does not tell us how Strepsiades will solve the problems with which the comedy began. Strepsiades must accept his son's love of horses, and even his wife's lasciviousness. Does this not mean that rustic virtue is doomed by the luxury of the city?

Aristophanes' inability to defend the psyche by an exaltation of the body has already been suggested, and may now be documented by his own words. The indictment of logos can be accomplished only through the use of logos. In the revised version of the parabasis Aristophanes praises the *Clouds* as "the wisest of my comedies," which cost him "the highest degree of labor" (522–24). It is with this wisdom that he seeks to defend Athens against the wisdom of philosophy. But the champion of traditional piety and virtue is forced to use the same words as the Unjust Logos in praising his wisdom. He plumes himself, not for the repeated use of the same stories, a mark of inferior poets, but because "I show my wisdom (σοφίζομαι) by always bringing in new ideas [i.e. "forms": καινὰς ἰδέας], none the same as the others, and all clever" (545–48). In order to defeat the Unjust Logos Aristophanes is forced to publish it. In order to defend tradition he is forced to introduce change.

Aristophanes, who hates sophistry, is yet in a decisive way

closer to it than Socrates. Like Hippias, Aristophanes must say
new things in a new way, whereas Socrates always repeats himself.[16] Aristophanes' new speeches are addressed to the clever
members of the Athenian audience, whose approval he will
never betray, and "to whom it is pleasant to speak" (527–28).
They are not addressed to the forgetful Strepsiades, for whom
"the rustic life was most pleasant" (43).[17] Thus, although he
makes Pheidippides condemn the Socratics as "the earth-born"
(853)—that is, as the race of giants who tried to attack the gods
(and who reappear in his speech at the banquet)—Aristophanes
seems to come perilously close in the parabasis to hybris or a
declaration of his own divinity. His direct discourse to the
Athenians blends smoothly into the speech of the Clouds, who
say: "Although we benefit the city most of all the gods, we are
the only daimons to whom you neither sacrifice nor pour a
libation, we who watch over you" (877–79). Aristophanes shows
that he recognizes his own daimonic nature. Men like himself
can find their completeness only in the city which is the home
of the highest intelligence and sophistication, and therefore of
corruption as well. If Aristophanes must become the victim of
his obscenity rather than its master, would this lead him to sacrifice poetry for the barnyard virtue of a Strepsiades? If not, how
can he avoid an alliance with those who challenge the gods?

Aristophanes, like Plato, practices the double irony or logos
which is based upon the distinction between the few and the
many. Unlike Plato, he has no enduring basis for the preservation of that distinction. As a result the difference between his
advice to the few and to the many is difficult, perhaps impossible, to discern. He counsels the many to repudiate clever speech
and to find contentment in the body and the silence of piety. At
the same time, he demands that they acknowledge his own cleverness, and so the superiority of the psyche to the body, if only
by accepting his advice. His message to the few is similarly contradictory. The articulateness of philosophy leads to disaster;

16. Cf. Xenophon, *Memorabilia* 4.4.5–6 and Strauss, *SocrArist*, p. 33.

17. Cf. *Birds* 255–57, where the Hoopoe calls Peisthetairus τις ὁρμὸς πρέσβυς/
καινὸς γνώμην/καινῶν ἔργων τ' ἐγχειρήτης.

we must guard against it by the articulateness of poetry. The implication here is that the speech of poetry is actually a kind of silence, and for that reason therapeutic in a way that the speech of philosophy is not. It remains to be seen whether the silence of poetry can defend itself from the silence of technicism.

Eros, pederasty, and the revolt against the gods are also linked together in the *Birds;* here, as in the *Clouds,* sky-dwellers replace the Olympians. The divinization of physical or atmospheric, rather than heavenly, phenomena leads to the divinization or hegemony of man. This is more evident in the *Birds* than in the *Clouds.* The revolution is successful; Peisthetairos marries Basileia (the power of Zeus) and is worshiped as king. Whereas the Eros of his passive companion, Euelpides, is directed toward women, the active Peisthetairos is a pederast and is prepared to copulate with a goddess.[18] He orders, and the others follow (846 ff.). He persuades the Hoopoe, and so the birds; he expels the old-fashioned poet, the oracle, the land-measuring geometer, the tribute inspector, and the seller of decrees. Peisthetairos is a man of erotic hybris, as Iris, Zeus' messenger, points out (1259). The connection between Eros and the birds is apparent in Aristophanes' revision of the cosmogony of Hesiod.[19] The main step here is the mating of Eros and Chaos in Tartarus to produce the birds (685–702). In sum, the pederast of erotic hybris leads the revolt against the old gods in the name of the new (848); the new gods are sprung from Eros and Chaos, or human striving plus physics.

Eros is the force of darkness in man's psyche, and its ultimate sterility or destructiveness is indicated by its ungenerated genesis from a wind-egg (695). Heaven and Earth, and so the order of the cosmos, are generated by Eros or man's pride. Similarly Heracles, the product of sexual intercourse between a god and a human, plays the leading role in urging the surrender of Zeus'

18. For Euelpides' love of women, cf. 137 ff., 669 ff. The references to Peisthetairus are 137 ff., 1254 ff. Euelpides is cowardly compared to Peisthetairus (354 ff.) and plays the role of a Strepsiades in giving homely examples of Peisthetairus' cosmic theses (466 ff.). I am indebted to Mr. Robert Charles for first calling to my attention the significance of Peisthetairus' pederasty.

19. *Theogony* 116 ff.

authority to Peisthetairos.[20] Peisthetairos is also assisted by Prometheus, who covertly informs him of the difficulties faced by the gods and gives him the crucial advice of insisting upon the hand of Basileia in negotiating the peace treaty. Aristophanes tacitly identifies Zeus' power with fire, the principle of technē. In Hesiod the theft of fire resulted in woman, an evil thing for man,[21] thus raising the question of how men reproduced prior to her generation.[22] In Aristophanes this theft is associated with pederasty. In both writers the link between Eros and Eris is easily recognizable, and Hesiod's doctrine of the good and bad Eris is undoubtedly one of the antecedents for the doctrine of the double Eros in the *Symposium*.[23] Aristophanes' conception of Eros is nowhere more beautifully anticipated than by Hesiod three centuries earlier, who tells us that it breaks the mind and wise counsel in gods and in men.[24]

The danger of Eros is identical with the danger of logos. As Peisthetairos says, "the mind is raised heavenward by logoi and man is elevated." [25] The Hoopoe, who taught the birds to speak (200. cf. *Clouds* 1320), was himself once a man of erotic violence who retains human tastes and human knowledge.[26] He perverts what is obviously the Aristophanean code of excellence (what is "common, safe, just, pleasant, beneficial") by applying it to Peisthetairos' proposal (316). And finally the Hoopoe, in describing the two humans, or the double Eros in which the active element is dominant, draws a dangerous distinction between nature and mind: "if they are enemies by nature, they are friends by their mind" (371).[27] It is just this distinction which permits

20. E.g. 1603 ff., where Heracles votes to dethrone Zeus in exchange for a dinner invitation.

21. *Theogony* 600.

22. Cf. K. Reinhardt, "Prometheus," in *Tradition und Geist* (Göttingen, 1960).

23. *Works and Days* 11 ff.

24. *Theogony* 120.

25. *Clouds* 1447–48: ὑπὸ γὰρ λόγων ὁ νοῦς τε μετεωρίζεται/ἐπαίρεται τ' ἄνθρωπος.

26. Tereus, a Thracian prince, raped his sister-in-law and was turned into a Hoopoe for this act of erotic hybris (15). He and Peisthetairus "speak the same language." For the Hoopoe's human tastes, see lines 75 ff. His wisdom is Odyssean or Herodotean: he has seen all lands and the ocean. Cf. Nietzsche, *Menschliches*, par. 519.

27. 371: εἰ δὲ τὴν φύσιν μὲν ἐχθροί, τὸν δὲ νοῦν εἰσιν φίλοι. This notion is given a

them to soar heavenward, borne by the wings of logos. Whether we call the link between men and gods Eros or logos, human excellence is at the same time human defectiveness. From this brief inspection of Aristophanes' own writings, then, we should be prepared to discover that the most articulate of Greek poets praises Eros in such a way as to restrain its power by silence.

The Logos of Poetry

As the spokesman for the city, Aristophanes opposes the Socratic enterprise by employing the logos of poetry rather than of philosophy. The meaning of this opposition is shown by the fact that whereas Aristophanes is never portrayed in direct conversation with Socrates,[28] he engages in two exchanges with Eryximachus, whose own encomium is thus the center of a dialectic between medical technē and political poetry. Stated technically, the issue is whether logos or *mythos* gives us a more adequate speech of the whole. Of course, this technical formulation is in fact an oversimplification, as is suggested by Plato's own use of both logos and mythos. In this light, Eryximachus and Aristophanes represent a fatal sundering of logos from mythos, or of both technai, medicine and poetry, from philosophy. This may be understood as Plato's correction of the Aristophanean account of the division in human nature. Neither logos nor mythos alone can give an adequate account of the whole.

Although the allegiance between poet and city has long since been suppressed by the course of history, the quarrel between logos and mythos continues to occupy the center of contemporary speculation. In contemporary terms, the issue is whether science or logic must finally be regarded as a myth or poem. If, for example, poetry speaks for the whole man, and logic for his

---

prudential interpretation in the context: cf. 375 (ἀλλ' ἀπ' ἐχθρῶν δῆτα πολλὰ μανθάνουσιν οἱ σοφοί), 376. But the deeper results, at least for men, will be disastrous. Aristophanes anticipates the dualism of seventeenth-century philosophy, which was used to justify the unlimited mastery of the body by mathematical science.

28. I shall mention another implication of this fact in Chapter 6.

reasonable component, then the latter derives its significance from the former. Logic is thus a purified extraction of reason, which, however, is itself a derivative of "sensations, passions, and emotions," [29] or unreason. It would not be difficult to show a fundamental relationship between "existentialistic" condemnations of rationalism and the most positive empirically oriented defenses of logical reason today. If logic is the articulation of the formal structure of Chaos, then it must surely apply to poetry for information concerning its beginning and its end. Logic is silent about its own significance, thereby forcing its extreme partisans to a corresponding silence, in which they refuse to speak all words or sentences that might compromise its autonomy. But this silence does not rescue them from the myths of poetry.

It has thus become increasingly common today to hear talk about the "mythical" nature of science,[30] and still more so about "the poetry of logic," "the poetry of mathematics," or "science as an enterprise of the creative human spirit." Those who speak in this way tend to draw a discreet veil over the irrational origin of poetry. Poetry is now conceived as originating in the spontaneous activity of human imagination as directed by the will. The most immediate source of this view is Nietzsche, according to whom all thinking is perspectival, or the willful creation of "human" order where none "objectively" exists.[31] If logic is free creative activity, then logical forms, as relative to the "productive imagination," are like poems. The rule of logic over poetry is thus dependent upon the transformation of logic into the highest kind of poetry. Whether high or low, however, the component of silence or unreason has not been banished from, but rather pushed more deeply into, the center of the project.

29. D. Hume, A Treatise of Human Nature (Oxford, 1955), p. 1.

30. Cf. S. Freud, "Why War?," in *Collected Papers* (New York, 1956), p. 283 and P. Rieff, *Freud, the Mind of the Moralist* (New York, 1959), p. 204, for an example taken from the modern authority on Eros.

31. Nietzsche's theory of "perspectivism" is a consequence of Kant's distinction between the noumenal and phenomenal. Nietzsche disposes of the a priori status of the noumenal by extending the power of the imagination and linking it with instinct.

One way to summarize the detachment of the poet from the city is to observe that if every decision is relative to the will, then any choice is an arbitrary one. To be free means to be the slave of chance or an arbitrary universe. Of any two alternatives, man can never say which would be best, since he himself generates the standards of excellence by the very act of choosing.[32] The poetic art, in which Aristophanes sees the salvation of the city, is unable to prevent itself from being absorbed into logic or into the power of technē stripped of philosophical orientation and regulation. The content of poetry surrenders to the poetic technique (as in the case of Agathon), and this in turn to technique simply. Aristophanes will be conquered by the spiritual descendents of Eryximachus. And as the first dialogue between the two makes clear, it is Aristophanes' body that betrays him.

In the second dialogue Aristophanes, having recovered from his hiccoughs, ridicules Eryximachus. The poet is wittier than the doctor, which leads him to forget that his wit was rescued from silence by the doctor's technē. Aristophanes suggests that the virtuous Eros cured his hiccoughs, i.e. the god rather than the man. This can be understood in two ways, both contradictory to Eryximachus' main premise. The cure depended upon sneezing: in hiccoughing, we breathe in; in sneezing, we breathe out.[33] The cure rests upon the love of opposites, whereas Eryximachus found health within the context of pederasty, in the love of similars. Or we may say that hiccoughing plus sneezing produces silence rather than speech. Eryximachus understands at least that Aristophanes' jest is a sign of war, and responds accordingly; if the poet does not speak "in peace," the doctor will become "the guardian of your speech" (189a7–b2). The threat of force is thus opposed to the weapon of laughter. Laughter based only upon ridicule is a substitute for thought. Eryximachus prefers sobriety because he wants men to face up to their

32. Cf. J. Milton, "Areopagitica," in *Complete Poetry and Selected Prose of John Milton* (New York, n.d.), p. 697: "For reason is but choosing." Milton did not mean that man chooses the standards by which he will then choose; this is a later development of the initial version of the modern conception of thinking.

33. Cf. Chapter 4, n. 3.

cares and to remove them by work. The development of technique, like the mastery of nature to which it leads, is a serious business requiring sobriety and industry.[34]

Aristophanes accepts the offer of peace with laughter (189b2); he is sure that he will trick the coarser Eryximachus. He forgets that peace cannot, as in comedies, be obtained by the laughter of sexual obscenity; the professional soldier thinks rather than laughs.[35] Laughter relaxes us, while sobriety is a precondition for effective action. In these terms, tragedy is politically more effective than comedy because it is based upon the virtually universal fear of death. Men struggle to master nature because they wish neither to suffer nor to die. We shall find that even Aristophanes' "comedy" depends for its effectiveness upon the fear of genocide: at bottom, his speech is a tragedy.[36] In either case, however, it is a mythos rather than a logos. Aristophanes emphasizes, in response to Eryximachus' eristic hectoring, that he follows the custom of his muse.[37]

One can learn a technique but one cannot learn to be a genius. In science or art it is the muse or goddess who speaks through the lips of the genius. No one can predict where she will appear, or compel her to do so; thus the widespread feeling that there is a link between divinity and chance.[38] In the domain of art more clearly than in science, this leads to the view that one cannot capture the shape or form of genius in logos. In Greek terms, if it is the muse rather than the poet who speaks, then the poet is silent even as he speaks.[39] Aristophanes accepts

34. For this reason, once the modern project moved past its initially Platonic inspiration into the domain of "work," the philosophy of Aristotle tended to replace that of Plato as the implicit base of the enterprise. Cf. I. Kant, "Von einem Neuerdings Erhobenen Vornehmen Ton in der Philosophie," in *Werke, 3* (Wiesbaden, 1958), pp. 378–82, 387 (Plato was the father of *Schwärmerei;* "Die Philosophie des Aristoteles ist dagegen Arbeit").

35. Cf. *Republic* 388e5.

36. Cf. Rettig, *Symposion*, pp. 21 ff. and Krüger, *Einsicht*, pp. 130, 138.

37. 189b6–7; the opposition is to Eryximachus' attempt to restrict laughter by technē (189b4–5).

38. In the modern science of genetics, divinity is replaced by mechanism, which, when mastered, may be applied to the political end of the production of geniuses.

39. This is the theme of Plato's *Ion*. Hence also the "darkness" of Heraclitus,

Eryximachus' supervision with a reference to silence: "let the things which have been spoken be unsaid" (189b4). The dimension of silence plays a dominant role in his own teaching as well: the human psyche is characterized by a desire "which cannot be spoken, but it must prophesy or hint at what it wants" (192c7–d2). Speech is merely a means for hinting at what we have silently understood. The poetic mythos is thus the surface of inner silence. He might also accept the definition of a logos in the scientific sense as speech with a surface of silence; that is, speech which is unaware of its own definition by silence.

For Aristophanes, there can be no "logical" account of understanding, no rational speech about the cosmos but only riddles, and so no rational speech about poetry: no mythology in the literal sense of the word. This is unacceptable to Eryximachus, who in effect demands that Aristophanes "give a logos" of what he has to say, if he wishes to be released from bondage (189b8–c1). Aristophanes begins by linking Eryximachus and Pausanias (189c2–3), with whom he "intends" to disagree, and whom he cleverly identifies with humans in general. Aristophanes and Socrates are distinguished from the other symposiasts in that each disagrees altogether with everyone else (189c4, 198c5). One might be tempted to suggest that this makes their own disagreement the radical opposition between mythos and logos, but this view is obviously false, since Socrates himself tells the mythos of Diotima. It would be more accurate to say that both employ mythos to effect a religious revolution, but that Socrates' new religion has a component of logos that Aristophanes' does not. Even this suggestion seems to be contradicted by the fact that Aristophanes is a spokesman for the traditional Olympian gods.[40] It is true that he makes Eros subordinate to the Olympians. On the other hand, it is no mere accommodation to the cir-

who draws the same distinction within the domain of philosophy: οὐκ ἐμοῦ, ἀλλὰ τοῦ λόγου ἀκούσαντας . . . Diels, Vorsokratiker, 1, Fr. 50. The same distinction is in a way present in the Platonic dialogues, but the logos of Socrates does not normally speak in the poetic idiom of Heraclitus.

40. It is thus significant that Aristophanes uses the word for "sense perception" to refer to "thought" at the beginning of his speech (189c5: ἠσθῆσθαι, αἰσθανόμενοι). The gods as he and the tradition understand them are bodies.

cumstances that leads him to begin with Eros. When we unravel the details of Aristophanes' speech, we find an untraditional interpretation of the tradition.

Aristophanes begins by dropping the distinction between the double Eros; he will divide mankind, instead:

> For [Eros] is the most philanthropic of gods, the ally of human beings and the physician of those [ailments] through whose cure there would be the greatest happiness (μεγίστη δαιμονία) for the human race. I shall then try to introduce his power to you, and you shall be teachers of the others. (189c8–d4) [41]

The friendship of the single Eros belongs to the race, or to each human being, in whom the division is now to be located (and not, as in Diotima's speech, between the few initiates and the many). For Eryximachus the disease is in the cosmos and, to exaggerate slightly, must be healed by man. For Aristophanes, the disease is in man and can be healed only by the friendship of the god. In keeping with his reference to the genus rather than to a special few, Aristophanes is the first speaker who asks that his teaching be disseminated beyond the banquet to "the others." [42] On the other hand, although intended for the whole city, Aristophanes' teaching is not simply the old orthodoxy, but has been introduced by him. Aristophanes mixes tradition with innovation.

In the previous speeches praise of Eros and human ingenuity was silent about divine philanthropy; the gods were by and large absorbed into cosmic forces. Aristophanes, the first to speak under the inspiration of a muse, preserves the human form of the gods. He replaces nature or the whole as defined by physics, with nature as understood by the poetic tradition; and so he says: "first it is necessary for you to understand human nature and its affections" (189d5–6). The theory of the so-called hu-

---

41. Cf. *Peace* 394, where Hermes is called ὦ φιλανθρωπότατε καὶ μεγαλοδωρότατε δαιμόνων with 192d2–e6 and Chapter 3, n. 14.

42. Pausanias asked for a change in the law, but not for public discussion of the reasons for that change.

manistic Sophists leads to the disappearance of human phenomena. Whether or not Aristophanes' Eros is "a purely human appearance" [43] will depend upon the status he gives the gods, who
are responsible for the presence of Eros among men. If the gods
do not possess an enduring status, then the question must arise
as to the principle by which Aristophanes in fact differs from
his predecessors, in addition to their initial difference in orientation.

The question is raised by Aristophanes' next words: "our nature was formerly not the same as it is now, but of another kind
(189d6–7)." Aristophanes' "likely story" concerns the mutability of human rather than cosmic nature. In traditional terms,
if the gods are also mutable, then nature is identical with genesis. What then is the basis for Aristophanes' new teaching? This
question cannot be answered until we have studied Aristophanes' speech. But it is possible to anticipate his answer by re-
calling the distinction between logos and justice. According to
Aristophanes' misology,[44] there can be no rational way to distinguish justice from injustice; the technē of logos can defend
either side, and indeed it gives injustice a distinct advantage.
Since man stands or falls with justice, it and the polis are better
defended by myth than by logos. For logos undermines their
roots in looking beyond men to heavenly or superhuman phenomena. Since these roots cannot survive in the sunlight, man
must be defended by a kind of noble lie. Whether the defense
of man is at the same time the defense of truth will depend
upon whether Aristophanes really believes that human nature
changes.

To summarize: despite his misology and preference for the
speech of mythos, Aristophanes is a teacher with a message for
mankind that can be formulated in essentially rational terms. In
logos as practiced by Eryximachus or Socrates, man rises up to
the divine; in mythos the divine descends to man. Eryximachean
logos shares with Aristophanean mythos an exaltation of the

43. Hug, *Symposion* 189d5; cf. *Birds* 700 ff. and Bury's note: "This is the
order of A.'s exposition—περὶ φύσεως 189D–190C, περὶ παθημάτων 190C–193A."
44. Cf. *Phaedo* 89d1 ff.; *Republic* 411d7.

body. While Eryximachus is concerned with the human body as a gateway to the body of the cosmos, Aristophanes is concerned with the cosmos for the sake of the human body. The position of the psyche as the speaker of mythos thus becomes problematic in Aristophanes' teaching. Aristophanes' teaching is persuasive to the extent that it is reasonable. Aristophanes must prove that it is rational for man to celebrate the irrational or that the psyche is preserved thanks to the wisdom of the body.

The Circle-Men

According to Aristophanes, there were originally three kinds (γένη) of circle-men: male, female, and androgyne. The androgyne took its shape (εἶδος) and name from the other two sexes: "now only the name is left; the thing itself has vanished" (ἠφάνισται: 189e2). Aristophanes thus substitutes three kinds or sexes of primordial man for the Platonic principles of the One (Monad), the many (Dyad), and a Third which binds together the first and second.[45] Just as Aristophanes caricatures Socrates' teachings with corporeal imitations, so one may suspect that Plato satirizes himself in Aristophanes' doctrine of the three sexes. The more important point is of course that Aristophanes employs Eros, and so the body, to describe the whole, whereas Plato has recourse to noetic principles which constitute the structure of psyche and body. Just as the One holds together the multiplicity of matter, so the male transmits the form of the race onto the matter contributed by the female womb.[46] But the form and the matter are disparate in nature, and must be brought together by psyche or Eros. The sexual desire of the body is Aristophanes' counterpart to the psyche's erotic striving toward the Ideas.[47]

45. Cf. Chapter 4, n. 56.

46. The fact that this account is physiologically inaccurate does not affect the point at issue, since male and female still furnish us with examples of two principles which require juncture by a third. For remarks which are relevant both to the present passage and the next, cf. J. S. Morrison, "Four Notes on Plato's Symposium," *Classical Quarterly*, *14* (May 1964), esp. 48–54.

47. Cf. Aristotle, *Metaphysics* 1072b3 ff. The "Third" is not a univocal term

The disappearance of the androgyne is the most interesting result of the sundering of the circle-men that Aristophanes is about to describe.[48] It would seem that sexual generation is an accidental by-product of the absence of true harmony between men and women,[49] who in their longing for each other seek to recapture the unity of the androgyne rather than an imperfect reduplication of their sundered selves in children.[50] Sexual generation is thus the mark of imperfection in man's current nature; the circle-men had genitals but sprang initially from the sun, earth, and moon, and reproduced by spilling their seed on the ground, like grasshoppers (190a8 ff., 191b6). They were truly cosmic beings, like the Uranian gods discussed by the first three speakers. Aristophanes replaces these gods by the cosmic circle-men, whom he then proceeds to cut in half. In other words, the cosmic must be replaced by the Olympian gods, who are noted for their sexuality and human form: they thus mirror the incompleteness of man as well as the "remedy," or rather solace, for that imperfect condition. The sexual medicine leads to the generation of the city as an artificial whole which, although not the true end of human desire, is necessary in order to preserve mankind from the dangerous and ultimate consequences of that desire.

The city is thus an unstable or erotic harmony of opposites, whose defect is symbolized by pederastic or homosexual love. The pederast's pride or hybris is needed in the form of political

---

in Plato. It could be the ἰδέαι in one context (the purely noetic) and psyche in another (the cosmic).

48. According to Empedocles, the androgynes actually existed: Diels, *Vorso-kratiker, 1,* Fr. 61. This suggests a further point of contact between Eryximachus and Aristophanes.

49. Cf. Neumann, *Diotima,* pp. 43–48: Diotima advocates a "selfish" attempt to reproduce in the psyche for the sake of fame. The reproduction of bodies (children) must then be a by-product: i.e. the city is necessary for the happiness of the individual, who is thus intrinsically separate or transpolitical.

50. Cf. Delcourt, *Hermaphrodite,* pp. 28–29: ". . . les artistes et les poètes, d'un bout á l'autre de la tradition, l'ont toujours conçu et représenté [Eros] comme androgyne, et les cosmogonies orphiques insisteront sur ce caractère." Delcourt concludes that bisexuality was linked to man's aspiration for "perennité" (p. 64). The androgyne represents physical completeness, and the ability to generate from oneself seems to symbolize the power of rejuvenation.

ambition, but his Eros contradicts the principle of the city. The coupling of pederasty thus resembles the circular form (εἶδος) of the hybristic star-men; union or unity is not directed toward reproduction nor does it lead to its own moderation by means of the accidental by-product of reproduction.[51] In the case of both pederasts and circle-men, Eros is replaced by or transformed into hybris—or the desire to be divine.[52] The "high thoughts" of the circle-men, associated with their bodily strength, lead them to attack the gods (190b5). The high thoughts of pederasty lead either to philosophy or tyranny, unless checked by the mechanisms of the city.[53] The instability of these mechanisms, and so the sense in which Aristophanes' speech is a tragedy rather than a comedy, is prefigured in the cosmic or corporeal ground of hybris. Aristophanes objects that the Socratic Eros leads man to attack the gods;[54] yet in his own myth the attack takes place despite the absence of Eros.

By making Eros fundamentally sexual, Aristophanes illustrates two inseparable principles of his teaching. Human striving, whether for truth or fame, is essentially physical: the psyche is defined by and depends on the body. In order to counter the baneful effects of Eros, one must employ some kind of physical satisfaction. The body can be controlled only by the bodily, and not by the psychic or mental.[55] Since men wish to be gods rather than philosophers, the consequence of logos is unreason or absurdity. Aristophanes fights fire with water: he teaches us the need to quench our sexual appetites, by a variety of physical

51. On the form of circularity, cf. Morrison, *Notes*, pp. 48–49. Consider also Aristophanes' use of εἶδος. The Ideas are present, yet he cannot see them.

52. For a discussion of the historical antecedents to Aristophanes' circle-men, and their connection with Orphic cosmogony, cf. J. Stenzel, "Über zwei Begriffe der platonischen Mystik . . . ," in *Kleine Schriften* (Darmstadt, 1957), pp. 23 ff.

53. The mode of reproduction of the circle-men (191b7–c1) links them to the earth in a double sense; not only are they starlike or cosmic in their genesis, but autochthonous like the Athenians. Reference to the grasshoppers thus reinforces the ambiguous status of the city as both natural and artificial.

54. This is the traditional poetic wisdom; cf. Pindar, *Olympian* 5.25–27.

55. This principle is destined to assume fundamental importance in modern philosophy; cf. Spinoza, *Ethics* IV.7 and Hume, *Treatise*, p. 415: "Nothing can oppose or retard the impulse of passion, but a contrary impulse . . ."

or immanent means, in order not to kindle the transsexual
Eros. This Eros is just a perverse form of sexuality; if man could
have the perfection he desires, it would be physical and tyrannical rather than mental and just.[56] And so man conceives of the
gods themselves, the most powerful tyrants, in physical rather
than spiritual terms.[57]

The corporeal and human form of the Olympians should remind us that in the traditional mythology they sprang from the
Uranian gods, just as the present race of man is said by Aristophanes to have sprung from the cosmic circle-men. Aristophanes' silence about the Uranian gods indicates that he is also silent about the genesis of the Olympians. So far as one might
guess from his speech, the Olympians have ruled forever. In
other words, according to Aristophanes' explicit religion, genesis and generation are the same or coeval. The defective component in genesis is represented by the circle-men, who also
generate, albeit in a peculiar manner. Throughout the ramifica-
tions of Aristophanes' speech, it is important to grasp the fact
that sexual generation, despite its ultimate danger, is the source
or ground of justice. Thus it will not do to institute the rule of
Zeus by reference to the traditional story of violence against
his father. This also explains Aristophanes' association of Ephi-
altes and Otus with the circle-men. These giants who attacked
the gods and who were sufficiently powerful to chain Ares in a
bronze cauldron,[58] are said by Homer to have been slain by
Apollo,[59] the surgeon in Aristophanes' speech. Aristophanes tacitly criticizes Homer for making the sons of human generation
into enemies of the Olympian gods.

56. In the myth of Er (*Republic*, Bk. 10), the nonphilosophically virtuous man
chooses the life of the tyrant for his next incarnation.

57. M. Nilsson, *A History of Greek Religion* (Oxford, 1949), p. 179, states the
importance of anthropomorphism in Homer for later Greek thought: it prevented the Greeks from conceiving of the gods as magical and wonder-working.
But the "sobriety" of Greek religion, from the viewpoint of Aristophanes'
speech, is a consequence of the physical or natural status of hybris.

58. *Odyssey*, 10.305 ff. Note that Ares was also bound in chains by Hephaestus,
a myth to which Aristophanes will later allude.

59. *Iliad*, 5.385 ff.

The stars are the gods of the barbarians. By cutting the circle-men in half, the Olympians indirectly refer to their victory over the cosmic or barbarian gods. The origins are barbarian; man becomes truly human, civilized, or Greek through submission to the Olympian gods. Aristophanes apparently distinguishes between the divine cosmos or order, and man's barbarian (although also cosmic) origins, but the connection is in fact present in the initial relations between Olympians and circle-men:

> So Zeus and the other gods counseled what it was necessary to do with [the circle-men], and they were at a loss. For neither were they able to kill them, as they had the giants, making the race disappear by striking them with lightning—for then their honors and the sacrifices from [the circle-men] would disappear as well—nor could they allow them to go on behaving licentiously. (190c1–6)

The circle-men, despite their cosmic origin and whatever their communal life, worship or render homage to the Olympians. And the Olympians need this homage; they needed it prior to the appearance of man (if we are to believe the myth). Their link with barbarism, which also leads them to make man in his present form, is thus selfishness and not philanthropy: the philanthropy of Eros is rooted in the selfishness of the Olympian gods.[60]

The inability of the Olympians to kill the circle-men means either that they had become entirely habituated to honor and sacrifice, or that their very existence is dependent upon being worshiped. In the first case, the question arises of how they ac-

60. Cf. *Birds* 1603: the gods will starve without sacrifices from man; Peisthetairus uses a dinner invitation as a means to attain the surrender of their enemies. Aristophanes is not so explicit in the *Symposium*, but the situation is different. In Hesiod's *Theogony*, 535 ff., Prometheus devises the technique of tricking the gods by sacrificing bones wrapped in fat. Man thus keeps the meat for himself, and starves the gods. Prometheus is not mentioned by Aristophanes in the *Symposium*; his role is divided between the pride of the circle-men and the friendship of Eros.

quired so dangerous a habit, and what they were like before this addiction. To conjecture further along this line would lead presumably to primeval barbarism, and once again to the cosmic or Uranian gods. But the end result is the same as that of the second case: the Olympian gods are generated by the civilizing consequences of being worshiped. And these consequences are in turn rooted in selfishness, or the barbaric form of (corporeal) hybris. There is a circularity in the gods that corresponds to the circularity of the star-men. The Olympians need men in order to exist, but men exist thanks to the Olympians. By the simple assumption that Aristophanes' circle-men are a metaphorical symbol for unchanging human nature, the divine circle becomes immediately intelligible. Primitive man brings the gods into being by worshiping the stars. But these gods serve in turn as an instrument by which man civilizes himself. Unfortunately, when this process of civilization develops past a certain point, men wish to rebel against, dispense with, or replace their gods. This wish is in fact self-destructive since, without the regulative influence of the gods, men will lose justice, and so too the condition for their humanity. They will become like the stars but thereby revert to barbarism, not to divinity. If this consequence can be prevented at all, it is only through a self-restrictive act of piety. Just as Zeus needs men, men need Zeus.

The foundation of the civil religion is the descent of mankind from the gods. Men and gods literally dwell together; their συνουσία is sexual as well as spiritual. If men were like the stars, there would no longer be a spiritual, but only a physical, bond between them and the divine. Aristophanes' major step is to show the dependence of spirituality, in both men and gods, on sexuality. At the same time, Eros is the source of man's corruption as well as of his preservation. Aristophanes' vision of human life is essentially tragic because he denies the possibility of the transcendence of the body. Man is perpetually restrained within the self-contradictory dimension of desire and satisfaction: self-contradictory because perpetually cyclic.[61]

61. Cf. Krüger, *Einsicht*, pp. 125–30.

The Contrivances of Zeus

In Aristophanes' speech the function traditionally assigned to Prometheus is fulfilled by Eros.[62] Furthermore, while Prometheus stole fire—the principle of technē—from Zeus on man's behalf, according to Aristophanes Zeus willingly gives man sexuality—the principle of piety. Unfortunately for both Zeus and man, the principle of piety is also the principle of hybris. Sexuality is also a technē, directed toward the generation of human beings, and thus inevitably of high thoughts. The selflessness of sexual pleasure and parental love is also the selfishness of carnal desire and ambition for one's own offspring. This defective dualism in Eros is prefigured by the origin of philanthropy in Olympian selfishness:

> Zeus, having thought with great pain, then said: "I believe that I have a contrivance ($\mu\eta\chi\alpha\nu\dot{\eta}\nu$) whereby men may continue to exist but, having become weaker, will cease in their licentiousness. For now," he said, "I shall cut each one in two; they will become weaker, and at the same time more useful ($\chi\rho\eta\sigma\iota\mu\dot{\omega}\tau\epsilon\rho\sigma\iota$) to us through their increase in number." (190c6–d3) [63]

The comic aspect of Zeus' speech has been noticed before[64] but not adequately explained. Zeus' perplexity is not altogether incompatible with his intelligence. In fact, Zeus faces a serious dilemma: he cannot destroy his rebellious subjects without destroying the Olympians as well. By cutting the circle-men in half, he gives humans the powerful friendship of Eros. What if Eros and Prometheus should form an alliance on behalf of their

---

62. Cf. Chapter 3, n. 14.

63. As Leo Strauss has pointed out, the first two words of Zeus' speech ($\delta o\kappa\tilde{\omega}$ $\mu o\iota$) are also the first two words of the dialogue. I am not sure that this makes Zeus' speech the theoretical center of the whole work. The repetition also serves to establish a connection between the tragicomic Apollodorus and Aristophanes.

64. For example, by Rettig, in his note to 190c6. Bury says of this passage: "Notice the comic touch: the omniscient Zeus has to cudgel his brains over the business!"

two-legged friends? This is of course precisely what Aristophanes fears. The effort with which Zeus propounds his solution is in fact the effort of Aristophanes, who ironically identifies himself with the king of Olympus. Zeus' speech is comic because Aristophanes' cleverness is in vain. That Zeus recognizes the danger is shown by his threat to cut men in half once more, should they refuse to "keep still" (190d4–6: ἡσυχίαν ἄγειν). Silence is Aristophanes' ambiguous remedy for the corrupting alliance between logos and hybris. But in communicating this remedy, he himself cannot keep silent.

Aristophanes does not realize that Zeus' contrivance (μηχανή) is already a result of the technē of logos.[65] He does not seem to appreciate the fact that the speeches he assigns to Zeus are much franker than the mythos in which they are set. For example, in the myth of Protagoras Zeus gives men "shame and justice" because he fears that the human race will perish without them.[66] According to Aristophanes, Zeus rearranges man's "shameful parts" so as to make possible sexual generation, because he takes pity on the futile longing for union and consequent perishing of the severed halves (191a5 ff.). But Aristophanes does not actually say whom Zeus pities, or why he regards the human dilemma as pitiful. Zeus may be concerned exclusively for his fellow gods, whose need for sacrifice and honor "generated" the present situation. In any case, sexual generation and Eros take the place filled by shame and justice in Protagoras' myth. The psychic is corporealized: shame before the gods is transformed into shame before the genitals. The shameful parts of the body engender the public shame of the city.

For the optimistic Eryximachus, man is the physician. For the pessimistic Aristophanes, man is the patient. Apollo, the god of medicine and Zeus' surgeon, takes the place of Hermes, Zeus' messenger, as the link between Olympus and man. Again speech is subordinated to the body, locus of the operation. Zeus

---

65. *Phaedrus*, in a parallel passage, criticized the contrivance of Orpheus, but himself wished for a contrivance whereby one might form a city or army of lovers: 178e3, 179d6.

66. *Protagoras* 322c1 ff.

cuts men in half as though they were fruit or eggs (190d7–e2), a simile that reminds us that mankind is the source of divine nourishment. The nourishment of the gods is safeguarded by the absence of genuine physical unity, which is replaced by temporary copulation. One commentator has suggested that by using Apollo to sew up the newly divided men, Plato shows that the new condition is salutary, "genuinely willed by the divinity." [67] But salutary for whom? It would be more accurate to say that Apollo's needle stitches together man's perpetual incompleteness in accord with the pattern of utility to the gods.

Unfortunately the pattern is in principle defective, an unstable harmony of opposites, as it were. Zeus orders Apollo to turn man's face toward the cut side "so that, seeing his division, man might be more orderly" (190e4–5). Apollo also gathered together the cut skin, smoothing out the wrinkles except for a few at the navel, where the skin is tied together, "to be a memorial of the former condition" (191a4–5).[68] Man is thus the animal who is aware of his navel and what it signifies. Yet in looking down toward his navel, he also sees his shameful parts; the vision of his incompleteness drives him on to overcome it. But we have here combined what are in Aristophanes' account two separate operations. Let us return to Apollo immediately after he has turned man's face toward the evidence of the first operation:

> When nature had been cut in two, each half yearned to be with its other self, and putting their arms around each other and becoming entwined, they desired to grow together; they died of hunger and idleness in other respects through not wishing to do anything when separated from each other. (191a5–b1)

Three stages must be distinguished here: We begin in the circle-men with barbarism, to which corresponds divine selfishness. The division of the circle-men gives rise to mutual yearn-

67. Rettig, *Symposion* 190e2.
68. Hug, *Symposion* (190e6), seems to have noticed an ambiguity in Aristophanes' account; he says that Apollo binds together "der, wie es scheint, dehnbaren Haut des bisherigen νῶτον . . ."

ing, or the precondition for political (civilized) friendship—
now the divine selfishness is modified into pity, whether for
gods, men, or both. In the third stage physically incoherent
yearning is replaced by the more efficient Eros: men may now
generate after their own kind and thereby form genuine cities.
The presence of Eros as the gift of the gods means that divine
pity has now taken definite shape as philanthropy. In sum: as
man is modified, so too are the gods. Consequently Aristophanes
says "nature" in the passage just translated, and not merely "human nature." He, or Plato, thus provides an additional clue for
the careful reader, pointing toward the deeper meaning of his
mythos: the conception or interpretation of the order of nature
is decisively, although not completely, dependent upon or relative to man. Since there is no logos of the cosmos, there can be
no cosmology for Aristophanes, as there is for the first three
speakers. Yet the net result is curiously similar: the absence as
well as the presence of order in flux endangers the very existence of mankind.

Aristophanes no doubt wishes to suggest that the failure of
the first contrivance is due to the absence of friendship between
man and the gods, which is inseparable from friendship among
men themselves. The philanthropy of Eros brings the gift of
intercourse with gods as well as men, or the generating of heroes
and the establishment of noble houses as the foundation of the
city. Man does not become truly human without a perception
of the divine, the heroic, the noble. Without this, he has no
perception of himself, no desire to preserve himself through
work (191b1), no desire to reproduce but only to disappear. In
brief, man does not yet understand the significance of his navel,
which becomes intelligible only through the visibility of the
genitals. Hence the necessity of the second operation, which
Zeus had no doubt hoped to avoid because of the dangerous
consequences of genuine sexuality: "He moved their shameful
parts to the front. . . . and through this he effected genesis in
each other, through the male into the female . . ." (191b6–c4).
According to Socrates and his pupils, philosophy begins in the
wonder which men feel when they look up at the stars. Accord-

ing to Aristophanes, man first becomes human through the erotic awareness that is dependent upon looking downward, and not at the stars but at himself.

Whereas Apollo performed the first operation, Zeus himself is the surgeon in the second, which suggests its greater difficulty and importance. Zeus, the father of the gods, is also the father of mankind. This means that he is also the father of pederasty, or the unresolvable dualism within Eros: He introduces the second contrivance

> for these reasons, in order that if man would come to-
> gether in intercourse[69] with woman, he would beget,
> and the race would continue; but if male with male,
> surfeit ($\pi\lambda\eta\sigma\mu\sigma\nu\dot{\eta}$) from the [desire for] intercourse would
> occur; there would be a pause, and they might turn to
> work ($\tau\dot{\alpha}$ $\check{\epsilon}\rho\gamma\alpha$) and attend to the rest of life. (191c4–
> 8) [70]

Zeus is a tragic hero who strives to preserve gods and men, but whose contrivances are flawed by contradictions inherent in nature. The tragedy arises, not from a want of intelligence in Zeus, but from the absence of logos in the natural origins of gods and men. Preservation requires not merely the work of sexual generation but of noble deeds as well. The surfeit which arises from the intercourse of males stands for the freedom from merely corporeal concern or the selfishness of parental love. They are free to think high thoughts, to make the city their family, and so finally to endanger the bodies entrusted to their care. Thus Aristophanes' later praise of homosexuals (191e6 ff.) is not merely ironical, as some commentators have believed.[71] Man's dedication to politics (192a6), regardless of his personal

69. Cf. the $\sigma\upsilon\mu\pi\lambda\sigma\kappa\dot{\eta}$ $\epsilon\dot{\iota}\delta\tilde{\omega}\nu$ in *Sophist* 259e5.

70. For heterosexual intercourse, Aristophanes speaks of $\dot{\alpha}\nu\dot{\eta}\varrho$ and $\gamma\upsilon\nu\dot{\eta}$, whereas for homosexual intercourse he says $\check{\alpha}\rho\rho\eta\nu$ $\check{\alpha}\rho\rho\epsilon\nu\iota$, thereby suggesting the "human" character of the first, and the biological or animal character of the second. Note also the use of $\pi\lambda\eta\sigma\mu\sigma\nu\dot{\eta}$ in the context of homosexuality: probably this is a reference to Eryximachus, and perhaps to Agathon as well, who both are associated with the word.

71. E.g. Hug, *Symposion* 192a3.

sexual habits, is itself the highest manifestation of the dualism of Eros.[72]

The Imperfect Origin

Both Plato and Aristophanes are concerned with the existential origin of man.[73] The difference between philosophy and poetry should not blind us to a certain similarity between the two thinkers. Since speech is by its nature determinate, every theoretical discourse calls our attention to a specific set of forms. By so doing, it inevitably draws our attention away from the environment or horizon of those forms.[74] A complete speech would be one which comprises both the horizon as a whole and also the detailed structure of the parts falling within it. It would give equal satisfaction to the demand for conceptual precision and to our sense of the "texture" of wholeness in existence. Unfortunately it seems that precise speech differs in kind from speech that conveys a sense of wholeness. In the Platonic dialogue the dramatic structure and the use of mythos serve to complement, and even to complete, the defects inherent in the virtue of precision. In the speech of Aristophanes, however, mythos replaces logos. For Aristophanes, the defects inherent in precision can be healed not by completion, but by suppression. He does not wish man to have or to strive for a perfect awareness of his own nature. There can be no perfect awareness of what is by nature imperfect. In other words, clarity about the whole leads to the dissolution of the mystery and obscurity upon which human existence depends.

Man originates in the darkness of the body rather than in the light of the psyche:

72. Another difficulty which Aristophanes faces in his defense of Athens is suggested by the fact that Athena both is the goddess of technē and is non-erotic. In addition, she sprang full-grown from the body of Zeus: her birth was not by normal sexual generation. Cf. Otto, *Götter*, pp. 51–52, 55, 58, and n. 53 above.

73. Cf. Chapter 1, pp. 1–5.

74. This point, implicit in Plato, has been made a basic theme by Heidegger, both in his distinction between *Sein* and *Seienden*, and in his conception of *Welt* (where he seems to follow Husserl).

Ever since, the Eros in human beings for each other is inborn (ἔμφυτος), the one who unites the original nature (τῆς ἀρχαίας φύσεως συναγωγεὺς) by trying to make one from two and to heal the human nature (τὴν φύσιν τὴν ἀνθρωπίνην). (191c8–d3)

The original nature, however, is the pre-human or barbarous condition of circularity. If Eros were to succeed in making one from two, he would not heal human nature but destroy it. Aristophanes' real teaching is that cure and ailment constitute a perpetual cycle wherein human genesis gives birth to disease in the act of quenching it. Eros is not merely man's friend, but his enemy as well.[75] The instability of human nature, prefigured in Zeus' perplexity, is evident from the statement that Eros is inborn ever since the second operation: in other words, not before. As Zeus himself warns, it is possible for human nature to change again, by means of a third operation. If men are cut in half once more, the genitals will be destroyed. The disappearance of Eros will then lead to a condition even worse than the original, since the circle-men (whose genitals were on the outside) were able to reproduce by spilling their seed into the earth. The origin is not only imperfect but altogether inaccessible. Man is a contradiction balanced precariously between two forms of oblivion.

Thus when Aristophanes says that "each of us is a half-token (σύμβολον) of a human . . . each searches perpetually for his matching half" (191d4–5), we must understand him to be alluding to the permanently incomplete nature of man. The merits of the search for one's matching half are contained in its necessary failure. It must fail because the division of the body is a better image of the cosmos than is the Socratic articulation of the psyche.[76] The parts of the cosmos are at war with each other, and so too the "parts" of the psyche. Mind cannot impose peace because there is no logos. Hence the ambiguous

75. Cf. Reinhardt, *Prometheus*, pp. 197–98. Speaking of Zeus' punishment of man for Prometheus' theft of fire: "Aller Liebreiz, alles Schöne dem Menschen geschenkt von Zeus—um ihn zu betrügen."

76. Cf. Marcel, *Ficin*, Oratio Quarta, 11. 30r.

status of the pederasts.[77] "By nature they do not turn their minds toward generating children" (192b1–2). That is, they are not content to "keep quiet" (190d5) since "they are by nature most courageous [manly]" (192a2). In other words, they flaunt the one principle of regularity in genesis but thereby do most to preserve the human race. More generally, the best is also the worst. That this is Aristophanes' meaning is clear from his exaggerated claim that all who engage in politics are pederasts 192a6–7).

Given the perversity or ambivalence of nature, the defense of virtue must rest upon convention; the health of the city arises from the constraint placed upon its leaders by nomos (192b2: ὑπὸ τοῦ νόμου ἀναγκάζονται). It is up to man to ameliorate the defects and dangers of his natural condition by the enactment of prudent laws. Eros is therefore subjected to the constraint of reason; his friendship and counsel must be partly repudiated. The speech of nomos must lead us away from the silence of nature. In terms of the mythos, it would be possible for the severed halves to find their corresponding segment only in the first generation. If two male halves were to reunite, they would cease to reproduce after the human and "better" or pederastic kind. In brief, from the second generation following, all humans are "half-men" by nature. The present form is now for humans the whole form. Man is not simply divided within himself, but he exhibits a division simply within nature.[78]

That Eros or nature, the origin of humanity, does not supply us with a coherent speech about the origin, is now explicitly stated by Aristophanes. All successful lovers

> are the kind who associate with each other throughout life, who would have nothing to say about what they desire to happen to themselves through each other. No one could suppose this to be sexual pleasure, for the

77. Aristophanes says nothing about lesbian love (191d6–e5) or heterosexual promiscuity, thereby emphasizing the special problem which the male Eros presents.

78. Aristophanes alternates between "nature" and "human nature": the two are equivalent for him.

sake of which one enjoys being with the other with such great zeal. It is clear that the psyche of each desires something else which it is unable to speak, but it prophesies what it desires, and speaks in riddles. (192c2–d2)

Sexual pleasure and children are riddles or hints of the genuine but humanly inexpressible longing. The status of man is best expressed by the power of prophecy. Since man is in the deepest sense inarticulate, philosophy can only be dangerous for him. But since man is not merely a brute, he needs some form of spiritual sustenance. The mode of expression appropriate to man's "in-between" state is religion. At the same time, if the object of religious longing were granted, it would lead man to rise up against the gods. It would seem to be best from Aristophanes' viewpoint that man never even knew the object of his longing. The mythos, with its recourse to hints and prophecies, is equivalent to a veil drawn across that object.

In Aristophanes' comedies the whole as cosmos is replaced by the whole as city. In his mythos at the banquet, nature simply is transformed into human nature; religion replaces physics. As Aristophanes is himself forced to admit, just as man is the speaking animal, religion is not simply silence. The language appropriate to religion is poetry. But poetry, like prophecy, is notoriously ambiguous. Although this ambiguity may be a genuine reflection of the imperfect character of the origin, it leaves man a prey to the danger of false prophets. The entire situation is summarized by Aristophanes, who adopts the persona of Hephaestus, the god of technē. If Hephaestus were to ask the lovers what they wish from each other, they would be at a loss to tell him. But should the god offer to melt them together, making one from two, both in life and in death, even though he might warn them to be certain that this is indeed their desire, "we know that, hearing this, no one would deny it or seem to want anything else . . ." (192d2–e6).

The speech of Hephaestus echoes an episode in Homer.[79] According to the bard Demodocus, Aphrodite was married to

79. *Odyssey*, 8.266 ff.

Hephaestus, who trapped her in adultery with Ares by means of "unbreakable, indissoluble bonds." Upon seeing the guilty lovers locked together by the guile of his technē, Hephaestus says to Zeus and the other Olympians:

> I expect that they will lie like that only a short time, however great their love. Soon they shall not desire to sleep together. But my trick and bond will confine them . . ." [80]

Hephaestus, although lame and slow, has captured Ares, the swiftest Olympian, by means of his technē.[81] Similarly, one may anticipate that Eryximachus, despite his clumsiness, will overcome the mercurial Aristophanes. One reason for this is the difficulty in understanding mercurial speech. The poets seem to stand apart from the general inarticulacy of mankind; they can speak for the gods. But the speech of Homer is not compatible with the speech of Aristophanes. More accurately, Homer's version of the Hephaestus story is a much clearer illustration of Aristophanes' teaching than is the latter's. The offer which Aristophanes attributes to Hephaestus and which is part of his public revelation through the intended instrumentality of his immediate auditors, an offer which he says all men would eagerly accept, is one that guarantees their destruction.

By making man inarticulate Aristophanes renders him a potential victim of bad advice. His own Hephaestus cautions human lovers to be sure that they wish corporeal union but does not explain that this means the end of man. Homer's Hephaestus is less subtle but more helpful. We can learn from him that man will never be satisfied by the bondage of circularity (cf. 192c–d2). To the extent that the chains of Hephaestus represent Aristophanes' solution, they force him to draw man's attention to human dissatisfaction, and thus to the fact that the friends of Hephaestus are more powerful than those of Ares.[82]

80. Ibid., 315–17.
81. Ibid., 330–32.
82. In the *Odyssey*, 8.334–42, Apollo encourages the lust of Hermes, messenger

Speech about the Whole

The chains of Hephaestus bind Aristophanes in the sense that he is forced to publish the true teaching so as to protect mankind from self-destruction. Since the true teaching is itself dangerous, Aristophanes must present it in a disguised form. But the disguise he chooses makes his teaching excessively ambiguous; it is open to false interpretations. On one point Plato is undoubtedly in sympathy with Aristophanes: the answer to the dilemma of education cannot be mere straightforward logos. The key to education is a perception of the divine. Just as we do not first prove that sense perceptions exist but argue about the mode of their existence on the basis of prior perceptions, so too with the gods.[83] For Plato, however, man's intuition (νόησις) of the divine, however intermittent, serves as the basis for speech about the divine (διάνοια). Aristophanes on the other hand does not seem to be in any better position than the lover he describes, who would not seem to want anything else than corporeal unity with the beloved. Aristophanes does not know what is desired. The best he can do is give a false account of desire that is redeemed by its favorable practical consequences. Aristophanes' account of Eros is his "noble lie." But since that lie is not grounded in logos or intuition of the Ideas, its nobility is compromised by the existence of rival accounts.

Aristophanes "divines" the truth about the nature of Eros. He says of the lover's apparent desire:

> This is the cause, that our original nature was the same and we were wholes. Eros is thus the name for the desire and pursuit of the whole (τοῦ ὅλου οὖν τῇ ἐπιθυμίᾳ καὶ διώξει ἔρως ὄνομα). (192e9–193a1)

The defect in the divination of truth is this: Aristophanes cannot explain what he means by "the whole." By this time we

---

between gods and men. In Aristophanes' speech Apollo is the surgical assistant to Zeus in the operation whereby man acquires Eros. Apollo's "irony" is more visible in Homer than in the *Symposium*.

83. Cf. n. 41 above.

do not need to be reminded that Eros desires bad as well as good things, destruction as well as life. Erotic desire is not self-sufficient but requires direction by the vision of noetic order. In the *Symposium* the question of noetic order is discussed almost entirely in terms of human experience rather than in the language of epistemology or ontology. For this reason the *Symposium* is not altogether free of the dangers implicit in Aristophanes' mode of speech. As I have already indicated, the *Symposium* is not a complete or self-sufficient account of the whole. But the teaching of the *Symposium* is a necessary element in the complete speech about the whole. The *Symposium* is a more effective mythos than the speech of Aristophanes because it points beyond itself as Aristophanes' speech does not.

Although the *Symposium* does not actually mention the Ideas, it leads us upward to the boundary of their domain by reference to the vision of beauty in itself. This upward Eros is associated regularly with hybris, and so with injustice.[84] The upward Eros, as Aristophanes has correctly divined, transcends the nomos of the city. Whereas justice means "minding one's own business" or "keeping quiet," the upward Eros encourages man to mind "everyone's" business, to engage in the synoptic vision of philosophy rather than submit to the perspectival vision of justice. The philosopher cannot "keep quiet" but is characterized by being a "busybody": he suffers from πολυπραγμοσύνη. Aristophanes contends in effect that the philosopher minds the business of the gods, although he is silent about the fact that he does the same:

> And formerly, as I say, we were one, but now we have been forced by the god to live apart, thanks to [our] injustice, as have the Arcadians by the Lacedaimonians. One may fear that, unless we are well-behaved (κόσμιοι) toward the gods, we may be split in two again. . . . [Hence] it is necessary for all to exhort every man to be reverent toward the gods, in order that we may escape (bisection), and hit upon those things of which Eros is our guide and general (193a1–b2)

84. Cf. Chapter 1, pp. 14–15, and n. 35.

The presence of an anachronistic reference to a political event of 384 B.C. has prevented commentators from appreciating the importance of this passage.[85] The idea of cosmos or order, and the danger of division or *dioikismos,* are stated in explicitly political terms, in opposition to the previous speakers' reliance upon physics. The connection between politics and Eros means that the pursuit of honor through the performance of noble deeds is a consequence of the severed man's search for his other half. Such an incentive would be altogether lacking among the circle-men. If human beings, dwelling in a city and ruled by divinely sanctioned nomoi, were to rise up against the gods, it would be an act of injustice. But how can the pre-political (because pre-human) circle-men be accused of injustice? Aristophanes has already indicated that the Olympians demanded the subservience of the circle-men on grounds of self-interest rather than justice. It was only after great perplexity that Zeus initiated the events leading to the founding of cities and justice. In fact Zeus acted from the same motive as did the Spartans against the Mantineans in 384. The dioikismos of Mantinea was not a punishment of injustice but the ruthless act of a stronger enemy for the sake of his greater security in war. Aristophanes tactfully mentions a Spartan rather than an Athenian example, but the theoretical point is clear. Humans, together with justice, emerge from a pre-human state of nature which can best be described as a condition of war and selfishness.[86]

The origin is not merely imperfect, but nasty and brutish as well. Hence the need for dissembling in a teaching intended for public dissemination. It must be expressed in such a way so as to say one thing to the many and another to the few. The men of hybristic natures must be warned not to disturb the peace of the city, but they cannot be restrained by mere repetition of conventional pieties. The mythos tells the truth that there is no safety beyond the walls of the city, but it tells the truth in a way that is designed to remain within those walls.

85. Cf. Bury's note.

86. Cf. Plato's teaching in the *Laws,* where the Athenian stranger deduces an initial condition of peace and friendship from the natural state of poverty and desolation: 678e6 ff.

There is no Enlightenment for Aristophanes; the veil which covers the face of his teaching is in fact an integral part of that teaching. The cosmos is fundamentally a dangerous home for mankind; it cannot be escaped, but its dangers may be mitigated by construction of a just and stable city. Thus man must be perpetually on his guard, not simply against the cosmos, nor even his enemies, but against himself. Man is perpetually at war with self, gods, and cosmos. There is a sense in which he can bring the war to an end, by using technē to enchain Eros, but the result will be a loss of his humanity. So far as men are concerned, "war is the father of all things" because the cosmos is a harmony of unresolvable opposites.[87]

The inadequacy of the Heraclitean foundation of Aristophanes' thought was already surmised by Eryximachus. If the form of the harmony of opposites (the double Eros) is itself at war with itself, then it is perpetually dissolving, being and ceasing to be. But at any instant of dissolution the whole or cosmos would literally fall apart. Diotima corrects this deficiency by giving Eros an intermediate status; its peculiar resemblance to "the power of the negative" arises from the fact that it is other than the whole which it desires. In human terms, Aristophanes is right to make human nature in accord with the nature of the cosmos, but he is wrong in his understanding of the cosmos. Therefore he does not understand the truth of his own statement that "whoever opposes [Eros] is hateful to the gods" (193b3). For Aristophanes obedience to Eros means the self-forgetting of sexual love (193b3–6); for Plato the obedience of Eros to the gods means the self-forgetting of man in the vision of the Ideas.

We come then to the conclusion of Aristophanes' speech, which has proved to be a tragedy rather than a comedy. The situation is as dark for Zeus as it is for mankind. The second operation was a failure as much as a success. But Zeus cannot carry out his threat to bisect men again without incurring total disaster. The quarter-men, whom Aristophanes compares to profiles on tombstones, would indeed symbolize the end for men and

87. Heraclitus, Fr. 44 in Diels, *Vorsokratiker, I.*

gods alike (193a4–5). The gods, like mankind, must live in the present dilemma. On the basis of his own teaching, we cannot accept Aristophanes' claim that happiness for the human race lies in a return to the "original nature" (193c5). Aristophanes comes close to giving the correct interpretation of this claim himself; he says that, if a return to the origin "is best, it is necessary that the best for presently existing man is to come as close to it as possible" (193c5–7). We know what this means: temporary surcease from erotic striving in sexual intercourse for everyone, "men and women alike" (193b6–c3).

As is appropriate for the *defensor pacis,* Aristophanes concludes with a reference to the benefit which is greatest in the present life: being led by Eros "to one's own" family or home (193d1–2). If we mind our own erotic business, we may have "the greatest hopes" of happiness in the next life, or a return to "the original nature" through death (193d2–5). Thus Eros is our friend in this world, but not in the next. The origin is death; the beginning is the end. Life and the cosmos are out of joint. Human existence occurs within this discontinuity, from which it cannot escape without a perception of noetic order.

CHAPTER SIX

❖ AGATHON ❖

The Androgynes

Agathon, the effeminate[1] beloved of the soft but clever Pausanias, follows the pessimistic Aristophanes with a doctrine of optimism.[2] The beautiful host, however, is a more intricate character than his lover and, as we shall see, his speech contains a radical and explicit version of a teaching that is implicit in Aristophanes. For Aristophanes the purpose of innovating speech is to preserve traditional stability. The contradiction to which this gives rise is solved in Agathon's speech by the emancipation of novelty. Instead of political justice, Agathon advocates autonomous innovation; instead of tradition, he praises youth.[3] As the most radical representative of poetry, Agathon deserves to speak immediately before Socrates, who draws him into two dialogues, and accommodates his own mythos of Diotima to the need for peace between poetry and philosophy.[4]

1. Cf. Aristophanes, *Thesmophoriazusae* 191 ff. et passim.

2. Cf. Krüger, *Einsicht*, pp. 134, 138.

3. E. Hoffmann has pointed out (*Symposion*, p. 16) that, on the basis of the number of lines, Agathon's speech is exactly in the middle of the dialogue. This important position, the base of Socrates' own speech, is explained as follows: "Agathon kommt dem, was Platons Vorhaben im *Symposion* ist, näher als irgend einer seiner Vorredner. Denn Platons philosophische Hoffnung gründet sich auf den jungen Eros. . . . Dazu leitet Agathon gewissermassen schon über, weil er das Wesen der Liebe mit dem Jugendlichen verbindet." Hoffmann is right to emphasize the importance of youth for Agathon, but he does not see the importance of the connection between youth and innovation. This position is indeed crucial, but if it were closest to the teaching of Diotima, then Eros would strive for poems rather than for the stability and permanence of the noetic order. There is a similarity between the teaching of Agathon and Diotima, as I shall later show, but this raises the question of the degree to which Diotima speaks for Plato (or Socrates).

4. Very few commentators have discerned the importance of Agathon's speech.

The intricacy of Agathon's nature is a mixture of softness or effeminacy and the hardness of hybris. From the beginning his "refinement . . . and social tact"[5] are mitigated by a certain flustered peremptoriness in connection with Socrates' delayed arrival.[6] When Socrates does arrive Agathon shows that he recognizes the philosopher's hybris but, far from yielding to it, he is eager to compete and promises to take Socrates to court about wisdom (175e7 ff.). Of course, Agathon's hybris is soon shown to be passive in comparison with that of Socrates.[7] And one may agree with Friedländer, who calls him a representative of "that *dolce stil nuovo,* in which a music and rhetoric, become arbitrary, negates all tragic strength."[8] But as is clear from the occasion of the banquet, Agathon is a poet of considerable talent and an innovator of importance in the development of Greek drama.[9] Agathon is a softer version of Alcibiades: the one innovates in speech, the other in deed.[10] However, for us the decisive statement concerning Agathon's nature is made by Socrates himself. Amidst the gathering of Sophists and their pupils at the home of Callias, Socrates sees Pausanias seated near Prodicus. With him is

> a young lad whose nature, as I thought, was noble and good, and whose form was very beautiful. I seem to have

---

Thus, e.g. Brentlinger, *Cycle,* p. 18, can say that it has almost no content, although he then observes that "the real point of the speech, however, lies in the *self-glorification* Agathon is able to achieve in it. . . . a blurring of identities between himself and the god" (p. 19). According to Isenberg, *Order,* p. 37, Agathon is placed next to Socrates only because he raises the discourse from Becoming to Being. In principle this is the same mistake as is made by Hoffmann.

5. Bury, *Symposium,* p. xxxiv.

6. Cf. Chapter 1, pp. 26–27 above.

7. Aristophanes is explicit about the passive character of Agathon's eroticism. Cf. *Thesmophoriazusae* 35 (καὶ μὴν βεβίνηκας σύ γ', ἀλλ' οὐκ οἶσθ' ἴσως), 50, 157–58.

8. *Platon* (Berlin, 1954), 3.19.

9. P. Lévêque, *Agathon* (Paris, 1955), contains all of the evidence and references. Lévêque summarizes Agathon's contributions as follows: "il transporte dans la tragédie des innovations qui sont alors en plein vogue et qui font le succès d'autres genres: la philosophie, l'éloquence ou la musique instrumentale; il greffe ces rameaux pleins de sève sur le tronc antique de l'art théâtral."

10. Ibid., pp. 78–79.

heard that his name is Agathon, and I should not be
surprised if he were the sweetheart of Pausanias.[11]

The excellence of Agathon's nature must have been tempered
by a softness at least sufficient to render him accessible to
Pausanias. Yet Agathon is harder than Pausanias in the sense
that he generates poems worthy of awards by the Athenians,
while Pausanias seeks his gratification in a softening of the
Athenian nomos. Although Agathon is the beloved of Pausanias,
he offers a more radical version of his lover's teaching. As Plato
makes clear in the *Laws,* it was originally innovation in music,
or a softening of tradition, that generated *paranomia* in the
whole political domain.[12] An earlier reference to the Egyptians
shows that proper legislation of music is possible, if linked
with religion and piety.[13] This helps us to understand why
Socrates will make use of Diotima, a priestess, in his effort to
contain the innovations of Agathon. But it also suggests that
poetic innovation arises because of an inadequate foundation
for virtue. In order to guarantee the virtue of religion, and
so the stability of poetry, a virtuous lawgiver is required.
Agathon's theory of poetic innovation is not really autonomous,
but is generated by a theoretical interpretation of the city and
cosmos. The lawgivers in this case are Agathon's teachers, represented by Prodicus and Gorgias.

As we already know, Prodicus lacks an adequate theoretical
basis for his defense of conventional virtue.[14] If virtue is dependent upon linguistic distinctions, rhetorical skill permits
innovations in its conception or definition. In Platonic language, "one's own" comes to mean "one's own taste" rather
than "the nomos of one's own city." But Prodicus, like Pau-

11. *Protagoras* 315d8 ff.

12. *Laws* 700a3–701b3. This process is associated with freedom, democracy,
and the rule of artists by the theater audience. Cf. 658a4 ff.: comedies are said
to entertain older boys best; tragedies, educated women, young men, and
τὸ πλῆθος. Old men prefer to listen to recitations of Homer and Hesiod.

13. Ibid., 656d ff. The laws of the Egyptians were insufficient, but not altogether bad.

14. Cf. Chapter 3, pp. 60–64 above.

sanias, whatever his weaknesses, stays within the horizon of the city. The more radical position of Agathon seems to be inspired by Gorgias of Leontini.[15] Whereas Prodicus defended the conventional virtue, we are told by Meno, an appropriate student,[16] that Gorgias never taught virtue, and laughed at those who claimed to do so.[17] The strength of the rhetorical technē seems to arise from the absence of any basis for distinguishing virtue from vice or truth from falsehood. There is no need to dwell upon the self-refuting character of Gorgias' proof that either nothing is, or else nothing is knowable, or if knowable, incommunicable.[18] What Gorgias "proves" is not the absence of Being or the presence of chaos, but a primitive version of *esse est percipi*.[19] "To be" is to be a singular and private sense-perception. As a consequence, any statement about a sense-perception must also be a unique and private *individuum*.

Gorgias' argument is a distant precursor of Nietzsche's doctrine of creativity, which is also based upon the radical uniqueness of physical events and the personal character of knowledge.[20] Entirely apart from the self-contradictory character of the argument, it is not Gorgias but Agathon who draws the radical inference of continuous innovation. The rhetoric of Gorgias is like cooking rather than medicine,[21] but meals are made to be eaten. Stated differently, Gorgias is still the chef of the city; he conforms to the nomos by teaching the rhetoric of persuasion. Despite his nihilistic inclinations, Gorgias per-

15. Agathon's complexity is in a way symbolized by the fact that his two teachers, Prodicus and Gorgias, were professional rivals: cf. *Phaedrus* 267a4 ff.

16. Cf. Xenophon, *Anabasis,* 2.6.21 ff.

17. *Meno* 95c1–4. Cf. *Isocrates* 15.155 ff. (Diels, *Vorsokratiker,* 2, Fr. A18): Gorgias never married or settled down in one city, but wished to be free from all "political" ties.

18. Diels, *Vorsokratiker,* 2, Fr. B3.

19. Ibid., par. 83 ff.

20. Cf. Nietzsche, *Jenseits,* pars. 231, 43; *Götzen-Dämmerung* (Streifzüge), par. 26; *Der Wille zur Macht* (Bauemler), pars. 357, 337, 381 et passim. All in *Werke,* ed. Schlecta.

21. *Gorgias* 462d.

suades by reference to common goals, pleasures, and passions. Agathon, however, advocates that each man, or at least each erotic man, become his own chef. It is Eros or poetry who persuades the city, destroying it by dissolving it into its constituents. Agathon's doctrine of a soft Eros is generated by his poetic hybris, a hard attribute which he shares with Socrates. In his peculiar combination of soft and hard music, Agathon exhibits clearly what was already implied by the first three speakers. The hybris of pederasty stands for the circularity of the star-men in Aristophanes' mythos.

According to Aristophanes, there were three kinds of circle-men: male, female, and androgyne.[22] Aristophanes makes a special point of the disappearance of the androgyne,[23] although strictly speaking there can be no circle-men of any kind after Zeus' contrivance. As the combination of male and female, the androgyne represents better than the other two species of circle-men the idea of human completeness. One of the most important themes of the *Symposium* is that the androgyne is at least potentially present and constitutes both the greatest danger and the greatest hope of the human race. Let me state the issue in a preliminary form. Agathon, the most effeminate of the reported speakers, called the "man-woman" in one of Aristophanes' comedies,[24] makes the strongest claim in the dialogue: identification of himself with the ruling god. In order to refute this "religious" teaching, Socrates has recourse to a mannish woman, who prefers children of the psyche to those of the body[25] and is hard in her treatment of her young pupil. Whereas the mystery of Eros is revealed by Diotima, the mystery of Socrates is revealed by Alcibiades, the effeminate exemplification of masculine hybris. And Socrates himself, the hybristic midwife, is the paradigm of the psychic androgyne. Thus it is no accident that the three people in the *Symposium*

22. Cf. Chapter 5, pp. 138–43 above.

23. 189e2: Aristophanes says the androgynes are "invisible" ($\dot{\eta}\phi\acute{a}\nu\iota\sigma\tau\alpha\iota$). Plato shows that they may still be discerned in men of outstanding hybris.

24. *Thesmophoriazusae* 136: $\dot{o}$ $\gamma\acute{v}\nu\nu\iota\varsigma$.

25. 209c7.

with whom Socrates engages in direct and extensive dialogue are Agathon, Diotima, and Alcibiades.[26]

Agathon Drugged

Agathon's speech is preceded by two brief dialogues. The first is between Aristophanes and Eryximachus. Thus Aristophanes' speech is between two exchanges with Eryximachus, just as Agathon's speech is between two dialogues with Socrates. With a slight exaggeration we may say that Eryximachus lays siege to the city, whereas Socrates encompasses poetry. In the first of their exchanges Eryximachus warned Aristophanes not to make his audience laugh (189a7 ff.). In the second Aristophanes falsely claims to have been the one who demanded seriousness: "as I required of you, don't turn my speech into a comedy" (193d7). Eryximachus accepts this transposition of roles; he is persuaded by Aristophanes' present request, but not by his speech, which pleased but did not convince him (193e2–3). Despite the variety of the speeches thus far, Eryximachus is courageous in believing that something more remains to be said (193e4–7). This is not simply a vote of confidence in the "terrible" skill of Agathon and Socrates, but an indication that he fears them as little as he does Aristophanes. The eristic or agonistic undertone of this exchange is now made explicit by Socrates:

> But you have fought nobly for victory, Eryximachus.
> If you were where I now am, or rather perhaps where I
> shall be when Agathon has also spoken well, you would
> certainly be afraid and at your wit's end as I now am.
> (194a1–4)[27]

26. In this light, the implication of Alcibiades as the ringleader in the castration of the Hermae assumes a special significance. For a Christian interpretation of sexual inversion as the striving for superhuman status, cf. G. Fessard, *De l'actualité historique* (Paris, 1960), *1*, pp. 187 ff.

27. Bury says in his note to this passage that Socrates "implies that the various encomiasts are engaged in a rhetorical contest . . ." This should be put more strongly, since from Plato's viewpoint the "contest" is rather a war for the conquest of the human psyche.

Socrates praises the martial prowess of Eryximachus and prophesies the excellence of Agathon; he is silent about the speech of Aristophanes.[28] In terms of the *agon,* he thereby indicates who are his dangerous opponents, or who gives him cause to fear; he does not thereby comment on the intrinsic merits of the speakers.[A]

Socrates shows that he has understood Aristophanes by keeping silent about him, in ironic obedience to the comedian's instruction.[29] In a parallel vein Agathon responds to the hybristic irony of Socrates by stating his comprehension explicitly:

> You want to drug me, Socrates, so that I may be confused into thinking that the audience has great expectations of my speaking well. (194a5–7)

When Socrates describes the effect of his conversation on others in the Platonic dialogues, it is generally in flattering terms: the gnat who stimulates lethargic Athenians,[30] or the midwife who tests the merits of her patients' offspring.[31] Frequently, however, the impression of the patients is the reverse: like Agathon, they detect in the midwife's drugs a narcotic rather than a stimulating effect.[32] And indeed, as we have seen, Socrates sanctions the useful lie precisely on medical grounds:

> Does it not become useful with respect to enemies and so-called friends whenever they try to do anything bad

28. Socrates' silence is emphasized by the fact that Agathon, but not the comedian, is warmly applauded by the symposiasts at the end of his speech (198a2). The applause signifies that Agathon's views will appeal to a wider audience than does the teaching of Aristophanes.

29. Aristophanes is never shown in direct conversation with Socrates. E.g. at 212c4 ff. he is cut off by the noise of Alcibiades and his party.

30. *Apology* 30e4–5.

31. *Theaetetus* 149a4 ff.

32. In *Meno* 80a4 ff. Socrates is compared by Meno to a torpedo fish who stuns whomever he touches, thereby making them forget what they were previously able to say. The purpose of stunning or drugging dialectic is to achieve agreement rather than truth; cf. 75c8 ff., 76e3 ff., 81a5 ff. In *Republic* 487b1 ff., Adeimantus discusses the step-by-step process through which Socrates reduces his interlocutors to silence, or to an inability to defend what they believe to be correct.

through madness or any folly, diverting them like a drug? [33]

As a spy in the camp of the enemy,[34] Socrates will employ drugs and charms which are useful in the prevention of evil caused by that other sorcerer, Eros.[35]

Like many of Socrates' other patients, Agathon understands that he is being drugged but his intelligence is obscured by vanity. Already he visualizes the symposiasts in terms of a theater audience before whom his brilliance will shine once more. Socrates plays upon this vanity by referring to it as "courage" or "manliness" (ἀνδρείαν) and "greatness of mind" or "arrogance" (μεγαλοφροσύνην); he is not so forgetful of Agathon's previous behavior as to suppose that the present audience will confuse him (194a8–b5). Agathon's "courage" is in fact narcissism;[36] he cannot be frightened by an audience, which is for him only a mirror. As a result, Agathon is more "forgetful" than Socrates:

> But really, Socrates, you don't think me so full of the theater as to be ignorant of the fact that, to a man of intelligence, a few sensible people are more frightening than a multitude of fools? (194b6–8)

This is a careless remark for two reasons. In deprecating the theater audience Agathon cheapens his own triumph. And even if we attribute the comment to politeness, it remains true that Agathon also insults his guests, since he forgets that they too were included in the theater audience.[37]

Socrates is not taken in by the urbanity of Agathon's statement. His reply is extremely intricate and must be quoted in full:

33. *Republic* 382c6–10.
34. Cf. Chapter 1, pp. 23 ff. above.
35. Cf. 203d8.
36. Narcissus not merely fell in love with his own reflection, but was changed into a flower, thereby indicating his softness or delicacy. This mixture of egoism and softness is very characteristic of the author of *Flower*.
37. Hug, *Symposion* 194b6 ff.

I should not act nobly, Agathon, in supposing you to be boorish.[38] I know well that if you should happen to encounter any whom you consider to be wise, you would pay more attention to them than to the many. But we are not such—for we were also present there and were among the many. If you should chance upon others who are wise [i.e. as we are not] you would perhaps feel shame before them, if perhaps you would suppose yourself to do anything shameful. Or what do you say? (194c1–7)

Socrates contrasts his own nobility with Agathon's boorishness in a way that reveals his hybris without passing beyond the formal boundaries of verbal politeness. Still, it is necessary for him to be somewhat outspoken, in order to instruct his auditors, whomever they may be.[39]

Each sentence of the above speech both discloses and conceals. Socrates grants that Agathon would pay more attention to the wise than to the stupid but implies that he does not seek out the wise, but encounters them only by chance. This suggests that his own appearance at Agathon's home is not a usual occurrence.[40] Socrates politely denies his own wisdom, and not so politely that of the other guests, while quietly exposing Agathon's thoughtlessness. And then in the most intricate sentence of the passage he raises a doubt as to whether Agathon would feel shame even before the wise, whether he would ever suppose himself to have done a shameful deed. The recognition of wisdom, like the distinction between shame and nobility, depends upon the rooting of communication in community, whether with the cosmos or the city. In the last analysis Agathon, like his teacher Gorgias, dissolves that community, and so has no basis for praising anyone but himself. His deeper narcissism, however, wears the mask of the hypocrite or actor in a comedy of innovation. In acquiescing to Socrates' speech

38. See Bury's note to περὶ σοῦ τι ἐγώ: Socrates is explicitly contrasting his own nobility to the boorishness of Agathon while ostensibly contrasting his paltriness with Agathon's importance.

39. Cf. *Republic* 327c12–13.

40. For a similar passage cf. *Republic* 328c5 ff.

(194c8: "you speak the truth"), Agathon wishes to convey the fact that his accommodation to the audience's taste for novelty is compatible with his ability to distinguish the wise from the foolish. Since he still must prefer the company of the foolish many who adulate him by honoring his plays, the further implication arises that Agathon does not regard the distinction between the wise and the foolish as really important. One may say that for him it exists or is rooted in convention.

As a playwright Agathon is dependent upon the many, not because they are wise but because no one is, or rather because wisdom lies in self-gratification, which is intensified by an increase in numbers. Agathon has 30,000 lovers, all in a way equivalent to himself. Socrates next asks whether "you would not feel shame before the many if you should think yourself to do something shameful?" (194c9–10). If Agathon were to answer this question honestly, it would be in the negative. What the many approve cannot be shameful. Still more radically, what gratifies Agathon cannot be shameful. Such a direct answer, however, would be embarrassing to Agathon in the presence of the spokesmen for noble pederasty, who include his own lover. Fortunately for him, Phaedrus intervenes to terminate the dialogue, for the sake of which, especially with someone handsome, Socrates would neglect everything:

> I myself listen to Socrates with pleasure when he is engaged in dialogue, but it is necessary for me to take care of the praise of Eros, and to receive a speech from each one of you . . . (194d1–7)

Phaedrus' action here on behalf of the logos is at the same time a revelation of his passivity; he is pleased to listen to, but not to participate in, Socratic dialectic. That is, he treats it as though it were oratory. In the same way, he demands a speech about Eros from each guest, but nothing from Eros himself.

Phaedrus' own speech is not a praise of Eros but rather of self-gratification by means of the lover's passion. In this way he prefigures the narcissism of Agathon, or the extreme consequence of the separation of Eros from philosophy. Again, as an essentially passive listener, Phaedrus comes close to representing the audience of Agathon's tragedy. The opposition of Eros to philosophy generates narcissism, or a selfishness in which poet and audience can scarcely be distinguished. Just as the poet sees himself in the audience's applause, so the audience correctly assesses the poet's splendor as a function of its own approval. In this dialectic of seeing and being seen, the mutual dependence of gods and men, as suggested by Aristophanes, is transformed into the divinization of man the creator.

Agathon's Method

By distinguishing between "method" and "content," the first sentence of Agathon's encomium is an innovation in the proceedings. Agathon is also the first speaker to begin his encomium with the pronoun "I" and an assertion of will: "I want ('Εγὼ δὲ δὴ βούλομαι) first to say how it is necessary for me to speak, and next to speak" (194e4–5). From the perspective of the history of modern philosophy, it is impossible not to be impressed by the prophetic conjunction of ego, will, method, and technical innovation.[41] Needless to say, Agathon is not a Cartesian, but it would be the worst sort of anachronism to refuse to see what lies before our eyes because of historical piety. We misunderstand Plato's manner of writing if we either affirm or deny that Agathon is the paradigm of a technical or academic philosophical position. Philosophical positions are posed by a synoptic vision of the cosmos which has its ground in pre-philosophical experience. The portraits in the *Symposium* (to say nothing of the other dialogues) are intended to assist us in the reflexive act of grasping the origin of philosophical positions, by concentrating our vision upon the texture and structure of everyday experience.

To understand Agathon we have to consider his character

41. Pausanias and Eryximachus mention δόξα in their first sentence, and Aristophanes in his second. Eryximachus seems to cancel out δόξα by ἀνάγκη, as is fitting in a student of φύσις, but since necessity is impersonal or transhuman, his speech is a δόξα about ἀνάγκη. Agathon also mentions necessity, but in conjunction with the will. His first word is ἐγώ, and opinion is replaced by will.

169

and the nature of his technē. Such a consideration has nothing to do with the importing of modern technical developments into the ancient world. On the other hand it may show us the stratum of experience which is common to all technical innovation. Every technē, however primitive, includes as an essential component the assertion of the will. Man strives to modify his environment in the simplest effort to preserve his existence. To live in accordance with nature is to recognize that her benevolence, because it extends to all beings, is also the cause of work and war. In those arts which are directed by daily necessity, the exercise of will is subordinate to satisfaction. But poetry arises from the satisfaction of necessity. When man sings about work and war he comes to a consciousness of his acts as the consequence of intention. He moves within the dimension of freedom. For example, the song arranges the details of work and war not as they actually or historically occurred, but in order to express some general meaning, or perhaps a wish that was not granted by the events themselves. It is easy enough for philosophers to speak of the necessity that underlies the illusion of freedom. But since that illusion is coextensive with human experience, they succeed only in strengthening man's belief in the superiority of illusion to fact. The poet, in exercising his technique, believes himself to exemplify the inadequacy of the doctrine of necessity. Taking poetry in the general sense, one may define it as consciousness of innovation as the language of the will.

The belief that experiment is an expression of freedom, whether correct or not, is thus rooted in the simplest activities of daily life, and it is this root by which science and art are related. From this viewpoint of poetry it would be senseless to criticize Agathon simply because he deviated from the procedures of Aeschylus and Sophocles. At the same time, if innovation is implicit in the poetic activity, the question arises whether and how we are to evaluate Agathon's deviations. Men claim that the wars they fight are both just and useful, and the products of their work they deem beautiful if not just. To speak of a just or beautiful innovation seems to be an appeal to a standard other than technique; in the most obvious sense to ends other than utility. If these ends coincide with the autonomous exercise of the innovating will, then one innovation is not only as beautiful and just as another, but also as useful. For this reason those who praise the autonomy of innovation are in fact asserting the superiority of "one's own" innovations. I must innovate, not because I am a great poet, but because greatness is "making for oneself," or the solitude of narcissism.

The pride or hybris of the poet is thus very close to that of the philosopher. Whereas the philosopher wishes to see or know the whole, the poet wills to generate it. In the portrait of Agathon, this similarity comes to light as a concern with method. Agathon admits that there is a "right" and "wrong" way in which to generate speeches. What we may call his egoism is inseparable from a pride of workmanship that necessarily takes him beyond himself. His self-intoxication, which leads him to portray Eros in his own image, is at the same time an intoxication or drugging of the self by Eros: a love of beauty. Thus Agathon's statement of method is a demand that we consider the nature of the god:

> For all those who have spoken previously seem to me not
> to have praised the god but to have called men happy
> because of the goods (τῶν ἀγαθῶν) of which the god is
> for them the cause. (194e5–7)

Instead of the Idea of the good, Agathon, employing the language of genesis, speaks of the cause of goods. His implicit claim is that the goodness of genesis is visible as beauty.

Unlike the philosopher, however, Agathon does not wish to suggest that men become happy by the vision of beauty. Instead he means to say that happiness arises from the imitation of genesis through the making of beautiful speeches. In philosophical terms, this is closer to the assertion that *dianoia* (discursive thinking) is superior to *noēsis* (noetic intuition). Whereas the philosopher also advocates the generation of beautiful speeches, he is clearly cognizant of the fact that genesis is not itself a speech.[42] The defect in Agathon's position is not that his description of god is automorphic, but rather that it is autogenetic. Agathon claims to possess knowledge of god as ground or cause, whereas in fact he is describing the effects or acts of that cause. If we choose to defend him by the identification of god as pure activity, then Agathon must himself be reduced to the status of a speech or poem. Accordingly, the freedom of innovation is transferred altogether from man to genesis. Human poems (and poets) are symbols rather than explanations of god. The need to interpret the symbols in order to understand the cause and guarantee the possession of human happiness, is due to the fact that for man, if not for god, poetry is subordinate to philosophy.

Thus Agathon's initial remarks on method, as Socrates will later claim, are superior to his encomium, because they imitate the language of philosophy (which means that Agathon does not really understand what he is saying):

> What sort he himself is who gives these things, no one has said. There is one right way of any encomium about anything: to go through in speech (λόγῳ) what sort of cause there is of those things concerning which the speech (λόγος) is about. In this way is it just for us to praise Eros first as to what sort he is, and next the gifts.
> (194e7–195a5)

According to Agathon's method, it is just to philosophize first and then to write poems on the basis of knowledge.[43] If we do not know the nature of the giver, it is impossible to be sure that his gifts are praiseworthy. Aristophanes, the spokesman for justice, was therefore unjust in presenting us with an interpretation of human rather than divine nature. He began with a poem or mythos, instead of a logos, about the divine. Not only does Agathon challenge Socrates to battle, but in so doing he rebukes Aristophanes for his timidity. To this we may add in summary that if happiness is equivalent to the generating of

42. For a related problem cf. *Parmenides* 132c9–12.
43. This was the procedure followed by Socrates, who spent his life philosophizing, and wrote poetry in the last hours of his life: *Phaedo* 60c9 ff.

beautiful things, then Agathon's method teaches us that the happiness of generating is dependent upon the happiness of knowing.

Happiness as Beauty

If man may be defined by pity toward his fellows and fear of the gods, then the purging of these emotions would seem to make him something other than human. In somewhat different terms, if the function of tragic catharsis is to generate happiness among men, it is also to raise him up toward the divine. Divinity is happiness:

> Thus I say (φημὶ οὖν ἐγώ) that of all the happy gods,
> Eros, if it is right to say so and does not anger the gods,
> is the happiest, being most beautiful and best (195a5–7)

Agathon explains the nature of all the gods and not simply Eros, or more accurately, all those who are happy, by which he no doubt means that to be a god is to be happy. His qualifying phrase ("if it is right . . .") indicates that, like Aristophanes, he is aware of the danger in revealing knowledge of the gods. Unlike Aristophanes, Agathon is willing to take the risk. One might suspect that, in his subsequent conjunction of happiness with peace or softness, he will seek to propitiate Nemesis. However this may be, there is a more fundamental reason for Agathon's daring.

When Agathon comes to speak of Eros' wisdom, he identifies it as poetry or making, rather than as knowledge of the cause. Eros makes men poets, which is to say that he generates in them the technē by which they obtain knowledge of his nature (197a3 ff.). The wisdom of Eros consists in generation (not merely of man) rather than in thinking or knowing. Eros is poetry making itself: as such, it has no knowledge of itself, but simply enjoys its own activity. In fact, this lack of knowledge is the condition for Eros' happiness, since divine knowledge in Platonic terms would be perfect vision, not of oneself, but of

173

the Ideas.[44] To "know thyself" is then not to know oneself as a person or individual, but (to summarize a complex problem) to know the "Idea of man." To the extent that Agathon knows the god, he ceases to be himself. Actually, what he wishes for is a union with the god that brings happiness rather than knowledge. Agathon does not fulfill the promise of his methodology because to do so would be to contradict his genuine teaching. Still, insofar as he has a teaching, he reveals the difference between himself and Eros. The gods will show no anger at Agathon's revelation of their nature because they have no knowledge of this revelation. Agathon wishes for or loves Eros in the sense that philosophers love wisdom but do not possess it. In Agathon's own terms, his defect is that he is too wise.

If the gods are not angry at the revelation of their nature, it does not follow that the same is true of men. The Greek word θέμις, which was translated above as "right," refers primarily to law or custom, and so to rightness or piety in the sense of obedience to the nomos about the gods. Like his lover Pausanias, Agathon innovates with respect to nomos, and he claims that men will become happy or peaceful if they follow his teaching. If the gods have no self-knowledge then they cannot be concerned with whether or how men honor them.[45] But this means that no nomos is sanctified by the gods: *themis* has no sanction beyond that of human agreement. Rightness may then be identified as "what men want" and is accessible through the force of persuasion or rhetoric. The most righteous man is the most powerful rhetorician, which, as interpreted by Agathon, means the most skilled innovator. In this way righteousness and happiness combine in the poetic activity. But the highest happiness belongs to the innovator who persuades men of the principle of innovation itself.

According to Agathon's new teaching, Eros is the happiest of gods because he is "most beautiful and best." He begins with a demonstration of Eros' beauty:

44. On this point Plato differs from Aristotle, for whom the divine perfection is a νόησις νοήσεως. But even for Aristotle, one could scarcely say that the divine mind is analogous to an ego.

45. The same idea is later expressed by another poet, the materialist Lucretius.

In the first place, he is the youngest of the gods, Phaedrus. He himself furnishes a great sign for this account
by fleeing old age, which, as is clear, goes quickly; in any
case, it comes upon us faster than is needful (τοῦ δέοντος). (195a8–b3)[46]

Agathon's emphasis upon youth is in sharp opposition to Socrates as well as to Phaedrus. Both Socrates and Phaedrus praise
what is "oldest" and "ungenerated." Nevertheless, the difference between the two is sufficient for Agathon to make a tacit
appeal for the allegiance of Phaedrus: "you are happy because
you are beautiful," he implies, "but your beauty depends upon
your youth. It is not to your advantage to praise old age!" In
contrast to Socrates, Agathon preserves beauty and (in a sense)
goodness ("the best"), but truth is replaced by poetic genesis, which is for Agathon a cause in the sense of "principle"
(ἀρχή). If the youngest god is the happiest, Eros' happiness may
well be transient, lasting only until some new god is generated.
But the advocacy of poetic genesis cannot be replaced by another doctrine, since any new doctrine would itself be a poem.
The rule of poetry, if once accepted, cannot be overthrown by
its own offspring, as were the Olympians.

Since beauty is essential for happiness, it follows that old age
is man's enemy. Agathon says that Eros flees old age, not that
men do. But he adds that old age comes upon men "faster than
is needful." The phrase τοῦ δέοντος might be translated by some
as "than is right" or "than is suitable," but the point remains unchanged. As we have already seen, "rightness" and "suitability"
mean for Agathon something like "the result of human persuasion." At best, it would have to be claimed that he intends by
τοῦ δέοντος the right as established by the gods; but this would
scarcely preserve the notion of traditional piety. The only sensible translation is the literal one: if old age moves faster than is
needful, then something can be done to slow it down. There is
a subtle connection between Agathon and Eryximachus. Agathon, however, does not wish to slow down old age by medi-

46. Bury's comments throughout this section are especially helpful concerning
rhetorical devices and possible allusions to other writers.

cine;[47] his technē is poetry. One must conform to the youthfulness of the innovating Eros in order to escape the old age of the psyche. As Agathon might argue, a youth which depends upon medicine is merely a corporeal arrestation of death, and so only a negative condition. Medicine must be subordinate to poetry because the psyche is the principle of life.

Agathon is thus attempting to win Phaedrus away from Eryximachus. While ostensibly rebuking Phaedrus he actually refers to the internal inconsistency in Eryximachus' position:

> It is Eros' nature to hate old age, and not to come anywhere near it; he exists always in association with the young (μετὰ δὲ νέων ἀεὶ σύνεστί τε καὶ ἔστιν). For the old saying puts it well: like draws near to like. (195b3–5)

The "old saying" is in fact the principle of Eryximachus (186b5) who, not to repeat all the complexities, interpreted it to mean that the healthy love the healthy. But if nature draws like to like, then the art of medicine is superfluous. In addition, there is a practical difficulty: if like desires like, then Phaedrus should love the young and beautiful Agathon. Eryximachus' technē, as Agathon implies, is at odds with nature. Agathon is thus better able to appeal to Phaedrus' selfishness. Phaedrus need not desire the young and beautiful but may merely associate with them to his advantage. Phaedrus can turn Eros to his advantage only so long as he is young, and thanks to poetry the psyche can remain young as the body cannot. Agathon is appealing to Phaedrus' love of beautiful speeches, of which he, and not Eryximachus, possesses the technē.

The principle that like seeks like is associated throughout the *Symposium* with hybris or rebellion against the gods, and usually with pederasty. But the tendency of Agathon's innovation is toward peace with the gods. Physics, medicine, perhaps even philosophy, are war-like; poetry is peaceful. Science "puts nature to the torture," whereas poetry celebrates or honors her. Thus Agathon denies the connection between Eros and cosmology:

47. Cf. Chapter 3, n. 18, and Chapter 4, n. 11 above.

But I, although agreeing with Phaedrus about many other things, do not agree with this, that Eros is older than Kronos and Iapetus,[48] but I say that he is the youngest of the gods and always young, and the old deeds concerning the gods, which Hesiod and Parmenides recount, were generated by Necessity and not by Eros, if indeed they spoke the truth. (195b6–c3)

Agathon in a way restates the implication which we detected in Phaedrus' speech: there are two kinds of genesis, one of which (the older) is not erotic but the principle of (cyclic) cosmogony. In other words, cosmogony and physical science generally are concerned with, and so characterized by, necessity, while poetry is the genuinely erotic activity of freedom. Man cannot act significantly, cannot generate, or exercise his (autonomous) will in the domain of physics or the body, because he has not created the cosmos.

According to Agathon, the psyche is the principle of freedom, and the body that of necessity. One might object that man no more created the psyche than he did the body, but this does not meet Agathon's point. For the position which Agathon represents in the *Symposium* is that the nature of the psyche is creativity. The psyche manifests itself in generative activity, the lowest form of which issues in and is limited by bodies, but the highest and freest form of which is poetry. Whatever the difficulties in such a view, it is both defensible and persuasive. But Agathon makes his own task much more difficult by linking psychic creativity to peace, or by denying the connection between youth and war. The difficulty is dramatically evident in the eristic character of Agathon's own relationship to Socrates. For even if war in the most obvious sense is connected to the body, ambition, the root of war, is a trait of the psyche and is especially characteristic of the young.

One might defend Agathon by arguing that his quarrel with Socrates is a war to end all wars: a war for the sake of perpetual peace. Thus he suppresses the hardness of youth on behalf of

48. See Bury's note.

the softness which one normally associates with effeminacy, thereby making quite a different use of homosexuality than did his predecessors. This suppression takes place with respect to both god and man:

> For neither castrations nor enslavement of each other would have occurred, nor many other acts of violence, if Eros had been among them, but there would have been friendship and peace, as there is now, ever since Eros has ruled the gods. (195c4–7)

The immediate object of this sentence is the speech of Aristophanes. At 191a5, Aristophanes summarizes the operation of Zeus with the words "when nature had been cut in two"; the word τέμνω can also be translated as "to castrate," and appears in the sentence just quoted (ἐκτομαί). For Aristophanes, there is an essential opposition between the divine and the human which is the precondition of the presence of Eros in human nature. Eros is the mark of the war between gods and men, and of the perpetual victory of the gods. In addition to his initial operations, Zeus threatens the present race of men with castration if they should continue to exhibit hybris. Agathon denies this interpretation of Eros: the mutilations occurred because of Eros' absence. They are the mark of the barbarian, warlike nature which preceded the civilized and peaceful reign of Eros.

The soft Eros replaces the hard, warlike Zeus, and so renders the other gods soft as well. Traditional theology must be changed, and so too the link between gods and men. Eros is not only young but "delicate" (ἀπαλός: soft, sensitive):

> It requires a poet such as Homer was to reveal the delicacy of a god. For Homer says that Atē is both a god and delicate—or at least that her feet are delicate—saying, "Her feet are delicate, nor does she approach the ground, but she walks on the heads of men." (195c6–d5)

Agathon mentions "softness" in one form or another fourteen times in his own name and once in the quotation from Homer. He is of course thinking of himself when he says that another

Homer is needed to reveal the nature of the gods; and we may add that he seems to regard himself as fourteen times superior to Homer, with respect to the central virtue of softness! This Platonic joke is accompanied by another. In his quotation from Homer Agathon improves upon the ancient poet by omitting certain crucial points. If we consult the original we find that Agathon has suppressed the name of Zeus, Atē's age, and her accursed function of misleading or destroying mankind.[49] The softening of Atē is symbolical of the new nature of the gods. Homer sings of the reign of Zeus and so of war, the hardness of hero-soldiers, and necessity. Agathon sings of the reign of Eros and so of peace, the softness of poets, and freedom.[50]

One might suppose that if Agathon replaces Homer, the heroes and their descendants will all become as soft as the gods. Such, however, is not the case. In applying the softness of Atē to Eros, Agathon says:

> For [Eros] walks neither on the earth nor on heads, which are not very soft, but he both walks and dwells in the softest of all things (ὄντων); he has established his home in the characters and psyches of gods and of men: not, however, one after another in all psyches, but whenever he happens upon one with a hard character, he departs; when he happens upon one that is soft, he colonizes it. Since he grasps always the softest of the soft both with his feet and as a whole, he is necessarily most delicate. (195e2–196a1)

Agathon imitates and therefore challenges Socrates by subordinating the body to the psyche, and he is the first speaker to do so clearly and explicitly. He also imitates Socrates by drawing a firm distinction between erotic and nonerotic men, and indeed much more sharply than Socrates. For Socrates all men, al-

49. *Iliad* 19.91–94.
50. At 195c7, after the first mention of "soft," the word "of the poet" follows immediately: . . . ἁπαλός· ποιητοῦ δ'ἐστιν . . . Whereas Agathon softens Homer, Aristophanes retains his "hard" view of human existence. Cf. Hesiod, *Theogony*, 1.3: the Muses dance πόσσ' ἁπαλοῖσιν. Agathon's "soft music" or teaching concerning genesis is also a tacit correction of Hesiod. Cf. Chapter 2, pp. 45–50 above.

though few are philosophers, exhibit an erotic nature to one degree or another.[51] For Agathon on the contrary, some men are not at all erotic in the sense represented by poetic creativity.

This natural distinction between the young and the old, or soft and hard, is a serious defect in Agathon's soft music of hybris. His teaching, despite its repudiation of cosmology, is grounded in the attempt to reverse the order of nature by making the young soft and the old hard. There is no reason to believe that the hard men will let the soft men live in peace. Agathon has made Eros too delicate and so deprived him of the ability to soften or colonize the hard, whom we may conjecturally identify as the allies and descendants of Eryximachus. Agathon's Eros is an aesthete; he judges men by their character rather than by their intelligence; hence Agathon's silence concerning mind even in the discussion of Eros' wisdom.

The softness or self-indulgence of Eros is not the same as complacency, which in a way would serve as a basis for peace among men. Similarly, Eros' fluency permits him to distinguish between soft and hard psyches rather than to encompass them all. We see here another aspect of the divisive nature of Agathon's aestheticism:

> Eros is youngest and most delicate, and besides these, the form (τὸ εἶδος) is fluid (ὑγρός).[52] For if it were hard, he would not be able to embrace anything, nor entering into each psyche at first to be unnoticed, and also when leaving. A great mark of his harmonious and fluid shape (ἰδέας) is [his] elegance, which Eros is agreed to possess to a degree greater than anyone; for there is always war between Eros and gracelessness. (196a1–7)

Here Agathon admits that he has not only failed to establish universal peace but that his principles guarantee perpetual war.

51. *Phaedrus* 248a6 ff. Note also that at 245a1 Socrates says the manic enthusiasm which comes from the muses affects soft and pure psyches.

52. See Bury's note for various senses of ὑγρός, including the erotic. This passage is very close to double entendre and is reminiscent of the description of the horses' wings in the *Phaedrus*.

Agathon's fluency is rhetorical rather than noetic or theoretical, and this fact is exhibited in the form of Eros. The fluency or suppleness of mind permits it to identify with the forms of all things, whether soft or hard: in this sense, mind and form are akin; there is peace between them. But the fluency or suppleness of Eros permits him, according to Agathon, to "enter into" (rather than "identify with") all psyches in order to select the soft ones for colonization. Eros cannot dwell in graceless psyches; his criterion is elegance rather than knowledge or understanding. Therefore poetry is less fluent than philosophy, precisely because of its greater elegance.[53] Agathon is the first speaker to mention the form ($\epsilon\tilde{\iota}\delta os$, $\iota\delta\epsilon a$) of Eros, but instead of defining it he lists a stream of characteristics. And this is in keeping with his technē, the function of which is to exemplify rather than to define.

The beauty of Eros is characterized by his youth, delicacy, and suppleness or fluidity. Stated differently, his home is in elegant or graceful characters. In an obvious allusion to one of his own plays,[54] Agathon compares elegance to flowers, and these in turn to "the beauty of the god's complexion." One may suspect that this is Plato's way of saying that the beauty of Agathon's Eros is only skin-deep. Agathon then continues:

> For Eros never sits on anything, whether a body, a psyche, or anything at all, which cannot bloom or from which the bloom has departed. But in whatever place is flowery and fragrant, there he sits and stays. (196a6–b3)

The power of Eros to make men poets, and presumably also to imitate states of the psyche in poetry, is restricted to psyches which share his nature. In the concrete terms of the dialogue, this means that there is a war between the beautiful and the ugly. The freedom of innovation is bound by a kind of snobbism, just as it lacks a theoretical or noetic base for the determination of the beautiful. As a result freedom becomes a function

53. Cf. S. H. Rosen, "Thales," in *Essays in Philosophy* (University Park, Pa., 1962).
54. Cf. Bury's note to $\chi\rho\delta as$ $\delta\grave{\epsilon}$ $\kappa\acute{a}\lambda\lambda os$.

of convention and chance. Agathon's particular conception of beauty cannot withstand the assault of the graceless psyches he so despises. Unfortunately, his weapons in the war against gracelessness are too soft to kill. Agathon wishes to fight a war by rising above the battle, an act of elegance if not of martial cunning. And here, as so often in the *Symposium*, Agathon's defect, when seen from a different angle, becomes a kind of virtue. Elegance is the aesthete's imitation of philosophical magnanimity. In shunning the hard or graceless, Eros slips delicately away from the ugly or uncouth without giving voice to his scorn.

Happiness as Virtue

Aesthetic magnanimity refrains from punishment and thereby expresses the unpolitical element in Agathon's teaching. A good citizen practices justice, and it is the task of justice to punish the evil as well as to reward the good. Agathon's Eros does not regard ugliness as evil, and therefore he must also distinguish between beauty and goodness. He defines the "virtue" (ἀρετή) of Eros in keeping with his passive or apolitical nature: "The most important point is that Eros neither does nor suffers injustice, whether with regard to god or man" (196b4–7). By using ἀρετή at 196b5 to replace ἄριστος at 195a7 and 197c2, Plato emphasizes Agathon's distinction between beauty and virtue or goodness. At the same time, Agathon's failure to attribute justice in a positive sense to Eros shows that the excellence of the god is not the same as that of the citizen.

In a political context magnanimity is a way of asking for less than one's due. Whatever may be the reasons which motivate such conduct, the least one can say is that it is passively political, or practically in accord with the principle of justice. The magnanimity of Agathon's Eros, however, is due to his possession of the powers of an absolute tyrant:

> Neither does he suffer by force, if he suffers [undergoes] anything—for force never touches Eros; nor in acting does he use it, for everyone willingly serves Eros in ev-

erything. And where the willing agree with the willing, the saying "the nomoi are king of the city" is just. (196b7–c3)

In this intricate statement, the link between Eros and the will is explicit. But the substitution of persuasion for force, or seduction for rape, is not the same as free obedience to the nomoi. Agathon quotes from a Sophist[55] in order to indulge in sophistry. The servants of Eros are a disguised version of those who in Pausanias' speech were said to surrender completely to passion.[56] Thus Agathon hints that Eros may not "suffer" or undergo anything at all. "To be obeyed" is not the same as "to honor one's agreements" but is more like "to be known," the manner in which Being "suffers." [57]

Again, Agathon has now described Eros as both an absolute and a limited tyrant. He is absolute because everyone willingly obeys him, but his tyranny was previously limited to the young and supple. In slipping away from the hard or ugly, he leaves them to their own devices. Agathon's apparent failure to understand the limitation he himself has placed on Eros' powers is confirmation of his failure to grasp the consequences of the war between the beautiful and the ugly. The elegance which gives Eros the appearance of magnanimity is in fact an egotistical self-indulgence. Like all acts of self-indulgence, it decreases rather than increases Eros' power. Just as the philosopher must know the ugly and the beautiful, so the effective king or tyrant must govern the bad and the good. He must be able either to punish his enemies or to transform them into friends. It is incumbent upon Agathon to show that the softness of Eros is a satisfactory substitute for punishment. To do this, however, he must modify the exclusiveness with which Eros was previously said to avoid the hard. In the terms of his speech, Eros cannot be both beautiful and virtuous (best) because the beautiful is entirely free from the ugly, whereas the most virtuous is just, and justice entails punishment or a concern with ugliness.

55. The quotation is attributed to Alcidamas, a student of Gorgias.
56. Cf. 184d5. The same verb, ὑπηρετέω, is used there.
57. Cf. *Sophist* 248d10 ff.

Agathon wishes to give a soft interpretation to the hard teaching of Gorgias that, according to the law of nature, might makes right.[58] Eros is both hard and soft. The paradox is most easily perceived in terms of virtue, and especially in terms of justice (which is the fourth of seven qualities attributed to Eros). Eros cannot be just, and yet he must be. Agathon's explicit solution to the problem is to infer his justice from the fact that he neither does nor suffers injustice. "Besides justice, he participates fully in temperance" (196c3–4). Not only are these two virtues closely connected, but temperance presents Agathon with the same problem. No one who possesses it can be entirely delicate or free of force:

> For it is agreed that temperance is the mastery of pleasures and desires, and that no pleasure is stronger than Eros. But if they are weaker, then they may be ruled by Eros; he may then rule and, ruling over pleasures and desires, Eros would be unusually temperate. (196c4–8)

Agathon's use of the potential optative reveals the dilemma he faces. The exercise of virtue depends upon force and hardness, and Agathon wishes to preserve the former while repudiating the latter.

In addition, Agathon has not proved that Eros is temperate. He would be, if pleasures and desires were all weaker than he. In any case Agathon's argument is an equivocation on the word "stronger." He claims that (1) temperance is the mastery of pleasure and desire; (2) Eros is stronger than all pleasure; and (3) Eros masters pleasure and desire and so is unusually temperate. But an immoderate man may also be stronger than all pleasures, ruthlessly subordinating them to his untrammeled will. Thus it is no accident that in this premise Agathon fails to add that no desire is stronger than Eros. Whatever Eros' domain, he must rule it by force. The peculiarity of Agathon's general position lies in his deduction of an ethics of softness from the hy-

58. *Gorgias* 483d–e.

bristic principle of the absolute strength or tyranny of Eros. The ethics of softness is the practical consequence of his theoretical use of soft rhetoric rather than hard logos. Poetry contains no implicit principle of argumentation; even the principle of autonomous creativity is philosophical or religious.

Agathon's inability to forge a valid harmony of opposites between the soft and the hard vitiates his discussion of each of Eros' virtues. It is unmistakably the case with respect to his analysis of courage. How can so manifestly hard a virtue be defined in terms of softness? As Hug points out in his commentary, Agathon does not even attempt to define courage.[59] Instead he gives an example:

> And with respect to courage, "Ares is no match for" Eros.[60] For Ares does not hold Eros, but Eros holds Ares —[in love] of Aphrodite, as the story goes—and the one who holds [or captures] is stronger than the one being held. So he who masters the bravest of all others should be the bravest altogether. (196c8–d4)

The story to which Agathon refers was mentioned previously by Aristophanes, who, however, follows the spirit of the original account by making Hephaestus rather than Eros responsible for the capture of Ares.[61] Homer does not mention Eros in speaking of Ares' love ($\phi\iota\lambda\acute{o}\tau\eta s$) for Aphrodite. Agathon revises the story by reducing Aphrodite to a passive role, and by eliminating Hephaestus altogether.

Agathon corrects both Homer and Aristophanes, who give too much power to the god of technē. If Hephaestus is most courageous, then Eryximachus' teaching will triumph. Agathon sees that praise for one's own technē is not the same as praise for technē simply. He rebukes previous poets for not having prop-

---

59. In his note to 196c8. But Hug explains this omission by saying that courage is somewhat harder to define than moderation. It should be added that Agathon does not actually give a definition of justice, either.

60. A quotation from Sophocles' *Thyestes*.

61. Cf. 192d ff. and *Odyssey* 8.266 ff.

erly praised or understood their own art. As the suppression of Hephaestus suggests, poetry for Agathon is not simply or decisively a technē, but the free activity of man's nature. A technē is employed for an external end, but poetic activity is its own end. This is illustrated in Agathon's revision of the story of Ares' capture. It seems at first as though Hephaestus is a genuine master, with Ares and Aphrodite as his subjects. But the appearance is misleading: it was Hephaestus' love for Aphrodite and his desire for vengeance that drove him to forge the trap for his wife and her lover. Hephaestus, like Ares and Aphrodite, is in bondage to Eros. Eros is the highest force that drives both gods and men to use their trickery and techniques. He is both the beginning and end of conscious activity. In this way Agathon comes close to a successful definition of soft courage. Eros conquers the hard and the strong by making them weak or soft. Agathon fails, however, in reconciling the definition of beauty with the definitions of the virtues. It is barely possible to reconcile temperance with the exclusiveness of elegance, but not justice or courage. The elegant man who is just and courageous must be hard rather than soft.

We come now to wisdom, or the step at which Agathon most directly competes with Socrates. Success here may lead us to overlook earlier inadequacies; thus Agathon dismisses the other virtues by saying of wisdom alone: "So far as is possible, I must try not to leave anything out" (196d4–6). Agathon is most confident of his case with respect to beauty and wisdom, and he glides over justice, temperance, and courage. In effect the structure of his speech suggests that for the poet there is a relationship between beauty and truth, but some difficulty in the relationship between beauty and goodness. But in its relationship through poetry to beauty, the truth must be redefined to conform with the primacy of perpetual renewal through innovation. If we follow the traditional division of wisdom into theory and practice, since Agathon makes generation primary he must redefine theoretical in terms of practical wisdom. And practical wisdom in his sense must be compatible with injustice, intemperance, and cowardice.

Happiness as Wisdom

The discussion of wisdom is divided into three parts, each of which corresponds to a mode of making or generating: the musical, the sexual, the arts and crafts.

> And first, then, in order that I may honor our technē just as Eryximachus did his, the god is so wise a poet that he can make another [a poet] as well. At least everyone becomes a poet "even if he were unmusical before," should Eros touch him. It is fitting for us to use this as evidence that Eros is a good poet generally with respect to every kind of musical making. For what someone does not possess or does not know, he cannot give to another nor teach to another. (196d6–e6) [62]

The reference to Eryximachus and "our" technē shows that the quarrel is not simply between two individual speakers, but between poetic and scientific technique. The touch of the doctor may heal the body, but it does not teach the psyche, as does the touch of the poet.

Agathon begins with an example rather than a definition of wisdom. In this example knowing is equated with making through the medium of touch. Agathon continues to believe that wisdom may be imparted by touching (cf. 175c8 ff.), by making or generating rather than by the theoretical grasping of the principles of making or generating.[63] He therefore poses the alternative of giving what one possesses or teaching what one knows. It is evident that the touch of Eros is a kind of giving rather than teaching, just as the touch of sexual generation is a giving of life rather than a teaching about life. From the fact that Eros makes or generates poets, it does not follow that he is himself a wise or good poet. A moment's reflection suffices to show that, precisely in the domain of Eros, making is not equivalent to knowing.

In the passage just quoted, Agathon tries to suggest that a

---

62. Agathon's quotation is from Euripides; cf. Bury's note.
63. Cf. S. H. Rosen, "Thought and Touch," *Phronesis, 6* (1961).

"wise maker" is thereby good by using the word ἀγαθός in place of σοφός (196e1, e4). The word "good" (ἀγαθός) appears four times in Agathon's speech: at the beginning (194e7) in the sense of "benefits" or "advantages"; in the middle (196e4), where it means "competent" or "clever" and twice at the end, once in the sense of "gracious" (197d5) [64] and once in an indeterminate sense (197d8). Moral goodness disappears; instead, we are given the making and loving of the beautiful. If goodness means to be a clever poet, if this in turn entails dwelling with the beautiful and shunning the ugly, and if the beautiful is the young, then there are no obstacles to pederasty. Sexual generation may then presumably be left to the hard or ugly. Agathon minimizes the importance of this kind of making. He can better afford to do this than the previous pederasts, because he has presented a theory of psychic generating which attempts to account for man's highest aspirations. Sexual love is then quietly sublimated into poetic activity.

More specifically, sexual generation as a corporeal making is the least important of the three kinds of *poiēsis* for which Eros is responsible. Thus Agathon says briefly:

> And as for the making of all living things, who will deny that without Eros there is no wisdom by which all living things come into being and grow? (196e6–197a3)

Human sexuality is absorbed into cosmic or natural genesis. Agathon's main interest is in artificial genesis:

> But in the case of the making of the technai (τὴν τῶν τεχνῶν δημιουργίαν), do we not know that he for whom the god becomes a teacher turns out to be of high repute and famous (φανός) but he whom Eros does not touch turns out to be obscure? (197a3–6)

In the *Timaeus* the Demiurge tells the gods that if He were to make men, they themselves would be equal to the gods. In or-

64. The mss. give ἀγαθός at 197d5, but see Bury's note for the grammatical difficulty. He accepts the reading ἵλεως ἀγανός, which would yield "graciously mild."

der to avoid this He instructs the gods to turn to "the making of living things" (τὴν τῶν ζῴων δημιουργίαν) in accordance with nature, but to imitate His own power as it was exercised in the generating of their kind.[65] Agathon replaces the natural demiurgy of living things by the technical demiurgy of poems. When speaking of the genesis of living things, in the previous passage, Agathon did not explicitly state that Eros is the generator or demiurge but rather suggested that Eros is needed for the "wisdom" of genesis.

The Demiurge of Timaeus makes both men and gods. In Agathon's speech there is some ambiguity with respect to the gods. Since Eros is the youngest of the gods, he could be responsible only for the genesis of their children. We are left to wonder whether Eros is not perhaps the only as well as the youngest (in the sense of perpetually self-renewing) god. Moreover, Timaeus' Demiurge, once having made the cosmos, rests. Eros, on the contrary, is perpetual innovating activity, both in his own right and within the activity of man. The depreciation of cosmic or natural genesis, and the importance of technical innovation, also leads Agathon to assign to Eros the role traditionally played by Prometheus. Eros teaches men and especially gods how to discover the arts (which further suggests that both may be his offspring), and he is directly present in their activity or functioning. This direct presence is the touch of Eros (197a5).

Eros' technical demiurgy is never at rest; its work is never done. Incomplete erotic striving which expresses itself in the making of new and mortal products is connected by Agathon to visibility or fame. Agathon is more concerned with being known than with knowing; "to be knowable" means literally "to be seen" through one's "poems." There is no knowing because there are no deathless forms to be seen. Man is thus what he makes. He who makes nothing is as good as dead, for when he dies it will be as though he had never been. But he who makes badly is not seen or remembered. Eros steals softly away from him and so renders him invisible or nonexistent. Agathon's de-emphasis of sexual generation is intimately related to

65. 41c2 ff.

the fact that he does not regard mere bodily existence as genuine visibility or being.

Of the various things which a man may generate, children bring one less fame, and so less immortality, than erotically inspired works of art. The fathers of Homer and Hesiod are forgotten, whereas Homer and Hesiod live for as long as their poems are read, and even for as long as it is remembered that they were once read. In a strange but real sense the inanimate poem is more alive than the animate descendant of the poet. Nevertheless, if being or enduring is dependent upon being known, then the being of a poem is finally dependent upon the living audience. The source of the poet's immortality is not in his poem, but in the opinion of the audience; if the poet wishes to endure, he must consult the taste of the audience. It is all very well to say that great works of art create their own audience. Taste is still variable; if fame is the spur, the artist has no assurance that his works will stand the test of time. In seeking to please his contemporaries, he may offend their descendants; yet if he does not please his contemporaries, he may never become known to their descendants. This is especially the case since Agathon stresses youth or innovation: the young flee from the old. Eros hates old age. Agathon's principle does not permit even the consolation of believing that one will continue to exist as a memory. The narcissism of youth precludes the development of spiritual history.

There is then a contradiction between perpetual youth and immortality (except for Agathon, teacher of the one true doctrine which must be preserved: Agathon is the sole tyrant of all other, virtually anonymous men). Continuous rebirth is at the same time continuous death. And indeed, one dies in the very moment of being applauded. If Agathon is a narcissist so too are the 30,000 Athenians; each is a mirror for the other. The Athenians do not applaud Agathon but Eros, who appears momentarily in his words. They are applauding themselves as brought momentarily to life, made young and splendid by the Eros of drama. Time, the middle term between youth and innovation, is thus the same as cosmic war. The replacement of one

novelty by another is a hard rather than a soft exchange. The ultimate victory of the hard is already prefigured by the very
formulation of delicacy and elegance. It is not the beautiful but
the fit that survive, a process that leads to the identification of
the fit as the beautiful. War rather than peace is the condition
of beauty. The young are by nature warriors; peace is for the
old. The very idea of technē is that of mastery: a bending of
things to one's will. Thus in an absolute sense Agathon is wrong
to close his discussion of Eros' wisdom by mentioning only the
peaceful arts, although his teaching forces him to do so.

While Prometheus is said to have taught the arts to man, Agathon makes Eros the teacher of both man and gods. In fact he
emphasizes the gods who were Eros' students, naming five examples. Of man he says simply that Eros' tutelage brings fame.
And yet by not naming any great artists he reveals the difference between human and divine glory. The gods are visible in
a way that men, who dwell in the shadows of time, can never be.
To the extent that man becomes truly poetic, or is possessed by
Eros, his visibility as an individual is obscured by the light of
the god, who is identical in Agathon's fantasy with himself.
Agathon is the only man to achieve genuine immortality, and
he is a god. He would undoubtedly wish us to think that the
five pupils of Eros must be his own pupils, in the sense that he
has explained the nature of their achievement as no one else
has ever done:

> Apollo discovered archery, medicine and divination un-
> der the guidance of desire and love, so that he may be
> called a pupil of Eros; and the Muses are so in music,
> Hephaestus in the blacksmith's art, Athena in that of the
> loom, and Zeus in the government of gods and men.
> (197a6–b3)

Eryximachus attributes the founding of medicine to Asclepius, "as the poets say, and I agree" (186e2–3). But neither of
the two poets present says so. Aristophanes makes Zeus the chief
surgeon and Apollo his assistant; Agathon gives credit to Apollo
for the discovery of medicine. Both poets correct Eryximachus,

but Agathon corrects Aristophanes as well. Again, Eryximachus mentions the art of divination, which he says is concerned with "friendship between gods and men" (188d1). But he makes it a branch of medicine and so of the art of Asclepius. Aristophanes attributes the power of divination to the psyche, where it is the result of the operation performed by Zeus and Apollo (192d1–2). Agathon mentions only Apollo as the master of divination, thereby transforming it into a divine rather than a human property. Finally, Eryximachus does not mention the technē of archery, but he does allude to a bow in his central image of the harmony of disharmonies. Here, however, the reference is to Heraclitus, a man rather than a god (187a3 ff.). Aristophanes is silent about archery and the bow, perhaps because they symbolize the specific function and independent status of Apollo, whom he wishes to subordinate to Zeus.

Aristophanes emphasizes the predominance of Zeus by making Apollo, the second most powerful Olympian, his assistant.[66] Agathon, although he recognizes Zeus as the master of government, restores individuality to Apollo. He shows the prominence of Apollo in three ways. He is the first of Eros' five divine pupils to be mentioned; whereas the others are each assigned one art, Apollo is given three; Apollo's arts identify him as the god of the whole individual. Medicine tends to the body and divination to the psyche. Zeus, by way of contrast, is assigned only the art of government, which has as its proper object the health or completeness of the city (or community of gods) rather than of the individual. Furthermore, whereas Ares, or the art of war, is not mentioned, archery comes close to representing the individual manifestation of what is itself a political function. One might almost dare to suggest that in Agathon's speech the bow of Apollo represents the harmony between the disharmony of body and psyche. However this may be, Apollo, the sun-god, the god of purity and the lyre, exemplifies the connection between visibility and poetry.[67] In the next chapter we

66. Cf. Otto, *Götter*, p. 62: "Apollon ist neben Zeus der bedeutendste griechische Gott . . ."

67. There is also a connection between Heraclitus, Apollo, and perpetual

shall also see the close connection between Socrates and Apollo. In emphasizing the god of the lyre, Agathon not only underlines the fact that he is the champion of human individuality, but he also challenges Socrates to a war of music and prophecy.

Agathon distinguishes between Apollonian divination and the song of the Muses because he wishes to draw a distinction between the perfection of the individual and that of the city. Eryximachus also distinguished between music and divination, but for him divination deals with bodies, as music in itself does not. The prominence of Apollo is meant to suggest the possibility of transcending the body, and thereby the city, through the divination of poetry. If divination is connected to bodies, then the prophet, in discovering the "will" of the gods, is actually discovering the behavior of the physical cosmos. He discovers the regular order of motion, or the rule of Necessity (rather than the rule of free will), and it is upon this that the universal effectiveness of technē is founded. For Agathon, on the other hand, divination means the perception of the rule of Eros as poet, in the sense that a teacher always rules his students. Eros is the master Sophist who rules by persuasion; his rhetoric is the principle of freedom. The man whose psyche is touched by Eros is free because he can bend others to his will. Men are persuaded by beautiful innovations.

The Olympians, especially Zeus, owe their rule to the poets.[68] According to the teaching of Agathon, the poets are the real legislators of gods and men: the rule of Zeus is the rule of Eros. But here too, Agathon preserves the distinction between the private and the public. It is not Eros but Zeus who sits upon the throne, and his reign is one of peace:

> In that way also the affairs of the gods were [peacefully] arranged when Eros was born—doubtless of the beautiful (κάλλους) since there is no Eros for the ugly. Before that, as I said in the beginning, many terrible things

youth. Cf. Diels, *Vorsokratiker*, *1*, 157, Fr. 6: ὁ ἥλιος . . . νέος ἐφ᾽ ἡμέρηι ἐστίν . . .

68. 2.53. Cf. S. H. Rosen, "Herodotus Reconsidered," *Giornale di Metafisica, 18* (1963).

came into being among the gods, as is reported, through the rule of Necessity. But when this god was born, all good things (πάντ' ἀγαθά) came to be, both among gods and men, through love of beautiful things. (197b3–9)

The birth of Eros is at the same time the end of the rule of Necessity. Necessity is associated with the cosmic wars or catastrophes of the Uranian age. The rule of Necessity is the rule of the body.

Although in one sense the motions of bodies are orderly, it is an aspect of their order that bodies collide and decompose. Disorder is implicit in corporeal order, and therefore the rule of the body means a reign of war. A necessary order is necessarily disorderly, because corporeal Necessity is blind or unconscious. But the free order of the psyche banishes the ugliness of disorder; the poet exercises his will in arranging the parts of his poem as beautifully as possible. Order is peace, and beauty is order; hence the love of beauty is also a striving after peace. The order of the physical cosmos is an inferior presentiment of the order of poetry. Poetry may imitate cosmic order, but the imitation, as the product of divine intelligence freed from the necessity of matter, is superior to the original. The love of beauty or peace is therefore the source of all good things: goodness is a consequence of beauty. We need not repeat the defects of this conclusion; suffice it to say here that Agathon is silent about the parents of Eros. No criterion is given for the preservation of the rule of Eros, or for the preservation of the superiority of the psyche to the body. The origin of poetry cannot suffice to transform the cosmos into a poem. If the wisdom of Eros is persuasion, it is not merely a rhetorical persuasion. Eros rules by means of the necessity of the body rather than by dissolving it. This is perfectly clear from the examples which Agathon himself gives. His argument thus suffers from an internal contradiction. He believes that Eros can rule the whole by persuasion, but the capacity to persuade is based upon the Necessity that the rule ostensibly overcomes. And the rule is over the whole, but half the kingdom is left to its own devices.

The Peroration

The wisdom of Eros is a self-delusion, or what Socrates calls in the *Republic* the lie in the psyche. Now Agathon introduces his peroration, in which he is carried away by self-delusion, with an illustration of Eros' power. Overcome by poetic inspiration, he sings of Eros as the one who makes

> peace among men, and calm stillness upon the sea, a bed for the winds, and sleep in mourning. (197c5–6)[69]

Some scholars have been puzzled by "the reversion to human κῆδος after mentioning waves and winds."[70] There is, however, an obvious explanation. Agathon's verse has four phrases: the two in the middle refer to Eros' power over nature, and they are surrounded by references to his power over men. The psyche is able to contain the force of nature. Much more puzzling is the fact that, although Agathon links gods and men throughout his speech,[71] when he is moved to poetry the gods are replaced by nature. Perhaps we may detect here the irony of Plato, who inspires Agathon to prophesy the real consequences of his interpretation of Eros.

The verse and the balance of the peroration emphasize the delicate peacefulness of Eros, but there are one or two jarring notes. Thus at 197d8 Agathon says that Eros is "careless of the bad," which implies a languorous magnanimity but in fact reveals the breach in Eros' kingdom. At 198e1 Agathon calls Eros the "best soldier," an attribute which is apparently evoked in times of fear (197d8). A still more important point is Agathon's claim that Eros is "visible to" or "contemplated by the wise" (197d5). The word for theory or contemplation is related to the word "theater." We see the gods and heroes on the stage in the splendor of their beauty, a splendor which is inseparable

69. See Bury's note for difficulties in the punctuation and reading of Agathon's verse. Bury does not comment on the curious fact that both κοίτη and κῆδος have sexual meanings.

70. See previous note.

71. As Hug observes at 197e4.

from their universal significance or function. The hero in a play is not an abstract concept but, like the Platonic Idea, universal and particular.[72] Agathon is concerned with the particularity rather than the universality of beauty. It is his beauty which illuminated the vision of 30,000 Greeks; it is his beauty which shines forth in the innovations of his tragedies. Since Agathon is unwilling to surrender himself to the universality of Eros, he does not understand the full import of his own poems.

The *Symposium* begins and ends with the theme of corporeal Eros. Eros acts primarily through the force of beauty. Beauty is more visible than goodness or truth, just as the body is more visible than the psyche. It is possible to feel the attraction of beauty while remaining indifferent to truth and goodness; hence nature has employed the impulse toward the beautiful to guarantee the continuation of the race. For the most part, we obey the exhortation of Agathon that

> It is necessary for every man to follow [Eros], singing beautifully of him, and sharing (μετέχοντα) in the ode which he sings, charming the mind of all gods and men. (197e3–5)[73]

Instead of participating mentally in the Ideas, we share in the song that charms our thoughts away. If Eros is simply beauty, then its power lies simply in persuasion. Such an Eros is a master Sophist. Strangely enough, in this situation, the body rather than the psyche provides us with a constant or natural base in the midst of flux. The Eros of the body operates by Necessity. Agathon wishes to dissolve the rule of Necessity in order to give complete freedom to persuasion. The sophistic Eros can then persuade us of the beauty of anything at all— even of the ugly, the base, and the false.

72. Cf. Aristotle's famous judgment that poetry is more philosophical than history: *Poetics* 1451b5 ff. (The names of both Agathon and Alcibiades appear in conjunction with this passage.)

73. This is a softening of Hesiod, *Theogony* 120 ff.

CHAPTER SEVEN

❧ SOCRATES AND DIOTIMA ❧

Visibility and Invisibility

As we approach the most difficult section of the *Symposium*, it seems prudent to reflect upon the long and complex journey that has already been completed. Were this reflection to take the form of a mere summary of conclusions, it would be false to the very spirit of Platonic dialectic. A dialogue is the articulation of a question into a family of questions; it asks more than it tells, both of us and of the themes under discussion. In this sense a Platonic dialogue may be compared to a great poem or to a fruitful set of mathematical axioms. No description of the poem or axiom-set is equivalent to what each contains or implies. There is no substitute for the concrete work of analysis and speculation, as governed by an accurate grasp of the most minute particulars. Nevertheless, we must be sure that the particular deductions and analyses are coherent steps in the gradual unfolding of the central question of the dialogue. In gaining a synoptic vision of the first six sections of the *Symposium*, we may try to acquire a general perspective on the nature of the Platonic dialogue, provided that we are not deluded into regarding such a perspective as equivalent to the study of the dialogues in detail.

With this qualification, I risk the observation that every dialogue is the result of a "dialectic" between intuition and discursive reason. Dianoetic logos is not fully adequate to the content of noetic vision: the psyche is open to and tends toward the Ideas, but it also obscures them.[1] To some students of Plato,

1. For the similarity between Plato and Heidegger on this issue, as well as the difference between them, cf. S. H. Rosen, "Heidegger's Interpretation of Plato," *Journal of Existentialism* (1967).

this leads to an insoluble *aporia* and finally to the split between the two worlds of Ideas and things.[2] In my view the aporia may be overcome by a more careful consideration of the dialogue as a third or unifying element which is not reducible to pure intuition or discursive speech. Within the dialogues themselves this third or unifying element is given different forms, depending upon the context. In the *Symposium* the form of the bond is Eros. Eros is one of the daimons, and certainly one of the most important forms assumed by the divine principle of mediation between the lifeless Ideas and the mindless motion of matter or the spatio-temporal "receptacle." As the prime example of the daimonic in the *Symposium*, Eros corresponds to the harmony of opposites which came to light in the speech of Eryximachus. One may go so far as to say that Eros is the light of each speech in the *Symposium*, provided we remember that Eros is polymorphous perverse, and so not necessarily self-sufficient. There is, in other words, more than one daimon.

Every speech within the *Symposium* attempts to make something visible, or as visible as theoretical and practical circumstances will allow. Phaedrus and Pausanias are concerned with the visibility of deeds, Phaedrus almost entirely in terms of self-interest and Pausanias more from the viewpoint of style. Eryximachus' central theme is the visibility of the body, and Agathon's the visibility of the psyche. Socrates pursues the visibility of beauty in itself. Diotima makes visible the mysteries of Eros, and Alcibiades those of the nature of Socrates. Even Aristodemus, virtually invisible throughout the dialogue, has the task of making visible the speeches and deeds of the banquet. This leaves us with the gods, and brings us to the speech of Aristophanes. Aristophanes' intention sets him in opposition to all other spokesmen in the dialogue. He reveals the gods, or makes visible the speech of Zeus, whose message is that men

2. This is the interpretation to which Plato has been submitted by modern German philosophy through Nietzsche and Heidegger. It has been widely influential among scholars as well. Ultimately, of course, it goes back to Aristotle's formulation of the "separateness" of the Ideas.

must be content with invisibility. As the most radical opponent to rational speech or philosophical investigation, Aristophanes teaches that the revelation of divine speech obscures rather than enlightens man's mind.

Socrates, on the contrary, although not simply a spokesman for enlightenment, is engaged in a reconstitution of religion in order to preserve both philosophy and political virtue. The daimonic Eros (whether alone or through the assistance of a further divine gift[3]) directs man's thought toward beauty in itself rather than toward the Olympians. At the same time, however, Eros as a daimon is an emissary of the divine, which therefore sanctions the enterprise of philosophy. By turning reason toward the divine, Eros attempts to make peace between men and gods. Philosophy is presented in the *Symposium* not as a sophistic revolt against the Olympians, but as a divinely sanctioned and directed employment of psychic hybris. The question of the philosophical significance of "divine" is thus obscured to a considerable extent by a reconciliation with religion. The speech of Diotima is a poetic mixture of visibility and invisibility.[4]

The Eros of Diotima's teaching, as the striving for completeness or immortality, is not a simple, unilinear phenomenon. It leads us both toward the gods and the Ideas,[5] which could be identified only at the price of excluding life from the cosmos or, equally erroneously, by making the Ideas living.[6] The bridge between life and the Ideas is represented in the *Symposium* by the theme of beauty. In man's daily existence the power of the beautiful is immediately perceptible, as the power

3. *Phaedrus* 244a6 ff.

4. A failure to consider Diotima's speech within the specific context of the dialogue as a whole leads an otherwise acute interpreter like Neumann (in *Diotima*) to oversimplify the structure of her teaching. He dwells upon the "selfish" aspects of Diotima's conception of divinity, without considering the "impersonal" nature of the divine, or the general consequences of the fact that Eros squanders his possessions.

5. The Ideas are not mentioned in the *Symposium;* as for "beauty in itself," I shall return to it at the end of this chapter. Still, there can be no doubt that, according to Diotima, Eros points us toward the Ideas.

6. Hoffmann, *Symposion,* pp. 24–25, commits this error.

of the true and the good is not.[7] Within the flux of existence, the power of the beautiful not only endures but is itself the cause of the perpetuation of human existence. As such, the beautiful comes to be regarded as the direct presence of the divine in man and the cosmos. The orderly and regular is beautiful because it endures the flux of genesis; it remains visible in the midst of decay and obscuration. It is the light by which we are able to see the decaying and the obscure.[A]

That which both endures and is the cause of endurance, that which itself shines forth and illuminates all else in the splendor of its light, is the divine.[8] Both religion and philosophy originate in the recognition that beauty is divine. But the manner in which philosophy recognizes the divinity of beauty differs in principle from that of religion. The main business of the *Symposium* is precisely this difference as it is expressed in human rather than abstract terms. This means that the full nature of the difference is not expressed, except obliquely. For that matter, no human speech can ever be complete, but speeches are incomplete in various ways. The *Symposium* speaks in the philosophical idiom of poetry, as the dialect which is appropriate to beauty. Poetry, however, is speech which communicates partly through silence: it means more than it explicitly says. Unlike prose, poetry intends to be silent as it speaks.

There are at least three different kinds of poetry in the *Symposium*. Aristophanes speaks for the traditional or Olympian religion of the city. The poetry of Agathon is an attempt to transform traditional religion into a religion of poetry. The poetry of Aristophanes is a defense of justice; Agathon is unconcerned with justice and attempts to usurp the prerogatives of philosophy. Socratic poetry, however, is designed to give justice to both philosophy and poetry. As the dispenser of justice, it must be free from the obsession with novelty that super-

7. Cf. E. Hoffmann, *Platon* (Zürich, 1950), p. 95 and *Phaedrus* 250b1 ff.
8. For a recent survey of the almost complete diversity of scholarly interpretations of Plato's conception of θεός, cf. G. François, *Le polythéisme et l'emploi au singulier des mots* Θεός, Δαίμων (Paris, 1957), pp. 295 ff.

sedes respect for the fitting or due. In other words, it is not poetry in the usual sense but what we may call inspired religious or even erotic musical [9] speech. This kind of speech is adequate to build the bridge of beauty between the living and lifeless dimensions of the divine. But the bridge which it builds reflects the mixture of visibility and invisibility in poetic speech.

That is, dialectic as "measurement according to kinds" occurs within a horizon of experience that cannot be reduced to the sum of those kinds. To measure is to divide; wholeness must precede measurement. Since measurement is a necessary component of complete vision, philosophy shares the human limitation; like Moses it can point out, but not enter, the promised land. Man can never adequately or completely return to his origins. He can never achieve the unity which is the pre-condition for completeness. For fundamental human experience, the ground of unity, unifies in and through the activity of diversification. The very attempt to seek unity is at once a mark of incompleteness.[10] Plato accepts Aristophanes' claim that man is divided by nature but adds that philosophy, or reflection upon what division implies, is the only medicine for man's wounds.

Philosophy is like a doctor who knows which salves or drugs to apply to the various afflictions from which man suffers. Man can never be whole, well, or wise without a vision of the unity which expresses itself as diversity. But as a result of that expression of diversity, he can never entirely obtain such a vision, and certainly not by a repudiation of diversity. The ultimate purpose of the dialogues is to present man's complex fate in terms of philosophy's inference from its own incompleteness. The dialogues are the counterpart to the just city of the *Republic*: the wishes of those who love wisdom. A wish has something in common with a game or a daydream, to use the phrases which Socrates frequently applies to his own words. But the dreams of philosophers are dreamt while they are fully awake. Compared to the dialogues, wakefulness or reality is but a

9. *Phaedrus* 248d3 ff.
10. Cf. *Phaedrus* 248b1 ff. The psyches lose their wings in the struggle to see the hyperuranian *ousiai*.

dream. One could do worse than to define the dialogue-form with the words in which Agathon characterizes his encomium: "Let this my speech, O Phaedrus, be dedicated to the god, sharing in a proper amount of playfulness and earnestness, to the best of my capacity" (197e6–8).

Socratic Praise

Agathon's closing words are a challenge to Socrates and prepare us for the dialogue in which the men are about to engage. As Aristodemus observes, the audience applauds Agathon's performance as a fitting speech "about himself and about the god" (198a1–3); no objection is made to Agathon's hybris, of which the symposiasts, including Aristophanes, are connoisseurs. In a brief exchange with Eryximachus, Socrates responds to Agathon's challenge by claiming to be both afraid and a prophet. Eryximachus agrees that Socrates spoke prophetically in predicting Agathon's success; "but I do not believe that you will be at a loss" (198a3–10).[11] In claiming the mantic gift, Socrates speaks as a student of Diotima. This combination of male and female is necessary in order that Socrates may conquer the androgyne Agathon.[12] As we have already seen, Agathon's pederastic hybris, linked to the praise of poetry, makes him the appropriate mediator between the previous speakers and Diotima. Socrates' maieutic technē [13] is the political surface of his erotic technē. Socrates subordinates himself to the nature of his interlocutor in the rhetorical form of his dialectic.

In the practice of safe rhetoric Socrates is passive or feminine. On the other hand he dominates his interlocutor through the power of refutation, which is thus akin to eristic or the mascu-

---

11. Rettig, *Symposion*, points out (p. 28) that Socrates' exchange with Eryximachus is in rhythm, and also that Eryximachus is closely associated with his father. Cf. *Phaedrus* 227a5, where Phaedrus mentions Acumenus to Socrates as "your and my comrade." Note also that Socrates' claim to mantic powers is not unusual. Cf. *Theaetetus* 142c5, *Phaedrus* 242c4, *Apology* 40a4.

12. Cf. Chapter 6, pp. 159–64 above.

13. *Theaetetus* 149a4–150c8; cf. *Symposium* 206c1 ff.

line art of war.[14] Socrates' Eros is "bisexual"; in political terms, it combines war and peace. The rhetorical seductiveness of Socrates is clear in the *Symposium* from the fact that he has more lovers than any other character,[15] including Agathon and Alcibiades, the two most beautiful men at the banquet. This seductiveness is the external or human expression of the hybristic psyche whose synoptic vision reconciles opposites in its fidelity to the divine harmony. Socrates, however, is a philosopher rather than a pederast. In the *Phaedrus* the philosophical or erotic madness is distinguished from both the prophetic and the poetic species: Socrates' Eros differs from that of both Diotima and Agathon.[16] Despite this difference, philosophy remains a divine gift; both the *Symposium* and *Phaedrus* show Plato's intention to reconcile or make peace between philosophy and religion.

The net result of all this is that Socrates' conquest of Agathon is at the same time an accommodation to his teaching. Poetry is needed for the establishment of peace between philosophy and religion. In his second dialogue with Agathon, Socrates will transform Agathon's principle that Eros abstracts from the ugly, into the teaching of Diotima. Diotima is not a thinly disguised Plato, but a purified Agathon, generated by the bisexual dialectic of Socrates. Instead of a womanly man, we are presented with a masculine woman, who dominates Socrates, prefers children of the psyche to those of the body, and herself aspires to synoptic vision.[17]

Socrates emphasizes the beauty and intricate construction of Agathon's speech as the cause of his fear that he will not be able to distinguish himself. More specifically, it is the peroration which he praises:

14. Cf. *Sophist* 225a6 ff. and S. H. Rosen, "Wisdom," *Review of Metaphysics,* *16* (December 1962), pp. 200–02. At *Sophist* 222d10, the *eidos* of the erotic technē is said to be the hunting of men by giving presents.

15. We are informed of Socrates' seductiveness when Aristodemus is called one of a number of Socrates' lovers.

16. *Phaedrus* 265a9 ff. This provides evidence for Neumann's distinction, not adequately documented by him, between Socrates' behavior and the Eros of Diotima (*Diotima,* p. 54).

17. Cf. 201e10, 202b10, 204b1, 207c2 ff., 209c7.

> Of course, the rest of the speech was not equally marvel-
> ous. But who would not have been astonished at hearing
> the beauty of the language and syntax toward the end?
> (198b3–5)

Socrates approves of the beginning, which raises his favorite question "what is . . . ?," and (more ironically) the end, but he rejects the middle of Agathon's speech, or its actual teaching. Still, the speech is "marvelous" and "astonishing"; the power of beautiful rhetoric functions by "stunning." It drives the listener out of his senses (198b5: ἐξεπλάγη), paralyzes his wits: in a word, it turns him to stone.[18] But one cannot think with stone wits; the attraction of beauty is somehow opposed to philosophy. At least this is true of Agathon's sophistic rhetoric, the rhetoric of Gorgias, which Socrates compares to the Gorgon's head.[19]

The comparison between Gorgias' rhetoric and the Gorgon's head (198b6–c5) refers us to Homer.[20] Odysseus is sent by Circe to Hades in order to confer with Tiresias, the blind prophet "whose mind is steadfast still," the sole shade in possession of reason (νόος). Tiresias will tell Odysseus the journey he must follow and the risks he must run on his way home.[21] After his consultation with the prophet, Odysseus has a number of encounters, the last with Heracles; these are interrupted by the "marvelous song" of the gathering dead. Odysseus is seized with terror "lest the Gorgonic head of a terrible monster" be sent by Persephone from the house of Hades. Once again Socrates compares himself to Odysseus, and Tiresias reminds us of the approaching confrontation with Diotima. Socrates, however, is not simply in the same situation as Odysseus.

Odysseus has somewhere to go, namely, to his wife and home in Ithaca. But Xanthippe is no Penelope, nor is Socrates a

18. Cf. Chapter 6, n. 32 above.
19. Perhaps it is true of philosophy as well. Cf. W. J. O'Neill, *Proclus' Alcibiades I* (Hague, 1965), p. 18. He says that Eros leads toward beauty and dialectic toward the good.
20. *Odyssey* 11.632.
21. Ibid., 10.492–5, 538–40.

homesick prince. There is a homelessness about philosophy, a detachment from the city which is essentially alien to the wily Odysseus. Having "somewhere to go," Odysseus does not wait to confront the Gorgon's head but flees from Hades. Socrates, on the other hand, remains, and is not turned to stone. He does not suffer from the voicelessness of the severed humans in the speech of Aristophanes, when Hephaestus asks them the purpose of their erotic striving.[22] Socrates' fear is a reminder that he is in the midst of enemies. The war between Socrates and the other speakers may be stated in terms of the analogy between the city and the body. Socrates' predecessors are all insufficiently daring; the principle of the gratification which each seeks is the body rather than the psyche. By failing to go beyond the body,[23] the previous speakers are in the end prisoners of the rhetoric of the city. The "visibility" which each praises is inseparable from the public audience. If truth is "presence" or "visibility," each defines truth relative to public taste or custom: the wits of each are turned to stone by custom.

The popular method of encomium is to attribute qualities to one's subject which will be praised by the audience, whether or not the attributes are true. Socrates bluntly repudiates this method, along with his agreement to join the others in praising Eros, as absurd:

> For I in my silliness supposed it necessary to speak the truth about each thing being praised, and that on this basis, one would select the most beautiful aspects of the thing and arrange them in the most seemly manner. I was presumptuous enough to think that I would speak well, since I knew the truth about how to praise anything. (198c5–d7)[24]

22. 192d1: οὐ δύνατοι εἰπεῖν, ἀλλὰ μαντεύεται.

23. Cf. *Republic* 509b9: ἐπέκεινα.

24. See Bury's note to 198d7: some scholars bracket τοῦ ἐπαινεῖν ὁτιοῦν and understand something like περὶ τοῦ ἔρωτος in its stead. My general impression is that the text should remain unaltered. Plato frequently writes something unexpected or bold as an important clue to his meaning. With Socrates' view of the proper method for praise, cf. Aristotle, *Rhetoric* 1358b27; epideictic rhetoric is concerned with τὸ καλὸν καὶ τὸ αἰσχρόν and not with justice or injustice.

The correct method of praise is to speak the truth; Socrates hybristically accuses his predecessors of lying. But still more important, he does not advocate telling the whole truth, but only the beautiful aspects of the truth.[25] And even these should be arranged in the most "seemly" manner. The truth then is the foundation of the encomium but not entirely visible in the superstructure. Beauty thus seems to result from an appropriate suppression of aspects of the truth.

The preceding disjunction between beauty and truth suggests that true encomium is not merely the same as a true speech. Praise is truly beautiful when it is so constructed as to make visible to an audience as much of the truth as it is able to perceive. The "whole" truth would then be beautiful only to him who can see it as it is. To the nonphilosopher the whole truth would be ugly rather than beautiful.[26] Thus philosophical is distinguished from sophistic encomium by its dual allegiance to the truth and by the capacity of the audience. The Sophist praises only what he believes the audience will find praiseworthy, regardless of its truth or virtue. Socrates identifies himself as a philosopher by claiming to know the truth about how to praise anything at all. In so doing he does not entirely disavow all the techniques of the Sophist.

The need to praise Eros thus leads Socrates to contradict his famous claim to know nothing but his own ignorance. Knowledge of the bond between men and gods entails knowledge of both men and gods.[27] Again, Eros is the daimonic capacity of the psyche; Socrates claims to know the psyche, and thereby to possess knowledge of the whole.[28] In both the *Symposium* and

25. Isenberg, *Order*, p. 45, notices that Socrates advocates omitting the ugly in praise. He understands this to mean that praise must come as close as possible to Being. But if a thing is ugly, and one suppresses that fact, how can one approach its Being?

26. Consider *Phaedrus* 267c7 ff. The rhetorician Thrasymachus excels at beguiling the multitude, as Socrates, in other words, does not. With this, cf. *Sophist* 229a3; and *Phaedrus* 269e1 ff., especially 270b1, where rhetoric is compared with medicine, should be compared to *Sophist* 228a4 ff.

27. For a parallel series of passages, cf. *Phaedrus* 228a5 ff., 229e5, 270c1 ff.

28. Cf. Gaiser, *Ungeschriebene*, p. 25: the psyche, like the objects of mathematics, exhibits the whole; mathematical structure and psychic capacity are two aspects of one and the same thing.

Phaedrus this claim is associated with prophecy or divine in-spiration. Eros is not the same as prophecy, but both are species of divine madness.[29] As one would expect from the *Symposium,* the *Phaedrus* exhibits the "madness" of the philosopher.[30] To summarize: the psyche is mantic, but it is also philosophical or erotic.[31] The madness of the psyche, already a gift from the gods, is the link between religion and philosophy. The apparent contradiction between Socratic knowledge and ignorance can be restated in these terms. Philosophy, as the pursuit or love of knowledge, is ignorance. But one cannot pursue that of which he is altogether ignorant. Prophecy is that aspect of the divine madness which allows us to surmise what we seek to know. The disjunction between intuition and discursive reason is bridged by the mantic art, which expresses the link between the human and cosmic psyche.

Socrates' knowledge of erotics is then a divine madness, from which it does not follow that he has knowledge of divine mad-ness itself. The difference between knowledge and madness is parallel to that between explanation (giving a logos) and praise. A mathematical determination of the formal structure of an entity is by itself insufficient basis for the decision as to whether the entity is praiseworthy. In condemning the previous encomia of Eros as rooted in opinion and appearance, Socrates in effect compares them to "moving logoi" (198e2–199a3).[32] A true logos, however, "stands still" in its exhibition of the unchanging form it describes. Moving logoi are in fact mythoi. But this criticism of his predecessors in no way implies that Socrates can himself furnish a logos of either psyche or Eros. In fact, the Platonic dialogues give ample reason to doubt the possibility of such a

29. *Phaedrus* 265a9 ff.

30. Ibid., 249c6–d2 (where madness and philosophy are linked to language of mysteries and initiation, reminiscent of the *Symposium*). Cf. 257a7, 266b3–c1. That philosophy is not simply a form of madness or enthusiasm, is indicated at 263d1.

31. Ibid., 242c3, c7: μαντικόν γέ τι καὶ ἡ ψυχή. At *Republic* 499b7–c2, Socrates says that the Eros of the true philosopher comes ἔκ τινος θείας ἐπιπνοίας. For a criticism of prophecy, cf. *Philebus* 71e1 ff., *Timaeus* 71d3–e2.

32. He says that the speakers πάντα λόγον κινοῦντες, and they attribute the results to Eros.

logos. We must be content here with a sampling of the evidence. According to the *Phaedrus*, "all psyche is immortal." [33] The proof offered for this proposition, whatever one may say about its merits, is followed shortly by this remark about the psyche's "form" or "nature" (ἰδέα) "what sort it is, is altogether a divine matter and a long account [i.e. one which only a god could tell]; but as for what it resembles, that is a human and a shorter affair" (246a3–6). Socrates then introduces his "likeness" of the charioteer and the two horses. In the course of this mythos, he says:

> as for the immortal, we cannot give an account of it in any logos, but since we can neither see nor grasp mentally god in an adequate way, we imagine him to be somehow immortally alive . . . (246c6–d1)[34]

Psyche as independent of the body is virtually identified as god in this difficult passage. But the main point for our purpose is clear enough: there is no logos of the psyche. Essentially the same view is present in the *Phaedo*. Students of this dialogue seem to agree that the proofs for the immortality of the psyche prior to Socrates' "hypothesis" of the Ideas are either incomplete or not altogether seriously meant.[35] At 80e2 ff. Socrates unmistakably makes immortality contingent upon the previous practice of philosophy. This passage may be said to prepare us for the hypothesis of the Ideas. As the term indicates, and as Socrates expressly warns,[36] a proof which is dependent upon such a hypothesis is necessarily incomplete until the hypothesis has been "discharged." [37] Such a proof cannot be called a logos

---

33. 245c5: ψυχὴ πᾶσα ἀθάνατος. For the ambiguity of this sentence and the following passage, cf. Hackforth, *Phaedrus*, pp. 64 ff. and Stenzel, *Zwei Begriffe*, p. 15.

34. Cf. *Timaeus* 26e4: . . . τό τε μὴ πλασθέντα μῦθον ἀλλ' ἀληθινὸν λόγον εἶναι. The imagination is associated with myth, not with logos.

35. Especially interesting in this connection are Socrates' remarks at 77e and 91a, where he says that the fear of death, which is childish, must be "charmed" away, and that he is behaving unphilosophically or trying to persuade without considering the true facts. Cf. R. S. Bluck, *Plato's Phaedo* (London, 1955), p. 20.

36. *Phaedo* 107b5.

37. Bluck, who thinks that Plato regarded the proof as decisive, himself com-

in the technical sense unless we raise doubts as to the status of all logoi.[38]

Finally, we may refer to Timaeus of Locri, who tells his interlocutors and audience that we must first distinguish between "what is always and has no genesis, and . . . what always becomes but never is." Timaeus adds that "what can be grasped by noetic intuition together with a logos is always in the same way."[39] If we apply this passage to the *Symposium*, it is evident that there can be no logos of Eros, which perpetually comes to be and passes away. Accounts of what is not steadfast, certain, and evident can be not logoi but images or likely myths; and this, according to Timaeus, is true "concerning many things, [such as] the gods and the genesis of the whole."[40] The *Phaedrus, Phaedo,* and *Timaeus* all teach us that it is impossible to grasp the immortal and divine by means of logos. But the *Timaeus* joins the gods to genesis, and so places them outside the domain of the steadfast and unchanging.[41] This is compatible with the *Symposium*, at least so far as psyche and Eros are concerned. It seems to be in disagreement with the *Phaedrus,* in which immortality is linked to perpetual motion.[42] In either case, however, psyche is not susceptible to logical determination.

For the present at least, we may leave it open whether the psyche has a form in the sense of an Idea. Its internal motion requires an account that is also moving. The real defect of the speeches before that of Socrates is not that they were moving, but that they were moving in the wrong direction.[43] The principle of the motion in the speeches at the banquet is Eros, and

pares the passage with *Republic* 509d ff. I agree with him that the hypotheses are Ideas, and not existential propositions.

38. The parallel passage in the *Republic* is permeated with language of incompleteness and dependence upon metaphor. Cf Rosen. *Eros Repub,* n. 63.

39. *Timaeus* 27d5 ff.

40. Ibid., 29b3–d3.

41. Cf. 34b8: διὰ πάντα δὴ ταῦτα εὐδαίμονα θεὸν αὐτὸν ἐγεννήσατο.

42. 245c5: ἀεικίνητον. Cf. J. B. Skemp, *The Theory of Motion in Plato's Later Dialogues* (Cambridge, 1942), pp. 83, 88.

43. Cf. *Theaetetus* 206d1–5, where speech altogether is compared to flowing water. There is an anticipation here of the reality of motion, to be developed in the *Sophist*.

in itself, Eros has no form. Precisely if we regard it as desire of Ideas, it cannot be an Idea or an instance of an Idea. Eros is continuously coming to be and passing away; it is and is not at the same moment. A logos, however, is of something; it gives a determinate account of a particular being, work, or power.[44] To think, perceive, or speak is for Plato to think, perceive, or speak of a particular "something." [45] The "whatness" of a "something" is granted to it by its form, which in turn arises from the interwovenness of Ideas; and it is of this "whatness" that we speak in rational logoi.[46] Whatever may be the case with psyche, Eros is not merely moving but is formless; hence the extraordinary difficulty in speaking about it at all. Little wonder that recourse to prophecy is necessary!

Phaedrus, we may recall, is said to be the "father of the logos." With the single exception of Aristophanes, the previous speakers err in attempting to construct a logos about Eros. It is therefore "just" for Socrates to break his promise to share in the common method of encomium. At the same time, the problem implicit in Socrates' claim to tell the truth (199a5), and in his deeper rivalry with Aristophanes, is shown by his quotation from Euripides of the notorious phrase, "my tongue promised, but not my mind." [47] In terminating the original covenant (177d6), or rectifying the injustice to which it led, Socrates must employ duplicity. By demanding permission to speak in his own way, Socrates invites the symposiasts to enter into a new covenant. The old covenant found its climax in the speech of Agathon; by grounding his speech in a dialogue with the defender of pure poetry, Socrates will try to transform the previous results into a more satisfactory common agreement (199a8–10: "in order that, having come to an agreement with Agathon, I can speak").

Socrates thus begins his second dialogue with Agathon by

44. *Republic* 438c6 ff., 476e7 ff., 477a9 ff. Cf. *Symposium* 194e4–195a3 with *Phaedrus* 237b6–d1.
45. *Theaetetus* 188e2 ff., *Sophist* 237d1, 237d6–8, 262a5.
46. *Sophist* 259e5; Oehler, *Noetischen*, pp. 74–79.
47. *Hippolytus* 612.

leading him back "to the hypothesis," [48] or the nature and function of Eros. Agathon began as though he were about to give a logos in the technical sense about "what sort of being Eros is, and next his work." [49] He ended by referring to his encomium as "my logos" (197e6). Agathon was right to wish to exhibit the nature of Eros but wrong to combine logos and poetry. Some other method for praising Eros must be employed. Agathon's speech was a poem or myth which pretended to be a logos: it was the speech of a Sophist.[50] And indeed, the problem of how to describe Eros, let alone praise it, is closely related to the problem of how to say what is not, or to attribute being to nonbeing.[51] Hence the connection between the teachings of the Sophists and speech about Eros.

A Digression on Incest

Socrates' initial formulation of the nature of Eros poses the fundamental problem of incest, albeit in so ambiguous a manner as to have led some scholars to emend the passage:

> I don't ask if Eros is [desire for] a mother or a father—
> for the question whether Eros is erotic desire for a
> mother or father would be laughable." (199d2 ff.)[52]

The surprising thing about a dialogue on Eros is not that it should contain references to incest, but that these references are infrequent and brief. Now that Socrates has at last mentioned the obvious, let us try to think through the dramatic and thematic significance of incest in the *Symposium*.

To begin with, why does Socrates say that incestuous desire

---

48. Cf. Xenophon, *Memorabilia* 4.6.13–15.

49. 199c3–d2: ὁποῖός τις ἐστιν and τὰ ἔργα αὐτοῦ. Cf. n. 44 above.

50. Cf. *Sophist* 239c4 ff.

51. Ibid., 241b1–2.

52. In his note to 199d, Bury discusses the various interpretations placed upon οὐκ εἰ μητρός τινος, and convincingly defends the explanation of Ast, which I have adopted: the genitive is objective and the reference is to the absurdity of incest. But Bury does not explain why incest should be mentioned here, nor why it is laughable rather than somber or frightening.

is laughable? The peculiarity of this judgment to a Greek audience, and especially to a tragic poet, should be evident from the *Oedipus* trilogy of Sophocles. Perhaps Socrates is obliquely criticizing the violent and somber manner in which incest is treated by the poets.[53] Or perhaps he means to suggest that the silence of the poets and rhetors thus far on the subject of incest is laughable to the philosopher. We know from the *Republic* that Socrates is willing to countenance incestuous love between brother and sister as a possible consequence of the community of women. He takes steps to prevent intercourse between parents and children, but the fact that he does so is a reminder that such erotic desire occurs by nature. Incest is similar to pederasty in that both are forbidden by nomos more than by nature; at least neither is forbidden by nature in the simplest and most obvious sense as derived from the body. Socrates, then, is franker and more daring than the ostensibly enlightened Sophists in his consideration of the connection between Eros and politics. The spokesmen for pederasty in the *Symposium* praise the pre-Olympian gods as part of their campaign to change the nomos, and this is related to their dependence upon the physical sciences. As is especially clear in the speeches of Pausanias and Eryximachus, the defense of pederasty as a natural appetite leads inevitably to a sanctioning of all appetites. Yet none of the pederasts dares to defend incest.

The speeches prior to that of Socrates are "laughable" because they are inconsistently cautious. Agathon, for example, said nothing about the nature of Eros' own genesis. Perhaps his silence was due to the fact that Eros must necessarily desire his beautiful, because divine, parents. Neither natural desire nor aesthetic perception militates toward the exclusion of incest. So far as science is concerned, there could be no genetic objections to pederastic incest, or the love of father and son. Why, we must repeat, are the pederasts so tactful? The answer lies in a fundamental limitation of their project to revise the nomos. They do not intend their criticism of old-fashioned morality to be an uprooting of the political foundations. Just as they do not

53. Cf. *Laws* 838c1 ff.

understand the anti-political consequences of their physical theory, neither have they attained to the transpolitical consequences of hybris. Sophistry is essentially a political enterprise designed to gain power and therefore to determine the meaning of "right" in accord with one's own tastes.[54] Since the whole project depends upon the existence of a city, one taste must be rigorously excluded because it endangers the city's existence.

The Sophists conceive of being as becoming, and of becoming as that which is visible to man. Power to coerce, whether via the body or psyche, is needed because genesis comes to be visible in different ways for different men. This mutability of the visible permits the most persuasive men to establish agreement or nomos in conformity with their own vision. The physics of flux serves as the basis for the interpretation of "visibility" as "appearance," and hence is intended to lead to dominance over, not destruction of, the city. This raises the theoretical problem which sophistry is in no position to resolve. If the mutability of the visible makes possible the persuasion of the many by the few, then there is a difference between the appearance of conformity (nomos) and the reality of flux or genesis (*physis*). One may perhaps doubt whether the Sophists were even aware of this problem. But there is no reason to doubt their awareness of the political importance of the prohibition against incest.

Incest is destructive of political life for at least two reasons. First, it makes the family self-sufficient, whereas the city arises from exogamy.[55] Second, the respect which children owe their parents is symbolic of the relationship between citizens and the mother city. If this distinction is bridged by sexual union, intimacy and passion—not to mention the viciousness of lust— must surely corrode the feeling of awe which is the condition for respect. Of course, it is a simple matter to conceive of special circumstances in which incest might be necessary. But general approval and encouragement of incest is politically even more

54. Cf. Chapter 6, n. 58 above.
55. Cf. S. Benardete, "Sophocles' Oedipus Tyrannus," in *Ancients and Moderns* (New York, 1964), p. 3.

unthinkable than the public or legal recognition of pederasty. The defense of pederasty, although logically linked to the defense of incest, requires a strict silence about the sanctity of the prohibition against incest.

Agathon's principle of continuous innovation expresses in human terms the generated character of reality, or the primacy of becoming. It comes close to furnishing a principle by which the difference between nomos and physis may be suppressed. Whether consciously or not, Agathon tries to avoid this consequence by distinguishing between beautiful or poetic and ugly or nonpoetic psyches. We have already noted that this distinction is highly unsatisfactory, since it amounts to a war between the soft and the hard. If the beautiful and soft psyches all become poets, each concerned with his own innovations, Agathon's audience will then consist of the hard, ugly, or nonpoetic psyches, who can scarcely be expected to appreciate and applaud him. Agathon's entire argument is "laughable" because it amounts to a defense of incest, or a love of one's own productions. The radical defense of poetry terminates in a necessary dissolution of the city or communal audience because it introduces the distinction between "mine" and "not mine" in its most radical form.[56] The defense of pederasty is at bottom a defense of like loving like, and so its root is narcissism: the love of self for self.

In place of this radical, incestuous narcissism, Diotima will substitute the selfless love of beauty in itself.[57] But this substitute is by no means free from peril. If man were altogether free of love of one's own, the city would be as completely destroyed as if he loved nothing but his own. A proper pursuit of what is best by nature requires an accommodation to the equally natural desire to regard one's own as best. There is, then, a fundamental ambiguity in "nature" as it is accessible to man. Nature includes both the "facticity" of genesis, and the ends by which facts are praised or condemned. Differently stated, nature includes both body and mind as the central and

56. Cf. *Republic* 462c4 ff.
57. See n. 4 above.

irreducible dualism of human existence. To be a man is to be divided against oneself, and so to be torn between love for what one has generated and what is best. The sexual perversion of incest is merely an external form of the inner or psychic desire to combine these two kinds of Eros, and so to achieve unity. We rightly fear incest because it is nothing less than the self-destructive aspect of the desire for divine perfection. But those who wish to be gods, or *causa sui,* must come to terms with, or laugh at, that fear.

Desire and Possession

Having laughed at incest, Socrates goes on to show that desire (ἐπιθυμία) is an attribute of Eros, directed toward what it does not possess (200a5–7).[58] If this is true, then Eros must be ugly rather than beautiful; hence Agathon's grudging acquiescence: "as seems likely" (200a8–b8). Socrates apparently inverts Agathon's teaching; in fact, he will accept its most outstanding feature. Let us pause for some preliminary observations about this most important step in the argument. If Eros is a desire for what one does not possess, it follows that what we desire erotically must itself be nonerotic. In the case of erotic love, we do not desire the erotic desire of the beloved, but rather (as Aristophanes showed) the satisfaction or completeness which is a consequence of, but not the same as, physical union. If Eros were the desire for Eros, it would be a striving for incompleteness or dissatisfaction. Those who condemn erotic love as intrinsically unsatisfying have divined something of the truth. In philosophical terms, the nonerotic character of the state of completeness is an image of the nonerotic character of the Ideas.

The same point may be made in terms of beauty. Erotic desire

58. Hug, *Symposion* 200a3, is mistaken in saying that Socrates' argument depends on a "von ihm als selbstverständlich vorausgesetzten Identifizierung der Begriffe ἐρᾶν und ἐπιθυμεῖν." In fact, Socrates clearly indicates that Eros has desires, not that it is desire simply. Note also the ambiguous sentence at 200a1–2 in which Socrates seems to warn Agathon to remember the consequences which we have just discussed.

for a beautiful body is desire for the beautiful as exhibited within the body, rather than for the body itself. Suppose now that one actually possesses, either through carnal union or physical proximity, the body of the beloved person or object. Presumably he will discover that physical possession is an inadequate form of ownership, thanks to the transience of bodies or the vagaries of time. If, however, the lover's desire may be transferred from the body to the instance of beauty reflected therein, his desire is itself transformed to admiration or friendship. Friendship, of course, may be a consequence of erotic gratification.[59] Even so, however, it is distinguishable from the desire which precedes such gratification. Friendship may be defined as that form of love in which there is no erotic desire for the friend, but a shared possession of desire for some other thing. More simply stated, friends love the same things; the affection they feel toward each other is like a possession rather than a desire because it arises from the recognition of shared love. When the objects loved are noetic rather than physical, the possession of or union with one's friend depends only upon the degree to which both may "see" the inexhaustible, indivisible, or universally accessible beloved.[60]

Friendship is higher than desire because it has attained its end. The object of friendly love is present to the lover in a way that cannot be dissolved into the past. Our friendship with a man does not properly cease with his death, and it is perfectly intelligible to speak of friendships in which both persons are dead. Of course one may object that death terminates consciousness of friendship, but this need not decrease the amount of satisfaction possessed by friends during their lives, provided they recognize that and how their friendship derives its shape and significance from what transcends time. In the case of a shared love for noetic entities, whether these be scientific laws,

59. Cf. *Phaedrus* 231b7–e2, 232e3–233a5, et passim. These passages show that Gould, *Love*, p. 144, incorrectly asserts: "In Plato's last years, however, the paler word for friendship, φιλία, seems once more to have replaced ἔρως, his word for friendship in the *Symposium* and *Phaedrus*." Eros does not mean *friendship* in any of the dialogues, nor is φιλία paler than ἔρως.

60. Cf. Aristotle, *Nichomachean Ethics* 1156b4 ff. (esp. 1156b19 ff.).

mathematical demonstrations, or Platonic Ideas, the transience of the friends is irrelevant to the certitude of their perception of the excellence of their beloved. And this certitude is possible even when perfect knowledge of the beloved is impossible. One may know that wisdom is superior to ignorance even if one is not himself wise.

The root of the difference between friendship and desire is therefore the difference between time and timelessness. If the latter difference does not obtain, neither does the former. Socrates develops this theme in terms of the difference between the future and the present. Whoever possesses any quality "at the present time" (ἐν τῷ παρόντι) cannot be said to desire it:

> Consider then, when you say this: "I desire what I possess at present (τῶν παρόντων)," whether you mean anything other than this, that "I want what I now have (τὰ νῦν παρόντα) to be present in the future" (καὶ εἰς τὸν ἔπειτα χρόνον παρεῖναι). (200b10–d6)

As in the case of time itself, each moment of desire is radically incomplete, other than itself, a striving or motion, a genesis. In Platonic language genesis is held together, and so kept moving, by the "intentional" structure of Eros, which strives for its completion or satisfaction through possession of or friendship with the noetic order.[61] In this sense the generated cosmos is "a moving image of eternity."[62] As so erotically constituted, genesis is midway between nonbeing and being.

Present desire is then implicitly oriented toward the future. But what of present possession, as in the example of friendship? The Greek phrase for "the present" (τὸ παρόν) contains the verb by which Plato designates the "presence" of formal properties

61. *Metaphysics* 1072b3. Cf. *Phaedo* 65c9.

62. *Timaeus* 37d3–7. Cf. Gould, *Love*, p. 122. W. Jaeger, *Aristotle* (Oxford, 1962), p. 142, commenting on *Laws* 898e and Aristotle's conception of the unmoved mover, says: "The bodiless soul of the third hypothesis is obviously a transcendental Form, moving the star as final cause, as the beloved moves the lover. It is the principle of the unmoved mover. The wonderful power of which Plato speaks may be imagined as similar to the longing of sensible things for the Idea, or to Aristotle's *orexis*."

in a nontemporal sense (παρουσία).[63] When a property is "present in" an entity, the entity "possesses" or "is" that property. Thus the visibility of the form is due to the presence of the appropriate Idea or Ideas. This presence or *parousia* of *ousia*, however, is not a desire for the future, or a present absence; if it were, the form would not be visible or identical to itself. There would be no entities.[64] One must therefore distinguish two senses of parousia, and in so doing it will be helpful to cite a passage from the *Timaeus* which refers to temporal units such as days, nights, months, and years:

> All these are parts of time; both "was" and "will be" are forms of time which have come to be, and in applying them incorrectly to the eternal ousia, we forget this. For we say that ousia was, is, and will be; but "is" alone (τὸ ἔστιν μόνον) belongs to it according to the true logos. . . . But that which possesses the same state forever immovably, cannot properly become older or younger through time, nor can it ever become so; it cannot have now become so, nor will it be so in the future. In general, nothing (belongs to it) of the things which genesis attaches to what is being borne along in sensation . . .[65]

The presence of a property in a form is not the same as the presence of the form to man. Ousia is present to itself or in itself, but it does not present itself to man in its entirety.[66] Differently stated, the mind to which form presents itself is part of a psyche, and so within the generated or temporal world. Even the *parousia* accessible to the gods is said by Socrates to occur "after a time," and the gods are part of the moving or

63. Cf. *Sophist* 247a5 and F. M. Cornford, *Plato's Theory of Knowledge* (New York, 1957), p. 233, n. 1. Also *Phaedo* 100d5.

64. For the use of οὐσία, see Ast, *Lex. Pl.*

65. *Timaeus* 37e4 ff. For a "Heideggerean" interpretation of Plato's distinction between the temporal and the timeless present, expressed in the idiom of "ordinary-language analysis," see G. E. L. Owen, "Plato and Parmenides on the Timeless Present," *The Monist*, 50 (July 1966).

66. *Phaedrus* 248a1 ff.

temporal world.[67] Even the "instantaneous" [68] noetic possession of the self-presentation of form or Ideas is bounded by the time which it momentarily transcends. It is like the instantaneous bloom of pleasure which completes human activity, or a whole which is and is not but never comes to be.[69]

The *Symposium* is devoted primarily to a consideration of the erotic nature of psyche. As I have tried to indicate in the preceding paragraphs, if Eros is equivalent to, or defines the essence of, psyche, then man can never possess but must constantly desire. This means that man is radically temporal, and among the consequences of such a condition, friendship in its various forms is impossible. But philosophy is one of the forms of friendship, as the name itself states. The erotic parousia is not intelligible in itself but only upon the basis of the non-erotic parousia as just described. The intentionality of desire is insufficient to determine apprehension in any degree of intelligible form, because for Plato mind or psyche does not generate these forms by the act of intending. In the passage presently under analysis, Socrates repeats the distinction between desire and possession several times, thus emphasizing its importance. But he retains the temporal framework of the discussion, as is appropriate to the dominance of Eros. In reading the *Symposium* we must also take into account what lies beyond its borders. It is a mistake to regard Eros as simply equivalent to philosophy. The absence of the eternal is a mark of the incompleteness of the teaching of the *Symposium*.

I have already explained the intentional incompleteness of the *Symposium* in terms of Socrates' desire to effect a rapprochement with Agathon. Let us return to the text:

> "Now besides this, recall those things which you said in your speech to be [the objects of] Eros. If you wish, I shall remind you. For I believe you said something like this, that the difficulties among the gods were resolved

67. Ibid., 247d1 ff.
68. I shall return to τὸ ἐξαίφνης at 210e.
69. Aristotle, *Nichomachean Ethics*, 1174b15 ff.

through love (ἔρωτα) of the beautiful. And you said that there could not be love (ἔρως) of the ugly. Didn't you say something like this?" "I did," said Agathon. "You speak properly, comrade," said Socrates. "And if this is so, will Eros be anything but love (ἔρως) of beauty, and not of ugliness?" Agathon agreed. "Is it not then agreed that he loves what he lacks and does not possess?" "Yes," he said. (201a2–b3)

The main point[70] of this crucial passage is as follows. The distinction made previously by Socrates between desiring and possessing leaves open the possibility that Eros is both presently beautiful and desirous of preserving his beauty in the future (cf. 200d3 ff). But Socrates states, as an inference from an immediately preceding question, and so as an indirect question: "So Eros is a lack of, and does not possess, beauty"; to which Agathon replies, "Necessarily." But there is no need for Agathon to agree to this strong conclusion, except in terms of his own teaching, to which Socrates is accommodating his argument. The separation of Eros from the possession of beauty is equivalent to the suppression of the eternal from the psyche. This means that Socrates is going to pursue the vision of beauty in itself by starting from the same total acceptance of genesis that defined the horizon of the previous speakers. More specifically, he begins by accepting Agathon's abstraction from the ugly. His two premises are thus those of poetry: continuous innovation and exclusive pursuit of beauty.

One could perhaps say that Socrates intends to show the superiority of philosophy to poetry on the basis of the ends of poetry itself. But it is more immediately important to insist upon the fact that the description of Eros which follows is an inadequate account of philosophy. In order to make peace with religion, it is necessary to exaggerate the poetic character of the philosophical enterprise. An exaggeration is not simply a lie but neither is it simply the truth. The necessary defect in

70. In his note to this passage, Bury changes λέγεις to ἔλεγες, thereby destroying part of the irony of the passage. Socrates makes use of Agathon's contention without actually affirming it himself.

writing about extremely complicated subjects is that one can discuss adequately only one aspect at a time. If we restrict our attention merely to the *Symposium,* the result is a distorted understanding of Plato's conception of philosophy. On the other hand, in order to obtain a rounded understanding of that conception, it is necessary to restrict our attention to the *Symposium* in the sense of concentrating our energies upon the task of grasping its meaning. The proper method for the interpretation of a Platonic dialogue is thus a continuous expansion and contraction of vision.

Young Socrates

Socrates is about to modify the position of Agathon by means of a recollection from his youth. As a young man Socrates resembled Agathon in believing that Eros is beautiful, but Diotima set him straight. We may prepare ourselves for the speech of Diotima by the following reflection. In the *Symposium* we are shown two stages in Socrates' career. The first or pre-Diotiman is in principle the same as the position of Agathon. According to Socrates, the second or post-Diotiman stage is merely a development of Agathon's position. As we have already seen in part, the irony of this claim is not restricted to the immediate need to correct Agathon politely. It is coextensive with the dialogue as a whole. Consequently the second stage in Socrates' career, or the teaching of Diotima, is not the final stage of Socrates' teaching as presented in the corpus of Platonic dialogues.[71] (I am of course referring to stages in the career of the "mythical" Socrates who is a persona in the Platonic dialogues; the point has nothing to do with "historical" development or the "historical" Socrates.)

Agathon's principle led to war rather than to peace. But if Eros is the desire for completeness, and the adjunct of synoptic vision, it must encompass the ugly as well as the beautiful, or somehow make peace between them. Just as the physician is concerned with disease and the judge with crime, so too the

71. Cf. note 16 above.

philosopher must be concerned with falsehood and "the thing which is not." The Eros of Agathon and Diotima could be said to desire the whole only through beautification of the ugly. But this is to distort the whole and so render it partial. Such a tendency seems to have characterized the young Socrates, as is suggested by the *Parmenides*, too. The aged Eleatic asks the young Socrates whether he believes that there are Ideas of "hair, clay, dirt, or any other least honorable and most trifling thing." [72] When Socrates expresses his doubts, and his fear that to assert such Ideas would be "to fall into a depth of drivel," he is chastized by Parmenides:

> "you are still young, Socrates," said Parmenides, "and philosophy has not yet taken hold of you as it will, in my opinion, when you will not dishonor these things. But now you still pay attention to the opinions of humans, because of your age."

Before his study with Diotima Socrates did not understand Eros. As a young man he was unable to distinguish between the beauty of Ideas and the ugliness of their spatio-temporal instances. He did not understand the intermediate zone, or the complex relations between the daimonic and the human in genesis.[73] The same can be said of the motives which led him to study the materialistic physics of Anaxagoras.[74] If we identify the intelligible with an essentially mathematical order of the physical cosmos, we render invisible the intermediate web of the daimonic-human. Socrates must have wished to associate beauty and purpose, or a hierarchy of ends, with respect to numbers, proportions, and forms, but without separating these from their physical instances. However, he was troubled by the baseness and ugliness of many of these instances. Apparently he later abandoned physical explanations and turned to definitions, a step intermediate between bodies and Ideas. He could then progress to an acceptance of the Idea of dirt without attribut-

---

72. *Parmenides* 130c5 ff.

73. Cf. Brumbaugh, *One*, p. 34.

74. *Phaedo* 96a6 ff. Cf. *Apology* 26d4: Meletus accuses Socrates of sharing Anaxagoras' view that the sun is stone and the moon is earth.

ing the beauty of the Idea to the dirt itself. Until then, he could not do justice to the whole.

The philosopher must neither scorn the ugly nor mistake it for the beautiful, but desire it as the way to the genuinely lovable or beautiful. At the same time, he must know how to make others desire the beautiful as well. This is the "political" counterpart to theoretically inflected desire. Within the limits of irony one may suggest that Socrates, as a relatively young man, was instructed in this art by another woman.[75] In the *Menexenus* Socrates tells us that his teacher in rhetoric is Aspasia, who also counts Pericles among her pupils.[76] Aspasia's role as mistress of Pericles is thus replaced by her function as master. In addition, she is said to be sharptempered and accustomed to beating Socrates because of his poor memory. Aspasia shares with Diotima a masculine toughness, obviously a necessary trait for those who would educate potential philosophers. At some risk to himself, Socrates, presumably moved by Eros, recites Aspasia's funeral oration; its main characteristics are an exaggerated praise of Athens, even through lies, and an equally strong praise of patriotism generally.[77]

At the beginning of the *Menexenus* Socrates says that it is not difficult to praise Athenians among Athenians. To this we may add that it is not difficult to praise beauty among lovers of beauty. Aspasia's speech exemplifies the rhetoric of patriotism, or self-praise transformed into the common interest. Perhaps Socrates learned from her how to transform pederastic selfishness or narcissism in a similar manner. Aspasia distinguishes between the Attic soil and the Athenian *politeia;* the country of the autochthonous Athenians alone is like a natural mother to her residents, whereas other countries are like stepmothers. Aspasia is mother-Athens, praising her children with edifying, if not

75. Robin, *SymBudé,* p. xxv, notes the resemblance between Diotima and Aspasia. See now Ehlers, *Eine vorplatonische Deutung des sokratischen Eros,* in *Zetemata, 41* (Munich, 1966), 131 ff.

76. *Menexenus* 235e4 ff. Socrates also names Connus, the son of Metrobius, as his teacher in music.

77. Cf. G. Vlastos, ΙΣΟΝΟΜΙΑ ΠΟΛΙΤΙΚΗ, in *Isonomia* (Berlin, 1964), pp. 22 ff.

precisely noble, lies.[78] This is the political counterpart to Agathon's praise of one's own poems or speeches. Human existence depends upon the addition of more than a tincture of each rhetoric to the love of the best.

We may playfully but instructively regard Diotima, Anaxagoras, and Aspasia as Socrates' early teachers concerning beauty, truth, and goodness respectively. It is no accident that Socrates learnt physics from a man, but politics and the erotic mysteries from women. The domain of the political-religious is essentially that of peace, associated with the womanly arts of child-rearing, housekeeping, weaving, and the like. The masculine component in Socrates' female teachers corresponds to the need to protect the city by the art of war. The pure study of physics, on the other hand, symbolizes the male or pederastic hybris by which the city is not merely transcended but threatened with destruction. The example of Aspasia thus helps us to see how Diotima corresponds to the noble lie in the *Republic*. Peace, and therefore justice, is impossible without the mediation of the female element. In the political context woman is connected with the mother-earth; in the theoretical context she mediates between man and the heavens.

The preceding remarks bring to a focus a problem that has been implicit in our entire analysis up to this point. It is by no means self-evident, as many readers of Plato have concluded, that beauty, truth, and goodness simply coincide at the highest stage of his teaching. In his dialogue with Socrates it is Agathon who asserts that the good is beautiful, or rather, that it seems to him to be beautiful; Socrates merely posed the question (201c1–9). Again, when Socrates accuses the poets of lying in the *Republic,* he does not say that their lies are ugly. The noble lie upon which the just city is founded must certainly be good, and as noble, beautiful; yet it is not true. If truth and beauty are identical, then every false speech is ugly. Just as the beauty of the good does not preclude the possibility of the beauty of the bad, so the goodness of the true does not necessarily exclude the possible goodness of the false.

78. *Menexenus* 237a4, 237b6.

Perhaps we may suggest that the speech of Diotima, like any noble lie, is intermediate between the true and the false, just as Eros is intermediate between the divine and the human. The *Symposium* explicitly teaches that Eros is rooted in the body or genesis. By itself Eros is insufficient to explain the ecstatic or transcendent nature of the psyche. The illumination of beauty which Eros generates, as derived from the body, is not false, but it is incomplete. The incompleteness of beauty, which depends for its visibility upon the corporeal,[79] both illuminates and obscures. This very incompleteness characterizes the *Symposium* and any other dialogue; they all partake by virtue of their form in poetry or *mythos,* and so are a mixture of noble lies and truth. Among her many functions Diotima symbolizes the transformation of Socrates' mythical youth into a beautiful version of the truth.

Eros as Intermediate

As both prophet and woman, Diotima is passive with respect to the gods. She cannot rebel against them, but neither can she explain them. Her function is to receive and deliver their revelations. Her activity is directed toward men; like Socrates, she is a midwife who assists others in giving birth to their own divine revelations. As her name indicates, she stands for the honor due to god.[80] Diotima is a stranger from Mantinea, and yet she served Athens in arranging for a ten-year postponement of the plague of 430,[81] something which the Athenians

79. According to Moravcsik, *ReasonEros,* p. 8, one may begin to love the beauty of incorporeal things without loving bodies. This misses the main point of the *Symposium.* The psyche is "attached" to the body, which supplies it with the "notion" of beauty. The meaning of the "ascent" is precisely that we ascend from the body.

80. Rettig, *Symposion* 201d2: "Wie in dem Mythus von der Geburt des Eros Διὸς κῆπος die menschliche Seele bedeutet, welche die Idee in sich aufnimmt, so bedeutet Διοτίμα die dieser Aufnahme gewürdigte Seele . . . Aehnlich wie mit ihrem Nahmen, dass er eine Bezeichnung ihres Wesens und ihrer Bedeutung ist, verhält es sich mit ihrer Bezeichnung als Μαντική, worin zugleich eine Anspielung auf ihre Prophetengabe liegt."

81. See Bury's note to 201d3 ff. W. Kranz *Diotima, Die Antike* (2) (1926), and

were apparently unable to accomplish without her mediation (201d3 ff.). Her art is thus related to the technē of medicine and links her to Apollo, god of prophecy and medicine. At the same time, she is bound by necessity; the plague could be postponed, but not altogether averted.

In anticipation of Diotima's teaching that Eros is born of need and cleverness, Socrates himself gives birth to the prophetess from the marriage of wisdom and the need to persuade:

> as for the account (λόγον)[82] she gave, I shall try to go through it for you, proceeding on the basis of what has been agreed by Agathon and me, but by myself, insofar as I am able. (201d5–8)

Socrates and Agathon have agreed that Eros pursues the beautiful, and therefore the good, while shunning the ugly and the bad. By virtue of their further agreement concerning the nature of desire, it follows that Eros himself cannot possess any of these qualities. Socrates relates how he learned of Eros' peculiar intermediate nature from Diotima. In addition to the aforementioned qualities, Diotima explains that Eros is neither wise nor ignorant; that is, although he does not possess the truth, he is not ignorant:

> "Or don't you perceive that there is something between wisdom and ignorance?" "What is that?" "To have right opinion without being able to give a reason (λόγον). Don't you realize that this is neither to know—for how could knowledge be something without logos?—nor is it ignorance—for how could what hits upon the thing as

---

Taylor, *Plato,* both accept the historical existence of Diotima. Kranz regards the story about the plague as poetic (p. 321), whereas Taylor says that it would not have been cited unless Diotima were a real person (p. 224). Neither author gives the slightest justification for his opinion on the basis of the *Symposium* itself, and Taylor's "principle" commits him to belief in the historical existence of all gods and other mythical beings who are mentioned in connection with specific events.

82. Perhaps it should be mentioned that the precise meaning of λόγος must always be determined from the context of each occurrence of the term. It does not always stand in opposition to μῦθος.

it is be ignorance? Instead, right opinion is just this: between prudence (φρονήσεως) and ignorance." "You speak the truth," I said. (201e6–202a10)

Socrates shows himself to be as docile toward Diotima as was Agathon toward himself; when a young man, the intermediate was evidently terra incognita for him. He was therefore ignorant of human nature and of the way in which genesis becomes visible to man. His mathematical and scientific orientation prevented him from understanding the realm of "opinion" or δόξα, the peculiarly human atmosphere through which the light of reason or logos is filtered.[83] This attitude is represented, in the initial exchange with Diotima, as an ignorance of the difference between contraries and contradictories: a "logical" version of the ignorance of the intermediate.[84] Those who, because they see only the divine, fail to perceive the human, are not ignorant, but impractical or imprudent. This is why Diotima, in the passage just cited, shifts from wisdom (σοφία) to knowledge (ἐπιστήμη) and finally to prudence (φρόνησις) as the contrary to ignorance.

According to Diotima, it is impious to suppose that whatever is not beautiful must be ugly. Similarly, she demands of Socrates:

"Tell me, wouldn't you say that all gods are happy and beautiful? Or would you dare to deny that any of the gods is beautiful and happy?" "By Zeus, not I," I replied. (202c6–9)

Socrates' oath is a proper response by a docile student to Diotima's implied threat.[85] Presumably his lack of daring prevented him from observing that if Eros desires what he lacks,

83. *Sophist* 227a7 ff.

84. Cf. Souilhé, *Intermédiaire*, pp. 52–54: μεταξύ is the point of contact between contraries, making a continuity between them. See *Phaedo* 71–72, *Parmenides* 156d, *Theaetetus* 188a.

85. Cf. E. Brann, *The Music of the Republic* (Annapolis, Md., 1966), p. 2, for an explanation of Socrates' favorite oath, "by the dog." A study of the function of the various oaths in Plato would be most useful.

he must love the ugly as well as the beautiful.[86] Nor does he comment upon Diotima's striking failure to mention wisdom or truth as a possession necessary for happiness. Instead, he asks:

"What then might Eros be? Mortal?" "Least of all!" "But what?" "As in the previous instances," she said, "between mortal and immortal." "Well what, Diotima?" "A great daimon, Socrates; everything daimonic (τὸ δαιμόνιον) is intermediate between god and mortal." "Having what power?" I asked. "To interpret and convey the things from humans to gods and the things from gods to humans: from the one, needs (δεήσεις) and sacrifices; from the others, orders and recompense for the sacrifices. Being in the middle, and so filled up with both, it thus binds together the whole to itself." (202d8–e7)

As an intermediate entity, Eros must be of indeterminate shape. It can bind together the whole, Ideas and instances, because it is neither the one nor the other, not a self-identical unity.[87] The problem in understanding the account of Eros so far is to reconcile the terms "between" and "filled up with" the divine and human, with the negativity or indeterminacy of desire. If Eros were filled with both in the sense of being "half of each," it would decompose into two irreconcilable parts. The reconciliation is possible if we identify the daimonic with the tendency of genesis to be continuously other than it is. The formal or visible element in genesis is the reflection of the domain of ousia; but that in which it is reflected lacks the capacity of continuity or coherence. At any specific point or instant, genesis exhibits a coherent structure, but the discontinuity of points or instants means that it is also losing that structure. Genesis altogether is not immortal because each of its parts dies. But it is not mortal because each moment of death occurs as a birth of something else.

86. *Republic* 474d4.

87. Thus Aristotle says in *Physics* 192a16 ff. that εἶδος cannot desire or strive toward itself διὰ τὸ μὴ εἶναι ἐνδεές. Cf. *Phaedo* 65c9, *Metaphysics* 1072a24, *De Anima* 406b24, 415a26 ff. (the psyche πάντα ὀρέγηται to participate in τοῦ ἀεὶ καὶ τοῦ θείου), 433a9 and notes 61 and 62 above.

Eros is one of the daimons who constitute the intermediate or syndesmotic domain.[88] It is by the work of the daimons that genesis is saved from dissolution into nonbeing; but that same work prevents it from achieving union with ousia. The structure of the whole is identical with the structure of necessity. Both gods and men are bound by necessity through the bonds of their being. Despite her ironical reference to religion as a kind of barter between gods and men,[89] Diotima endorses its function in terms close to those of Aristophanes. We have already learned from Aristophanes that the religious striving toward wholeness is doomed to failure. Diotima's account of Eros makes the same point in more fundamental terms: the success of genesis or becoming in achieving the goal of ousia would amount to its cessation or negation: hence the famous Socratic remark that philosophy is a preparation for dying.[90] Wholeness for man would be a total vision of the Ideas. In the activity of such vision, however, the self would not be cognizant of itself.[91] Thus man is perpetually intermediate between two species of nothingness: the death of the body and the perfection of the psyche.

Diotima both accommodates to and revises the traditional religion. As part of her accommodation she suppresses the fact that the perfection of the psyche is a progressive loss of personality, and so a falling away from personal immortality. Related to this suppression is the restriction of technē to "all prophecy . . . and the technē of priests concerning sacrifices and initiation into mysteries . . ." (202e7 ff.). As part of her revision she makes the daimonic intermediate between the dis-

88. Robin, *SymBudé*, p. lxxviii. Thus it is an oversimplification to say, as does J. Derbolav, *Erkenntnis und Entscheidung* (Vienna, 1954), p. 172, that the "Eroslehre" is the *syndesmos* of Plato's philosophy.

89. Cf. Festugière, *Contemplation*, pp. 268 ff. In traditional religion the δαίμονες "sont donc les dieux pour autant qu'ils nous assignent ce qui nous revient." They are related to μόρος and μοῖρα, and function as the distributors of human shares.

90. *Phaedo* 64a4 ff.

91. As has often been noted, there is no technical concept of the ego in Plato (e.g., Hoffmann, *Symposion*, p. 24.)

tinct realms of the divine and the human. We have already commented upon this separation in terms of cosmology or the nature of genesis. In human terms, there is no more direct intercourse, whether sexual or noetic, between gods and men:

> God does not mix with human, but all intercourse and conversation between gods and men occurs through [the daimonic], both in waking and in sleeping . . . (203a1 ff.)[92]

Man's link with the gods cannot be understood solely in terms of his empirical or generated existence: there are no more divinely sired heroes. The vision of the divine is a gift from above, through the mediation of special, daimonic individuals, whose wisdom is not commensurate with the empirical or "vulgar" technai.[93]

By its denial of immortality to the human psyche,[94] the teaching of the *Symposium* agrees with the cosmology of the *Timaeus*. Man's psyche is bound by its daimonic nature to the cosmic psyche, the *syndesmos* of genesis altogether. And the cosmic psyche itself "comes to be" from a series of mixtures by the demiurge.[95] This genesis of psyche is prior to the genesis of body.[96] It is a mixture of kinds of being, including those kinds that are present in the body. This seems to mean that psyche, with respect to its being, is unchangeable and eternal, "but in respect of its thoughts it is in change and in time." [97] Since personal immortality depends upon thoughts, whereas these are subject to the change of time, it follows that the coherence of individual identity is dissolved by the temporal sequence within the enduring cosmic psyche. On the other hand, the human psyche has a genesis of its own, as derived from the cosmic psyche rather than from corporeal genesis. Let us now turn to

92. Cf. Bury's note to 203a for the difficulty in translating this phrase.

93. Cf. Krüger, *Einsicht*, pp. 152 ff. See also *Meno* 100b2 ff., where Socrates says that virtue comes to us, it seems, θείᾳ μόιρᾳ.

94. 206e7–8, 208b2 ff., 212a5 ff.

95. *Timaeus* 35a1 ff.

96. Ibid., 34c4.

97. Cf. F. M. Cornford, *Plato's Cosmology* (London, 1948), p. 63.

the account of the genesis of Eros, which is the counterpart in the *Symposium* to Timaeus' likely myth about the genesis of psyche.

The Birth of Eros

Eros is not simply equivalent to psyche, but is its striving for wholeness, and so for immortality. If this striving is itself generated, then it must also pass away; as we saw in the previous section, success is identical with failure. Diotima begins her myth as follows:

> When Aphrodite was born the gods were feasting, both the others and Poros, the son of Mētis.[98] After they had dined, Penia came begging, because of the feast, and stood by the door. Meanwhile Poros, drunk from nectar —for there was no wine—going out into the garden of Zeus, was overcome by sleep. So Penia, contriving because of her need to give birth to a child by Poros, lay down beside him and conceived Eros. (203b2–c4)

Diotima, like Aristophanes, associates the praiseworthy Eros with the Olympian rather than the Uranian gods.[99] Unlike Aristophanes, she presents the birth as a purely celestial phenomenon, having nothing to do with human beings.

The situation on Olympus prior to the birth of Eros may remind us of the distinction between pre-erotic and erotic genesis, already visible in the speech of Phaedrus. In mythological terms, the birth of Aphrodite takes us back to the castration of Uranus by Kronos. [100] Diotima, of course, is not following the "orthodox" tradition; in fact, she is silent about the manner of Aphrodite's birth. But this very silence forces us to ask about the significance and manner of generation among the gods prior to the closely related births of Aphrodite and

98. *Theogony* 886 ff. Is he the god who will overthrow Zeus?

99. For some of the most famous interpretations of Diotima's account, see Bury's note to 203b, and C. Huit, *Études sur le Banquet de Platon* (Paris, 1887), pp. 62–63.

100. *Theogony* 167 ff.

Eros. In order to explain the birth of Eros, Diotima herself invents new gods.[101] This, of course, is part of the charge later to be leveled against Socrates by the city of Athens. The cryptic reference to the birth of Aphrodite reminds us of the heavenly gods or pre-Olympians, and the account of Eros introduces what we may call post-Olympians into the society of the traditional gods. One can only surmise that Diotima regards the traditional account as defective with respect to Eros; the link between cosmic genesis and sexual generation needs a more elaborate explanation than she or any of the other speakers has given or will give.

The defects of the Olympians are symbolized by drunkenness and the seduction of Poros by Penia, and consequently by the conception of Eros. If the gods were perfect, Eros would never have been generated; he is therefore an expression of their incompleteness as well as mankind's. The humans at the banquet of Agathon, for example, are able to restrain their drunkenness in order to give speeches in praise of Eros. Granted the difference between praise and explanation, one may still say that speech, even about enthusiasm and erotic striving, needs sobriety as much as madness. The actual presence of Eros seems to be closely related to intoxication, and to stand for the absence, even the impossibility, of logical explanation. At the divine or cosmological level, this may mean either that belief in gods does not constitute an explanation of the origins, or that only mythical accounts of the origins are possible, and then only through the help of inspired madness.

Drunkenness is a vice of excess, whereas abstinence is a vice of deficiency. Although Socrates does not abstain from wine, the speech of Alcibiades indicates that he is more than sober with respect to pederasty. Socrates' erotic deficiency seems to be a condition of his verbal fluency; instead of making love, he talks about love. But there is a shortage of logos on Olympus, as is symbolized by the parents of Eros. Consider the names of his father and grandfather. "Poros" means "a way," as for ex-

---

101. See Bury's note to 203b for the known personifications of Poros (by Alcman), Penia (by Aristophanes), and Mētis (an Orphic alias of Eros).

ample by boat across water, and thus generally "contrivance." It reminds us of technē as well as *hodos:* "way" or "road" and the root meaning of "method." And it is also used to refer to "a way of raising money," which is interesting in view of Diotima's following identification of Eros as a Sophist. "Mētis" is an epic word meaning "wisdom" in the primarily practical senses of "craft" or "skill." [102] Thus Poros, the unwitting father of Eros, is himself the son of poetic or pre-philosophical technē or practical wisdom. Were Poros a philosopher like Socrates, he would have been immune to excessive drink. But in that case, presumably, Eros would not have been born. In other words, as is certainly implied by Plato's invention of Diotima, the origin of philosophy cannot be explained in purely "logical" terms.

At least since the time of Ficino[103] it has been observed that the description of Eros is reminiscent of Socrates. In view of the tension between sobriety and intoxication, or logos and madness, it would be surprising if there were not also differences between Socrates and Eros. Let us first consider Eros' inheritance from his mother:

> Since Eros is the son of Poros and Penia, he has been established in the following fate (τύχη): first, he is always poor, and very much lacking in the softness and beauty which the many suppose [him to possess]. Instead, he is hard, dry [=weatherbeaten], shoeless, homeless, always sleeping on the ground and uncovered, going to bed in doorways and in the open roads, having the nature of his mother to be always wedded to need. (203c5–d3)

The connection of ugliness with poverty suggests that need is in itself unable to determine the location of beauty. Penia was driven to conceive a child, but the selection of the father was a matter of fate or chance.[104]

102. Μῆτις is the first wife taken by Zeus after he becomes king of the Olympians (*Theogony*, 886). The "defectiveness" of Eros is thus related to the beginning of Zeus' rule.

103. Marcel, *Ficin*, Oratio septima, 11. 105v–106r.

104. Perhaps this is why Kuhn, *Tragedy*, 1. 3, says of these lines that "the air

Although Eros is the consequence, and presumably the agent, of divine intoxication, like Socrates he is not himself intoxicated. The resemblance extends to the attribute of poverty, but thereafter qualifications are necessary. For example, the many do not suppose Socrates to be beautiful, as Alcibiades will forcefully remind us. We may agree that Socrates is hard and dry, but the *Symposium* testifies to the fact that he is not always shoeless, as is Aristodemus (173b2). This is related to the quality of homelessness. The philosopher must be free from the tyranny of nomos to a considerable degree but not entirely. Socrates retains his loyalty to the city both in theory and practice, whereas Eros is intrinsically apolitical.[105] In other words, Socrates is a citizen of Athens, whereas Eros may be found in every city. Or again, Eros seems to point toward the transpolitical unity of the human race, and in so doing to threaten the stability of the political virtues upon which the safety of philosophy depends.

Eros' inheritance from his father is much more complex; it makes him

> skilled at plotting against the beautiful and good, since he is brave, bold, and eager, a clever hunter, always weaving some contrivances (μηχανάς), a resourceful desirer of prudence (φρονήσεως), philosophizing throughout his whole life, a clever sorcerer, poisoner, and Sophist. By his nature he is neither immortal nor mortal; but on the same day he will bloom and live, whenever he prospers, and then he will die, being brought back to life by the nature of his father. Eros always wastes away what he has acquired, so that he is at no time poor or rich, but is in between wisdom and ignorance. (203d4–e5)

of tragedy hovers over Eros . . . ." That Kuhn himself recognizes the inadequacy of such a characterization is apparent from his general conclusions; e.g. 2.52.

105. Eros, of course, manifests himself in the political relation but is not intentionally directed toward this or any other limitation on his striving. The Socratic moderation of this political rootlessness seems to have weakened among many of his later disciples and offspring, especially the Cynics and Skeptics. Cf. V. Brochard, *Les Sceptiques Grecs* (Paris, 1922), p. 18.

We may note in passing a slight incompatibility between the maternal and paternal inheritance; while previously Eros was said to be always poor, now he is described as never poor or rich.

The main feature of the paternal inheritance, however, is that Eros' philosophical nature is manifestly practical rather than theoretical. The emphasis throughout is upon trickery, and even worse. He does not love the beautiful and good, but he is skillful in plotting to possess them. In this respect he resembles the "nonlover" as described by Lysias' speech in the *Phaedrus*. Lysias points out that the lover, as overcome by his desire, is the most needy, whereas the nonlover is his own master. Eros seems to combine the need of the lover with the cleverness of the nonlover. Need alone is scarcely a guarantee of merit; thus Lysias advises: "when we give a private banquet, we should not invite our friends, but the importunate, and those needing to be filled up." [106] In other words, the emptiness of the erotic appetite is dependent upon the bounty of the possessors for its satisfaction. Whether this appetite deserves or is capable enough to be filled up is another question, which cannot be answered merely by pointing to the existence of need.

According to Diotima's teaching, those who possess beauty and goodness must be tricked into sharing these attributes. Whether we interpret "trickery" in a practical or theoretical sense, the man who is a slave to his desire is not in a good position to exercise cunning. Those whose desire drives them to a skillful use of duplicity, such as sorcery or poison, exhibit the strange fact that Eros is also the opposite of himself. In philosophical language: sobriety without madness is without purpose, but madness without sobriety is self-destructive. Eros, like other philosophers, uses questionable methods in his pursuit of beauty and goodness (here placed on the same level, whereas previously goodness was a species of beauty). The erotic hunt-

---

106. *Phaedrus* 231d4, 233d5 ff. There are numerous echoes of the *Symposium* throughout this section of the *Phaedrus*; e.g. 234d1 (*Symp.* 178b5), 234e5 ff. (*Symp.* 198b1 ff.), 236d4 (*Symp.* 198c5–6), 237a4 ff. (*Symp.* 216d1 ff.). Consider also 236e7–8.

ing of beautiful bodies by morally ambiguous methods is somehow transformed into the pursuit of goodness as well. And the
hunting is not precisely or entirely erotic.

Eros is by nature a harmony of opposites. For example, he is
said to be philosophical and brave, but not just or moderate.
Eros combines the virtues of the guardian and soldier class but
lacks the virtues of the workers and the city as a whole. He is
unjust (and so apolitical) because his desires are immoderate;
like Socrates, Eros is hybristic. The philosopher is the most ef-
fectively selfish man since he is most skilled at getting beautiful
and good things for himself. On the other hand, like Eros, he
also squanders freely what he has obtained.[107] This generosity
gives an added dimension to his cleverness, in which he resembles Orpheus and Zeus, at devising "contrivances" to trick
others and gain his own ends.[108] Eros combines the selfishness
of Phaedrus, the cleverness of Pausanias, the pharmacy of Eryximachus, and the sophistry of Agathon. As for Aristophanes, is
he not a sorcerer whose words transform serious and good natures into absurd and base caricatures? Eros is reminiscent of
Proteus; his skill and need combine in an ability to assume a
variety of shapes.[109]

Eros vacillates between the cleverness, which resuscitates, and
the need, which vitiates him. His cleverness brings him closest
to the gods, who are beautiful and good, and therefore happy,
or free from desire. His need, on the other hand, is not simply
human, but more than human, rooted as it is in the nature of
becoming or genesis. The cosmic origin of need reinforces the
ambiguity of the pre-erotic origin of the gods, whose happiness
would seem to depend upon their sharing in neither corporeal
nor psychic appetite. Yet the very birth of Eros is a sign that
the gods are not so privileged. The problem may be stated in
terms of the nature of divine happiness. Whereas in an earlier
passage, divine happiness was associated with beauty, and consequently with goodness, Diotima now asserts that the gods are

---

107. Cf. n. 79 above and Xenophon, *Memorabilia* 1.2.60.
108. Cf. 179d6, 190c7.
109. Cf. *Republic* 380d1 ff. and *Symposium* 203d8: Eros is a γόης, god is not.

wise, although she doubts whether anyone else may be (204a1–2; cf. 202c6–9). If the gods, however, are living and sentient beings, for whom wisdom is a perfection of mind, then they must possess psyches, and thereby partake of genesis or need.

Both the intermediate status of Eros and the divine gift of philosophy are evidence that the gods desire human happiness. We are faced with a dilemma: if the gods desire anything, they are not wise—and it becomes open to question whether man should love or emulate them. If, on the other hand, they are wise, they cannot desire anything—and the function of Eros, or the status of philosophy, becomes suspect. Although the Platonic dialogues are by no means consistent in their portrait of the gods,[110] they never present philosophy as anything but a divine gift or the expression of the divine in man. To question whether the gods can be wise means that we do not yet know what Plato understands by the terms "divine" and "wise." [111] The teaching of Diotima amounts to the assertion that man can never possess an adequate account of these matters. Complete satisfaction is possible only for the wise and the altogether ignorant (204a4). Even further, if wisdom is the same as complete satisfaction, it then becomes impossible to distinguish between the wise and the altogether ignorant.

In sum: a satisfactory description of a god could be given only by a god, and only to a god, yet neither would have any need for such a description. One must suspect that the happiness of the gods, like their beauty, stems from their lack of logos; they speak and dwell in mythos. The gods do not need to give an account (λόγον διδόναι) of the whole, whereas man may be accurately defined by this need. The closest man can come to giving an account of the gods is by saying that they lack the need which decisively defines his nature. At the same time, man's nature is such that the lack of this need must necessarily appear to be a defect rather than a mark of perfection. Man's own

110. Cf. *Republic* 379c2 ff., 382a1 and *Timaeus* 24c7.

111. In the *Parmenides* 133c ff., Parmenides says that the theory of Ideas raises the problem of god's knowledge. If there is an Idea of knowledge, then god will know it, but nothing of the spatio-temporal world. Socrates regards this as "too strange."

striving for a perfect logos, if successful, would result in the disappearance of logos, and so too of man. If man should become a god, it seems that he would lose all knowledge, and perhaps even all consciousness, of his wisdom and divinity. Intelligence is necessary for the recognition of need, but it also seems to guarantee unhappiness. The gods, if they are happy, must lack intelligence but not, presumably, beauty and goodness. Do they not, under this hypothesis, become strangely like stars or heavenly bodies, or perhaps even Ideas? [112]

Love of the Good

According to Diotima, philosophers, like Eros, are neither wise nor ignorant. The young Socrates, who does not understand the intermediate, is puzzled as to who the philosophers may be. Prior to his instruction by Diotima, Socrates seems to have believed that men rather than gods are wise, or that men are gods. But this divine status is dependent upon the possession of, in the sense of identification with, the order of intelligibility. Socrates now discerns that the gods may be happy, but not wise in the sense of possessing knowledge. And apart from this, if there is no mixture between gods and men, while only gods are wise, how can man distinguish between wisdom and ignorance? How is philosophy, or the love of wisdom, possible? What faith can be placed in the messages of Eros? Does not the mutually conflicting character of these messages cast doubt upon the coherence of their source?

Diotima gives Socrates an insolent answer: "it is clear even to a child that [the philosophers] are intermediate between [wisdom and ignorance], and among them is Eros" (204b1–2). However clear the answer may be, it does establish an extremely important point. If Eros is not the only philosopher, then there must be nonerotic philosophers. And from this it follows in turn that, contrary to the main thesis of the *Symposium*, it is not necessary to love beauty in order to be a philosopher. Therefore, Diotima's next argument is misleading:

112. Cf. Chapter 5, n. 52.

> Wisdom is one of the most beautiful things, and Eros is love (ἔρως) for the beautiful; so Eros is necessarily a philosopher, and as such, between wisdom and ignorance. (204b2–5)

Since there are a number of beautiful things, it would be possible for Eros to love one of them other than wisdom. Socrates is the only speaker at the banquet who could reasonably be said to love wisdom, and even he is ambiguously presented as a beloved who is strangely cold toward, or lacking in natural understanding of, Eros.

In this light, Diotima's next words have a peculiar aptness:

> Indeed, the beloved is truly (τῷ ὄντι) beautiful and delicate and perfect and to be regarded as happy, but what loves has another nature (ἰδέαν) altogether, such as I have just described. (204c4–6)

If philosophy is a divine share or gift, making the recipient as close to the gods as possible, then the philosopher, as possessed by divine madness, is beloved by or passive with respect to the gods. Human perfection seems to be a function of divine imperfection. As the term "delicate" suggests, this perfection is also inseparable from imperfection. If the gods are conceived of as unconscious initiators of the process whereby man "delicately" submits to the vision of the Ideas, in a way like Aristotle's passive mind, it seems possible to reconcile these disparate results. But that would be to go beyond the teaching of the *Symposium*.

If philosophers are daimons, how can human beings be philosophers? If, on the other hand, human beings are philosophers, and so the beloved of the gods, what need have they of Eros? Socrates therefore very reasonably asks: "since Eros is of this sort, of what use [χρείαν also contains the sense of "need"] is he to men?" Diotima requires about twice as many lines to answer this question (204c7–207a4) as she needed for Socrates' first three altogether (which concerned Eros' power, his parents, and the identity of philosophers). By way of anticipation, the crucial step in this section will be the replacement of the love of beauty by the love of the good.[113] The difficulty of this section of her teaching is clear from Diotima's own remarks. The first section was so "clear" that "even a child" could grasp it. Now Diotima will "try to teach" Socrates material which he can "perhaps" (209e5) understand (204c7–209e4). After 209e5, Diotima no longer knows whether she has transcended Socrates' comprehension. Her revelation, then, falls into three stages, the first and simplest of which depends upon Agathon's premise that Eros is love of the beautiful. It remains to be seen whether, in her ascent, she can altogether free herself from the defects of that premise.

The second stage of the initiatory rites begins with a partial rejection of Agathon's premise. The love of beauty is not an end in itself. When asked "why love beautiful things?" Socrates replies:

> "So that one will come to possess them." "But," she said, "the answer still needs the following question: what will belong to him to whom the beautiful comes to be?" (204d7–9)

Socrates has no clear response to give to this question. He cannot think of an end for the sake of which we desire to possess the beautiful. It is for him neither an end in itself nor (to anticipate) a cause of happiness. He is more successful when Diotima suggests that they inquire instead about the love of good things: he to whom good things belong or become will be happy. Diotima agrees:

> "Because," she added, "the happy are happy in the possession of good things, and there is no need to ask: for the sake of what does someone want to be happy? But the answer seems to be complete." "You speak the truth," said I. (205a1–4)

Two observations are in order here. First, for the young Socrates, it is neither *the* beautiful nor *the* good, but the possession

113. Cf. Neumann, *Diotima,* p. 30.

of good things (τἀγαθά; 204e5) that brings happiness. So far as this passage tells us, the only property shared by all good things is that they make us happy. For Agathon, all good things come from the love of beautiful things, for gods and mortals.[114] Agathon is apparently ready to equate beauty with goodness, as the young Socrates, prior to Diotima's instruction, is not. Second, from Socrates' acceptance of her assertion that, although not everyone agrees, all mortals not only love, but love the same things always (205a9–b4), Diotima goes on to infer that "in general, every desire (ἐπιθυμία) for good things and for happiness is the greatest and entirely deceitful Eros."[115] At this point in her teaching, Diotima replaces beauty with happiness as the end of Eros: happiness via the possession of good things. Beauty has been silently demoted, although it will return at a later stage of the discussion.

If beauty is not the same as goodness, then the suspicion that love of beautiful bodies is not necessary for philosophy is strengthened. Furthermore, Diotima insists, with a plain reference to Aristophanes, that "Eros is neither of the half nor of the whole, should it not happen to be something good" (205e1–3). Eros is properly just one species of love (εἶδος: the point has nothing to do with the so-called theory of Ideas) that takes the name for itself. We do not apply it, for example, to the love of gymnastics or of philosophy, although these too are species of love for good things and hence for happiness (205b4–7, 205d1–8). All men love only good things, and (as Diotima's examples show) these are as diverse as money and wisdom. Human beings are made happy by radically different things, as is reinforced by the example of those who will allow the amputation of their legs or arms if they suppose them to be harmful (205e3–5). This raises a serious problem for Diotima. On the one hand, she denies that the whole is good, and hence that it is lovable. On the other hand, she seems to allow the possibility that everything, even amputation, is good or lovable.

Either alternative leads to trouble for the doctrine of Eros. If

114. 197b8–9; again cf. *Phaedrus* 244a7.
115. 205d1–3. See Bury's note for the grammatical justification of the manuscript reading.

only part of the whole is good and lovable, how can philosophy
be knowledge of all things, including dirt, hair, and other low
things? How can philosophy know what it does not desire? If
knowledge of the whole is distinct from, and does not require,
love of the whole, what is the connection between Eros and philosophy? Even more pressing, what, if Eros desires happiness,
is the connection between philosophy and happiness? If everything is good or lovable (as would seem to follow, incidentally,
from the doctrine in the *Republic* of the Idea of the good), or in
other words, if there are as many roads to happiness as there
are types of lovers, then there is no necessary connection between philosophy and happiness, and the regular Socratic distinction between philosophers and nonphilosophers dissolves.

One might suggest that, by desiring happiness, all mortals are
implicitly striving for wholeness, that is, philosophy. But few
comprehend the nature of their desire; they mistake the part
for the whole. The definition of Eros as the love of beauty is in
fact a misdefinition that obscures rather than illuminates the
truth about human nature. When Socrates asks for an example
of how men define the whole of Eros by a part, Diotima cites
poetry:

> Every cause by which anything at all comes from non-
> being into being is poetry (ποίησις), so that the work in all
> the technai is poetry, and all the craftsmen (δημιουργοί) in
> these are poets. (205b8–c2)

The significance of the example is as follows: since genesis is
equivalent to poiēsis, and the ugly comes into being as well as
the beautiful, it is wrong to define poetry as merely the love of
the beautiful.

Diotima's example underlines the importance in the *Symposium* of poetry, which functions as the middle term between
cosmic genesis and human technē. Just as parents love their own
children, in whom they see their completion, more than all

116. Socrates implies in the *Phaedrus* that there are no nonlovers when, in
his first speech, he makes the nonlover a lover in disguise, and, like the Dioti-
man Eros, wily or deceitful (αἰμύλος: 237b2–4).

other offspring, so the artist, craftsman, or technician loves the fruit of his own skill beyond all else. The poetic love of one's own leads man to identify his offspring as the good things upon which his happiness depends. This equivalence between genesis and happiness differs from Agathon's position in that it allows us to regard ugly productions as good things. In cosmic terms, whatever comes to be is good; being is better than non-being because anything may make its contribution to someone's happiness. Hence the aforementioned dilemma.

Parallel to the importance of poetry, the love of beautiful bodies is the paradigm of Eros in the *Symposium*. Whatever comes to be and passes away is either a body or a modification of a body. Diotima mentions the love of money, gymnastics, and philosophy as three species of the erotic desire for good things and happiness, which correspond approximately to love of property, love of the body, and love of the psyche (205d4–5).[117] Given the primacy of genesis, the psyche is an epiphenomenon of the body, one which we may designate as its most precious possession. Thus far at least in the teaching of Diotima, the psychic lover may be the highest type of erotic (although even this is conjectural if "highest" means "happiest"), but he cannot be acorporeal. Just as it is hard to distinguish the lover from the nonlover, so it continues to be hard to distinguish the psyche from the body.

To the example of the species of Eros, Socrates replies: "you seem to speak the truth" (205d9), instead of "you speak the truth," his answer in three previous steps of the discussion.[118] Socrates is quite clear about the truth of the statements that happiness is the end of desire, that genesis is the same as poiēsis, and that the name "poet" is normally given to those who work in music and meter. His uncertainty at the fourth step is due to the aforementioned difficulty in identifying the true or properly named lover. As we also saw previously, Socrates is puzzled by sexual love. But there is a more fundamental problem here. If all men are lovers, then the object of every desire must be at

117. Cf. Socrates' first speech in the *Phaedrus* and n. 113.
118. 205a4, c3, c10, d9.

least potentially good. Given the polymorphous nature of Eros, it becomes impossible to say that some bodies or modifications of bodies cannot make anyone happy or contribute to anyone's happiness. As we noticed previously, it seemed as though Diotima was making just this point, by means of the substitution of "good" for "beautiful." But then, as though in response to Socrates' puzzlement, she said something quite different.

> Indeed, a story is told that lovers look for the (other) half of themselves, but according to my account, love is neither of the half nor of the whole, unless, comrade, it should happen to be good. For men desire to have their own legs and arms amputated if these parts seem to them bad. (205d10–e5)

Diotima cannot affirm consistently, and in fact has denied, that the whole is good. Even if we assume that Diotima accepts the doctrine of Ideas, and further that the Ideas are both beautiful and good, only parts of genesis are good, and these parts differ for different kinds of lovers. The connection between which parts one regards as good, and love of the Ideas, remains, to say the least, dubious. The doctrine of erotic ascent, as described by Diotima, becomes irrelevant, and perhaps even an impediment, to the love of Ideas. In fact, the only candidate for the status of Idea in her teaching is beauty itself. Assuming that beauty is everywhere the same, goodness is not. If beauty is then the key to happiness, goodness (contrary to her thesis) is irrelevant. But if goodness is the key, then beauty is secondary if not irrelevant.

As her reference to Aristophanes' speech shows, Diotima is currently attempting to define "the good" in terms of the body. At the simplest level, the difficulty she faces is evident from the phrase "if these parts seem to them bad." There are some men who would prefer to die rather than to live without their limbs. On what basis do they sacrifice the good part of the body after the bad part? Somewhat more generally, a good lover may choose to die when deprived of his bad beloved. If good and bad are to be defined in terms of the body, then nothing could be easier than to multiply examples of men who love the bad simply because it is their own. At best, Diotima might claim that men suppose whatever they love to be good and, we may add, beautiful. But this amounts to the admission that the difference between good and bad, or between beautiful and ugly, is a matter of seeming or opinion. We are once again faced with the consequence that whatever is, is potentially good. Happiness, as a function of the body, is a private affair.

The substitution of the love of the good for the love of the beautiful thus leads to exactly the same result: namely that men love the part rather than the whole, and the part that belongs to them. If the whole is both corporeal and good, one cannot own it all but must settle for some part which then seems especially good to him, and which he struggles to preserve. If it is partly good and partly bad, and if men love only the good, then, as Diotima says, the bad is "unwelcome" to them (205e5). In either case the result is the same: war between the good and the bad. Since Diotima claims that men will refuse to own the bad, this amounts to a war between one's own and another's conception of the good. And this conception, as a resident of genesis, or a modification of body, cannot be clearly and distinctly established as a perpetually present standard of the wisdom or ignorance of the warring owners.[119] It is important to emphasize in Diotima's own statement that men not only love the good, but they love its possession (206a6–7). What, then, is to prevent them from coming to love their possessions more than, or as though they were, the good?

Perpetuity and Physiology

Diotima's definition of Eros is presented in the second section of her teaching and is divided into three parts. Eros is love of the good, love of the possession of the good, and love of perpetual possession of the good (206a9). As we saw in the preceding section, the love of the good is an ambiguous improvement on Agathon's definition of Eros as love of the beautiful. The ambiguity stems from the fact that, so far at least, Diotima re-

119. Cf. *Republic* 470b4 ff.

mains within the limits of genesis, and so gives primacy to the
body, in terms of which the psyche must be understood. Since
the body is the principle of private property, the attempt to
define the good as the whole is not successful. Stated differently, if the whole of genesis is good, this goodness cannot be
understood as a possession of man, or at least of an individual
man. And even if an individual were somehow able to possess
the whole of genesis, he could not do so perpetually, since that
which is generated must also die. The problem, if it can be
solved at all, depends for its solution upon breaking the link
between Eros and genesis, or by directing Eros toward what is
ungenerated.[120]

Little wonder, then, that the young Socrates is at a loss when
asked for an illustration of the work (ἔργον) by which to illustrate the essence of perpetual eros (ὁ ἔρως . . . ἀεί) as just defined (206b1–6).[121] Diotima is again forced by Socrates' ignorance to answer her own question. The work of Eros is "childbirth (τόκος[122]) in the beautiful, both by the body and the
psyche" (206b7–8). Socrates is still baffled: "what you say requires prophetic power, and I don't understand" (206b8–9).
Before his instruction by Diotima, Socrates lacked this prophetic power and understanding, which he afterward frequently
claimed to possess.[123] We should bear in mind that the capacity
to understand the work of Eros is not the same as the ability to
work erotically. The mature Socrates, shortly before his death,
tells the young Theaetetus that he is himself sterile, and cannot
bring forth children of the psyche.[124] In any case, at this moment, Socrates is not even a midwife.

Diotima presents Socrates with the following explanation:

> Socrates, all men are pregnant, both in the body and in
> the psyche. When they arrive at a suitable age, nature

120. Cf. *Phaedrus* 245d1, 247d7.

121. Socrates says that he "frequents" (ἐφοίτων) the company of Diotima to
learn the answer to this question; the word also means "to have sexual intercourse." Note also that the ἔργον of Eros is called a σύντασις (206b2).

122. Cf. *Republic* 506e1 ff., 508b12.

123. Cf. n. 11 above.

124. *Theaetetus* 150c7–8, 150d2, 157c8.

in them desires to give birth. But she cannot give birth in the ugly, but rather in the beautiful. Childbirth is a communion (συνουσία) of man and woman.[125] This deed is divine, for thus immortality inheres in the mortal animal: by pregnancy and generation. But these cannot occur in discord. The ugly is in discord with the divine altogether, but the beautiful is in tune. Beauty is the fate of childbirth at genesis. (206c1–d3)

In this curiously "Aristotelian" statement, we find decisive confirmation of the claim that the *Symposium* abstracts from the ugly. Diotima beautifies the phenomena of childbirth or genesis altogether, in accord with the teaching of Agathon. If her teaching were true, only beautiful people could procreate. The passage sheds ambiguous light on the "sterility" of Socrates' psyche,[126] but it is refuted by the fertility of his body.

One might claim that sexual desire leads lovers always to regard each other, and so too their offspring, as beautiful. But this claim leads directly to all the problems of private ownership, or the reduction of goodness to opinion. Diotima does not in any case deny that the ugly exists, only that it is fertile. The discord between the ugly and the divine means perpetual war within nature, as well as the impossibility of an explanation for the existence of the ugly, and so of an account of the whole. This is approximately the situation which obtained in the speech of Agathon. There is one important difference, however. Despite her lack of an explanation for the existence of the ugly, Diotima wishes to claim that Eros is equivalent to genesis or nature altogether. Since Eros is said to lack beauty, it follows that beauty is somehow beyond genesis. This is the basis for the third or highest stage of Diotima's teaching.

If that which desires beauty must thereby be other than beautiful, if the whole as erotic is neither beautiful nor ugly, then it is impossible for the body to be genuinely beautiful. De-

---

125. Many editors excise this sentence as a "meaningless intrusion" (Bury), but it has the obvious function of serving as transition from homosexual to heterosexual generation.

126. Cf. *Theaetetus* 149b10: midwives are never barren.

sire for corporeal beauty is the striving for a medium or instrument rather than an end in itself. But the same must hold good
for the children of the psyche: the products of genesis cannot
be radically sundered from genesis. Genuine beauty can be no
more psychic than corporeal: as it is deathless, it cannot be living. It presides over genesis like fate (206d2), or something even
higher than a goddess. Unfortunately for the argument of Diotima, the same must be said for the ugly. Even if we accept the
third stage of her teaching, we require an explanation of how
the ugly and the beautiful are held together in one cosmos.
And we should have to know why and how Eros is able to avoid
desire for the ugly.

In sum, genesis is not intelligible in its own terms, whether
as simply beautiful or as both beautiful and ugly. Diotima
concerns herself exclusively with the beautiful, and makes clear
its instrumental status by saying that pregnancy precedes a
striving for the beautiful (206c5 ff.). She attributes the desire
to give birth to nature (206c4: ἡ φύσις), which is then replaced
by Eros. Prior to the love of beauty is the love of the perpetual
possession of the good. Whatever the good may be, the psyche
must desire deathlessness in striving to possess it forever. Eros
is then not the love of beauty, "as you suppose," but "of genesis
and of childbirth in the beautiful," because "genesis is the
mortal equivalent to everlastingness and deathlessness" (206d7–
207a4).

This account of genesis abstracts from the difference between
the sexes, but not from the body. Human reproduction seems
to be a species of natural or cosmic genesis. On the other hand,
the identification of nature with Eros suggests that it is conceived in anthropomorphic terms. The desire for beauty is
then a by-condition of the natural desire for immortality
through reproduction. Diotima now seems to have gone altogether beyond a mere change in the subject matter of the
conversation (204e1 ff.). In this section of her teaching, she
explicitly denies what Socrates and Agathon had agreed upon,
and so presumably the very premise which she had been invoked to illustrate. It is superficial to regard Eros as love of

the beautiful, because beauty is not an end in itself.[127] The perception of beauty seems to be a consequence of the work of Eros, and not the work itself.

So much for the use of Eros to men, and the nature of his work. We turn now to the third part of the second stage of Diotima's teaching:

> All these things she taught me, whenever she would give accounts concerning erotics; and once she asked me: "What do you suppose, Socrates, to be the cause of this Eros and desire? Or don't you perceive in what a strange condition all the beasts find themselves whenever they desire to generate, both those which walk and those which fly? All are sick and erotically disposed, first to commingle with each other, next to nourish what has been generated; and the weakest are ready to fight on their behalf with the strongest, and to die on behalf [of their offspring], and themselves to endure starvation in order to feed the young: and they do all the other things [of this sort]. Among humans," she said, "someone might suppose that they do all this through calculation. But what cause disposes the beasts so erotically? Can you say?" (207a5–c1)

The work of procreation is caused by the desire for immortality. As we have already seen, the link between the work and the cause is expressed by the identification of Eros and nature. Nature or genesis altogether desires immortality or being. Diotima now spells out a consequence of this identification.

Previously Eros was described as a messenger between gods and men. But from the viewpoint of physics or physiology, the difference between men and beasts tends to disappear.[128] As a mark of this disappearance, the erotic disposition is not

127. 204d3: ὡς σὺ φῄς: she dissociates herself from this view.
128. Cf. *Phaedrus* 248d1 ff. The same psyche may inhabit a human or animal body. But here the kinship between man and beast is described in mythical terms; hence it does not depend upon the body, but on the purity of psychic vision. This passage is a good illustration of the difference between the *Symposium* and the *Phaedrus*.

described in religious terms, but as a sickness. Similarly, she denies that the cause of erotic behavior in mankind is calculative reason. These two points bring her quite close to Eryximachus and Aristophanes; taken together, they amount to a reconciliation of elements from the teaching of each man. Just as goodness was substituted for beauty, so Diotima toughens up Agathon's soft teaching with some hard ingredients. The mixture of poetry and physiology continues to baffle Socrates (207c4–7). Socrates is "ignorant and mindless" (207c2–4) concerning Eros. He is "erotic" in the sense that he desires enlightenment about Eros, but by the same token, he is also unerotic. The two passages in which he stresses at some length his need of Diotima for enlightenment concern the activity (206b1: πρᾶξις) or deeds (207b6: ποιεῖν) of those who are driven by Eros. Socrates does not deny that he has noted the "sick" behavior of erotically stricken creatures. But he has not been instructed in these matters by his own bodily nature.

Philosophy, as Socrates will later assert,[129] begins in wonder. Socrates does not express wonder in the first or third sections of Diotima's teaching. In the middle section, however, he does so on three occasions; and on a fourth, Diotima tells him that it is necessary to put an end to wonder. At 205b3 Socrates wonders why, if all men love the same thing always, we say that some men love and others do not. He is puzzled by the various senses of "love" or Eros; in other words, Diotima awakens in him the recognition of his ignorance concerning the heterogeneity in human nature. He grasps what is common to all, but not the differences; thus far, his study of man has been too abstract. We have already noticed the second reference to wonder at 206b5. Again Socrates is aware of the general truth that all men love the good, but he wonders at the specifically erotic seriousness and tension or straining, at the work of Eros in man's body. Finally, the long speech by Diotima, to which we shall shortly turn (207c8–208b6), begins and ends with the injunction not to wonder, which Socrates disobeys, since at its conclusion he wonders whether what

129. *Theaetetus* 155d2–3.

Diotima says is true (208b7–9). The general thesis of the speech is that since man is altogether in flux or genesis, he can share in immortality only through procreation, and that the aforementioned erotic seriousness is for the sake of immortality.

Socrates is aroused to wonder, not by the myth of Eros' birth, but by the ambiguities inherent in human nature as seen from a physiological or "scientific" perspective. He is a lover of nature and logos rather than of myth. He comes to philosophy from physics and cosmology rather than from religion and poetry. The conversion to philosophy is decisively prepared by the middle section of Diotima's teaching. It actually takes place in the final section, and Socrates no longer wonders. The first section of Diotima's speech is specifically designed as an accommodation to Agathon. It makes the transition from the poet to the physicist, but by retaining the best elements of both, it prepares each for the conversion to philosophy. Socrates needs the particular subtlety of myth as an essential ingredient in his education, but he is not in a position to make use of this ingredient until it has been joined to the object of his own Eros. Socrates is erotic for the divine, in the sense of the heavenly, the general, or the universal; he is not erotic for the human. But unlike most men, Socrates is aware of his defects. Hence he seeks out the "most wise Diotima" (208b8) in order to complete his education.

Diotima began this section of her teaching by redefining Eros as the desire for perpetual possession of the good. This desire in turn points toward happiness, which seems to be an end in itself. While linking happiness to the possession of the good, Diotima speaks of the Eros of men but not of animals. Socrates quickly agrees to the link between happiness and perpetual possession of the good. As a mathematically oriented investigator of divine phenomena, a physicist, and a cosmologist, young Socrates identifies happiness in godlike terms. But Diotima does not take this path, which incidentally is reminiscent of the *Republic*. Instead of ascending to the divine, she first descends to the level of what is common to man and beasts. The free, conscious pursuit of happiness is replaced by the constrained, unconscious or corporeal pursuit of what might perhaps be called "satisfaction." Since man is an animal rather than a god, he cannot acquire happiness without first dealing correctly with the demands of his nature for satisfaction.

The physiological and mathematical cosmology to which the young Socrates is devoted cannot deal adequately with the very corporeality it studies, because it inconsistently applies the divine science of eternal numbers to the domain of transience. This science first reduces man to a body and then transforms him into a god. By returning to the physiological or animal level of Eros, Diotima does not try merely to speak Socrates' language. She intends to correct that language with the lessons derived from the mythical section of her teaching. By studying physiology from the viewpoint of the stars, Socrates forgets that the human mixture contains the bestial as well as the divine. Diotima is more faithful to the phenomena of genesis than are the cosmologists or physicists. Nevertheless, at this level happiness is not present, because it is a specifically human or divine, but not bestial, quality. While waiting to see how Diotima will return to the heights from which she has here descended, we must observe that, in seeking to encompass the bestial, or to complete the account of the living, Diotima apparently ignores the distinction between beauty and ugliness which has hitherto dominated the conversation. This is connected to her lowering of Eros from the daimonic to the corporeal.

Socrates needs Diotima's wisdom in order to participate in immortality and so to achieve the happiness he desires. Without her he must remain in the flux of genesis. In that flux it is impossible to preserve the beautiful as distinct from the ugly, since all distinctions are equally transient. Socrates' recognition of this situation is expressed in wonder. Diotima says that he will cease to wonder only by believing Eros to be by nature what they have often already agreed:

> for here [in the case of animals] in accord with the same logos as before [in the case of humans], the mortal nature seeks to be always and immortal, so far as is possible.

And it is possible only in this way, by genesis, so that
[mortal nature] can always leave behind another new
[individual] in place of the old one . . . (207c9–d3)

Diotima again emphasizes that her account of Eros is the same
for all mortal nature. The generated cosmos holds itself together by a perpetual renewal. We have here Agathon's principle of poetic innovation, only restated in physiological terms.
The result is, to repeat, an "Aristotelian" position of the
eternity of the species through the continuity of generation
according to kind. But the form of the individual is generated
along with the individual by an unthinking, instinctual Eros.
For this reason no mention is made in the present passage of
the desire for goodness or happiness, but only of immortality.

Having established the fact that man is a creature of genesis,
Diotima turns from the class of animals to mankind in particular. She speaks first of the body and then of the psyche. Both
are suffused, and so "informed," by the principle of striving
to be or ceasing to become, and so to be other than what one
is. Just as the individual perpetuates himself in his children,
so too the elements of the individual are continuously reproducing themselves. The rest of the form of the individual is an
illusion, we may say, caused by the continuity of motion:
"although an individual is called the same, he never has the
same properties as such, but is always becoming new (νέος ἀεὶ
γιγνόμενος) . . ." (207d6–7). Each property of a generated individual thus exemplifies the behavior attributed by Agathon to
Eros, who flees old age and is always young (195c1: ἀεὶ νέον). The
cosmos altogether both is and is not. It is erotic, and therefore
daimonic, although the precise sense of "daimonic" depends
upon the sense in which "the divine" may be said to refer to
"gods."

This teaching is now applied to the human psyche:

And not only with respect to the body, but also with
respect to the psyche, the manners, habits, opinions,
desires, pleasures, pains, fears, each of these never remains (πάρεστιν: "presents itself") the same in each per-

son, but some come to be and others perish. And what is much more strange than that, with respect to knowledge (αἱ ἐπιστῆμαι), not merely does some of it come to be, while some is dying in us, so that we are never the same in regard to what we know, but each single instance of knowledge suffers the same. (207e1–208a3)

The inseparability of psyche from body, as reflected in the absence of any doctrine of personal immortality, as well as the equivalence between genesis and nature or the whole, means that psyche and mind are also in flux.

The crucial issue is of course that of knowledge. In the *Phaedo, Republic,* and *Phaedrus,* the immortality of the psyche is linked to the theory of Ideas by the doctrine of recollection.[130] The psyche is said to contain knowledge which cannot be derived from the world of genesis, and so must remember what it has seen "elsewhere." Such a distinction is in effect between what we may call immortal and mortal knowledge. Prima facie, it is not easy to see why this distinction, even if we accept it, should commit us to the immortality of the individual psyche. Can we not know that something is perpetually true—for example, that whatever comes to be must also perish—without ourselves existing perpetually? Whatever the case may be in the other dialogues, Diotima answers the preceding question affirmatively. Therefore she mentions "forgetting" (λήθη) but not "recollection" (ἀνάμνησις).

What we know is as transient as the fact that we know it. Our knowledge is continuously slipping away like a river: like the river Lethe itself.

What we call "study" (or "care": μελετᾶν) implies that knowledge is departing; for forgetting is a departing of knowledge, while study saves the knowledge by making a new memory (καινὴν ἐμποιοῦσα . . . μνήμην)[131] instead of the instance which departs, so that it seems to be (δοκεῖν εἶναι) the same. (208a3–7)

130. *Phaedo* 72e ff., *Republic* 614 ff., *Phaedrus* 248 ff.
131. Bury and others regard μνήμην as an interpolation; if so, it is one which perfectly expresses the central issue of the passage.

Memory is now understood as itself a "poem" or generated individual; the continuity of memory is one of δόξα or appearance. Since memory is a discontinuous flow of generated individuals, it cannot serve as the bond which holds the mind or psyche together throughout time by binding it to the timeless Ideas.

As a result, each new instance of memory is but an imitation of a preceding instance. Diotima does not discuss the origin of the first instance, but even if we assume that it arises from the vision of an Idea, this initial vision is instantly replaced by a transient replica. At each moment, then, we would be moving farther away from the Idea, and more inextricably into the world of appearance and opinion. Similarly (and here Diotima is explicit) man does nothing more than imitate immortality, just as genesis imitates ousia:

> In this manner, every mortal thing is preserved, not by being always altogether the same thing, like the divine, but by replacing what departs and becomes old by another new instance which is like its predecessor. By this contrivance, Socrates . . . mortal participates in immortality, both in its body and in all other respects . . . (208a7–b4)[132]

The word "contrivance" (μηχανή) appears in various key passages throughout the dialogue; it is used to describe the cunning of Orpheus, Zeus, Eros, and now of the mortal generally.[133] One may wonder whether Plato thereby links the Olympian gods to the daimonic poetry of mortals. They may be alike because they are bound by genesis, in contrast to the truly divine, for which all strive by cunning—the "wisdom" of imperfect (and consequently erotic) beings.

Love of Honor

Having reduced Eros to nature, and the striving for perpetuity to a physiological need of corporeal genesis, Diotima en-

132. The passage continues: "but is in another way immortal," which most editors correct to "impossible."
133. 179d6, 190c7, 203d6.

joins young Socrates not to wonder why mortals cherish their offspring. But he does not obey her command; wonder drives him to ask: "really, O most wise Diotima, are these things truly so?" (208b7–9). It is not difficult to see what puzzles him. Diotima's accommodation to physics is achieved at an excessive price. The denial of continuity excludes numerical identity and stable mathematical properties. From the perspective of Greek mathematics, even if numbers are themselves divine, the problem remains how they may be related to genesis. According to Diotima, mortal participates (μετέχει) in immortal by reproducing an initial imitation, itself already in motion or process of dissolution. The mathematical proportions of moving bodies are thus moving along with the bodies themselves; there can be no divine knowledge of the generated cosmos.[134] Diotima excludes the possibility of a reconciliation between Pythagorean mathematics and pre-Socratic "process" physics.

But mathematics is not the theme of the *Symposium,* nor for that matter is physiology. The erotic unity of generated things has been introduced to arouse Socrates' wonder. Diotima now returns to the specifically human Eros. The subject of her transition from physics or physiology to the highest "rites and revelations" is honor or political life. The city mediates between the sensible and the intelligible. At the same time, the city is here an object of "scientific" investigation. Diotima, a stranger and prophetess, speaks "like the perfect wise men" (208c1) or "Sophists," an ironical expression which points to the theoretical nature of her next speech. Of course, the scientific and theoretical character of her speech is mitigated by its essentially poetic language: we must never forget the general purpose of Diotima's teaching as a whole.

In order to prove her cosmogonic thesis that Eros is a striving for immortality, Diotima turns to ambition or the love of honor (208c2). By so doing, she deviates somehow from Eros; the term for "love" is now *philia.* Once we ascend from the physiological

134. For a discussion of this issue, cf. J. Klein, "Die griechische Logistik und die Entstehung der Algebra," *Quellen und Studien zur Geschichte der Mathematik, Astronomie, und Physik, 3* (B) (Berlin, 1936).

or unconscious to the psychic or communal, an element of possession is added to the fundamental stratum of desire. As opposed to the privacy of sexual desire, Eros becomes public as philia: love of wealth, honor, or wisdom. In the case of wisdom, the dimension of privacy again returns; hence the analogy between sexual and psychic Eros. But even here, the private is subordinate to the public nature of truth in itself, as contrasted to the problem of the communication of truth. The Ideas are in principle accessible to everyone; it is the body which interferes with this accessibility. The city, then, is a mixture of public and private, intermediate between sexual and noetic desire, or between need and possession.

Diotima shows the poetic mode of her investigation of the city by bursting into meter. Socrates, she says, will wonder at her teaching that Eros strives for immortality, unless he considers that the same impulse moves men to gain a reputation "and establish a deathless fame for all time" (208c5–6). The wonder which was aroused by physics cannot be satisfied without reflection on politics. Whereas previously men were described as behaving like beasts, they are now said to be more ready to run risks for fame than for their children (208c6–d1). Since political life was not visible from the previous perspective, it was necessary to settle for a corporeal imitation of immortality. But the existence of one's dependents is not the same as one's own immortality. The individual lives on as himself through his reputation. Children of the psyche are a truer expression of one's self than are children of the body. The love of honor is thus closer to the love of wisdom than is the love of children.

In this vein, Diotima reinterprets the examples of Alcestis and Achilles, introduced by Phaedrus, but emphasizes their love of honor rather than their material gain. She adds the example of Codrus, a king who is said to have sacrificed his life in order to propitiate "the god" [135] from enslaving Athens to the Dorians. Diotima introduces Athenian or public-spirited legend, as the selfish citizen Phaedrus did not. The king complements the

135. ὁ θεός: Bury quotes the scholium in his note to κόδρον.

wife and the warrior: these are the three "dimensions" of political life. In any of these dimensions, one may win "a deathless memory for virtue" (208d4–6): the political version of the recollection of the deathless Ideas. Reflection upon memory thus provides us with a bridge that reunites the discontinuous moments of corporeal genesis. The content of any member of a series of memories can always be the same, however different the spatio-temporal coordinates of the members of the series may be. This point was obscured by the previous discussion of memory as poiēsis. In other words, the continuous endurance of fame opens up a perspective on memory which was not visible in terms of physical genesis. So too our memories of bodies provide enduring objects through which divine numbers may be applied to the world of genesis.

To the extent that fame is incorporeal, it may be preserved continuously, and even resuscitated after a lapse of time. But we have already observed its defects. First, it depends upon bodies; and second, it is a version of immortality which is equivalent to the death of the person immortalized. If immortality depends upon continuity of consciousness or of corporeal identity, then it is altogether impossible for every product of genesis, which can inhabit only a segment of temporal duration. This is the basis for Diotima's erotic ascent. The principle of the ascent is this: a man is as excellent as the degree to which he is able to transcend temporality. Diotima herself introduces the principle by defining human excellence in terms of an erotic love for deathless fame (208d7–e1). In the specifically human domain, fame—and not, it would seem, the love of beautiful bodies—is the spur.[136]

In honoring love (212b5), we testify to the central agency of the love of honor. The banquet is itself evidence that men love their psyches more than their bodies. Previously Diotima made this statement about men generally (as living in cities: 208c6); now it is said to characterize the better class of men.[137] Preg-

---

136. Cf. Plutarch, *Alcibiades*, 6.2–3.

137. As Hug observes, ὡς οἴονται at 208e4 is ironical: the corporeal erotics suppose that, in their children, they achieve ἀθανασίαν καὶ μνήμην καὶ εὐδαιμονίαν.

nancy is the characteristic of the erotic desire for immortality. Those who are pregnant in the body tend toward women and the making of children (208e1–5). But those who are pregnant in the psyche give birth in a way appropriate to it:

> What then is appropriate? Both prudence and the rest of virtue. Of these things, all the poets are generators, and those of the craftsmen who are said to be inventive. And by far the greatest . . . and most beautiful part of prudence is the regulation of the affairs of cities and dwellings, which is named moderation and justice . . . (209a3–8)

As is clear to most commentators, the term "prudence" (φρόνησις) shows that the political Eros is intermediate between that of the body and the mind.[138] But it does not seem to have been observed that "the most beautiful part of prudence" contains the two virtues—moderation and justice—which are conspicuous by their absence from the initial account of Eros' nature (203c1 ff.). These two passages suggest strongly that the demotic virtues[139] of moderation and justice, although a consequence of the nature of Eros, are not a part of that nature. The Eros of the body is essentially directed toward sexual reproduction. In itself, the desire to mate and reproduce is not political but private. As directed indiscriminately toward any beautiful body, it may even be called antipolitical. As such, it is immoderate and unjust, and so must be regulated by nomos in order for men to live together peacefully.

Justice and moderation require an ascent from the body. At the same time, they depend upon a descent from the highest psychic activity. The Eros of the psyche is essentially directed toward the generation of thoughts and speeches, and so either to an excessive love of fame or a transpolitical love of Ideas. The characteristically psychic Eros is hybristic rather than moderate

138. E.g. Rettig, *Symposion* 209a3: "Auch die φρόνησις, von welcher hier die Rede ist, sowie die ἀρετή unserer Stelle, ist noch nicht σοφία, noch nicht die philosophische."

139. *Phaedo* 82a–b, *Republic* 500d7.

in its desire for the whole, and so it violates the definition of justice as "minding one's own business." The desire for self-perfection is not simply selfish, since it is both compatible with, and even depends upon, the same desire in others. But it is not directed toward, and may even interfere with, "the good of the whole" in the political sense. If then each individual were to abandon himself to Eros, whether of the body or psyche, it is easy to see that most men, and perhaps all, would soon come to grief. According to Plato we cannot simply "depend" upon nature. Human nature is such that the striving for self-perfection is at the same time a striving for self-destruction.

This paradox is discerned by Aristophanes, who advocates the intermediate or political life as the only salvation, however fragile. To a certain extent Diotima agrees with Aristophanes. The city, as intermediate between body and psyche, imitates, and so is in a way most in conformity with, the nature of Eros. It is natural in the derivative sense of being necessary to the strongest interests of man's corporeal and psychic Eros. The love of honor is thus intermediate between, or a blend of, the love of one's own and the love of the best. For this reason it is higher than the simply corporeal Eros, which, although excited by beauty, is essentially a desire for self-survival at any price. The love of honor, on the other hand, includes a "purifying" component of desire for noble self-survival. It therefore imitates the love of beauty in itself. The public appearance of Eros is inseparable from philia; its need is tinctured by possession. As Diotima carefully says, Eros desires prudence (203d6–7); the political man on the other hand is prudent. Indeed, he possesses the greatest and most beautiful part of prudence.

Poets and craftsmen are included as a subordinate species in the genus whose highest representative is the statesman. Poetry or "making" is a political rather than a theoretical activity, designed primarily to "civilize" human beings, not to make them wise. It is the musical logos of the Greeks which distinguishes them from the barbarians. Thus Diotima says that he who is pregnant in the psyche looks for the beautiful and shuns the ugly, "for he will never generate in the ugly" (209b3–4).

The political significance of this "physiological" principle is shown by the fact that the words for "beautiful" and "ugly" also mean "noble" and "shameful." In Diotima's purely physiological teaching, which is concerned with genesis altogether and in which she speaks of all mortals (208a7 ff.), beauty is not mentioned. Whenever Diotima refers to beauty (e.g. 206c5 ff.), it is as a divisive or selective principle. In the present section Diotima is silent about the problem of how to educate the ugly or shameful. And this is to say that Diotima's theoretical consideration of the city is practically defective.

This practical defect is a necessary consequence of Diotima's teaching in two different senses. In the first place it follows from her function as an accommodation to Agathon, or as a bridge between poetry and philosophy. Second and more fundamental, the narcissism of poetry is still present in the peculiar combination of selfishness and selflessness that characterizes philosophy. In contemporary terms, one might say that the *Symposium* denies the possibility of a complete reconciliation between theory and practice. If political virtue is defined as, or in terms of, the love of beauty and nobility, the results will be salutary for the moral and cultural health of the city. The same love, however, also points the best citizens beyond the city toward honor and wisdom. Man cannot live a truly human life which is not a political life, but political life is inconsistent or self-contradictory. The incompleteness of the philosopher is thus an extension of the more fundamental incompleteness of the citizen, or of man himself. The problem of completeness for the philosopher may be said to amount to the problem of how to reconcile the beautiful and the ugly. Whatever his limitations in this direction, it is Plato's final view, not clearly stated in the *Symposium,* that he is more adequate to achieve such a reconciliation than the citizen. In order to complete the portrait of philosophy in the *Symposium,* the reader must continuously remind himself of the ugly and the shameful.

Diotima indicates the defect of the political man by showing that a beautiful body is more important to him than a beautiful psyche. The political man insists upon a beautiful body; if chance provides him with a beautiful psyche as well, so much the better (209b4–c2). He devotes himself to the education of such an individual, but nothing is said about the case of a beautiful psyche in an ugly body, as for example Socrates himself. Since Diotima is educating the young Socrates, just as he will later educate the young and ugly Theaetetus, she is presumably not a political woman. We should also notice that prior to hearing the speeches about virtue, the doubly beautiful individual is called by the "zoological" name of *anthropos*. He does not become a real man (*anēr*) until he acts virtuously (209b7–c2). This distinction between anthropos and anēr does not appear in the physiological section, where the word "mortal" is used for humans and beasts alike.

Diotima gives three examples of the political life: the virtuous citizen, the poet, and the lawgiver. The citizen is reminiscent of the sketch which Pausanias gave of the virtuous pederast, except that Diotima suppresses altogether any mention of sexual union.[140] The end of virtuous speeches is a more secure friendship (209c6) or greater harmony than can be achieved through children of the body. Such a friendship thus imitates the possession of immortality or perpetual goodness. It is a condition of the psyche which to some extent frees man from the bondage of time. For example, like philosophy, it is not dependent upon the presence of a body but may exist in the memory (209c3–4). In such a condition the individual may himself "experience" the eternal or the good, even though the experience is limited and temporary. Thus Diotima points out that the "children" of virtuous friendship are "more beautiful and more deathless" than those of the body (209c6–7); that is, they are not simply or altogether deathless.

Diotima makes an easy transition from the speeches of friendly citizens to the speeches of poets (Homer, Hesiod, "and the other good poets": 209d1–2) and lawgivers (Lycurgus, Solon: 209d4 ff.), all of whom may be said to extend friendship by

---

140. G. M. A. Grube, *Plato's Thought* (Boston, 1958), p. 103, observes that Socrates—i.e. Diotima—does not exclude sexual intercourse.

their speeches to all citizens, and to citizens and gods.[141] The lawgivers are of course the highest type of political man. There are two noteworthy points in Diotima's brief discussion. First, even though she is addressing, so to speak, an audience of Athenians, she praises Lycurgus more highly than Solon. Lycurgus was the savior of Lacedaemon and, "so to speak," of Hellas, whereas Solon is merely said to be honored "among you" Athenians (209d5–7). Second, Diotima acknowledges that even the barbarians can produce lawgivers "who make many beautiful deeds show forth, generating the whole range of virtue" (209e2–3). In other words, it is possible for barbarians to be like Greeks, provided that they possess virtuous nomoi. Differently stated, the musical logos is not the same as the philosophical logos. Just as, with respect to the physiological Eros, all men are the same, so with respect to the political Eros they are potentially the same. So far as the whole domain of practice is concerned, the differences among men or races are conventional. The natural difference is between the individual who is capable of grasping the highest erotic teaching, or perceiving beauty in itself, and the many who are not. Again beauty functions as a divisive term. And thus we reach the highest stage of Diotima's teaching.

The Final Revelation

Diotima began her teaching with the premise that Eros is a daimon who inspires men to love the beautiful. At a very early point she linked beauty with goodness, and midway in her discussions she made the good primary and beauty an instrument to its achievement. From the time of this substitution, Eros ceases to be described as a daimon but has its source in the generated or corporeal instead. This means that Eros is no longer intermediate between men and gods as something other

141. Kuhn, *Tragedy*, 1. 11, says that there is no mention here of the tragedians among the true lovers of wisdom. But the present passage is not concerned with the true lovers of wisdom, and the tragedians would be included among the poets; their function is political or practical.

than either, but is a fundamental aspect of genesis itself. Despite her introductory myth, Diotima grounds the erotic ascent to perpetuity in nature and not simply in a gift from the gods. The beginning and end of her speech camouflage—and to a certain extent qualify—the teaching of the middle part. But the fact remains that poetry and religion are united in a nature which it is their task to render humanly intelligible.

The mythical, physiological, and political discussions were stages in a process combining examination and purification of the candidate for ultimate initiation:

> Perhaps even you, Socrates, might be initiated into the preceding erotic matters. But I do not know if you could [see] the perfect revelations for the sake of which the former exist, if someone should surrender to them rightly.
> (209e5–210a2)[142]

This most difficult part of Diotima's speech is delivered as a continuous revelation, to which Socrates is entirely passive. Diotima does not invite him to participate by so much as a question: "I will speak then . . . nor shall I be wanting in zeal. Try to follow me, if you should be able" (210a3–4). Despite the fact that the revelation is not dialogical, Socrates tells us that it persuaded him (212b2); he no longer expresses his wonder. At this point his erotic apprenticeship is presumably completed.

Or so it would seem. Since Socrates does nothing but repeat Diotima's words, we do not know whether her doubt as to his capacities is justified. Socrates is often made to say ironically, in other dialogues, that he has difficulty in following long speeches. It is not impossible that Socrates stands to Diotima as Apollodorus does to Socrates. With this in mind, let us inspect the details of the final revelation:

> It is necessary . . . for one who proceeds correctly in this matter to begin when young by heading for the beautiful bodies; and first, if his guide leads him correctly, he must love one body and generate beautiful

142. See Bury's instructive note to τὰ δὲ . . . ἐποπτικά.

speeches therein. Next, he must understand that the beauty in any body is brother to that in any other body, so that if it is necessary for him to hunt for beauty in form (τὸ ἐπ' εἴδει καλόν), it is altogether mindless not to suppose beauty to be one and the same in all bodies. Having understood this, he must establish himself as a lover of all the beautiful bodies, by this reflection relaxing his zeal for one, condemning [that zeal] and supposing it to be a trifle. (210a4–b6)

Socrates must be told that the first step in the erotic ascent is to head for beautiful bodies while young.[143] This is not the sort of advice which most young men require; it may be an ad hominem statement, showing that Diotima has grasped the peculiarity of Socrates' nature. In any case the prospective initiate has need of a guide, since the physiological Eros inclines us to all beautiful bodies, and for sexual rather than rhetorical purposes. In addition, the neophyte requires a guide to lead him away from women and toward a beautiful boy; the guide must see to it that Eros becomes "correct pederasty" [144] with logos as its end. That is, the guide draws the initiate away from the possibility as well as the desire to procreate via the flesh. It is then up to the novitiate to "understand" the beauty in one body as brother to the beauty in any other; the guide cannot perform this act of apprehension for him.

The fraternal relation between instances of beauty is itself

143. In a previously cited lecture (n. 79 above), Moravcsik says of Diotima's ascent: "We should not interpret the latter as entailing that each human has to traverse the entire path. For those whose life is dominated by physical eros each of the steps is a necessary condition for the attainment of the next one. But the more gifted need not begin at the bottom; Plato does not rule out the possibility of the young mathematical genius." This is contradicted by much of Diotima's speech, not to mention the nature of young Socrates. Eros in the *Symposium* is rooted in the body or genesis. A response to corporeal beauty is necessary for the understanding of genesis. The noncorporeally erotic "mathematical genius" is precisely the person who does not understand human existence, nor genesis itself. But Moravcsik's point is supported by parts of Diotima's speech.

144. 211b5–6; cf. *Phaedrus* 249a2, where "philosophical pederasty" is again a prelude to ultimate initiation (249c6 ff.).

expressed erotically.[145] There is then a distinction between perceiving the difference between beauty and a single body, and grasping the formal unity of beauty as exhibited throughout the manifold of its instances. Before this distinction can be drawn, the novitiate must extend his grasp of the brotherhood of beautiful instances from the body to the psyche (210b6 ff.), and then to the customs and laws of the city (210c3–4). We are still in the domain of the practical, but with this crucial difference. There is now a continuous and directed tendency toward formal unification within the domain of the practical. In her previous account of the city Diotima emphasized the potential unity of men with respect to virtue or the love of honor. She is now in the process of transcending the city and the love of honor as well. This is also shown by the omission from the present account of poets, who were mentioned in the first account as almost on a par with the lawgivers. The poet and inventor aim at novelty (209a4–5) and so cannot perceive the sameness and unity of beautiful instances.

On one extremely important point, however, the two accounts agree in principle, although they differ in degree. In both versions nothing is said about love for an ugly body, regardless of the quality of its psyche. The neophyte is able to make do with the smallest degree of psychic bloom (210b8), but he is not impervious to or emancipated from physical beauty. Even in the perception of the unity of beauty within the customs and laws of the city, he does not despise or ignore the body. In fact, Diotima says that this perception is necessary "in order that he may suppose beauty in the body to be a small thing" (210c5).[146] A small thing is still something. The irony of Diotima's teaching is that it leaves conjectural the way in which her pupil, who is notoriously ugly, could ever obtain the lovers we see pursuing him in the *Symposium*. In other words, although commentators are understandably eager to read more into her words than they convey, Diotima does not

145. Cf. *Republic* 506e1 ff. (esp. 508b12) and *Phaedrus* 249b6.
146. Krüger, *Einsicht*, pp. 178–79, notices this.

actually explain how the neophyte distinguishes between the body and the psyche.

From love of virtuous speeches, there is a necessary (210c3) transition to love of beauty in customs and laws. This stage is justified by the obvious dependence of virtuous speech upon the virtue and prudence of the founding "fathers." But Diotima next indicates that reflection upon the customs of the city will lead the neophyte "to the sciences" (τὰς ἐπιστήμας),

> in order that he may see beauty in them, too, and by looking at beauty on a great scale, not love it in a single case, like a slave, whether in a beautiful boy or some man or a single custom. (210c6–d3)

Or, we may add, in a single city. But Diotima does not say this: her careful phrase, "in a single custom," means that the love of science is intended to take place within the love of all customs in the virtuous city. Is there any necessity that patriotism should lead to theoretical love? Again, Diotima does not say how the neophyte moves from love of the body (in this case the city) to love of the psyche (the noetic consequences of the beauty of the city).

From the higher viewpoint of the sciences, Diotima refers to political piety as a slavish love. She thereby reminds us of the conflict between theory and practice, which we have met on several other occasions. The transition to "the vast sea of beauty" is a transcendence of the city, and therefore of the body in its own terms:

> by looking (θεωρῶν) at it, [the neophyte] may generate many beautiful and magnificent speeches and discursive thoughts (διανοήματα) in unstinting philosophy, until, strengthened and augmented thereby, he may see a certain single science, which is [knowledge] of the following beauty. And here . . . try to pay as close attention to me as you possibly can. (210d4–e2)

According to this passage, the transition from practical to theoretical looking comes about by the strength gained from the

267

genesis of many beautiful speeches. Philosophy is thus described as the process of generating speeches, and so as a locus of genesis simply. The vision of beauty in itself is a consequence of genesis, and so too of philosophy, which it completes or perfects. Presumably this "single science" is the science of wisdom, or so one would be tempted to surmise. But let us consider this point more carefully.

The sciences themselves are many, and so are the speeches and thoughts in which these sciences dwell. Diotima says that the generating cause of this manifold is a vision of the beautiful, not yet in its ultimate unity but as a kind of intermediate manifold (reminiscent of Kant's schematism), comparable to a vast or bounteous sea. The sea is at once formed and unformed; like Proteus it continuously changes its shape. The fluidity of water, which enables it to undergo all shapes or forms, is akin to the fluency of speech. The problem of how to reduce the fluidity or fluency of oceanic speech to its ultimate unity is the problem of the transition from discursive thought to intuition. Since Diotima's teaching is a description of an ascent from genesis (the bodily or multiple) to ousia, no account can be given of the factor or principle which guides the neophyte upward at each stage of the transcendence. This guide cannot be identified as Eros for reasons which have already been given: Eros is polymorphous perverse and himself stands in need of guidance.

We need to make the final ascent from beautiful particulars of the highest kind to beauty simply or in itself as the unity of those particulars. Unfortunately, such an ascent takes us from speech to silence. Every speech is a particular and generated individual, a wave of the sea rather than the sea itself; it is itself a unified manifold, but one which cannot speak its own unity. The visibility of the beautiful particular rests upon the prior intuition of beauty in itself; but every attempt to speak of beauty in itself merely generates another particular. Silently present within the interstices of Diotima's account of the ascent is an unspoken and unspeakable descent, the "guide" who directs Eros in the right way at each stage of transcendence.

Eros is the physiological or physical striving of genesis; not he but the guide has already seen that toward which the neophyte is being directed.

Little wonder that Diotima demands the closest possible attention from Socrates at this point, for her next step is really impossible: she intends to speak about the unspeakable. I repeat: speech about the unspeakable is not the unspeakable itself. We cannot bespeak the unspeakable. To speak it is to generate an example of it, and genesis is not ousia:

> Whosoever may have been thus far guided in erotics, looking at beautiful things one after another and in a regular way, coming now to the end (τέλος) of erotics, will see instantaneously (ἐξαίφνης) something wonderful, beautiful in its nature. And this, Socrates, is the reason for all the previous toils. (210e2–6)

The "wonderful" (θαυμαστόν) nature of beauty in itself is a sign that no logos can be given of it. Diotima's poetic account, with its emphasis upon visual imagery, is rather a prophecy of the step from philosophy to wisdom. The prophetic mode of discernment is like the poetic myths of a previous life or future redemption, a recollection of the necessary implications of the intelligibility of genesis.[147]

Diotima's prophetic vision is the counterpart to the role of the guide within her account of the erotic ascent. It is this vision which serves as the bond between discursive and intuitive reason. Prophecy emerges from the unchanging presence of ousia before the mind of cosmic psyche. It "opens the horizon" within which an ascent from particulars to the "instantaneous" vision of unity may occur.[148] The opening of the

147. In the *Phaedrus*, where the same visual imagery is combined with the language from the mysteries to describe the psyche's recollection of the hyperuranian ousiai, it is made clear that, in this world, the philosopher does not see the Ideas, but rather his memories of them; e.g. 249c6, 250a5.

148. Robin, *l'Amour*, p. 183, calls our attention to the uses of ἐξαίφνης in *Republic* 515c6, 516e5 (the allegory of the cave). More important, however, are the discussion of the instant in *Parmenides* 156c ff. and the passage in the Seventh Letter (341c–d) which is very close to the text of the *Symposium*. Cf. Festugière, *Contemplation*, pp. 343–44 and Oehler, *Noetischen*, pp. 88, 112, 125.

horizon is not discussed thematically by Diotima, but it is manifest in her revelation itself. Within that context one may agree that the "single science" mentioned above is dialectic. But every analogy between the ascent of the *Symposium* and that of the *Republic* should bear this in mind: Socrates states in the *Republic* (511b3 ff.) that the proper use of dialectic involves thinking with Ideas alone, apart from all sensible and imaginable things. Even more, it requires access to the good or principle of the whole. In the *Symposium* the beautiful is described in visual terms,[149] and it cannot be the principle of the whole.

Diotima begins her description of the goal of erotic striving in terms which have been called a kind of "negative theology":[150]

> First, then, it is always, neither coming to be nor passing away, neither increasing nor diminishing. Next, it is not beautiful in one part and ugly in another, nor at one time and not at another, nor [beautiful] in one respect and ugly in another, nor beautiful in one place and ugly in another, so as to be beautiful to some and ugly to others. (210e6–211a5)

We should not overlook the fact that throughout her speech Diotima never calls this kind of beauty an Idea. The word ἰδέα occurs in a "nontechnical" sense in her speech, referring to visible shape or nature. Diotima arrives at immortal beauty by an ascent from genesis; that which transcends genesis is not the process of vision of beauty, but the horizon within which the process occurs. Just as one can infer by negation the character of immortality from our desire for it, so one can "see" immortal beauty in its mortal instances by a similar negative induction.

Diotima's description of beauty does not presuppose the theory of Ideas, but may be understood as part of the preparation for its subsequent development by Socrates. Her proph-

149. Cf. Krüger, *Einsicht*, p. 200.
150. By Krüger, p. 201 ff.

ecy shows us how genesis points toward ousia. If we were to restate affirmatively what Diotima expresses negatively, beauty would be called eternal, stable, beautiful in all its parts and at all times, as seen by anyone in all places or from any perspective. The value of the negative description is that it suggests the "corporeal" origins of our vision without affirmatively identifying what we see as itself a body:

> nor will the beautiful be pictured (φαντασθήσεται) to him as a face or hands, nor does it share in any other part of the human body; neither is it a logos or any science, nor is it in anything else, such as an animal, or earth, or heaven, or in anything else . . . (211a5–b1)

The first half of the negative description excluded beauty from spatio-temporal change but not from spatio-temporal presence. For example, time and place are similarly exempt and yet spatio-temporally omnipresent. The second half of the description shows that beauty is neither a body nor a speech; but the fact that it cannot be "pictured" as a body does not mean that it does not "appear" at all. On the contrary, the beautiful, despite its uniqueness, is visible in its uniqueness. It is one of the "blessed appearances" (εὐδαίμονα φάσματα), to use a phrase from a parallel passage in the *Phaedrus* (250c3). It is a contradiction in terms to call beauty "invisible" or "nonapparent": beauty in itself appears or presents itself as that which is common to every appearing instance of itself. But that which is visible or apparent must be visible or appear in and through bodies, speeches, or whatever is bound by the spatio-temporal conditions of genesis.

Diotima terminates her description of beauty with a brief affirmative clause:

> but it is always itself in conformity to itself (αὐτὸ καθ᾽ αὐτὸ) with itself (μέθ᾽ αὐτοῦ), of unique form (μονοειδὲς); and all the other beautiful things share in it in such a way that, while the other things come to be and pass away, it becomes neither more nor less, nor suffers anything. (211b1–5)

I do not wish to overstate my point, but it seems to me fair to suggest that there is nothing in this brief description of beauty in itself which renders it in a realm altogether separate from its appearances to man. Its separateness is rather as a unique form, visible not in something else, but by virtue of those instances which dwell within it. Perhaps we may compare beauty to a number, which does not depend for its being on the act of counting but which is entirely present in any such act, even though no one could give a complete logos of its properties. Just as beautiful things share in beauty and do not change it by their changes, so too with enumerated things and number.[151] But apart from this brief remark, I believe it would be misleading to enter here into a long discussion of the logical, epistemological, or ontological difficulties implicit in the theory of Ideas. Even if it is true that Plato was in possession of such a "theory," it is certainly excluded from the *Symposium*. The thirteen lines devoted to the description of beauty in itself, about two-thirds of which are negative, are an indication of an implication of the nature of genesis, occurring within a context that makes abundantly evident the impossibility of furnishing a logos of what has been indicated.

As though to emphasize this point, Diotima returns to the process of ascent in such a way as to integrate the final vision into the accomplishment of the previous stages:

> so that when someone ascending from the previously mentioned stages through the correct kind of pederasty begins to see that beauty, he will almost grasp the end (σχεδὸν ἄν τι ἅπτοιτο τοῦ τέλους). This is the right proce-

151. One may seriously doubt whether the Idea of beauty (if there is one) is "beautiful" in the same sense that beautiful things are. An Idea is an absolute beginning which makes visible a property to which we give a name; this name is the "predicate" which stands for the property as it appears in spatio-temporal instances. The "predicate" is an application of the visibility of the Idea; it cannot be applied to the visibility of the Idea itself. That would amount merely to saying a = a, which in fact Plato does say by making Ideas self-identical. Beauty is then beautiful in the same sense that number is numerical or a tautology is tautologous: namely, as an apodictic exhibition of itself.

dure or way of being led by another in erotic matters . . . (211b5–c1)

The vision of immortal beauty is thus made dependent upon
correct pederasty, or a condition of corporeal genesis. And
Diotima now indicates that the instantaneous vision of beauty
is incomplete: the initiate begins to see the end but cannot
entirely grasp it. As a spatio-temporal being, man can begin
to perfect himself, just as genesis is constantly beginning to
transcend itself.[152] He cannot complete this process without
coming to an end or ceasing to exist.

Diotima's previous account of the ascent was governed by
the principle that the love of beauty is for the sake of immortality or the perpetual possession of the good. In the present account, which also serves as the peroration to her speech,
the good is not mentioned; the love of immortal beauty stands
alone as the completion of erotic striving. In other words, even
if we should see beauty in itself, we can never satisfy the desire
to possess the good perpetually. Stated differently, man may
see beauty but not the good, except inasmuch as the good is
exemplified by beauty. In the vision of beauty man enters into
the domain of the final or highest differentiation of the one by
the many. But he does not achieve the final unification of the
many by the one:

> beginning from the earlier beauties for the sake of this
> one, he must always ascend, as on the steps of a stair,[153]
> from one to two, and from two to all beautiful bodies;
> and from beautiful bodies to beautiful customs, from
> beautiful customs to beautiful knowledge, and from
> knowledge he will terminate in this knowledge, which
> is no other than knowledge of this beauty itself; and so
> initiated, he knows what beauty is itself. In such a life,

152. This shows that Gaiser radically oversimplifies (*Ungeschriebene*, p. 222)
in saying that Socrates asserts an ascent to the highest μάθημα of beauty itself.
And, as I mention in the text, μάθημα is not here ἐπιστήμη.

153. Cf. Hoffmann, *Symposion*, n. 24.

my dear Socrates . . . above all others, it is worth while for a human being to live, in the vision of the beautiful itself. (211c1–d3)

The peroration is more affirmative than what precedes; "almost grasping" is replaced by "knowledge" (μάθημα). In fact, *mathēma* or associated terms occur five times in this very brief recapitulation.[154] Although it would be tempting to see here an allusion to mathematics, or the similarity between knowledge of beauty and that of numbers,[155] we must bear in mind that the mathēma of the beautiful is a unification of physiology, politics, and the various kinds of human learning. Mathēma has replaced *epistēmē* because it refers, not to scientific knowledge, but to an understanding, which is broader than science. The understanding of beauty includes an appreciation of bodies. In summarizing the extraordinary character of beauty in itself, Diotima contrasts it with "gold and raiments, beautiful boys and youths," but is silent here about customs, laws, and virtuous speeches (211d3–5). The erotic appetite is essentially rooted in bodies, and especially in living bodies.

Whereas the striving of the body is for life, philosophy is a preparation for dying. The conflict implicit in human existence is dramatically resolved by "the correct kind of pederasty," or a love in which life comes closest to death. Such a "death" is the life most worth having for humans. The lovers of boys imitate this genuine life in being stunned by the sight of their sweethearts, wanting "to be with them always, if this were possible, neither to eat or drink but to see them only and to be with them" (211d5–8: συνεῖναι). The pederast is inclined toward the body as though it were an eternal being; his behavior, if carried out, would lead to his death from starvation. But the force of the body prevails over disinterested visual appetite: "to be with" also means to have sexual intercourse. The verb is used twice in this clause; in the second usage "always" is dropped: the purity of vision succumbs to the flesh.

154. Cf. n. 152 above and Brochard, *Banquet*, p. 80.
155. Cf. Krüger, *Einsicht*, pp. 212–13.

From the desire to look at and be with the body of the beloved, Diotima turns for the last time to beauty itself:

What then . . . do we suppose would happen to him who sees beauty itself, whole, pure, unmixed, not filled up with human flesh and colors and other mortal nonsense; what if he were able to behold divine beauty itself in its unique form? (211d8–e4)

The contrast is between corporeal and pure beauty, characterized for the first time by the terms "flesh" and "divine"; by contrast, at 206c6, human generating is called "divine." Now the body is daimonic, whereas the psyche is divine. Since there are various kinds of bodies (including acts and speeches), there is more than one form of corporeal beauty. The beauty perceived by the psyche, however, is unique in its form. The many forms of corporeal beauty share in the unity of psychic or noetic beauty. To see the noetic beauty is, then, to see the truth of the various instances of corporeal beauty.

Do you suppose . . . that a trivial life transpires (γίγνεσθαι) for a man who looks there, seeing [beauty itself] as one must and being with it? Don't you see . . . that there only will it happen (γενήσεται) to him, as he sees beauty with the faculty by which it can be seen, that he may generate (τίκτειν), not images of virtue, but true instances,[156] since he is not grasping an image, but the truth. When he has generated (τεκόντι) and reared true virtue, he will come to incur the condition of being loved by the god (ὑπάρχει θεοφιλεῖ γενέσθαι), and if it is available to any human being, immortality will also belong to him. (211e4–212a7)

In the last paragraph of Diotima's speech the word "become" occurs three times and "generate" twice; in addition, god is said to become the friend of man. These terms provide an unmistakable qualification to the way in which immortality is made hypothetically available to the successful initiate. Beauty

156. See Bury's note to οὐκ εἴδωλα . . . ἀλλ' ἀληθῆ.

is always, but man is not always with it.[157] Immortality is at best a "possession" of man for a limited time or part of his life, a possession that he loses with the others.

Man possesses the immortal only by seeing it; in so grasping the truth, he at once generates "true instances" of it. The immortal is silent; man comes closest to the immortal in a kind of silent vision, but he cannot adhere to this condition. He can only preserve or possess a memory of it by making speeches or giving an account of what he has seen. In giving an account of beautiful bodies, acts, and speeches, man generates the virtuous speeches of truth. The truth of that account is true beauty, which shines forth in virtuous speeches just as parents are visible in their children. As man sees or touches the truth, to that extent Eros is replaced by philia: man becomes a friend of god, for god is truth. In this sense Diotima succeeds where the previous speakers have failed. Without denying that man is essentially a resident of genesis, she shows how his desire for immortality may be satisfied. Diotima reconciles the human and the divine, and she does so on the premises of the previous speakers, thereby also reconciling rhetoric and philosophy.

The young Socrates is persuaded by Diotima's philosophical rhetoric:

> and having been persuaded, I try to persuade others also
> that no one could easily obtain a better co-worker than
> Eros for human nature with a view to this possession.
> (212b2–4)

Eros is not self-sufficient and, although extremely useful, he is not quite indispensable. As a coworker of human nature, Eros is not identical with it. If one tried hard enough, one could apparently find a still better assistant. The specific excellence of Eros is as an assistant in the attempt to grasp immortality via the perception of beauty. Perhaps better assistants are available

---

157. Some translators obscure the obvious by a gratuitous insertion of "ever" (Lamb) or "constant" (Hamilton) at 212a2 (συνόντος αὐτῷ). R. Hackforth, "Immortality in Plato's Symposium," *Classical Review, 64* (1950) correctly discusses the significance of this passage.

if one takes a different path. Socrates is persuaded of no more than that. His careful words point beyond the *Symposium,* or, if Eros is a mandatory coworker for man, to a possible short-coming in his own nature. The honor and assiduous exercise which Socrates devotes to erotics (212b6) are no doubt perfectly genuine, but they amount to a hunting for and testing of beautiful psyches. It is by no means self-evident that Socrates himself begins unambiguously at the level of the body.

This does not mean that he dispenses altogether with the body. Whatever may be his own erotic inclinations, in training potential philosophers and virtuous citizens, Socrates must of course appeal to that most accessible of coworkers. In his acts as in his speeches, Socrates conforms to the nomos of his fellow citizens as far as possible. He sits next to the beautiful Agathon, but he is not even tempted by the flesh of Alcibiades. How ambiguous is his remark that "now and always I praise the power and manliness of Eros as much as I am able" (212b7–8). So too his final remark to Phaedrus: "Believe, if you will, this logos to have been spoken as an encomium to Eros, or call it by whatever name you please" (212b8–c3). By leaving the task of identifying his speech to Phaedrus, the father of the logos, Socrates follows the advice of Alcmaeon: "This is why humans perish, because they cannot join the beginning to the end." [158]

158. Diels, *Vorsokratiker, 1,* Fr. 2.

CHAPTER EIGHT

★ ALCIBIADES ★

Alcibiades' Nature

In his perceptive study of irony Kierkegaard rightly observes that Socrates' account of Eros in the *Symposium* is theoretically incomplete: "He starts out from the concrete and arrives at the most abstract, and there, where the investigation should now begin, he stops." [1] Kierkegaard is writing from a Hegelian perspective, but this does not make his comment irrelevant. What he regards as incompleteness is for us a clue to Plato's intention. Kierkegaard correctly attributes the incompleteness of the discussion to Socratic irony, which he describes in terms of the relationship between Socrates and Alcibiades. Despite his sensitivity to the dramatic situation, Kierkegaard, as a disciple of Hegel, reveals a characteristically modern dissatisfaction with irony or reticence. Implicit in his conception of philosophy as system is the desire that Diotima's revelation be transformed entirely from myth into logos.

According to Kierkegaard, if the love between Socrates and Alcibiades had been complete, "then indeed would the Third have been given to them . . . namely, the Idea, and such a relation would never have generated about them such a passionate unrest." Kierkegaard implicitly compares the Platonic Idea to the Christian trinity or to the tripartite Hegelian dialectic, and thereby criticizes Plato (or the Greek age) for not having been able to give satisfaction to Eros. Hegel overcomes the difference between psyche and Idea by combining Greek thought with the Christian revelation; for Plato, as we have abundantly seen, such an *Aufhebung* is impossible. The satis-

1. Kierkegaard, *Ironie*, p. 48.

faction of Eros would mean the disappearance of man, and not his transformation into a selfconscious god.

In his later work, Kierkegaard frequently criticizes the philosopher for a failure to experience the infinite subjective concern for his individual immortality or perfection. It is curious that he did not remember his earlier study of Platonic Eros. Probably this is because he read Plato in the light of Hegel, and Hegel in the light of Christianity. But Plato's ironical silence with respect to the Third symbolizes his recognition of the irreducible stratum of concern by the individual thinker for his personal destiny.[2] For Plato, however, personal destiny depends upon thought as restricted by the privacy of the body. In the *Symposium* the privacy of prayer is replaced by the corporeal Eros. We cannot speak about our vision of divine beauty in universal terms because speech is inseparable from the particularity of genesis. Whereas the Christian god is the infinite synthesis of the universal and personal, in which man shares by love or faith, Plato's conception of "friendship with the gods" depends upon the cessation of love or the absence of personality.

The abrupt entrance of Alcibiades therefore represents the impossibility of remaining in the presence of the divine through the medium of speech. But it also brings us back to the central Platonic concern with the nature of the philosophical experience in man, or with philosophical religion, and so with the peculiar characteristics of the philosopher's erotic concern for immortality. The unsatisfactory character of the love affair between Socrates and Alcibiades is a necessary consequence of the peculiarity of Socrates' Eros, which can only desire divine things or beings. I have been implicitly suggesting throughout this study that such a peculiarity constitutes a defect in Socrates' nature. In order to understand Plato's conception of the philosopher, one would also have to consider his love for Socrates, and so the degree in which his praise of Socrates is also a criticism. This means that we have to understand the precise sense in

2. For the "third," cf. Rosen, *Ideas*, p. 410, n. 4. In the *Phaedrus* 248d3 ff. the nine kinds of life in order of their descent from the εὐδαίμων φάσμα are each described in terms of a specific caring (μελετή).

which the love of Socrates for Alcibiades is deficient or unsatisfactory. The problem is complicated by the fact that our
major witness to the nature of Socrates is himself of a most
peculiar nature.

To begin with, Alcibiades is another instance of the hybristic
circle-men, who imitate completeness by a harmony of opposites.[3] Although a licentious bisexual, he does not seem to have
been motivated by lust, but rather by "the love of conquest
. . . and of being first." Consequently (as Plutarch tells us),
Alcibiades' lovers appealed to his love of glory and reputation
rather than to his sensuality.[4] Socrates says that the young
Alcibiades surpassed all of his lovers in pride, although they
were many and high-spirited.[5] This pride is defined by Socrates
as a perpetual desire "to have more"; his *pleonexia,* however,
is neither for gold nor ousia, but for men. Alcibiades wishes to
rule "the whole of mankind"; he is by nature a potential tyrant.[6] In the service of this overmastering desire, Alcibiades is
capable of the most contradictory forms of behavior. He is an
Athenian to the Athenians and a Spartan to the Spartans; even
more, a Greek to the Greeks and a barbarian to the barbarians.[7]

Alcibiades imitates the whole, but in wholly human terms.
He can see into the psyche of Socrates, but he cannot see the
Ideas. He is himself a master of hunting and dissimulation, but
in a way which places him halfway between the Sophist and the
philosopher.[8] The philosopher's dissimulation is designed to
protect himself from the many, and the many from philosophy.
Alcibiades hunts the many or simulates their behavior in order
to dominate them. He is a true son of the democracy even in his
attempt to become its tyrant. He claims to have learned justice
"from the many" as a boy, and Xenophon regularly links him

3. Xenophon, *Memorabilia* 1.2.12.
4. *Alcibiades* 2.1, 6.2–3. Cf. 23.3. In the *Protagoras* Critias says of him (336e1):
'Αλκιβιάδης δὲ ἀεὶ φιλόνικός ἐστι πρὸς ὃ ἂν ὁρμήσῃ.
5. *Alcibiades I* 103b4–5.
6. Ibid., 104c2, 105a6–c4; cf. *Alcibiades II* 141a5 ff.
7. Plutarch, *Alcibiades* 23.3–5.
8. Ibid., 23.4: Alcibiades had a chameleon-like way of assimilating himself to
the customs and modes of life of others.

with Critias as characteristic of democratic and oligarchic licentiousness respectively.[9] Alcibiades' rivals, in linking him to the destruction of the Hermae, "offered as proof his licentiousness, especially his undemocratic habits." [10] These apparently contradictory judgments may be understood, from a Socratic perspective, as a sign that Alcibiades' extreme variability is itself a democratic vice. His entire life may be explained as hybristic insolence, in which conceit led to a self-destructive combination of daring and insolence.[11] He is a superb example of Thucydides' judgment on the defects of political life, and especially of the Athenian democracy.[12]

In the *Gorgias* Socrates describes his love for Alcibiades to Callicles: "Each of us loves two things: I love Alcibiades the son of Cleinias and philosophy, whereas you love the *demos* of Athens and the son of Pyrilampus." [13] The *Symposium* provides us with unmistakable evidence that Socrates and Alcibiades are compatible neither in psyche nor in body; although both are exceptional men, they seem to share only the attribute of hybris. For this reason it is not sufficient to interpret Socrates' "love" as a desire to make Alcibiades either a virtuous citizen or a philosopher. From the beginning of their relationship, Alcibiades is presented as obviously unfitted for either role. Of the various youthful interlocutors in the dialogues, he most resembles the spirited Glaucon, but exceeds him in hybris and seems to fall short of his modest patience for theoretical discus-

9. *Alcibiades I* 110e1; *Memorabilia* 1.2.12 et passim.

10. Thucydides 6.28.2.

11. Plato indicates the laziness or carelessness of Alcibiades' conceit by having him say with respect to Athenian statesmen: νῦν δ' ἐπειδὴ καὶ οὗτοι . . . τῇ γε φύσει πάνυ πολὺ περιέσομαι (*Alcibiades I* 119b5 ff.: his natural superiority makes it unnecessary for him to exercise and learn). Cf. Xenophon, *Memorabilia* 1.2.24.

12. Cf. J. de Romilly, *Thucydides and Athenian Imperialism* (New York, 1963), p. 322: "human nature being what it is, man allows himself to be so carried away by success that he conceives immoderate desires. This law is used by Thucydides to explain all the political mistakes described in his work, and those of Athens in particular." Cf. p. 333; de Romilly cites 2.65 for Thucydides' view that Athens was destroyed because ἐπιθυμία triumphed over πρόνοια.

13. 481d3–5. The son of Pyrilampus, a popular beauty, was named Demos; cf. Aristophanes, *Wasps* 98.

sion.[14] The Eros that Socrates bears toward Alcibiades is different from, but related to, his Eros for philosophy.[15] Alcibiades is neither philosophical nor prudent. He is outspoken to a degree that even the Athenian banqueteers find laughable (222c2: παρρησίᾳ). Nor can his lifelong appetite for tyrannical rule have recommended him to Socrates as a potential statesman, whether in peace or war.[16] Why, then, is Socrates erotically drawn to him?

The answer which Socrates himself gives is surprising only to those who have not understood the *Symposium*. He has been prevented by his *daimonion* from abandoning Alcibiades precisely because of the young boy's hybris or pleonexia.[17] Socrates pursues Alcibiades in order to provide him with the assistance needed for the fulfillment of his ambition to be king of all men.[18] Extreme hybris, or the desire to be a god,[19] is not simply a vice, but a quality deserving of study, and in a sense, of cultivation. Socrates' offer of assistance is not simply ironical, but expresses frankly his interest in hybris. Socrates loves in Alcibiades that which he shares with him: a kind of madness through which each in his way transcends his contemporaries. But though Alcibiades is jealous of the gods, his madness is not divine. The absence of divinity is the fatal flaw in one who can otherwise justly be regarded as the paradigm of the universal man.[20]

14. Cf. my portrait of Glaucon in Rosen, *ErosRepub*. Xenophon shows the young Alcibiades engaging Pericles in "Socratic" dialectic in *Memorabilia* 1.2.40 ff., but his impertinence is even more apparent here than in his conversations with Socrates.

15. That the excellence of Alcibiades is not theoretical may also be inferred from a remark by Socrates: Protagoras is more beautiful than Alcibiades (*Protagoras* 309c4 ff.).

16. Cf. *Alcibiades I* 135b6 ff. with *Gorgias* 515b5 ff.

17. *Alcibiades I* 103a5, 104e6 ff.

18. Ibid., 105d2.

19. J. Stenzel is right to say that Alcibiades represents φθόνος in the *Symposium* (he cites 213d), provided we realize that Alcibiades is jealous of the gods, and not of Socrates alone. Cf. Stenzel, *Erzieher*, p. 243 and F. Nietzsche, *Also Sprach Zarathustra* in *Werke*, ed. K. Schlechta (Munich, 1954), pt. 3, "Auf den glückseligen Inseln"; "was wäre denn zu schaffen, wenn Götter—da wären!"

20. Hence the appropriateness of the subtitle traditionally assigned to the *Alcibiades I*: Η ΠΕΡΙ ΑΝΘΡΩΠΟΤ ΦΤΣΕΩΣ ΜΑΙΕΤΤΙΚΟΣ.

Since Alcibiades can never rise to theory or vision of the Ideas, his hybris must necessarily be expressed in deeds rather than in speeches.[21] By the same token, his revelation of Socrates' nature is more concerned with the qualities of courage, temperance, and physical endurance than with speech. Alcibiades almost succeeds in transforming Socrates into a man of action, albeit one who is characterized by restraint or passive endurance. His speech cannot be adequately understood as intended by Plato to refute the public charge that Socrates was responsible for Alcibiades' political vices.[22] Alcibiades' praise of Socrates is to a considerable extent a defense of himself. He "revises" Socrates' nature, an act of hybris, in order to justify to himself his strange passion (213d6: τὴν τούτου μανίαν τε καὶ φιλεραστίαν) for the philosopher. It is also true that Alcibiades' profligacy is to some extent mitigated by his love for the paragon of virtue. But Alcibiades is the victim of a human mania where only a divine mania will do.

Enter Alcibiades

Alcibiades' sudden appearance at the banquet serves to rescue Socrates from the criticism which discussion of his speech would have engendered. In so doing, Alcibiades ironically repays Socrates for having saved his life at Potidaea. At the conclusion of his speech Socrates is praised by some (212c4: τοὺς μὲν) of the guests. As Bury observes, the response is less enthusiastic than the one which greeted Agathon.[23] Among those who refrain from applause is Aristophanes, who also wishes to object to a reference by Diotima to his own speech (at 205d10 ff.). At the point in question Diotima denies that the lover seeks his other half, or that Eros is love of the whole; instead, she says, it is

---

21. Plutarch, *Alcibiades* 10.3, in the act of praising Alcibiades as an orator, indicates by a reference to Theophrastus that he was not entirely fluent.

22. As claimed by J. Hatzfeld, *Alcibiade* (Paris, 1951), pp. 50 ff.: "Non seulement Alcibiade, en tant qu'homme politique, n'est pas le disciple de Socrate, mais c'est parce qu'il est devenu un homme politique qu'il a tourné le dos au Socratisme." Cf. Xenophon, *Memorabilia* 1.2.12 ff.

23. Cf. 198a1–2: πάντας . . . ἀναθορυβῆσαι τοὺς παρόντας . . .

love of the good. If Aristophanes had succeeded in registering his objection, Socrates would have been led into a discussion of the whole and the nature of the good, and thereby into a criticism of the city, which dilutes love of the good by love of one's own. Instead, thanks to the arrival of Alcibiades, we get an account of Socrates' political excellence.

Agathon is a poor dialectician, but he is more than competent to bewitch the crowd. Socrates, on the contrary, is a master at dialectic or the persuasion of individuals, but he lacks the ability to sway the multitude, whether at a banquet or in a courtroom.[24] This inability is related to his insistence that a poor memory prevents him from engaging in lengthy speeches.[25] In addressing the many, or by the use of long speeches, one cannot accommodate his remarks to the varied nature and continuously changing responses of the audience. As Socrates' remarks on popular encomia show (198b1 ff.), the problem is one of the selection of material. Socrates' method is not to say everything, but only the beautiful part of the truth. It is thus not the quantity of the material but its beauty which concerns him. When the content has been suitably prepared, Socrates is quite capable of speaking at considerable length. But the beauty of the selection depends upon the nature of his audience. He must say different parts of the truth to different people.

The Sophists and their students can sway the crowd, but only by failing to practice safe rhetoric. Their power is not due to a knowledge of the psyche but to a willingness to corrupt it.[26] Thus Protagoras, for example, who claims to be a master of the

24. In *Alcibiades I* 114b6 ff. Socrates tells the young Alcibiades that the same man can persuade the many and the one. But the relatively restrained response to his praise of Eros, together with such important examples as his failure to win acquittal before the Athenian jury, indicate that Socrates is unwilling or unable to excel in popular rhetoric. The response of posterity to the Platonic dialogues is evidence that, in this respect, the student surpassed the master. Cf. L. Strauss, "How Farabi Read Plato's *Laws*," in *What Is Political Philosophy?* (Glencoe, Ill., 1959), p. 153.

25. *Protagoras* 334c8 ff. Cf. *Gorgias* 474a.

26. *Phaedrus* 271c10 ff.: "since the power of speech is to win over the psyche, he who intends to be a rhetorician must know the various forms which the psyche takes."

long discourse, announces that he is the first wise man not to conceal his wisdom.[27] Later in the same dialogue, Protagoras is engaged by Socrates in a discomfiting conversation, which he tries to terminate by insisting on the need to make a long speech. Socrates protests, and when overruled by Callias, says he will have to leave. Just then Alcibiades comes to his rescue and so preserves the discussion.[28] Again, when Protagoras seems unwilling to continue the dialogue, he is stung into speech by the sharp remarks of the youthful Alcibiades.[29] In the *Protagoras* Alcibiades is young and sober; he defends Socrates against long speeches and speech against silence. In the *Symposium* he is mature and intoxicated; his sudden entrance again rescues Socrates from an inability or unwillingness to engage in popular rhetoric.

In the *Symposium* Alcibiades sings the swan song of his genius, delivered at the height of his power but only a step away from disaster. He has already ceased to frequent the company of Socrates;[30] although he is beyond influence, he continues to feel the attraction of Socrates' nature. His review of their relationship is thus made vivid by erotic hybris, but it also acquires a tincture of objectivity. And the entire occasion is heightened by its proximity to the castration of the Hermae and the profanation of the Eleusinian mysteries.[31] The accusation against Alcibiades that he mimicked the secret rites and revealed them to his uninitiated companions[32] is ironically represented in the *Symposium* by Alcibiades' encomium. He reveals the inner or secret nature of Socrates to the uninitiated guests at the banquet, almost immediately after Diotima has

27. *Protagoras* 316d3 ff.
28. Ibid., 336b7 ff. Cf. 347b3 ff., where Alcibiades interrupts Hippias.
29. Ibid., 348b2 ff.
30. Hatzfeld, *Alcibiade*, p. 33: *Symposium* 213.
31. Leo Strauss has suggested, in lectures he left unpublished, that the banquet is meant to take place on the very night of the religious crimes; thus the *Symposium* clears Socrates and his companions from implication in acts against the polis by showing "what really happened." I wonder whether, if this were true, Plato would have been so indirect in establishing the date.
32. Plutarch, *Alcibiades* 22.3 quotes the official indictment; cf. 19.1 and Macdowell's introduction, pp. 3–7, to his edition of Andokides.

described the stages of initiation into the mysteries of Eros and the revelation of divine beauty.

According to Thucydides, the profanation of the mysteries by drunken young men "in private residences" preceded the mutilation of the Hermae, and both were associated by Alcibiades' enemies with a plot to overthrow the democracy.[33] In the *Symposium* Alcibiades reveals Socrates' nature before an audience of essentially aristocratic taste, most of whom have already spoken against the demotic Eros or gods of the city. As the analogy with the speech of Diotima already suggested, Socrates takes the place of the divine, of beauty in itself, and not of Eros. Socrates is loved, but he does not love or desire in return; this coldness results in the "castration" of the young Alcibiades. Of course, Alcibiades compares Socrates to a satyr, and Socrates refers to Alcibiades' speech as a satyr play (223d3).[34] But the satirical dimension in Socrates' nature is his irony or feigned eroticism. His account of Diotima is a satire on the teaching of the tragedian Agathon, and it is also a satirical portrait of his own nature. Relative to the satyr play of Alcibiades' speech, it may also be regarded as a tragedy composed by Plato in order to indicate the defect in his teacher. The main point here is not to achieve a facile identification between the various speeches and the three kinds of drama, but to emphasize the peculiarity of Socrates' Eros. Depending upon how we view them, each speech in the *Symposium* is at once tragedy, comedy, and satyr play.

But Alcibiades' satirical revelation is preceded by a complex dialogue with Agathon, Socrates, and Eryximachus, the direct result of his sudden and drunken entrance. Phaedrus and Pausanias are altogether excluded from this dialogue; Aristophanes is mentioned as lacking in physical beauty, but he does not speak. The sudden knocking on the door is even more effective than the earlier attack of hiccoughs in silencing Aris-

---

33. Thucydides 6.27 ff.; Macdowell, *Andokides* 36.34; Hatzfeld, *Alcibiade,* pp. 177–81.

34. Krüger, *Einsicht,* pp. 283 ff., uses the phrase in the title of his excellent analysis of Alcibiades' speech.

tophanes, who seems to be especially vulnerable to chance outbreaks of physical force. In this vein Eryximachus plays a similar role in the two episodes. Previously his technē cured Aristophanes' hiccoughs; now he persuades Alcibiades to speak instead of leading the party into a night of drinking (214a6 ff.). Eryximachus alone seems to be immune to the compulsion of Alcibiades' entrance. The double exercise of his technē (the only one beside rhetoric actually practiced at the banquet) suggests the power of the physician when the body is given priority over the psyche.

Alcibiades, "very drunk and making a great noise," surrounded by revelers (κωμασταί) and "crowned with thick ivy and violets," is unmistakably portrayed as entering like the god Dionysus (212c7–e3).[35] He demands to see Agathon, whom he drunkenly announces he has come to crown with the wreaths from his own head, "as the wisest and most beautiful" (212e3–8). The guests laugh at Alcibiades, but he adds that "I nevertheless speak the truth" (212e8–213a2). Alcibiades is the Dionysus of comedy rather than of tragedy; he reminds us of Aristophanes rather than of Euripides. In the *Frogs* Dionysus goes down to Hades, where he judges a contest of wisdom between Aeschylus and Euripides, giving the crown to the older man rather than to the innovator. Alcibiades, although he praises Agathon as wisest before seeing Socrates, retracts the award immediately after; once again the innovator must yield to old-fashioned virtue.

Despite their laughter, the guests respond to Alcibiades' proposal that he join them, drunk as he already is, with the same unanimous applause that greeted Agathon.[36] Apparently yield-

---

35. Cf. Aristophanes, *Clouds* 606 (κωμαστὴς Διόνυσος); Euripides, *Bacchae* 81–82 (κισσῷ τε στεφανωθείς/Διόνυσον θεραπεύει) and 106. The *Bacchae* illustrates vividly the connection between wine and madness. W. Otto, *Dionysos* (Frankfurt-am-Main, 1960), pp. 159 ff., in discussing Dionysus' special relationship to women, reminds us: "Bei Aeschylus (fr. 61) heisst er geringschätzig 'der Weibische' (ὁ γύννις), bei Euripides (*Bacch.* 353) 'der frauenhafte' (θηλύμορφος) wird er zuweilen gennant." In this way, Alcibiades is related to Agathon, also called ὁ γύννις by Aristophanes. For the connection between Dionysus and satyrs, cf. H. J. Rose, *A Handbook of Greek Mythology* (New York, 1959), pp. 154 ff.

36. Cf. 198a1–2 and 213a3.

ing to the acclaim of his guests, in which he does not quite share (213a4: "and Agathon also invited him"), Agathon is as a result separated from Socrates by Alcibiades, who sits down between them. Distracted by the unwinding of his garlands, Alcibiades does not at first see Socrates:

> "But who is our third at table?" At the same time he turned round and saw Socrates; and seeing him, he leapt up and said: "O Heracles, look who's here! Socrates himself! So you lay here in ambush for me, showing yourself suddenly (ἐξαίφνης ἀναφαίνεσθαι) as is your custom where I least suspected you'd be!" (213b6–c2)

Alcibiades sits halfway between sophistry and philosophy; like Eros, he is "in between" (213b1) the human and the divine.

The dramatic situation between Socrates and his two table-mates sheds further light on the ambiguous notion of the bond (συνδεσμός) as it is exhibited in the *Symposium*. Up to the physiological section of Diotima's teaching, it seemed clear that Eros, as the intermediate between the human and the divine, was intended to represent the syndesmotic or cosmic psyche which holds together and thereby unifies the disparate zones of being and becoming. As a consequence of the physiological section, Eros loses his daimonic or intermediate status and is identified with nature or genesis simply. The two interpretations of Eros may be reconciled by the reflection that desire is intelligible only in terms of its object or end. The desire of genesis for ousia holds together or gives shape to the elements of genesis in their individuality and as connected modes of a persisting if changing domain. Although Alcibiades is in the middle, it is Socrates, the "third at table," who binds together his two lovers and himself as a unity. Socrates, despite his ugliness, is the dramatic equivalent in the *Symposium* to beauty itself; whereas Alcibiades, despite his beauty, is the dramatic equivalent to Eros.

Socrates becomes visible to Alcibiades "instantaneously" (ἐξαίφνης), the same word used by Diotima to describe the appearance of beauty itself. The *Symposium* presents us with the parousia of Socrates rather than the Idea of beauty; it is an "existential" statement of the nature of philosophy rather than an ontological description of the structure of Being. In human terms, the poetic and political hybris, without a clear apprehension of the object of their desire, point toward philosophy as the only genuine completion of man. The irony of Socrates' reference to his "Eros for this mortal" (ἀνθρώπου) is clear enough from his appeal to Agathon to protect him from the jealousy of Alcibiades' "madness and erotic devotion" (213c6–d6).[37] In demoting Alcibiades from the status of the god Dionysus to a mortal, Socrates now calls upon Agathon to play the role of intermediary. Despite the superiority of philosophy, the poetic and political forms of hybris each have their contribution to make to the wholeness of human existence. Still more specifically, the dangers of Eros or the Dionysiac are shown by Alcibiades' rejection of reconciliation. As he says to Socrates, "there is no reconcilement for you and me" (213d7–8).

In his very claim to be Alcibiades' lover, Socrates describes their relationship in such a way as to suggest that the roles are reversed.[38] It is the lover rather than the beloved who is jealous of his sweetheart's association with other beautiful persons. If Socrates' account of their previous relationship is correct, Alcibiades nevertheless shows by his response that the affair is virtually over. Instead of reconciliation, he will claim vengeance (213d8) for Socrates' accusation. Meanwhile, however, he offers Socrates a garland of flowers rather than violence, and the highest praise. In contrast to Agathon, Socrates "triumphs in speech over all men, not once the other day like you, but always" (213e3–4). Alcibiades thereby acknowledges that, in the end, he is not accessible to logos or philosophy. He cannot refute Socrates, but for him the silence of speech is not followed by acquiescence in action.

37. Note the obscene echo of ὄρρος and ὀρρώδης in ὀρρωδῶ.

38. Cf. Hug, *Symposion* 213c7: ". . . Freilich im vorliegenden Falle scheinen die Rollen umgetauscht zu sein; das Gefühl, das Alkibiades gegen Sokrates hegt, wird zwar nicht ἔρως genannt, was gegen den Sprachgebrauch wäre, wohl aber μανία τε καὶ φιλεραστία; die φιλεραστία hatte hier einen leidenschaftlichen Charakter angenommen, wie ihn sonst nur der ἔρως hat."

Alcibiades is the supreme example of the fact that the triumph of philosophy is something other than the triumph of logos alone. Still, he is the only character in the dialogue to whom Socrates attributes madness. Alcibiades is our best witness concerning the nature of Socrates, better than Apollodorus and Aristodemus, whose discipleship makes them suspect as accurate observers of the elusive ironist. And Alcibiades himself insists upon his uniqueness by ignoring the previous arrangements and hybristically electing himself the drinking leader (213e9).[39] The drunken Alcibiades thus replaces the sober Eryximachus, under whose informal rule the first six speeches were delivered. The madness of Eros was praised by sober men who become intoxicated despite themselves by the force of the god. The madness of Socrates will now be praised by a man who is both drunk and mad, but who becomes sober despite himself, if only for a little while, thanks to the force of the philosopher.

Praise and Accusation

Alcibiades' nature may be described as a mixture of contraries which approaches disharmony more frequently than harmony. He is both intoxicated and sober; one receives the distinct impression from the *Symposium* that it is his sobriety which drives him toward intoxication, a condition he is never quite able to achieve. I mean by this that his madness is human rather than divine, and, that despite the magnitude of his ambition he is never completely and genuinely possessed by it. Alcibiades is divided against himself; he lacks the coherence of genius and of fanaticism. This uncertainty is crystallized in his relations with Socrates, who may for that reason be regarded with some justice as the corrupter of Alcibiades. The initial enchantment of contact with Socrates produces confusion and self-doubt, but not virtue.

The unsteady character of Alcibiades' hybris is nicely shown in two small touches, immediately upon his assuming the role of drinking master. He downs a cooler of wine and orders it to

39. Cf. Hug 213e9.

be refilled for Socrates, but then admits that "my sly trick (σόφισμα) is in vain" (214a3). Socrates is immune to intoxication, just as he is immune to Alcibiades' beauty. At this point, Eryximachus intervenes, and Alcibiades yields his power of decision; the symposiasts must do "whatever you may command; for one must be persuaded by you: "one gentleman surgeon is worth the multitude." So prescribe what you will" (214b3–8).[40] The quotation from Homer is spoken by Idomeneus to Nestor on the wounding of Machaon by Paris.[41] In the *Symposium* the rival speakers are at war with each other; hence the power of technē generally, and medicine specifically.[42]

Alcibiades is an inconsistent tyrant who compromises with his subjects. Eryximachus calls him to justice (214c3): Alcibiades must speak rather than drink. But Alcibiades disobeys even in obeying, since he will praise Socrates rather than Eros. To justify his injustice Alcibiades observes that democratic equality cannot exist between the sober and the drunk (214c6–8: μὴ οὐκ ἐξ ἴσου ᾖ). This principle, however, is not invoked by Alcibiades in the role of judge or tyrant, but as potential accuser. Alcibiades is determined to take his vengeance on Socrates (214e2), even at the price of exposing his own vulnerability. His praise is at the same time an accusation, just as he is at the same time judge and plaintiff. Alcibiades seems to be pleading before the symposiasts for understanding of the harm Socrates has done to him; but in a more fundamental sense, he is condemning Socrates, or pleading to himself.

Alcibiades begins his accusation in a way that reveals his own vanity:

> does Socrates persuade you in what he says? Don't you know that the case is altogether the opposite of what he claimed? For this one, should I praise anyone in his presence, whether a god or any human other than himself, will not keep his hands from me. (214c8–d4)

40. Cf. *Phaedrus* 227a5 and *Memorabilia* 3.13.2.
41. *Iliad* 11.514.
42. Cf. *Republic* 405 ff. When war is limited to self-defense, the authority of the doctor is subordinated to the needs of political virtue.

He does not suggest that Socrates would be angry if anyone else were to praise a god or mortal in his presence. Socrates stands accused of hybris, but Alcibiades is the one man capable of bringing the charge. Alcibiades explicitly denies that anyone present but himself knows Socrates (216c7). What he knows is that Socrates, not he, is the most hybristic of mortals. Socrates takes this accusation quite seriously: "don't blaspheme" (214d5: οὐκ εὐφημήσεις), he replies. The only other occurrence of this phrase is at 201e10, where it is spoken by Diotima to Socrates. But the young Socrates was more obedient than the mature Alcibiades.[43] Thus Socrates is right to worry:

> "You there . . . what do you have in mind? Will you praise me in order to make fun of me? Or what will you do?" "I shall speak the truth. But consider if you will permit this." "Well . . . I permit the truth and I order you to speak it." (214e4–8)

He who is about to be accused in any case has no rhetorical alternative but to command that the truth be spoken. But the careful reader should not accept the rhetorical protestations of either party without reflection. What would be naïve in a court of law is equally so in the interpretation of a Platonic dialogue. Unfortunately, given the curious mixture of qualities in his nature, and the complexity of his motives, it is not easy to decide just how honestly Alcibiades will speak. Consider the following prefatory remark to Socrates:

> should I say any untruth, catch me up in the middle, if you like, and say that I lie in this. For I shall not willingly lie. But if I should mix up the order in my memory, don't be surprised. It is not easy for one in my shape to enumerate your oddities smoothly and in order. (214e10–215a3)

Under the circumstances this is a plausible statement, and Socrates does not in fact interrupt him at any point. At the close

---

43. In response to Socrates' command not to blaspheme, Alcibiades swears by Poseidon. Cf. Bury's note to 214D for the ironical pun on πόσις.

of Alcibiades' speech, however, Socrates accuses him in turn of having cleverly veiled himself, thereby rendering invisible his real purpose (222c4 ff.). Even if we accept the purpose mentioned by Socrates, it is still the case that Alcibiades has lied, or practiced inverted irony.

For whatever it is worth, then, Socrates denies that Alcibiades has "rendered visible" the intention of his encomium (cf. 217e4). This leaves open the possibility that the details of the encomium are themselves correct. On the other hand, Alcibiades invites Socrates to identify any lies "if you like"; it may be that Socrates, for his own motives, does not care to do so. Finally, there is apparently at least one factual error in Alcibiades' speech. Alcibiades reverses chronology in his account of the battle of Potidaea, placing it after the winter and summer campaigns.[44] If nothing else, this illustrates Plato's disinterest in historical accuracy. With this note of caution, let us turn to a preliminary survey of Alcibiades' ambiguous speech.

The speech falls easily into five parts of varying length. The first part consists of only one sentence, in which Alcibiades states the method he will employ (215a4–5). Second, there is a comparison between Socrates and Marsyas the satyr as well as the Silenus figures (215a5–216c3). Here, the emphasis is on Socrates' speech, but with respect to its practical end. Socrates' hybris and irony are portrayed essentially in terms of his relations with other men. The comparison with the Silenus serves as a transition to the third and longest part, the only one in which a dialogue between Socrates and Alcibiades occurs (216c4–219e5). Here Alcibiades relates his unsuccessful attempt to seduce Socrates; this account leads the audience to laughter and the charge that Alcibiades is guilty of excessive freedom of speech.

In the dialogue with Alcibiades, Socrates' hybris is portrayed as a sobriety beyond even the temptation of insobriety. In part

---

44. Hatzfeld, *Alcibiade*, p. 63, n. 1. He adds that, according to the *Charmides* and Isocrates 16.29, Socrates did not take part in the winter campaign, and Alcibiades went to war after the battle of Potidaea; Thucydides confirms the account given in the *Symposium*.

four we learn of Socrates' virtues in war (219e5–221c1). There are two sections to this part, which illustrate his endurance and courage respectively. Both sections repeat the point that Socrates is indifferent to the things which regularly affect mortals: physical hardship, fear of death, love of honor. Again, Socrates is portrayed as cold or indifferent: as a man of action, he is, so to speak, essentially characterized by passivity. Even the account of his courage concentrates on his calm behavior in retreat; nothing is said about aggressive feats of martial valor. Finally, Alcibiades discusses Socrates' absolute uniqueness among mortals, and returns to the Silenus image as a commentary on his theme that Socrates is not like a man but a satyr (221c2–222b7).

I may summarize Alcibiades' encomium or accusation as follows. Socrates is a dissembler, so full of hybris as to be indifferent to human things, even to the beautiful bodies by which he pretends to be erotically attracted. His hybristic indifference is justified in the sense that he is in fact superior to all other men. At the same time, it is unjustified or defective, because it impairs his effectiveness on behalf of philosophy among the nonphilosophers. Alcibiades' legalistic terminology, especially at 219c5–6, may then be understood as part of Plato's "indictment" of Socrates, in addition to the meaning those words have for Alcibiades himself. The hybris of Socrates is not properly in tune with the generated or corporeal nature of human beings. Only the dialogue as a whole is an example of the perfect or Platonic hybris.

Icons and Satyrs

The first two parts of Alcibiades' speech may be conveniently treated together, especially in view of the brevity of the first part. But it should not be forgotten that the first or methodological part is meant to describe the speech as a whole. It consists of the following words:

I shall try to praise Socrates, gentlemen, by way of images (δι' εἰκόνων). He will perhaps suppose that this is

to make fun of him [cf. 214e4], but the image will be
for the sake of truth, not for laughter. (215a4–6)[45]

We previously raised the question of whether Alcibiades is
speaking the truth in his account of Socrates.[46] The same question is raised from a different perspective by Alcibiades' use of
the word *eikon*. This word, which we can only briefly examine
here,[47] raises the same problem discussed earlier with respect to
whether there can be a logos or rational account of the psyche.
If every logos in the technical sense corresponds to an *eidos* or
web of eidetic relations, and if there is no eidos of the psyche,
then the most we can hope for is a "likely mythos" about Socrates' nature.[48]

This is not to suggest that a "likely story" is irrational or in
principle neither true nor false. Such a conclusion is unneces-
sarily severe with respect to icons as characterized by *eikasia*
in the famous passage of the divided line.[49] But the divided line
is itself introduced in order to illustrate the icon of the good,
and so too is the related icon of the cave.[50] Neither the image
of the sun nor of the cave is an icon in the sense of shadows or
reflected phantasms. A more relevant text is to be found in the
Sophist, where the Eleatic stranger subdivides "image-making"
(εἰδωλουργική) into two species: the *eikastic* and *phantastic*.[51] The
Sophist is eventually located within the latter species; eikastic
image-making is left undivided. The division of image-making
is a refinement of the lowest segment of the divided line. We
have seen that Alcibiades is neither a Sophist nor a philosopher.
The former may be inferred from the fact that his speech falls

45. We may observe in passing that the first word of Alcibiades' speech is
"Socrates" and the second (ignoring the particle) is "I." His "egoism" takes
second place to the philosopher.

46. Alcibiades asserts seven times that he is speaking, or has spoken, the truth:
214e11, 215a6, 215b5–6, 216a2, 217e4, 219c2 and 220e4.

47. For a longer and supplementary discussion, cf. Klein, *Meno*, pp. 112 ff.
(esp. p. 119).

48. *Timaeus* 29d2 and Chapter 7, pp. 202–11 above.

49. *Republic* 509e1 ff.

50. Ibid., 509a9, 514a4 et passim.

51. *Sophist* 235c8 ff.

under the eikastic species. Presumably the difference between Alcibiades and the philosopher could be conceptually fixed only by carrying out the diairesis of eikastic making.

Just as an image does not possess "real" being, so a verbal image is not genuinely true but, at most, merely like the truth.[52] Whatever may be said conceptually about the activity of image-making, the veridical character of a given image is not itself subject to logical confirmation. The act of confirming the accuracy of an image of a man's psyche is more like the assessment of the validity of a poem than of a syllogism or diairesis. No one could reasonably object to Alcibiades' method, then; but everything turns upon the adequacy of his icon. Iconic description is peculiarly appropriate to speech about the psyche, since eikasia is coextensive with *doksa* or the intermediate; and it is in this domain that the psyche, which both is and is not, dwells.[53] The coextensiveness between doksa and psyche makes it unusually difficult to distinguish speech about human nature from sophistry. If one does not persevere in the face of this difficulty, the "poetic" idiom of philosophy succumbs altogether to the "mathematical"; paradoxically enough, the result is a total victory for sophistry within the human domain.

Alcibiades wishes to illustrate the daimonic character of Socrates in an appropriate icon. The daimon he chooses is not Eros but that of a satyr or Silenus. The famous sexuality of satyrs tends to obscure the fact that Alcibiades wishes to show Socrates as unerotic with respect to bodies or human things; to that extent, the icon is defective. Still, we need only read Alcibiades' words to see that he is abstracting from the erotic dimension in the sense defined. His satyrs exemplify two different qualities: the concealment of divine beauty by external ugliness, and the ability to conquer mortals by astounding or hypnotizing them through speech. Alcibiades was primarily impressed by Socrates' dialectical skill; but he mistakenly inferred from Socrates' success in individual cases that it might be transferred to dealings with the multitude. Alcibiades confused his own

52. Ibid., 240b2, b11.
53. Klein, *Meno*, p. 119 and *Republic* 477a-b, 478e, 534a1-2.

susceptibility to Socratic irony with the response of the many to sophistic rhetoric. One may say that he did not understand his own nobility: he could not distinguish between the noble and base horses in his own breast. Therefore, in his practice of irony Alcibiades did not preserve himself apart from the many, but became like them. His ability to assume a variety of forms, which is more akin to poetry than philosophy, degenerated into unregulated instability. Alcibiades is an icon of the Athens he strove to dominate.

Alcibiades continues with the second part of his speech as follows:

> For I say that [Socrates] is most like the Silenus-figures that sit in the statuaries' shops, those which the craftsmen make holding pipes or flutes; when their two halves are disjoined, they are seen to possess statues of gods within. And I also say that he is like the satyr Marsyas. (215a6–b4)[54]

By his comparisons to the Silenoi and Marsyas, Alcibiades suggests a link between Dionysus and Apollo. It is the flutes and hybris, rather than the sexuality, of the satyrs with which he is concerned.[55] Again, the bipartition of the Silenus-figure reminds us of the myth of Aristophanes: Zeus directs Apollo to cut the hybristic circle-men in half. Now, however, it is Dionysus (Alcibiades) who cuts Apollo (Socrates) in half.[56] The Silenus-figure has a double nature, but these halves are not actually separated. Marsyas, however, is the satyr who challenged Apollo to a contest of flute playing, and upon his defeat, was

54. Silenus is variously portrayed in antiquity as companion to Dionysus, prophet, and father of the satyrs. The older satyrs were also called Silenoi. Cf. Rose, *Handbook,* p. 156; also Bury's note and references in Liddell and Scott.

55. K. Kerenyi, *Pythagoras und Orpheus* (Zürich, 1950), pp. 34, 38, makes a comparison between Apollo and Dionysus by way of Orpheus: Orpheus lives and works in a Dionysian world, but he uses Apollonian music to tame the beasts, and to purify or bind daimonic powers. "Orphisches Leben und Denken ist dionysisches Leben und Denken, jedoch in einer von apollinischer Reinheitssehnsucht bestimmten Atmosphäre . . . ."

56. For the connection between Socrates and Apollo, cf. H. Kuhn, *Sokrates* (Munich, 1959), p. 9.

flayed by the god. Alcibiades tactfully substitutes the bifurcated Silenus for this story, but the implication is obvious. By stripping Socrates' speeches of their skin of irony, by "opening" them up, Alcibiades likens himself to Apollo. He is a Dionysus who, in his intoxication, mistakes himself for an Apollo.

The confusion in Alcibiades' nature between Dionysus and Apollo has its parallel in Alcibiades' double role as judge and accuser. Now the charge is made explicit before the court of symposiasts:

> That your [physical] form is like these, O Socrates, not even you would dispute. But after this, hear that you are like them in other ways too. You are hybristic, aren't you? If you should not agree, I'll furnish witnesses. (215b4–9)[57]

Socrates' hybris takes two forms, which very generally correspond to his speeches and deeds: namely, irony and moderation.[58] In Alcibiades' view, Socrates' moderation or indifference is the reason why he himself has failed to capture the philosopher's irony. Like Agathon, Alcibiades believes in the physical transmission of wisdom. His desire for Socrates' speech is distorted by his tacit assumption that it is a deed or epiphenomenon of the body, directed entirely toward bodily ends:

> [Marsyas] was able to charm mortals by his lips, through the use of instruments. . . . You differ from him in this alone, that you can do the same thing without instruments, in plain prose. (215c1–d1)

The power of Marsyas' music, when it is played by mortals, is "to induce possession and show, through its being divine, those who have need of [yearn for] gods and initiations"

---

57. According to Bury, "for the present Alcibiades forebears to enlarge on this satyr-like quality," namely, hybris. But such an observation shows that he has misunderstood the nature of the indictment. Nor is he alone in this, as may be confirmed by inspecting the various translations of the *Symposium*, which attempt to soften the meaning of "hybristic," presumably confused by the application of the term to Socrates.

58. Cf. Aristotle, *Rhetoric* 1389b11–12: ἡ γὰρ εὐτραπελία πεπαιδευμένη ὕβρις ἐστίν.

(215c5–6). Alcibiades' fundamental obedience to the body makes it impossible for him to comprehend genuinely this insight into divine music. He sees the need for initiation but does not believe what he sees. Unlike Socrates, he cannot translate this music into philosophical mythos. Socrates possesses the capacity, thanks to his daimonion, to identify other daimonic psyches. His verbal irony is a technē in the service of his daimonic activity of discriminating psyches, and is therefore peaceful or defensive. Alcibiades, however, regards the process of musical possession as a "political" activity, directed essentially toward the body and useful for potential tyrants. This confusion of genuine insight and willful misinterpretation, so typical of his nature, is nicely shown by Alcibiades' next words:

> For whenever we hear another person's discourses, even
> if he is quite a good rhetorician, no one, so to speak,
> cares at all. But whenever one hears you, or someone
> else speaking your words, however bad a speaker he may
> be, and whether the hearer be a woman, a man, or a
> youth, we are stunned and possessed. (215d1–6)

Alcibiades ambiguously moves from "we" to "one," suggesting at the beginning and end of this passage that Socrates has the power to sway the multitude. But those who are unaffected by excellent rhetoricians must constitute a special group and can scarcely be identified with the many.[59] And the middle of the passage states that Socrates' words have their positive effect on individuals. Alcibiades' ambition prevents him from remembering and understanding the precise manner in which Socratic dialectic functions. The power to "stun and possess" is more important to him than the ability to distinguish those who yearn for gods and initiation. Alcibiades does not understand the significance of his own ability to penetrate Socratic irony, nor the meaning of his own transformation into more than Corybantic enthusiasm (215e1–4). This lack of self-knowledge leads him to attempt the corporeal seduction of Socrates. One may suspect that it was the failure of this attempt as much as

---

59. *Euthyphron* 9c1.

any accessibility to divine music that led him to be enslaved and shamed by Socrates' speech (215e6, 216a8–b3).

Alcibiades perceives that he is divided against himself, or that he is neglecting himself, but his ability to resist Socrates' enchantments is clear evidence that he lacks genuine comprehension:

> Even now I am aware that if I should be willing to listen to him, I would not endure, but would suffer the same effects. For he compels me to admit that, needy as I am, I neglect myself and conduct the affairs of Athens. So I restrain my ears by force, as though from the Sirens, and run away, lest I sit next to him until I grow altogether old. (216a2–8)

The comparison between himself and Odysseus is apt in one sense, but defective in another. Odysseus flees immortality for the political or "one's own," but Alcibiades desires a universal tyranny that makes political life finally unsatisfying to him. Alcibiades knows that he is needy but knows not what he needs; hence his virtual assertion that he knowingly desires what is bad for himself.

Alcibiades' confused perception of self-division achieves a moment of clarity with respect to the cause of his self-neglect: it is a form of selfishness which makes him run away rather than surrender to the selflessness of logos. It is this selfless defeat he cannot endure; even the enslavement to the demos is preferable: "I know and cannot deny that I must do what [Socrates] commands; but whenever I leave him, I am defeated by the honor of the multitude" (216b3–5). Odysseus, although he had himself tied to his ship's mast, left his ears unstopped and dared to hear the Sirens' song. Alcibiades can neither listen to nor look at Socrates with security because there is no inner center of coherence in his nature. The very sight of the enchanter reduces Alcibiades to shame, yet he cannot even endure the thought of never seeing him again (216b5–c3). Odysseus is a coherent or complete man in a way that Alcibiades is not; he can voyage safely through strange worlds because he knows his own home. The same is true of Socrates, although his home is elsewhere. But Alcibiades is a universal man who suffers from homelessness. He is a slave to Socrates and Athens because he cannot live freely with either.

To summarize: the main purpose of the second part of Alcibiades' speech is to charge Socrates with hybris. Alcibiades realizes that Socrates will not admit the charge; in fact he expects a denial, in keeping with Socrates' irony. Instead of his usual formula to the effect that Socrates cannot deny the truth of his words, Alcibiades threatens: "if you don't agree, I'll bring witnesses" (215b7). He is himself the principal witness concerning Socrates' "marvelous power," since none of the symposiasts perceives it (216c5–d1). Socrates "spends his whole life in irony toward and play with mortals" (216e4–5). He pretends to be an expert on human Eros, and to be erotically attracted toward beauties like Alcibiades, Agathon, Charmides, Euthydemus, and the rest (cf. 222a8 ff.). In fact, however, Socratic hybris consists of a secret scorn for human Eros (216d2 ff.; 219c4–5; 222a8). As proof positive, Alcibiades will show how Socrates is indifferent to his own beauty. Instead of being erotic and ignorant, as he pretends, Socrates is neither the one nor the other (216d2–5). His temperance is a scorn for human things and so for "us" mortals as well (216d7–e4).

The Attempted Seduction

Unlike his fellow Athenians, says Alcibiades, he "once" saw the divine, beautiful, marvelous statues inside Socrates' breast (216e6–217a2). He claims that as a result of this vision he had to obey Socrates' commands. Instead, however, he is moved to attempt the conquest of the philosopher:

> for supposing him to be seriously attracted by my youthful beauty, I thought it was a gift from Hermes and marvelous good luck for me, that it was possible for me, by gratifying Socrates, to hear all that he knew. For I was extraordinarily proud of my beauty. (217a2–6)

Alcibiades presents himself as obedient to Hermes rather than insolent or impious, an amusing touch in view of the imminent accusations to be leveled against him. He is the honest citizen, and Socrates is guilty of insolence for refusing his advances.

There are three preliminary stages in the courtship of Socrates. Alcibiades converses privately with him, wrestles with him, and then invites him to dinner (217b3–d3). Alcibiades notes that during these preliminaries it was he rather than Socrates who behaved like "a lover" (217b3, c7); Socrates is rather the sweetheart. Despite the various opportunities which he is afforded, Socrates' habits are unchanged by solitude with Alcibiades, whether clothed or naked (217b6, c2–4). Socrates is unaccustomed to pederastic love, but simulates it as an accommodation to the noble Athenians. Similarly, solitude with Socrates does not change the habits of Alcibiades; he continues to be obsessed by the love of victory (217c4). The various contrivances by which Socrates exercises his skill in hunting men are less than useless with one who is more—or less—than a man. Nevertheless, the most illuminating device, and the only one which results in a dialogue, is the third, the invitation to dinner.[60]

For the second time we are presented with a banquet within a banquet. The first was the gods' celebration of the birth of Aphrodite, at which Eros was conceived. At the second dinner we may compare Socrates to Poros and Alcibiades to Penia; only this time the beloved remains sober and no seduction occurs. Consequently nothing is generated. Socrates fails to convert Alcibiades to a life of virtue or philosophy. Can it be because his indifference is excessive toward someone who is not by nature a philosopher or a disciple? In any event, the banquet is the key to Alcibiades' revelatory accusation:

> Up to this point, the account could have been nobly spoken to anyone. But you would not have heard me telling what follows, were it not first, as the saying goes,

60. In one of his most perceptive notes (to προκαλοῦμαι δὲ . . .) Bury says: "For *three* as a climacteric number cf. *Phil.* 66D, *Euthyd.* 277C, *Rep.* 472A."

that wine, whether or not joined with children, is truth-
ful. Second, it seems unjust to me to leave invisible
Socrates' arrogant (ὑπερήφανον) deed, once I have begun
his praise. (217e1–6) [61]

Commentators regularly understand Alcibiades to imply that
the intoxication of the event has led to a suspension of the
modesty that normally veils the speeches and deeds of lovers.
Yet it is scarcely likely that a man of Alcibiades' habits, whether
drunk or sober, would have hesitated to continue a sexual
anecdote for reasons of modesty. He has already indicated his
intention to "gratify" Socrates; the new revelation in what follows, and the reason for his hesitancy, concerns his wounded
pride. In order to substantiate his indictment, Alcibiades must
humiliate himself. This is what he means by saying that the
prelude could have been "nobly" spoken to anyone. It is honorable to pursue, but shameful to fail in, erotic adventures, and
it is especially shameful to speak of such failures in the presence
of rivals like Phaedrus and Agathon.

In dealing with his shame, Alcibiades tries to mitigate it by
blaming philosophy, which he compares to a snakebite that
drives men to a frenzy of obedience in deed and speech. This
enables him to associate his own behavior with that of the
other guests: "you have all shared the madness and bacchic
frenzy of philosophy" (218b3–4).[62] The comparison, however,
is inaccurate; Alcibiades gives an unjust "justification" of his
behavior (217e5: ἄδικόν μοι φαίνεται). We have already given reasons for the belief that Alcibiades was bitten by ambition rather
than by philosophy. A genuinely philosophical Eros, one may
add, would never have driven Alcibiades to attempt the sexual
seduction of Socrates. And if we excuse Alcibiades' youthful
error as an exaggeration of the first step in the erotic initiation
described by Diotima, we cannot excuse the justifying interpretation given it by the mature Alcibiades. This interpretation is

61. For a discussion of the proverbs to which Alcibiades refers, cf. Bury's note.
62. In the dialogue bearing his name, at 79e5–80c6 Meno compares Socrates
to a torpedo fish which gains its way by numbing the adversary into silence.
Alcibiades, on the contrary, is stung into madness. He alone, incidentally, calls
philosophy a μανία in the Symposium.

a mockery or profanation of the erotic mysteries: Alcibiades is guilty of profaning philosophy rather than the Eleusinian rites. Aristodemus and the previous speakers are fellow conspirators (218b4: συγγνώσεσθε): "But the servants, and anyone else who is uninitiated and boorish, must close great doors over their ears" (218b5–7).

The dialogue between Alcibiades and Socrates takes place when the two are alone at night, in bed, with the lamp extinguished (218b8–9). We see here an intensification of the dramatic setting of the *Symposium*. Just as in the *Phaedrus*, Socrates is alone with a beautiful male,[63] there in the sunlight of high noon, here in the darkness of the night. In both cases, logos replaces Eros. Whether by day or by night, Socrates pursues his usual customs.[64] The youthful Alcibiades, who is himself accustomed to "speak freely" what he thinks (218c2), interprets Socratic habit as shyness. He therefore takes the initiative by "setting Socrates in motion" (218c2: κινήσας αὐτόν), just as Agathon had wished to do when Socrates was standing still in a neighbor's porch (cf. 175b3). It is part of Socrates' passivity or indifference in the *Symposium* to be unmoved except by such constraint or "shaking."

Socrates accepts Agathon's invitation, dresses appropriately for the occasion, drinks or not as the others suggest, endures Alcibiades' pursuit, the rigors of the weather, and the threats of the enemy. On the other hand, he takes the initiative in inviting Aristodemus, refuses to praise Eros in the style of the other speakers, will not have intercourse with Alcibiades, and rejects the decorations of the Athenians for valor. In these positive acts he shows his indifference to conventional etiquette, to which he may or may not conform, rhetoric, sexual behavior, and love of honor. This selection of evidence, although by no means exhaustive, suggests that the voluntary presence of Socrates in Agathon's home is intended by Plato to illustrate the ambiguity

63. Phaedrus is no youth in the *Phaedrus* but is called one. Cf. Hackforth, *Phaedrus*, p. 8.

64. It is necessary to mention that marriage and procreation are part of Socrates' political duties—duties not fulfilled by Plato.

of his master's attitude toward human things. Socrates is present as Plato's spy or warrior in the camp of the enemy, but his own methods of conquest seem to be the satiric skin of an inner indifference.

Having set Socrates in motion, Alcibiades attempts to accelerate the process. He urges Socrates not to allow shyness to interfere with courtship. "Prudence," or "practical intelligence" dictates a "moderation" of selective license, based upon a distinction between the few and the many. Similarly, it is "mindless" not to use one's properties and friends in the service of ambition (218c7–d5). Alcibiades has difficulty in distinguishing between friendship and ownership; he takes possession, however, in the sense of the body. Parallel to this is his assumption that the difference between the few and the many is one of calculative intelligence rather than virtue. The abstinent are presumably either stupid or shy. Alcibiades' hybris is thus apparent from the fact that, as Bury points out, he says the many disapprove of gratification. Pausanias, on the other hand, of whom this passage reminds us, said "some." Pausanias wished to legitimate pederasty, whereas Alcibiades wishes to legitimate his own superiority to the multitude.

Socrates responds to this encouragement with a large dose of his customary irony (218d6–7):

> My dear Alcibiades, you may really not be stupid, if what you say about me happens to be true, and there is some power in me through which you could become better; what an extraordinary beauty you must see in me, altogether surpassing your own good looks. (218d7–e3)[65]

The Greek text is ambiguous, and has been taken in various senses by editors and translators. But Socrates may be said to imply that he had previously regarded Alcibiades as stupid. In other words, Alcibiades may be intelligent if he correctly perceives Socrates' beauty. The attempt to cheat Socrates by exchanging a specious for a genuine beauty (218e5–219a1) is a

65. Cf. n. 15 above.

sign of a secondary and even vicious shrewdness. Socrates' irony is directed primarily against Alcibiades' high regard for his own intelligence, mindfulness, or prudence. It should not be taken as a disavowal by Socrates of his inner beauty, although one may wonder whether Plato is ironical concerning the power of that beauty to improve Alcibiades.

Socrates' language is ambiguous because he is giving Alcibiades the opportunity to test or find himself in the mirror of speech. The ambiguity goes beyond syntax. Socrates cites a famous proverb which originates (in its written form) in Homer. Through it he compares Alcibiades to Diomedes, who with the help of Zeus, cheated Glaucus of his golden armor in exchange for bronze.[66] At the beginning of the dialogue Socrates used another quotation from Homer in such a way as to identify himself with Diomedes.[67] The present passage (219a1) suggests that there is a relationship between Socrates and Alcibiades, on the basis of which Alcibiades was enabled to perceive the divine in Socrates, however he may have misconstrued it. The two bear a kind of resemblance to Diomedes, who appears in Homer as prudent and cunning, in addition to being brave and powerful. Needless to say, this is not intended to establish an identity between the two, but it adds a stroke to the portrait which the *Symposium* paints of Socrates. In this vein, it may be permissible to regard Socrates' warning to Alcibiades as a "Homeric" double-entendre: "but, happy one, look more carefully, lest I hide from you that I am nothing" (219a1–2: μή σε λανθάνω οὐδὲν ὤν). Is this a franker version of the words of Odysseus, who, while making the overconfident Polyphemus drunk and sleepy, tells him that his name is "no one" (οὖτις)?[68]

In his private conversation with Socrates, just as in the presence of the symposiasts, Alcibiades insists upon his own frankness or honesty (218c2, 219a5–6). He exercises freedom of

66. *Iliad* 6.236.
67. 174d2; *Iliad* 10.224.
68. *Odyssey* 9.275 ff.

speech, the great Athenian virtue (cf. 222c2), but for vicious
and undemocratic ends, whereas Socrates is ironical and dissembling, but for virtuous ends. Alcibiades asks Socrates to
consider what is "best" (ἄριστον) for them both: not quite a
frank expression, and so one which Socrates can turn to good
purpose: "there you speak well" (219a5–b2). There is something about Socrates which forces Alcibiades to speak euphe-
mistically. He is, as it were, already potentially ashamed of the
proposal he makes, but without really grasping, or being persuaded by, the shamefulness of his intentions. He therefore
assumes that Socrates is speaking in the same euphemistic or
veiled mode, or that both are agreed upon the significance of
the word "best."

Alcibiades thus enacts the ambiguous character of his ostensibly open speech by covering Socrates and himself with a cloak,
and passes the night with his arms wrapped round the philosopher's naked body (219b5–c2).[69] The young Alcibiades achieves
the physical contact with Socrates later to be desired by
Agathon, but wisdom cannot be transferred by touch. The
"daimonic and marvelous" Socrates (219c1) obeys the same customs whether naked or clothed. We see him in both guises in
the *Symposium,* and in both he is marked by hybris. "You
cannot say that I lie," Alcibiades again insists (219c2), but this
does not guarantee that his words are altogether true. Alcibiades
sees only what one may call the surface of Socrates' inner
nature:

> When I had done this, he was so superior that he scorned
> and laughed at my beauty, and was hybristic (ὕβρισε
> toward the very quality about which I was particularly
> vain, O gentlemen of the jury—for you are jurors con-
> concerning the arrogance of Socrates. (219c3–6)

This is the peak of Alcibiades' indictment, and so he explicitly identifies the symposiasts as jurors. It is not so much
their philosophical as their erotic mania upon which Alcibiades

69. Cf. Aristophanes, *Clouds* 727 ff.

counts for sympathy. Who could grasp better than they the injustice of Socrates' behavior? By scorning Alcibiades, Socrates refuses to worship Eros. To this extent at least, Socrates' hybris is akin to atheism. The magnitude of this crime overshadows the dishonor which Alcibiades feels (219d3–4); it is this which moved him to tell the story, and the shame of dishonor rather than of licentiousness which made him hesitate. The present trial of Socrates is then a preview of the historical trial of 399; Alcibiades here stands for his lover Anytus, or the Athenian demos. The love of Athens for Alcibiades is the political version of the apolitical narcissism we perceived in Agathon. Socrates is temperate with respect to the love of body and city; this is his virtue as well as his guilt.

Alcibiades invokes both gods and goddesses before the "jurors" to guarantee that "I arose, having spent the night with Socrates in no more extraordinary a sense than if I had slept with my father or older brother" (219c7–d2). The citation of goddesses as well as gods is sufficiently unusual to have been noticed by Bury, who correctly refers us to the *Timaeus*.[70] According to Timaeus, discourse on the whole should begin with an invocation to gods and goddesses. The whole, like the hybristic circle-men who mirror it, contains both male and female elements. Socrates and Alcibiades are alone among the speakers in linking the female to the divine. But whereas Alcibiades patriotically invokes the local goddesses, Socrates describes himself as the student of a foreign priestess. As has already been observed, Socrates shares in the political indifference of the scientific student. For example, in the exchange with Agathon, it was he who introduced the topic of incest. Not even Alcibiades is so bold; he compares the innocence of his night with Socrates by reference to father and brother, but not to mother or sister. The point is not simply that Socrates is a man, but that women are the divine source of the city's coherence. The incoherent Alcibiades depends upon the city as the coherent Socrates does not.

70. Bury, in his note to μὰ θεοὺς, μὰ θεάς, says: "Such an invocation of the whole pantheon is unusual, but cf. *Tim.* 27C."

Endurance and Courage

The hybris of Alcibiades is overreaching ambition (or πλεονεξία) whereas Socrates' hybris is temperance or moderation. In the fourth part of his speech Alcibiades expresses the Socratic hybris in terms which come closest to his own sphere of activity. He who loves victory more than anything else is essentially a warrior. Alcibiades interprets Socrates' indifference in the context of war as a kind of courage or endurance which makes him triumphant in the sense of being unconquerable. Previously Alcibiades had said that Socrates always wins in speech (213e3); for him, the Eros of dialectic is essentially eristic. Despite his brilliant description of Socratic irony, he did not give us an adequate example of dialectic. In keeping with the general intentions of the *Symposium*, his illustration was taken from the domain of practice rather than theory. We saw a "war" in which speech was entirely subordinate to deed.

But Socratic activity is "negative," and Alcibiades finds this mode of behavior almost impossible to grasp:

> After that, you can guess what was in my mind, supposing myself to have been dishonored, but wondering at his nature, at his moderation and courage. For I had chanced upon a man of a sort that I could never believe to encounter, with respect to his prudence (φρόνησιν) and endurance. (219d3–7)

He cannot find a reason for being angry with Socrates, although we may readily suppose that he is angry. He can neither deprive himself of Socrates' company nor find a way to "win him over" (219d7–e1). Alcibiades interprets Socrates' unwillingness to have intercourse as endurance or courage; in other words, as martial traits which bring Socrates a victory in the domain of practice, a victory which is undeniable but inexplicable. Why has Socrates deprived himself of the prize of Alcibiades' beauty? Socrates surpasses Ajax in fortitude; the warrior's shield protected him against spears, and this Alcibiades can understand. But Socrates is immune to both money and beauty of the flesh; this surpasses belief (219e1–3).

In reviewing Socratic fortitude, Alcibiades omits mention of friends, the third part of his initial offer (218c10–11). We may at least presume that Socrates is not immune to friends, or that Alcibiades is not his friend.[71] He cannot be Socrates' friend because he does not understand him. As always in Plato, a lack of knowledge is equivalent to slavery: "So I was at a loss, and I wandered around enslaved by the man as no one has ever been by another" (219e3–5).[72] This condition is intolerable to Alcibiades, and so he passes on to the battle at Potidaea, where the two men can compete in a more intelligible manner. Alcibiades' desire to understand Socrates is an unconscious admission by him that the psyche is superior to the body. The same result would obtain if Alcibiades could make a sufficient analysis of his love of honor. His inability to do this means that he will not really be able to explain Socrates' military virtues either.

The main lesson in this fourth section is Socrates' indifference to physical hardship, and most suggestively, his courage in retreat. Socrates does not attack or conquer; he saves or defends against the attack of the enemy. He practices a safe rhetoric in both speech and deed. Alcibiades first discusses Socrates' endurance with respect to food and drink, a frequent theme in the *Symposium*.[73] We have already been told of two banquets within the *Symposium*, one divine and marked by intoxication and seduction, the other human and marked by sobriety in drink and sexual conduct. Now we learn that Socrates and Alcibiades were messmates at Potidaea (219e7). Socrates surpassed both Alcibiades and the entire army in undergoing hardships. When food was unavailable, "the others were nothing with respect to endurance" (219e7–220a1; cf. 219a2):

> But in feasting, he alone was able to enjoy himself [i.e. he surpassed all the others in enjoyment], and al-

71. *Lysis* 211e2.

72. Ibid., 208c5.

73. Eating imagery is also very frequent in the *Phaedrus*, especially during Socrates' second speech. Strauss, *SocrArist*, pp. 173, 314.

though he did not wish to drink, when compelled to do so, he would conquer everybody; and what is most astonishing of all, no man ever saw Socrates drunk. I believe we shall shortly see the proof of this. (220a1–6)

Socrates excels in both excess and defect so far as eating and drinking are concerned, whereas he is abstinent or defective erotically. Why should a philosopher be able to imitate a toper or gourmand, but not a satyr? Is not Alcibiades' icon defective in the decisive respect? Indeed, Alcibiades emphasizes the fact that Socrates' resemblance to a satyr is only skin deep. Whereas eating and drinking are public acts and are necessary for the defense or preservation of the individual, sexual intercourse takes place in private, and is necessary for the generation of others, but not for the preservation of the self. Socratic indulgence in food and drink shares in both defensive courage and political irony. Socrates adjusts publicly to the habits of the Athenians, but not privately.[74] His wife and child satisfy political demands; as a pederast, Socrates speaks much and does nothing.

The next two episodes illustrate Socrates' behavior in winter and summer, or his indifference to the excesses of nature in the modern sense:

Most marvelous were his deeds of endurance in the winter, which is terrible there. Once, there was an extreme frost, when everyone either did not go out, or, if anyone did, he bundled up with unusual care. We would put on our shoes and then wrap our feet in felt and wool, but he walked around outdoors in the same clothing he was accustomed to wear previously. He passed over the ice unshod more easily than the others in their shoes. And the soldiers looked askance at him, thinking that he was contemptuous of them. (220a5–c1)

In preparing for the banquet, Socrates was willing to bathe and wear shoes. He meets the gentlemen part way in an effort to establish some rapport with them. So far as the footsoldiers are

---

74. For his public piety, cf. *Memorabilia* 1.1.2.

concerned, he makes no such attempt. Why this difference in behavior?

As Alcibiades shows, Socrates' tactics were not effective with the multitude, but only with those who responded in some way to logos. In this sense one may say that Socrates is an adherent of the noble, but not of the base Eros. Of course, the significance of "noble" and "base" differs from what the terms mean for the earlier pederastic speakers. The donning of shoes functions as a disguise, or part of a disguise, by which Socrates conceals the true nature of his noble Eros. Different as the aristocratically inclined pederasts may be from Socrates, they still resemble him more closely than does the multitude. The resemblance consists in hybris, however this attribute may be modified. Socratic hybris, or inner coldness, is like the ice of winter which cannot be negotiated by ordinary men without special footwear. To those who are largely or altogether without hybris, Socrates is a comic figure who excites suspicion because of his pretentious and odd ways.[75]

Socrates' summer behavior is introduced with an especially illuminating quotation from Homer: "Enough of that 'next, what the steadfast man did and dared' once on that campaign, is worth hearing (220c1–3)." The line is from the *Odyssey*; the beautiful Helen praises the wily feats of Odysseus.[76] Odysseus disguises himself in order to spy on and kill his enemies. Helen, whose beauty was disastrous for the Trojans, is here replaced by Alcibiades, whose beauty was disastrous for the Athenians. And for at least the second time, Socrates is made a warrior-spy among the enemies at the banquet. The attendant reference to killing is not simply ironical; that is, accommodation is a peaceful version of the violence needed to found a just city.[77] In

75. Cf. Klein, *Meno*, p. 5.

76. *Odyssey* 4.242. Cf. S. Benardete, "Some Misquotations of Homer in Plato," *Phronesis, 8* (1963), p. 178.

77. E.g. *Republic* 540e5 ff.: the just city depends upon the expulsion from the community of everyone over the age of ten. Cf. *Laws* 627d11 ff., a passage so strong that some editors and commentators (e.g. England, Ritter) have been led to soften it by emendations for which there is no textual or philological support.

the *Symposium* the only killings which take place are of mortals by immortals. But the dialogue is a spy story in the deepest sense of the term. The activities of Socrates, in their curious mixture of daring and dissembling, of doing and indifference, are a cover for the still more curious activities of Plato.

In the winter Socrates showed his superhuman powers by moving about in the snow. In the summer he stands still from dawn to dawn, in both light and darkness, "meditating something" (220c3-4). When others rest, Socrates is in motion; when others move, he is still. The whole anecdote takes us back in memory to the beginning of the dialogue (174d4 ff.); Aristodemus walks on to the activity of the banquet while Socrates stands still, wrapped in thought. Then Socrates was still for only an hour or two; in the present example, he spends the entire day in thought. The banquet and its participants make up a more pressing external circumstance for Socrates than the military campaign and his fellow soldiers. Alcibiades underlines the difference between Socrates and the soldiers by calling the philosopher a "gentleman" (ἀνήρ), whereas the soldiers are referred to as "humans" (ἄνθρωποι) (220c6). Socrates, like Odysseus, behaves differently toward gentlemen and enlisted men.

Again, whereas Agathon urged that Socrates' meditations be interrupted, the soldiers watch Socrates like an exotic spectacle, waiting to see whether he will last out the night (220c6, c8-d3). Although Alcibiades notes that it is the Ionians who stay up to watch Socrates (since presumably the Athenians are familiar with his odd ways), it remains true in general that Socrates is as great a marvel to the multitude in his external behavior as he is to the few in his speeches (cf. 216c7, 220c6). The difference lies in the greater hybris of the few, who try to interfere with Socratic behavior. The many leave Socrates alone, and thereby give him more time for uninterrupted meditation. In a democracy or among the multitude, the philosopher finds a kind of privacy which is absent among more hybristic men; for this reason, the democracy is the least bad of the corrupt regimes, whatever its defects in other respects.[78] Finally, we must note

78. *Statesman* 303a ff.

that Socrates' meditation is measured by reference to the course of the sun, and that he finishes with a prayer to the sun itself. As the many regard his body, so he regards the sun. Their concern with human marvels is replaced in him by concern with the divine.

So much for Socrates' endurance; Alcibiades concludes the fourth part of his speech by turning to the theme of courage. Here again there are two anecdotes, in both of which Alcibiades combines praise for Socrates with slightly concealed praise for himself. First, we learn that Alcibiades was wounded in battle:

> he would not leave me behind, but saved both my armor and me. At that time I demanded that the generals give you the prize for bravery; and here too you will neither blame me nor say that I lie. For when the generals, in view of my social standing, wanted to give me the prize, you were more eager than they that I should get it instead of you. (220e1–7)

Socrates is shown saving and retreating, but not attacking. Thus it is significant that not he but Alcibiades is wounded. The implication is that Socrates was by no means so zealous in military action as Alcibiades. In addition, Alcibiades demonstrates his own magnanimity by recounting how he tried to decline the prize for bravery on behalf of Socrates. On the other hand, Socrates' declination, as we are reminded by Alcibiades' insistence on his blamelessness and honesty, is due to hybris toward humans and their opinions.

According to Alcibiades' tacit argument, it is hybristic not to be concerned with honor. Even the Athenian generals bow to political opinion by their deference to Alcibiades' social rank. This difference in the social standing of the two men is mentioned indirectly by Alcibiades in his introduction to the second anecdote, which tells of an event at Delium, eight years after the battle of Potidaea.[79] "I happened to be present with a horse," i.e. as a knight, "whereas he was a hoplite" (221a1–2). The army is in flight, and Socrates is retreating in company with

79. The dates of the two events are 432 and 424.

Laches. This reference is scarcely accidental, since the dialogue *Laches* is concerned with courage and the technē of the soldier. In it two famous generals, Laches and Nicias, consult Socrates about the utility of an innovation in the handling of spear and shield. It is ironical that the man who is distinguished for his behavior in retreat should be consulted about matters of attack. Without going too deeply into the *Laches*, it is helpful to mention that its namesake is depicted as regarding endurance to be an adequate definition of courage. This definition, however, is rejected by Socrates as too broad; we need to know the difference between prudent and imprudent endurance.[80]

Alcibiades' account of Socrates' courage seems to resemble the opinion of Laches in linking that virtue with endurance; consequently, it suffers the defect of Laches' definition. It should not surprise us to see that Alcibiades is defective with respect to prudence. This leads him to mistake the appearance of courage for the virtue itself, as we shall see in a moment. Of course, the fact remains that Socrates saved Alcibiades' life at Potidaea. But the point is that Alcibiades places the two anecdotes at the same level; if anything, he stresses Socrates' behavior at Delium. The incident at Potidaea begins with the words "if you wish to hear of him" whereas the much longer account of the retreat at Delium is recommended in itself as "worth seeing," just as his endurance in meditation was said to be "worth hearing" (cf. 220d5–6, e8, c3). Apart from the fact that Alcibiades himself appears in a more valorous light at Delium, we may note that he is most impressed with Socrates as a marvelous spectacle in this section of his speech. In this way Plato shows his closeness to the many whom he seeks to rule. Both look at Socrates instead of the sun.

In the retreat Alcibiades appears as "superior" to Socrates: he is on horseback, whereas Socrates marches on foot. In addition, Socrates is fully occupied in retreating, while this time Alcibiades exhibits the active courage. He urges Socrates and Laches to be bold, "and I said that I would not leave them behind" (221a4–5). Alcibiades remains voluntarily, whereas

80. *Laches* 192c–d.

Socrates was in a way compelled to remain with Alcibiades (220e1) due to the latter's wound. Socrates unwounded needs Alcibiades' help; presumably Alcibiades unwounded could dispense with Socrates. But the main point of the anecdote is Socrates as a spectacle:

> I got a more beautiful view (κάλλιον ἐθεασάμην) of Socrates there than at Potidaea, for I had less to fear since I was on horseback. First I saw how superior he was to Laches in coolness. Second, it seemed to me, O Aristophanes, as you put it, that he walked along there just as here, "swaggering proudly, rolling his eyes sideways," looking calmly aside at friends and enemies, making it clear to everyone, even from afar, that if anyone touches this man (ἀνδρός), he will defend himself vigorously. As a result, he and his companion got away safely. For scarcely anyone of those who behave this way in war will be touched; [the enemy] pursue those who flee in headlong rout. (221a5–c1)

Once again, Alcibiades' description of Socratic beauty is highly ambiguous. Does his remark that "he had less to fear" mean "less than at Potidaea" or "less than Socrates?" In either case, Alcibiades is in better shape than before, both in health and elevation, to observe Socrates' behavior. Perhaps he did not accurately see how Socrates acted while rescuing him; after all, he was lying wounded at the time. Thus the clearest picture is of Socrates in retreat, and Alcibiades gives that picture an unfavorable connotation for Athenian eyes by quoting Aristophanes' description of the philosopher's arrogant and comical strutting.[81] We must not forget that Socrates' behavior was very annoying to most Athenians. The Socratic spectacle is thus presented by Alcibiades as antipolitical, even in the performance of political acts. Socrates' coolness or courage is related to his endurance of the cold. Furthermore, Socratic coldness looks like courage, and so suggests military prowess. It suggests to the

81. *Clouds* 362.

audience that Socrates is a "real man" (ἀνήρ), whereas in fact, he is unique or somehow not a man at all.

Socrates' Uniqueness

This brings us to the fifth and final section of Alcibiades' speech. Of the many other qualities he might praise, Alcibiades selects Socrates' uniqueness: "he is like no other human being" (221c4: τὸ δὲ μηδενὶ ἀνθρώπων ὅμοιον εἶναι). In the previous section, Socrates was called an ἀνήρ, a "real man" or "warrior," either directly or through comparison with someone else. The reason for this is to contrast him with the multitude or enlisted troops. Now, however, Socrates is called a "human being" (ἄνθρωπος), directly or through negative comparison, three times in one brief paragraph (221c4, d2, d5), and Alcibiades refers to the other guests as "real men" or "sirs" (222a7: ὦ ἄνδρες). "Human being" designates primarily the genus here, although it must be understood secondarily to apply to a nongentleman. Socrates constitutes a separate species within the genus, as it were; since he cannot be compared to anyone, he is not quite a human being himself.

There is no middle term connecting Socrates to other mortals. Socrates lacks the human Eros. Alcibiades regards this fact as the outstanding item in his analysis of Socrates' nature. That he is unlike anyone, whether among the ancients or his contemporaries, "is worthy of total wonder" (221c5–6; cf. 220c3, e8). Socrates is wholly wonderful because he is whole or complete if only in the negative sense of being unique or not needing anyone:

> Such as Achilles was, someone might compare Brasidas and others; as for Pericles, he is like Nestor and Antenor, and there are others. And so one might compare the rest in the same way. But as for this mortal's peculiarity, both in himself and in his speeches, no investigator could come close [to finding a parallel], whether among those now living or the ancients, unless perhaps if, as I put it,

one were to liken him, not to a mortal, but to the Silenoi
and satyrs, himself and his speeches. (221c6–d6)

Socrates is a Silenus, and his speeches (as opposed to his
deeds) are satyrs. He does not care for human, but only for
divine things. Since he is himself a mortal rather than a god,
his care (μελετή) is hybristic. If we look within the genus of
mankind, Socrates seems to have more in common with the few
than the many. Despite his low birth and lack of certain gentlemanly qualities, it is the sons of the upper class whom he generally pursues in the dialogues. The claim made in the *Apology*,
that he spends his time in the marketplace, pestering and in-
terrogating every citizen about virtue and knowledge,[82] is certainly not confirmed by the dialogues as a whole. Socrates is a
partisan of the upper class, and even a parasite in the literal
sense of one who lives by dining with the rich.[83] He neglects his
affairs thanks to the generosity of wealthy friends like Crito,
who thereby make possible the pursuit of philosophy.

The philosopher needs the well-to-do as the poets need (or
are fond of) tyrants.[84] Why, then, does Alcibiades not compare
Socrates, whether positively or negatively, with men like Parmenides, Protagoras, Homer, or Pindar? In part, the answer lies
in Alcibiades' obsession with politics and honor. Achilles,
Brasidas, Pericles, Nestor, and Antenor are examples of men
with whom Alcibiades would like to be compared. The special
importance of Pericles, the middle example, is suggested by
the fact that his name occurs twice, and that Alcibiades was his
ward. Undoubtedly Alcibiades hopes to eclipse the glory of his
uncle and guardian by combining statesmanship with the art
of war. We are, after all, only hours away from the Sicilian
expedition. But we learn a deep truth about Socrates, apart from
Alcibiades' own nature, from being told that the philosopher is

82. 30e7: ὑμᾶς . . . ἕνα ἕκαστον.

83. Cf. Xenophon, *Symposium*, where Socrates seems to have most in common
with Philip, the professional parasite and buffoon; Socrates calls himself a
pander at 3.10.13.

84. For the difference between ἄνθρωπος and ἀνήρ, together with the problem
of the relationship between the sage and the tyrant, see L. Strauss, *What Is
Political Philosophy?* (Glencoe, Ill., 1959), pp. 104 ff.

not a hero, a general, a statesman, or a political orator. The lesson, in fact, is obvious: Socrates is not a political man.

The absence of thinkers and artists from the examples of men with whom Socrates cannot be compared, is designed by Plato to underline the character of his master's uniqueness. Socrates practices the political arts of dialectic, but for altogether transpolitical ends. Alcibiades twice distinguishes between Socrates' self and his speeches; what Socrates says is not the same as what he is. But the dissembling is not for the sake of honor or power. The split between self and speech is restored to coherence when one penetrates into the speeches themselves:

> And indeed, I bypassed this point in my opening remarks, that his speeches are most like the Silenoi that open up. For if someone wishes to hear Socrates' speeches, at first they would seem most laughable. (221d7–e2)

Alcibiades began by comparing Socrates himself with the Silenoi: the inner Socrates is a statue or image, i.e. an imitation of a god (215a7), beauty concealed within a laughable, comically ugly figure. Next, Alcibiades turned to Marsyas and developed a comparison of Socrates' speech to the charming music of the satyr. This comparison emphasized the external effects of Socrates' speeches rather than their inner nature. Again, at 216d4 Alcibiades compared Socrates himself to a Silenus: he is outwardly erotic and inwardly moderate. Now Alcibiades turns to the interior of Socrates' speeches, and so invokes the Silenus once more. This use of the Silenus enforces the insight that Socrates' interior is coincident with the interior of his speeches. Inside Socrates are divine images (216e7: ἀγάλματα . . . θεῖα); inside his "most divine speeches" are many images of excellence (222a3–4: ἀγάλματ' ἀρετῆς). Consonant with the general theme of the *Symposium*, Socrates' excellence is presented as an image: as made or generated. The psyche is compared to a divine statue or true body concealed within the body of flesh.

The language of Alcibiades' "iconography" is on this point

in conformity with the teaching of Diotima. At 212a3–4 she describes how he who sees beauty itself becomes immortal: by generating images of excellence in another's psyche (τίκτειν . . . εἴδωλα ἀρετῆς). Socrates' teachers generated the images which Alcibiades perceived in the philosopher's psyche, but which he himself cannot reproduce in the psyches of the audience. Psyche and speech are both generated, and they are also analogous in structure. In Socrates' case the exterior of both is hybristic, like the skin of a satyr (221e3–4). In the case of the nonhybristic men, their speech will also mirror their psyches, but they do not figure in the *Symposium,* which is restricted to the kinds or shapes of hybris. To return to Socrates, his speech is externally ugly and erotic; internally it is beautiful and unerotic, like his psyche. Socrates talks of commonplace things—of asses, smiths, shoemakers and tanners—but he is really referring to the rare and exalted, the virtuous and divine things, which are alone suitable for the one who intends to be noble and good (221e4–222a6). If Socrates is the image of a god, then the gentleman is the imitation of Socrates, or "three steps from the king." And this is a good description of Socrates' uniqueness. He differs from all previous philosophers in being the paradigm of gentlemanly existence, although he is himself a hybristic nongentleman.

Alcibiades concludes his speech on Socrates by admitting that he has mixed praise and blame into the image. The blame is again said to be directed toward Socrates' hybris. But he also makes it clear that he objects to this hybris only as it is applied to himself (222a7–8). In itself, Socrates' ironic hybris is praiseworthy rather than blamable. Alcibiades' warning to Agathon and the other beauties not to be deceived by Socrates' ostensibly erotic pursuit is not given out of concern for the welfare of his rivals, but out of spite against Socrates. He says: "guard yourself by learning from our sufferings, and do not, as in the proverb, learn from suffering like the fool" (222a8–b3). Alcibiades, who learned, if at all, only after suffering, has been made into a fool by Socrates, and so too will be those who regard him as sexually erotic.

Intoxication and Poetry

Alcibiades is greeted by laughter "at his frankness" (222c1–2: παρρησίᾳ), rather than by applause. What is the reason for this? To begin with, of course, his speech shows that he still "seems to be erotically attracted toward Socrates," as Aristodemus suggests. It is comical to hear of the great beauty's failure to seduce the ugly Socrates. Most if not all of the listeners must have been wondering: why should Alcibiades be attracted to so unworthy a person? From their viewpoint, given Socrates' "oddness" (ἀτοπία), Alcibiades deserved to fail. The very attempt was absurd. By withholding their applause the symposiasts indicate the oddness of Alcibiades' speech. Their laughter may be an embarrassed response to the fact that Alcibiades insults them for failing to perceive the beauty of Socrates, just as Socrates previously accused them all of being liars.

Alcibiades' "frankness" refers as much to his denunciation of the audience as to the confession of his own sufferings. The proverb with which he concludes is first found in Homer's *Iliad*, where it is spoken by Menelaus to Euphorbus over the corpse of Patroclus.[85] Menelaus warns Euphorbus: "father Zeus! it is not noble for the insolent man to boast!" [86] In condemning the boastful son of Panthöos, whose pride and spirit are greater than those of the wild beasts, Menelaus himself engages in some boasting, which Euphorbus ignores at the price of his life. In his previous quotation from Homer Alcibiades spoke with the voice of Helen; now he takes on the persona of her husband. Alcibiades is himself an insolent circle-man. We can scarcely expect the audience to applaud a man who threatens to kill them.

According to Socrates, however, Alcibiades has not been frank at all. Socrates' interpretation of his speech amounts to this: Alcibiades (Menelaus) warns Agathon (Euphorbus) not to touch Socrates' (Patroclus') body or strip him of his armor (satyr-skin). There is a problem here, since in the analogy,

85. *Iliad* 17.33.
86. Ibid., 17.19; cf. *Odyssey* 1.368: ὑπέρβιον is closely associated with ὕβρις.

Patroclus is dead, whereas Socrates is alive. And yet, is not
Socrates "dead" to human things, in the sense that philosophy
is a preparation for dying? In any event, here are Socrates'
words:

> You seem to me to be sober, O Alcibiades. Otherwise
> you would not have wrapped yourself up so cunningly in
> a circle [veiled your meaning], trying to make invisible
> the purpose for having said all this. Nor would you have
> mentioned it as an afterthought, tacking it on to the end
> [of your speech], as though you didn't say everything
> with the intention of setting Agathon and me at odds.
> For you suppose it necessary for me to love you and no
> one else, whereas Agathon must be loved by you and by
> no one else. But you won't escape undetected: your
> satiric and Silenic drama has been revealed. But my
> dear Agathon, don't let him get the biggest share [suc-
> ceed: μηδὲν πλέον αὐτῷ γένηται]; take steps that you and I
> are not set apart. (222c3–d6)

Alcibiades is sober rather than manic or inspired because of
his duplicity: he covers over his speech as he previously
wrapped Socrates' body with his own arms (219b5 ff.). But the
veiling of speech or the psyche is designed to prevent genuine
contact, whereas the covering of the body by another has union
as its goal. The two modes of seduction thus differ as does separation from union. A genuine union of two psyches is not
seduction, but agreement or friendship in terms of the third
entity by which they are unified. Seduction is a kind of dissembling or ironic hybris, a use of force, if only in the mild
form of persuasive speech. Socrates warns both Agathon and the
others that Alcibiades' jealousy is a result of his overreaching
nature. Alcibiades wishes to be both the sole lover and the
sole beloved. His speech is a satyr play, not merely because of
the description of Socrates, but because it expresses Alcibiades'
own Silenic nature. Unfortunately the images concealed within
Alcibiades' breast are not of virtue in the moral sense, although

they do exhibit his excellence. Alcibiades is not genuinely
erotic; like Socrates, he shares an abstract resemblance to Phaedrus, and like Socrates, his ambiguous form of Eros is directed
toward the whole. Unlike Socrates, however, "wholeness" is
for him restricted to the human or political, since he is unable,
despite his psychic restlessness, to conceive of anything higher.

At the moment, Alcibiades seems to be less forceful or seduc-
tive than Socrates. Agathon, taking it upon himself to speak
for the others, passes an unfavorable verdict on Alcibiades'
charge:

> Socrates, you may perhaps speak the truth. I judge that
> he has reclined between me and you in order to divide
> us. But he won't benefit by it (οὐδὲν οὖν πλέον αὐτῷ ἔσται).
> I shall come and sit down next to you. (222d7–e3)

Socrates' Marsyan music succeeds in a few measures; Alcibiades'
lengthy composition has failed. Agathon will prevent Alcibiades
from cutting him off from Socrates; he implies that he and
Socrates form a whole or pair of natural lovers in the Aristophanean sense. Agathon is still hybristic, and as the first sentence
of his verdict shows, he is not really concerned with whether
Socrates is speaking the truth. The net result of Alcibiades'
long interruption, then, is to bring Socrates and Agathon closer
together than they might otherwise have been.

When Socrates urges Agathon to change his seat, Alcibiades
protests:

> O Zeus . . . how I suffer from the mortal (ὑπὸ τῶν
> ἀνθρώπου) He believes it necessary to surpass me in ev-
> ery way. But if nothing else, O marvelous one, let Aga-
> thon sit down between us. (222e6–9)

Alcibiades swears three times in the *Symposium;* previously,
he invoked Heracles (213b8) and Poseidon (214d6). Now he
completes his own ascent by calling on Zeus to witness his sufferings. Alcibiades' indictment of Socrates has boomeranged to
the advantage of the accused. The accuser, foiled by mortals,

has no recourse but to the king of the gods. And the mortal who is the principal instrument of his humiliation, Alcibiades calls "O marvelous one." Nothing less than Zeus can function as the third, or bond, between himself and Socrates; the power of Dionysus is insufficient to conquer Apollo.

Alcibiades applies the word "marvelous" to Socrates on twelve occasions. He thereby qualifies Socrates' head (213e2), his music (215b6), his immunity to Eros (216c7), the images within his breast (217a1), his ability to help Alcibiades satisfy his ambition (217a3–4), his daimonic nature (219c1), his sobriety (220a4), his deeds (220a7), his ability to stand in meditation for an entire day (220c6), his many praiseworthy traits (221c3), his uniqueness (221c6), and finally, Socrates as a whole (222e8). The word appears in his speech on three other occasions, one of which refers negatively to Socrates (215a2), one to Alcibiades' opinion of his own beauty (217a5–6), and once to the care with which the soldiers dressed in winter at Potidaea (220b3). We may safely say that, to Alcibiades, nothing is more wonderful than Socrates. Socrates, as it were, is twelve times more marvelous than Alcibiades, and by the latter's own reckoning. Alcibiades also underlines his astonishment at Socrates' erotic indifference by speaking only of his own beauty as "marvelous."

Philosophy should have begun for Alcibiades in his wonder at Socrates. Instead, this wonder led to frustration, suffering, and humiliation. The political character of Alcibiades' hybristic ambition was not amenable to the enchanting music of Socrates' divine rhetoric. This is due in part to Alcibiades' own defects, but in part it exhibits a tension between theory and practice. The cosmic harmony of opposites is achieved only intermittently in the human sphere. In the scene before us, Socrates is granted the position of intermediary between Agathon and Alcibiades, but only for a moment. Chance supervenes, and Agathon never completes the motion by which he would have changed his position: he is instantly interrupted by a party of revelers who march in through doors that chance to be open:

the whole place was full of noise. Nothing was in any order (οὐκέτι ἐν κόσμῳ οὐδενί); it became necessary to drink a lot of wine. (223b1–6)

For the third time the word "instantaneous" (ἐξαίφνης) plays a decisive role in the dialogue, but one of descent from the vision of beauty itself (210e4), to the appearance of Alcibiades (212c6), to the destruction of the "cosmos," which was the precondition for rational speech.[87]

The necessity of reason is replaced by the necessity of chance. Eryximachus, Phaedrus, and some others, all presumably weak drinkers, take their leave, and Aristodemus falls asleep, so that the irrational disorder need not be described (223b6–c1). But no Platonic dialogue ends in chaos. Aristodemus awakens at dawn, the symbol of hope, to the crow of cocks,[88] and finds that philosophy has survived:

> the others were either sleeping or departed, but Agathon, Aristophanes, and Socrates were alone still awake and drinking from a large bowl, from left to right. Socrates was engaged in dialogue with them. (223c3–6)

Alcibiades is replaced by Aristophanes, who at last has the opportunity to converse with Socrates, although intoxicated. The phrase "from left to right" suggests that Aristophanes is now between Agathon and Socrates; the function of religious or political poetry in preserving order has been acknowledged. Socrates is engaged in a new attempt to produce a cosmos by uniting tragedy and comedy; he is "forcing" (προσαναγκάζειν) his interlocutors to agree that "he who has the technē of making tragedy has it also for making comedy":

> while they were being forced (ἀναγκαζομένους) to this, and not easily following [the argument] through drowsiness, first Aristophanes fell asleep, and then at daybreak, Agathon. (223c6–d8)

87. Cf. 213c1.
88. Cf. *Phaedo* 118a7–8.

The new order recapitulates in surprisingly explicit terms the underlying theme of the entire dialogue. Poetry must be forced by the logos of philosophy to reach a harmony in its parts. The way in which this is done cannot be reported explicitly from first principles (223c6 ff.), but can only be presented mimetically or dramatically.[89] The division between tragedy and comedy is a mark of the incompleteness of mortals who, having been sundered by the gods, cannot transcend weeping and laughter by engaging in both at once. Men may be compelled in this direction by philosophy, but the very intoxication which is a necessary condition for achieving unity, interferes with its accomplishment. Those who are compelled toward wholeness fall asleep from the effort of constrained journeying. To this extent life is more like tragedy than comedy, as Plato indicates in two ways. In rephrasing the point under discussion, he writes that the tragedian can make comedy, but not vice versa. Second, Aristophanes falls asleep before Agathon. Once again we are on the way toward the whole, but do not reach it.

Philosophy (together with its disciple) alone is left, neither to weep nor laugh, but soberly to rise up after a night of enthusiasm and continue in its customary ways:[90]

> When Socrates had put them to sleep, he rose up and left, and [Aristodemus], as was his custom, followed him. On arriving at the Lyceum, Socrates washed himself, and then passed the balance of the day as usual. Having done so, at evening, he went home to rest. (223d8–12)

89. Cf. *Republic* 533c3.

90. Alcibiades refers to Socrates' customary ways with great frequency; the phrase ὥσπερ εἰώθει or some variant occurs five times in his discussion: at 213c1 (instantaneous and unexpected appearances), 217b6 (customary talk), 218d6–7 (customary irony), 220b5 (customary clothing), and 223a6 (customarily sits next to beauties). The phrase is almost present at 223d11 (ὥσπερ ἄλλοτε), where it follows immediately a reference to the usual behavior of Aristodemus in pursuing Socrates at 223d10. Alcibiades applies the phrase to himself negatively just once at 217a6: he goes to Socrates without the customary attendant. Socrates manages to combine ἀτοπία with stability, or an imitation of νόμος, whereas Alcibiades is closer to the modern conception of an "unusual" man.

It is interesting that the dialogue should end with this mention of the problem of writing. In the *Phaedrus*, which is dramatically later than the *Symposium*, the subject of Eros will be re-examined in terms of the differences between sophistic and philosophical rhetoric. There, too, we shall find a connection between Eros and writing, and Plato will give to Socrates the task of describing, as though prophetically, the nature of a philosophical writing which combines the technai of tragedy and comedy with the technē of division and collection. But that is another logos.[A]

NOTES TO THE SECOND EDITION

Chapter One

A. The *Republic* and the *Symposium* are inversely related; the former criticizes Eros and the latter praises it. The criticism of Eros is closely connected to the exaggerated praise of justice and indicates the grave danger posed by philosophical madness to political life. The praise of Eros is accordingly reserved for a private celebration of poetry, during which justice is rhetorically subordinated to hybris. For a deeper understanding of the *Republic*, it should not be forgotten that an exaggerated praise of justice is itself a consequence of philosophical madness. In the *Phaedrus*, which takes place during the daylight and outside the city walls, the praise of Eros, as well as its criticism, is connected to a discussion of political rhetoric (of which philosophical rhetoric constitutes a species). For a deeper understanding of the *Phaedrus*, it should not be forgotten that the exaggerated praise of Eros takes place in terms intended to please Phaedrus (257a3–6). This is why the dialogue bears his name.

B. The question naturally arises whether the *Phaedrus* is also a revelation, and if so, how this affects its relation to the *Symposium*. One should consider carefully that in the *Phaedrus*, Socrates attributes his praise of Eros to the poet Stesichorus, and that it is a recantation for his earlier criticism of Eros. Unlike most other students of the dialogue, I take this (and Lysias') criticism to have a serious content; see my two articles: (1) "The Non-Lover in Plato's *Phaedrus*" in *Man and World* 2 (1969), pp. 423–37; (2) "Socrates as Concealed Lover" in *Classics and the Classical Tradition* (University Park, Penn., 1970), pp. 163–78. I restrict myself here to the following observation: despite the fact that the *Phaedrus* takes place outside the city walls, it is much more political or "edifying" than the *Symposium* (see the final remark in A above). In the *Phaedrus*, the "transcendent" (literally, "hyperuranian") status of the so-called Ideas makes them inaccessible to logos (as is plain from the silence of the divine and philosophical charioteers); as a consequence, we must have recourse to myth or poetry, and this in turn leads inevitably to a politicizing of philosophy or to the production of edifying discourses. In the *Symposium*, the so-called Ideas are not transcendent. The ascent to beauty itself does not take us outside or onto the roof of the cosmos. Our vision of beauty itself is accordingly more stable than the intermittent, harassed, and moving or

329

perspectival vision accorded to philosophical souls in the *Phaedrus* (248a1–
6). Hence, according to Diotima, the philosopher can generate true instances of the perceived truth (beauty itself) and not merely true images
(*Symposium* 211e4–212a7). However, it does not follow that the speeches in
the *Symposium* are themselves true instances rather than true images. The
poetic nature of the dialogues, and especially of the *Symposium,* points
toward the second of the two alternatives.

Chapter Two

A. The distinction between cosmic genesis and erotic generation is
linked in Phaedrus' speech to a suppression of the Olympian gods, and
thereby to the denial of the natural basis of the polis. This denial is traditionally associated with the Sophists, but there is good reason to suspect
that Plato might have endorsed it as well. For an extended discussion of
Plato's treatment of the problematic status of political life, I refer the reader
to my article, "Plato's Myth of the Reversed Cosmos," in *Review of Metaphysics* 33 (1979), pp. 59–85. Unlike Aristotle, Plato's characters never assert that man is by nature a political animal. Some might wish to infer this
from the Socratic analogy in the *Republic* (II, 368c ff.), according to which
the city stands to the person as do large to small letters. This analogy is
questionable from many perspectives; for example, in the passage (especially 368e–369a), Socrates suggests that if we can see the origin of justice
and injustice in the city, as well as what kind of thing political justice is,
this will answer our questions about justice in the person. The word used
for "person" here is ἀνήρ (368e2), not ἄνθρωπος—in other words, the
political rather than the biological term. This implies the question-begging
nature of the investigation, or that we will be comparing convention with
convention. So too letters, whether large or small, are conventional rep-
resentations of a conventional articulation of sound. More obviously, what
needs to be shown is that there exists a natural political order, within which
justice is the expression of the position of justice within the natural order
of the human soul. But this depends upon our vision of the natural order
of the soul; Socrates begs the question by attempting to infer the nature
of the soul from his theoretical construction of the just city. It needs to be
shown that every "normal" human being (already a question-begging qualification) is by nature just. And this in no way follows from the thesis that
a just city is useful to all human beings. The just city may still be (and in
Plato, I believe, is) a construction or poem, the wish of good men, hence
a project of the will (to use an up-to-date expression). Even if we give the
name of justice to that order in the soul which obtains when reason rules
the other parts, the result, if applied to politics, is to transform the city
into a philosopher. And this brings out still more clearly the questionable
status of Socrates' analogy. It suppresses the distinction between private

and public or demotic virtue, a distinction which is central to Socrates'
entire argument. This point may be put in another way. Justice is not the
virtue of a single part of the individual soul *or* of the city, as are wisdom,
temperance, and courage; instead, it is the proper functioning of all three
parts of the soul or city. But why should we assume that there is not merely
an analogy but a formal identity (368e8–369a3) between personal and
political justice? Why should we assume that the same psychic order is just
for philosophers and nonphilosophers alike?

Our purpose here is not to provide an exhaustive analysis of the *Republic*,
but to clarify the political implications of the praise of Eros, that is, of the
association between Eros and philosophy. Eros is a desire (ἐπιθυμία), and
as previously noted, it is sharply criticized in the *Republic* and made subordinate to spiritedness as well as to reason. The unacceptableness of this
ranking to the philosopher does more than bring into question the surface
argument of the *Republic*. The erotic or manic nature of philosophy, the
highest human good, supports the thesis that there is a radical discontinuity between philosophy and politics, that is, between theory and practico-
production (the two being united in Plato). The discontinuity between philosophy and the city (which is entirely compatible with the usefulness of
the city to the philosopher) is itself a consequence of the discontinuity
between nature and convention. For this reason, it is senseless to advocate
a life in accord with nature, without very considerable qualifications. The
transnatural aspects of human existence arise directly from the exercise of
the peculiarly human faculties and are hence exemplified by philosophy
but are already quite visible in the political life. This is why Socrates calls
philosophy a preparation for dying (*Phaedo* 65e1 ff, 69b8–c3). If the pure
vision of pure form is possible at all, it cannot be possible for living and
thus erotic human beings. This is the most succinct formulation of the
transnatural dimension of philosophy. In a similarly succinct vein, one must
say that the very consequences of human nature that direct us toward
political association render necessary artificial constructions and modifications of natural desire by free productions of the will (as, for example,
the productions consequent upon philosophical desire).

It is therefore not simply the case that there is an opposition between
the philosophical and the nonphilosophical or political life. These two lives
necessarily intersect. The root of their common problems is that a life in
accordance with nature is impossible. Nature sanctions too much and not
enough. To come back now to Phaedrus, he is no philosopher but a lover
of the rhetorical art, to the extent that he rises beyond vulgar utilitarianism.
He is thus marked by a verbal imitation of the technical confidence of
enlightened atheists wherever they appear. The disjunction between genesis and generation, or the absence of the Olympian gods, opens a space
for persons like Phaedrus to engage in the pleasures of discourse or what

is today called *écriture*. To be sure, the same space also leaves room for the philosopher. The difference between Socrates and Plato, as well as Socrates' symbolic function in Plato's dialogues, now becomes clear for the first time. Socrates has no time for *écriture*, just as he aspires to become a divine voyeur (who admires, but does not possess, the bodies of beautiful youths). Plato writes about the desire to become a divine voyeur, thereby attempting to inoculate himself against *écriture* with a dose of the poison itself (as has been surmised by Derrida). This would be the basis for a proper contrast between Plato and post-modernism, which I shall undertake elsewhere.

Chapter Three

A. I add here some remarks concerning Protagoras' myth that are relevant to the themes of the *Symposium*.

1. According to Protagoras, the gods made human beings "inside the earth" (γῆς ἔνδον; 320d3–6). Exactly the same expression is used by Socrates to refer to the production of human beings by the god in the noble lie (*Republic* III, 415a2 ff.). However, in Socrates' myth, the god makes the soul as well as the body, thereby determining in advance the natures of the citizens. In the Protagorean myth, the gods make the living body, but Prometheus and Epimetheus are ordered to adorn it with suitable powers (320d3–6). As the sequel makes plain, human beings, who are distinguished from the brutes (τὰ ἄλογα) by the possession of logos, are unfinished by nature. When Prometheus inspects the results of the Epimethean distribution, he sees that humans are "naked, shoeless, without bedding or weapons" (321c5–6); these precise words are spoken of Eros by Diotima in the *Symposium* (203d1 ff.). In order to protect human beings against their natural incompleteness, Prometheus steals "the technical wisdom connected with fire" from Hephaestus and Athena (321c8–d3). The gods are unwilling to give τέχνη to humans: τέχνη is stolen divinity, an alternative to the vision of pure Ideas. This is the seed of the modern revolution against antiquity, a revolution in which Eros is given the dual role of corporeal desire and the will to power. In the words of Nietzsche's Zarathustra, man is the unfinished animal.

2. To return to Protagoras, his human beings now possess "wisdom concerning life" but not the political wisdom (321d3 ff.). Protagoras in effect distinguishes between a productive theory and practice. This distinction is of course necessary in order to justify his own "Promethean" invention (τὴν πολιτικὴν τέχνην; 319a3 ff.), which teaches human beings "good council" (εὐβουλία) concerning the affairs of one's household and city (318e5–319a2), so that the household may be most excellent and the city most powerful in deed and speech (and we may note in passing that the distinction between excellence and power contains the seed of the modern distinction between society and state). One function of the *Symposium* is to

show how perverse are the consequences of the sophistical teachings. Protagoras, on the other hand, says that Prometheus is prosecuted by the gods for theft, whereas human beings obtain "facility for living" (321e3–322a2). As it stands, this is an overstatement, since productive τέχνη is insufficient without its political counterpart (whereas pure theoretical τέχνη is superfluous). Also of considerable interest is the association of productive τέχνη with crime, but a crime of which human beings are absolved via the intermediate figure of Prometheus.

3. Subsequent to the acquisition of productive τέχνη, human beings establish religion (322a3–5) and then "articulated speech and names via τέχνη" (322a5–8). Protagoras is not entirely clear as to the precise connection between production on the one hand and religion and language on the other (cf. 322a3: Ἐπειδὴ δὲ ὁ ἄνθρωπος θείας μετέσχε μοίρας). Suffice it to say here that, on his account, religion and language are man-made, and further, they are prior to the acquisition of cities (322a8–b1) as well as of the political τέχνη. We can say that human beings are not at home within nature on the basis of their natural endowments alone, even if we include productive τέχνη among them. To be sure, Protagoras attributes the gift of the political τέχνη to Zeus, who is made to assert that without this gift, humans will perish (322c1). But this is a transparent way of attributing godlike status to himself: Protagoras is Zeus (but is not Hephaestus or Athena); he knows how to govern production, but also how to make the city most powerful, that is, how to preserve it from destruction in the crucial case of war (322b1–8). At a more general level, Protagoras is claiming that politics, and hence political wisdom, are not natural consequences of desire, thus certainly not of Eros, even though productive τέχνη may be so understood (depending upon how we come to understand the figure of Prometheus). Protagorean εὐβουλία is not the natural φρόνησις of Aristotle. The difference between Eros and politics is obvious from the difference between the *Republic* and the *Symposium,* but it can also be very specifically seen by a comparison of Protagoras' myth with the speech of Diotima. According to Protagoras, Zeus sends politics to human beings via Hermes, the messenger god, who brings "shame and right" (αἰδῶ τε καὶ δίκην; 322c2; cf. c4). According to Diotima, it is Eros who mediates between god and mortal, thereby fulfilling the "hermeneutic" function ('Ἑρμηνεῦον; 202d13 ff. and esp. e3). And the plain message of the *Symposium* is that Eros brings, or points toward, *private* happiness, certainly not toward political shame and right. At this point, I break off my consideration of Protagoras, who deserves an exhaustive study in his own right.

Chapter Four

A. This section of my original argument needs to be stated with greater clarity. Eryximachus constructs his speech on the basis of two principles.

The first is that there is a cosmic as well as a human manifestation of Eros, and hence a divine as well as a human medicine (186a2–b2). The second is that there is a noble or healthy as well as a base or sick manifestation of Eros (186b5–d5). It is clear from Eryximachus' exposition that the human soul is, not separate from, but a manifestation of, the divine cosmos. Still more specifically, Eryximachus distinguishes between the love of human souls and the love of natural bodies, both animate and inanimate (186a3–7). Health and sickness are originally attributed to the body (186b5–7). Next, Eryximachus draws an analogy between the gratification of human beings and of bodies, that is, between psychic and corporeal gratification, an analogy that adopts Pausanias' distinction between noble and shameful love (186b7–c3). What then is the relation between cosmic and human Eros, and consequently between divine and human medicine? The god (186b1) holds together the cosmos by a harmonizing of opposite forces, for instance, cold and hot, bitter and sweet, dry and moist (186d5–e1). If we apply the divine paradigm to human affairs, the mortal physician must produce a harmony or reconciliation between opposites. This would seem to require that he make the noble love the base, and in particular, that he makes males love females. It is obvious that both inferences are repugnant to Eryximachus, who is the champion of noble pederasty. Eryximachus is accordingly forced to introduce a third principle, like loves like, which he states in the oblique form "the unlike desires and loves unlike things" (186b6–7). On the basis of this principle, however, the art of medicine, in both its divine and human forms, is either superfluous, ineffectual, or both. It is superfluous, since the noble will love the noble by nature. It is ineffectual, since neither the cosmos nor the human race will be harmonized. And in fact, we soon see that this principle is inadequate to the effort to account for the cosmos as a harmony of opposites. Eryximachus has arrived at an apparent impasse. As a pederast, he needs the principle that like loves like. As a physician, he needs the principle that, by nature, like also loves what is unlike itself. Finally, as a cosmologist, or less pretentiously, given his attempt to derive the art of medicine from cosmological principles and thereby to imply his own quasi-divinity, he must both attribute health and sickness to the cosmos and equate health with nobility and sickness with baseness.

The art of medicine, as practiced by human physicians, turns out in Eryximachus' interpretation to *modify* nature, namely, to transform the base into the noble love. But this is not the same as the divine physician's ability to harmonize opposites. It is instead the removal of opposition, and thus the replacement of harmony with unity. The Eryximachean interpretation of noble and healthy love is of an ungenerating love. It cannot be derived from the paradigm of natural genesis. The fundamental inconsistency of Eryximachus' speech lies in his attempt to link divine and human medicine by the conception of noble pederasty. One need not go so far in the opposite direction as to say that pederasty is against nature. But Eryximachus' speech makes it explicit that nature is divided against itself; hence the image of the double Eros. The cosmos is preserved by heterosexual Eros, or by the harmonizing of opposites. If pederastic Eros is noble and healthy, then the cosmos, precisely as generated and preserved, is paradoxically base and sick. The highest form of human erotic activity is an expression of the fact that human beings reflect in their own natures the internal opposition of the cosmos. According to Eryximachus, the human physician has as his task the suppression of base and the affirmation of noble Eros. This is quite different from the work of the divine physician. Human medicine is a hermeneutical art, an expression of human taste as regulative of nature, and not at all as obedient to it. We cannot simply obey or live in accord with nature, because nature leads us at once in opposite directions. Nature is silent with respect to its own telos; so too is a τέχνη that merely follows nature. As a hermeneutical art, medicine is subordinate to rhetoric, and hence to human decisions concerning the noble and the base lives. To state this result more generally, the natural arts are subordinate to the poetic arts. The inner logic of Eryximachus' position is thus an anticipation of Nietzsche: science is at bottom poetry, regardless of how the cosmos is in itself.

Chapter Six

A. This point should be stated more sharply. The two poets, Aristophanes and Agathon, stand for two (not unqualified) extremes, which we may represent very generally as conservative and innovative. Aristophanes employs new speeches in the attempt to preserve the old way of life; more fundamentally, he teaches us that the soul can be preserved only through the political domestication of Eros. As we have seen in the previous chapter, this leads to the dominance of the body, and hence to the dominance of silence over speech. The subordination of Aristophanes to Eryximachus is therefore a sign of the relative ineffectiveness of Aristophanean conservatism. Unlike Plato's own use of music for political purposes in the *Republic* and *Laws,* Aristophanes' attempt is to combine artistic innovation and political conservatism in a way not altogether dissimilar to that of the most prominent English-speaking poets of the first half of the twentieth century. But innovation in diction and meter cannot be insulated from content; hence Plato's technical conservatism once the political revolution has been effected. In our own time, the line from T. S. Eliot to John Ashbery is disconcertingly short. Technical innovation, furthermore, cannot be restricted to poetry. Whereas the justification of technicism is always rhetorical and thus, in the broad sense of the term, practical, it is nevertheless true that the triumph of poetic rhetoric soon leads to or accelerates an unmitigated technicism when innovation (or creativity) is emancipated from its theological origin. As we are about to see, Agathon is certainly no champion of unmitigated technicism. But Plato is not a crude satirist who employs obvious symbols. Agathon serves the cause of technicism unwittingly in his attempt to emancipate youth from old age, beauty from ugliness, and the soft from the hard. Today we would no doubt refer to Agathon as an aesthete, a term that is normally associated with repugnance toward technology and a disinterest in politics. This is, however, a misunderstanding: the aesthete is both a consequence and a catalyst of political, that is, psychic, decay. In the late twentieth century, with our linguistic horizons, world views, and hermeneutical relativity, we are all aesthetes, that is, spontaneous makers of private worlds; to borrow a metaphor from Proust, the public world is the continuously changing waste product of our private productions. The waters of poetry have mingled with the current of history to furnish us with the fountain of youth.

What one may properly designate as Plato's attempt to combine tragedy and comedy is presented most explicitly in the *Symposium* as Diotima's endorsement of philosophical poetry, that is, the continuous production of beautiful speeches and thoughts in the light of the vision of beauty itself (cf. 210d4–e2 and 211e4–212a7). Diotima attempts to regulate the innovativeness celebrated by Agathon. She does this by replacing Aristophanes' traditional hierarchy of ends, or δόξα, with a pure, unchanging, and yet accessible vision of beauty. Unfortunately, this vision is empty of content; it is in fact powerless to regulate discourse, as is obvious from the history of philosophy. Philosophy is by its nature as revolutionary as poetry. To put the point with extreme caution, the Platonic doctrine of Eros leads inevitably to the subordination of truth to beauty, even if beauty is associated by Plato himself with mathematical order as well as with what is humanly appropriate. The history of mathematics shows even more plainly than the history of philosophy how beauty triumphs over truth to emancipate innovativeness and technicism from the domination of eternity. The comic nature of Diotima's teaching is represented dramatically by the intervention of the drunken Alcibiades, who reveals the truth about Socrates' unerotic nature. As always in Plato, the truth is revealed in the form of a riddle. The riddle cannot be resolved by pious assertions of the conventionally noble elements in Socrates' nature, especially since Socrates does not yet himself know whether he is bestial or divine (*Phaedrus* 230a1 ff.). Those who are sufficiently tough-minded to take seriously the comic episode of Alcibiades, and who are therefore immune to the excessive softness portrayed by the person and speech of Agathon, will accept the tragic nature of Platonic comedy without seeking refuge in the alternative tragicomedy of Aristophanes.

Chapter Seven

A. This paragraph, taken together with page 272 in the text, requires a further statement. When I first studied the *Symposium*, it was more or less clear to me that there were different kinds of presentations of the so-called theory of Ideas in the Platonic dialogues. It was not then sufficiently clear to me that the variation in the presentations corresponded to a variation in the content. Differently stated, I now regard it as certain that there is no theory of a uniform set of beings, usually called "Ideas" (ἰδέαι) or "forms" (εἴδη), in the Platonic dialogues. The hyperuranian beings of the *Phaedrus* are not the same as the beautiful itself; neither of these can be identified with the "greatest genera" of the *Sophist*. There is no need here to explore in detail the range of logical, phenomenological, ethical, and ontological instances of beings, natures, or powers that are introduced into the dialogues in the recurring attempt to account for identity, visibility, intelligibility, and the hierarchical ordering of nobility. I have done some of the work in my *Plato's "Sophist": The Drama of Original and Image* (New Haven, 1983). In this context, I want to make two points.

First: whatever interest may lie in a comparison of the various passages in the Platonic corpus that deal with Ideas, there is no substitute for studying each passage within its own dialogue. Plato did not write logical treatises, and he will never be understood by means of a crash course in elementary logic and set theory. There is no evidence in the dialogues of a theory of predication in the Aristotelian, let alone the Fregean, sense. And to think of the Idea of a cow or of justice as a mathematical set is to betray a standpoint that is alien to the textual evidence, not to mention our experience.

Second: the diversity of so-called Ideas is illuminating, not as evidence of an underlying and unifying theory in the modern sense of a construction (which contradicts what the Ideas are presumed to convey), but certainly of Plato's conviction that to be is to be intelligible and valuable, albeit in radically diverse ways. But it does not follow from the intelligibility of, say, beauty, a cow, and justice, that there is an underlying ontological structure, common to the three intelligibles yet different from each, that is itself intelligible, for example in the way that mathematical structure is intelligible apart from the diverse things we count or name. To put this in another way, to say that diverse things are diversely intelligible is not to say that intelligibility is separately and in the same way intelligible. The analysis of a cow's structure (assuming such an analysis to be possible) is not the same as the analysis of the structure of the Idea of the cow. What discursive sense can be made of the contention that the Idea of the cow has a structure other than the structure of the cow, which is common to all Ideas, and yet which shows itself in this specific instance as the structure or intelligible look of a cow? Ontological analysis, if it becomes sufficiently general, turns into logic, mathematics, or both. But that tells us nothing about beauty, cows, or justice.

What is the relation between intelligibility and beauty? This question is undoubtedly central to any understanding of Plato's portraits of Eros. Diotima claims that Eros is the desire for beauty (however, see the text, pp. 240 ff.), that knowledge (211c6) is not only beautiful but is the penultimate stage in the satisfaction of erotic desire, and that it leads directly to the ultimate stage of knowledge of the beautiful itself (211c7–8). Finally, she claims that this ultimate knowledge moves its possessor to live a life devoted to the generating of true instances of beauty (211e4 ff.). Diotima offers no arguments to support any of these contentions. She tells us nothing whatsoever of the nature of knowledge of beauty itself. Nothing is said to account for the ostensibly beautiful nature of knowledge of things other than beauty. Nor is the life to which she accords the highest praise, namely, parenting (τίκτειν) true virtue (212a3–5), the same as the life of pure theory or contemplation of the so-called Ideas. Finally, Diotima mysteriously shifts from beauty (τὸ καλόν) to virtue (ἀρετή), as though to echo the middle stage of her teaching, in which goodness is substituted for beauty. Surely the two are not synonymous. Should not the genuinely erotic mortal generate true instances of beauty, which in turn may be virtuous or vicious, or else neither the one nor the other?

It is all very well to say that, for the genuinely philosophical nature, knowledge is beautiful. This may be so, but it answers no questions. Instead it points to a disjunction between the philosophical and the unphilosophical natures, and thus returns us to the doctrine of the two Eroses (both of which may be struggling for dominance within the soul of the philosopher, as the Stesichorean myth in the *Phaedrus* suggests). If human beings, to employ a contemporary expression, are polymorphous perverse, then philosophers are those with an Eros dominated by philosophy. But this is circular; we require a distinct and reliable criterion in order to distinguish between philosophical and unphilosophical beauty. If the criterion is discursive, then it is itself subject to disagreement, as is obvious from the radical change in the course of time with respect to what constitutes knowledge, and concerning which type of knowledge is pertinent to philosophy. If the criterion is intuitive, as is the case with Diotima's vision of beauty, then it cannot be independently, that is, discursively, confirmed, whether to others or to oneself. One last consideration: Plato regularly speaks of beauty in conjunction with Euclidean order. If the order of the cosmos is non-Euclidean, then either Plato's "beauty itself" is an erroneous interpretation of a historical perspective, or else Platonism means nothing more than the perception of the beauty of whatever theoretical account of the cosmos is currently acknowledged. In the latter case, Platonism is the aesthetic enjoyment of the work of the human intellect. In neither case is it *Platonism*.

Chapter Eight

A. The word προσαναγκάζειν has an interesting role in Plato's dialogues. It is frequently employed to convey the notion of the resolution of a problem by technical force in such a way as to constitute a whole out of what might otherwise be construed as incompatible elements, or at least as elements that would not unite without the necessity imposed upon them by τέχνη. At 223d2 ff., Socrates is reported as forcing Aristophanes and Agathon to agree that the same person has the τέχνη for making comedy and tragedy. What one might almost call the natural division of talents may be overcome by technical force. The τέχνη in question, of course, is linguistic or discursive, not Hephaestean. Socrates' meaning may be clarified by considering a passage in the *Gorgias* (503d6–504a5). The context is political. Callicles, who is studying with Gorgias in order to prepare for a political career, has just cited Themistocles, Cimon, Miltiades, and Pericles as examples of superior orators. Socrates denies that they possess genuine ἀρετή (503c5), or the τέχνη (503d1) of fulfilling only those desires (ἐπιθυμιῶν) which make a man better. He then goes on to describe such a τέχνη. The good man who speaks for the best will say nothing at random; his discourse will on all points be guided by a specific intention (503d6–e1). He thus follows the procedures of the craftsmen (δημιουργοί), who select nothing at random, and who construct with a view to a specific form (503e1–4). Examples are painters, housebuilders, and shipwrights, and "whoever disposes whatever he does in a certain order, thereby forcing each part to be fitted for and to harmonize with the other, until the whole has been constructed (συστήσηται) as an ordered and well-arranged thing" (503e4–504a1). The τέχνη to which Socrates refers is described in still greater detail in the *Phaedrus* in an account from which I have previously quoted (p. lvi). The genuine rhetorical τέχνη, by means of which the same man will be able to produce all types of speech (261e12), requires every discourse to be constructed (συνεστάναι) like a living being (264c2 ff.), in other words, like a whole that is essentially different from its nonliving parts.

We do not adequately grasp the Socratic or Platonic conception of τέχνη if we think of it simply as mimesis of nature. In order to achieve the *eidos* of his intention, the craftsman must force an order onto the elements furnished by nature. This order is not present in nature, and neither are the forms, except in the sense that human intentionality is a natural endowment. A detailed analysis of the *Phaedrus* would show that the paradigm of the living being is not a reference to a natural model for philosophical rhetoric. I mention only two points here. First, there is no genuine analogy between the order of parts in an animal and the order of parts in a speech. Second, each speech must be constructed with a view to a definite intention that is independent of the speech, whereas the principle of intentionality is intrinsic, to one degree or another, to the animal. We need not pursue such an analysis here. For us the main point is that the rhetorical technician constrains his material to change its form, exactly as does the demiurge. This is not true merely of political or epideictic rhetoric; it is also true of technical philosophical speech. I will illustrate this with passages from Plato's two theoretical works par excellence, the *Sophist* and the *Statesman*. In these dialogues, the point is made by the Eleatic Stranger rather than by Socrates. This will support my contention that the thesis of forcing is not just Socratic but Platonic. In his attempt to resolve the problem of how to speak meaningfully of nonbeing, the Stranger introduces the greatest genera and tries to explain how they combine by their natural power. More comprehensively, "discourse comes to us from the weaving-together of the forms with one another" (*Sophist* 259e5–6). However, there is a difference between the greatest genera (being, rest, change, sameness, otherness) and the laws (as we may call them) of their combination and separation. The natural properties named by the first three genera are immediately obvious, as is plain from their introduction into the discussion. The Stranger has only to ask Theaetetus whether he is aware of them and to refer to them in discourse for his young interlocutor to agree immediately (e.g., 250a4–7 for change and rest; a8–10 for being). The natures of sameness and otherness are not immediately obvious because exactly what we mean by these names already depends upon what we have decided about the laws of combination and separation (254e2–255a3). Our "prophetic vision" of rest, change, and being (ἀπομαντεύεσθαί τι τὸ ὄν . . . ; 250c1–2) does not extend to these laws, and hence not to sameness and otherness. Therefore Theaetetus cannot directly say what he means by being, although he grants the vision of being itself. And he does not at all see "prophetically" how the forms combine (e.g., 251d5–e3).

What I have called the laws of combination and separation of the natural elements are not furnished by nature. They are furnished by a τέχνη analogous to the τέχναι of grammar or spelling and musical composition (253a8–b7). The Stranger calls this technique an ἐπιστήμη, namely, dialectic, the science of the philosopher (253b8–e7). For our purposes, whether the dialectical ἐπιστήμη is something more than a τέχνη (although it cannot be something less) is not the crucial point. What is crucial for us is that the ἐπιστήμη is not furnished directly by nature or by prophetic vision. Theaetetus is not alone in his incapacity to discern directly or easily the laws of ontological combination and separation. The genera commune with one another by nature (257a8–9), since otherwise there would be no whole, no cosmos or order, and hence no discourse (259d9–e7). But as to which genera combine and which do not, this knowledge depends upon our technical knowledge; more specifically, it depends upon our technical resolution of what is meant by nonbeing. However, the general communion of forms requires technical argumentation, and hence persuasion: "Note then," the Stranger says to Theaetetus, "how we have fought with and constrained (διεμαχόμεθα καὶ προσηναγκάζομεν) our opponents in the knick of time to allow one thing to mingle with another" (260a1–3).

The discursive construction of the whole is accomplished by a technical constraint, which in the present instance depends upon the resolution of the problem of nonbeing. I have discussed the details of this resolution in my book on the *Sophist* and need not repeat them here. Instead, I turn to the *Statesman* for the reference that will complete our present survey of passages bearing upon *Symposium* 223c6–d8. The Eleatic Stranger is now attempting to define the ἐπιστήμη or τέχνη (both terms are used) of the statesman. At a critical moment in the discussion, it is necessary to establish that the greater and the less are related, not merely to each other, but also to the measure or mean (τὸ μετρίον: the proper amount). A failure to accomplish this will destroy "the arts themselves and all of their works, including the political art, which we are now trying to define" (284a5–7). This is, as it were, the practico-productive analogue to the theoretical problem in the *Sophist*. In both cases we are concerned with an ordered and well-adorned whole. The Stranger then makes the following crucial assertion: "just as in the case of the Sophist we forced nonbeing to be (προσηναγκάσαμεν εἶναι τὸ μὴ ὄν) since the logos had escaped us at that point, so now must we not force (προσαναγκαστέον) the greater and the less to be measured, not only with respect to each other, but also with respect to the genesis of the measure (τὴν τοῦ μετρίου γένεσιν)?" (284b7–c1). We should also observe the Stranger's statement that the task with respect to the measure is much greater than was the work of forcing nonbeing to be (284c6).

The genesis of the measure is a technical or productive task, because what counts as the right amount in human affairs differs from case to case. There is no natural standard of the fitting, to be uniformly imitated in all cases. *Phronesis*, or practical intelligence, is a natural faculty, but its work is artificial. Hence argument, that is, war or constraint, is necessary in order to enforce agreement. The political whole is an artificial or technical construction or σύστημα. But so too is the ontological whole, since its intelligibility in discursive terms (as opposed to its merely theoretical visibility) depends upon the enforcement of a technical resolution to the problem of nonbeing, and hence of combination and separation. This is the indispensable background for a proper understanding of the culminating account of the banquet in the *Symposium*. The intention of the philosopher, or master of the comprehensive rhetorical τέχνη, enforces a whole onto human experience by way of a comprehensive account of human experience, namely, via the Platonic dialogues. And this of course is the achievement of Plato, not of Socrates. Socrates is an ἰδιώτης. He lacks the requisite τέχνη. But this is to say that he is erotically defective, as in fact follows from his very claim to possess the erotic τέχνη.

BIBLIOGRAPHICAL APPENDIX

Hartmut Buchner, *Eros und Sein* (Bonn, 1965)

This book reached me too late to be consulted as I was writing my own study. Because of its great philosophical interest, it deserves more elaborate discussion than a footnote would normally allow. Despite the very detailed disagreement which follows, I recommend Buchner's dissertation as perhaps the most important study on the *Symposium* that has come to my attention.

Buchner's dissertation, which might well be subtitled "Diotima as Heidegger," covers only the section 199c3–212c3, and offers to explicate "den inneren Zusammenhang von Eros und Sein bzw. Nicht-sein . . ." (p. 7). Buchner justifies this restriction of attention on the grounds that we must first understand the Diotima section before we can understand the previous speeches (p. 15: nothing is said of Alcibiades' speech), and that, whereas the dialogue form was necessary for Plato's contemporaries, in order to lead them gradually out of the erroneous beliefs of the time, it is unnecessary for us who live in a different world and age, and who want to enter into philosophical conversation with Plato. For us, it is better to start with the root of Plato's teaching (pp. 19 ff.).

As a consequence, Buchner misses almost entirely the dependence of Diotima's speech upon what comes before and after. Despite many acute observations, and occasional precision in noticing what Plato did or did not write, he becomes progressively more arbitrary in his choice of what parts of even the Diotima section are suitable for comment. This arbitrariness, together with an also progressively increasing dependence upon (or surrender to) Heideggerian interpretations and terms, leads to a radically unsatisfactory analysis, all the more frustrating in view of Buchner's manifest intelligence. Buchner begins with the Heideggerian notion of a distinction between the ontological and the ontic, which leads him to ignore the human details of the dialogue, or to restate them in language which obscures rather than illuminates their status as facts, and precisely in the Heideggerian sense of facticity. An "ontology," after all, is a λόγος about τὰ ὄντα. No ontology is satisfactory which does not "save the phenomena," or illuminate the ὄντα in the full detail of

343

their concrete specificity. Buchner misses altogether the connection in Plato between "ontology" and "politics"; hence, not only is he insensitive to the nature of the dialogue form, but he hastily transforms ἔρως into a "transcendental-ontological" *Geschehen,* as though Plato were a Heideggerianized Hegel!

Differently stated, Buchner equates Being, Eros, and philosophy (thanks to careless textual analysis), all defined as *Verweilen, Geschehen,* and even *Geschichte* (pp. 38, 53, 75 ff., 80, 82, 114, 119–23, 131). Consequently, the difference between γένεσις and οὐσία is obliterated, and ποίησις (frequently identified as "transcendental will") is given the central position in Plato's thought; that is, the Ideas are now in effect conceived as "made" or "posited," and the beautiful in itself (which Buchner identifies with the good in itself) is eroticized, or rendered indistinguishable from Eros as ascent (pp. 94–95, 100, 107 ff., 134, 144, 149–50, 161 ff.). In Buchner, as in Heidegger, it becomes impossible to distinguish between man and Being: both are transcendence; and, in Platonic language, there is no distinction between ἔρως and φιλία (pp. 91, 110, 120, 140–41). Man then becomes the transcendental will, or the erotic projection of beauty itself (= Being) by the very work of erotic striving (pp. 108–09, 119–23). That is, man makes Being, or is the (erotic) ground for the Geschehen of Being (p. 131). Hence, the distinction between γένεσις and οὐσία is "sublated" into the positing, uncovering-covering, poetic will of man as himself a *Geschehnis;* i.e. man is presented as making himself and the world, the latter (the generated cosmos) of which is identified with Being altogether.

Some of the "inadequacies" which follow from this construction are attributed to Plato (e.g. pp. 89–90, 113, 122–23); others Buchner does not seem to notice. Of the various errors, either of commission or omission, which Buchner makes, I shall mention only these. (1) On pp. 35–42, he establishes the "temporal" sense of οὐσία in Plato by quoting *Parmenides* 151e7 ff. But, as I have argued elsewhere (Rosen, *Ideas*), this passage is taken from Hypothesis II of a complex dialectic designed to show the paradoxes generated precisely by the identification of Being and Time. (2) In the same section Buchner says that Plato never raises the question of man as such, but always of *a* man determined in a specific way. This shows Buchner's inability to appreciate the function of the dialogue form as beginning always from δόξα, and is a strange deviation from his own interpretation of Eros as man, conceived "transcendentally-ontologically." (3) On p. 44 he says: Jedes ἀγαθόν ist, so sagt Sokrates, in sich zugleich auch ein καλόν (201c2)." But a glance at the text shows that Socrates asks a question of Agathon: τἀγαθὰ οὐ καὶ καλὰ δοκεῖ σοι εἶναι; It is Agathon, not Socrates, who asserts; and his answer is not independent of his name or dramatic function. (4) Buchner's discussion of Plato's "onto-theology" (pp. 75 ff.) shows no awareness of the political aspects to Plato's "theology," and certainly no recognition of the relevant quarrel between poetry and philosophy. For instance, he never mentions the absence of justice from the list of Eros' traits, nor the connection between Eros and hybris. (5) In making Eros equal the daimonic (or the Metaxy), and so sublating the difference between γένεσις and οὐσία, he does not explain the "positive" or "unveiling" component of the resultant Eros. How can the world present itself or hold itself together, even long enough to generate or "hand itself down" (Überliefern), when Eros is described by Diotima as lacking what he seeks? Even if Eros "squanders what he gets," how does he get it to begin with?

But perhaps I have said enough to indicate my objections to Buchner's stimulating dissertation. It is an excellent example of the dangers which ensue from a surrender to ontological μανία that forgets altogether the significance of θεῖα μοίρα.

BIBLIOGRAPHY

Apelt, O., *Platonische Aufsätze*, Leipzig, 1912.

Ast, F., *Lexicon Platonicum, Darmstadt*, 1956.

Aubenque, P., *Le Problème de l'être chez Aristote*, Paris, 1962.

Bacon, H., "Socrates Crowned," *The Virginia Quarterly Review, 35* (1959).

Benardete, S., "Some Misquotations of Homer in Plato," *Phronesis, 8* (1963).

———, "Sophocles' Oedipus Tyrannus," in *Ancients and Moderns*, New York, 1964.

Bluck, R. S., *Plato's Phaedo*, London, 1955.

Boeder, H., *Grund und Gegenwart als Frageziel der Früh-Griechischen Philosophie*, Hague, 1962.

Bourgey, L., *Observation et expérience chez les médicins de la Collection Hippocratique*, Paris, 1953.

Brann, E., *The Music of the Republic*, Annapolis, Md., 1966.

Brentlinger, J. A., "The Cycle of Becoming in Plato's *Symposium*," PhD Dissertation, Yale University, 1962.

———, "Sur le 'Banquet' de Platon," *Études de philosophie ancienne et de philosophie moderne*, Paris, 1954.

Brumbaugh, R. S., *Plato on the One*, New Haven, 1961.

Burn, A. R., *Persia and the Greeks*, New York, 1962.

Burnet, J., *Early Greek Philosophy*, London, 1899.

Bury, R. G., *The Symposium of Plato*, Cambridge, 1932.

Cornford, F. M., "The Doctrine of Eros in Plato's Symposium," in *The Unwritten Philosophy*, Cambridge, 1950.

———, *Plato's Cosmology*, London, 1948.

———, *Plato's Theory of Knowledge*, New York, 1957.

Delcourt, M., *Hermaphrodite*, Paris, 1958.

———, *Héphaistos ou la légende du magicien*, Paris, 1957.

Derbolav, J., *Erkenntnis und Entscheidung*, Vienna, 1954.

de Romilly, J., *Thucydides and Athenian Imperialism*, New York, 1963.

de Vries, G. D., "Apollodore dans le 'Banquet' de Platon," *Revue des Études Grecques, 48* (1935).

Diels, H., *Fragmente der Vorsokratiker,* 3 vols. Berlin, 1956.

Dover, K. J., "The Date of Plato's *Symposium,*" *Phronesis, 10* (1965).

Dupréel, E., *Les Sophistes,* Neuchâtel, 1948.

Edelstein, L., "The Role of Eryximachus in Plato's Symposium," American Philological Association *Transactions and Proceedings, 76* (1945).

———, "Platonic Anonymity," *American Journal of Philology, 82* (1962).

Ehlers, B., *Eine vorplatonische Deutung des sokratischen Eros, in Zetemata, 41,* Munich, 1966.

Fessard, G., *De l'actualité historique,* Paris, 1960.

Festugière, A. J., *Contemplation et vie contemplative selon Platon,* Paris, 1950.

———, *Hippocrate: l'ancienne médécine,* Paris, 1948.

Finley, M. I., *The Ancient Greeks,* New York, 1963.

François, G., *Le polythéisme et l'emploi au singulier de mots θεός, Δαίμων,* Paris, 1957.

Freud, S., "Why War?," in *Collected Papers,* New York, 1956.

Friedländer, P., *Plato: An Introduction,* New York, 1964.

Fustel de Coulanges, Numa D., *The Ancient City,* New York, 1956.

Gadamer, H. J., *Platos dialektische Ethik,* Leipzig, 1931.

Gaiser, K., *Protreptik und Paränese bei Platon,* Stuttgart, 1959.

———, *Platons ungeschriebene Philosophie,* Stuttgart, 1963.

Gilson, E., *Discours de la méthode (Descartes),* Paris, 1947.

Gould, T., *Platonic Love,* London, 1963.

Grube, G. M. A., *Plato's Thought,* Boston, 1958.

Hackforth, R., "Immortality in Plato's Symposium," *Classical Review, 64* (1950).

———, *Plato's Phaedrus,* Cambridge, 1952.

Hatzfeld, J., *Alcibiade,* Paris, 1951.

Hegel, G. W. F., *Die Philosophie Platons,* Stuttgart, 1962.

Heidegger, M., *Sein und Zeit,* Tübingen, 1953.

———, *Einführung in die Metaphysik,* Tübingen, 1953.

———, *Nietzsche,* Pfullingen, 1961.

Hobbes, T., *Leviathan,* Oxford, 1947.

Hoffman, E., *Über Platons Symposion,* Heidelberg, 1947.

———, *Platon,* Zürich, 1950.

Hornsby, R., "Significant Action in the Symposium," *Classical Journal, 52* (1956).

Hug, A., *Platons Symposion,* 2d ed. Leipzig, 1884.

Huit, C., *Etudes sur le Banquet de Platon,* Paris, 1887.

Hume, D., *A Treatise of Human Nature,* Oxford, 1955.

Isenberg, M., *The Order of the Discourses in Plato's Symposium,* Chicago, 1940.

Jaeger, W., *Aristotle,* Oxford, 1962.

———, *Paideia,* 3 vols. New York, 1943.

———, *Humanistische Reden und Vorträge,* Berlin, 1960.

Jeanmaire, H., *Dionysos,* Paris, 1951.

Jones, W. H. S., *Hippocrates,* 3 vols. Cambridge, Mass, 1947.

Kahn, C., *Anaximander and the Origins of Greek Cosmology,* New York, 1960.

Kant, I., "Von einem Neuerdings Erhobenen Vornehmen Ton in der Philosophie," in *Werke, 3,* Wiesbaden, 1958.

Kapp, E., *Greek Foundations of Traditional Logic,* New York, 1942.

Kerenyi, K., *Pythagoras und Orpheus,* Zürich, 1950.

———, *Prometheus,* New York, 1963.

Kern, O., *Die Religion der Griechen,* Berlin, 1963.

Kierkegaard, S., *Über den Begriff der Ironie,* Düsseldorf, 1961.

———, *Philosophical Fragments,* Princeton, 1962.

———, *Concluding Unscientific Postscript,* Princeton, 1944.

Klein, J., "Die griechische Logistik und die Entstehung der Algebra," *Quellen und Studien zur Geschichte der Mathematik, Astronomie, und Physik, 3* (B), Berlin, 1936.

———, *A Commentary on Plato's Meno,* Chapel Hill, 1965.

Krämer, H. J., *Arete bei Platon und Aristoteles,* Heidelberg, 1959.

———, "Retraktationen zum Problem des esoterischen Platon," in *Museum Helveticum, 21* (1964, Fasc. 3).

———, "Die platonische Akademie und das Problem einer systematischen Interpretation der Philosophie Platons," *Kant-Studien, 55* (1964).

Kranz, W., "Diotima," *Die Antike* (2) (1926).

———, "Platonica," *Philologus, 102* (1958).

Krüger, G., *Einsicht und Leidenschaft,* Frankfurt-am-Main, 1948.

Kucharski, P., *Les chemins du savoir,* Paris, 1949.

Kuhn, H., "The True Tragedy: On the relationship between Greek tragedy and Plato," *Harvard Studies in Classical Philology,* 1952, *52–53.*

————, *Sokrates*, Munich, 1959.

Kühn, J. H., *System- und Methodenprobleme im Corpus Hippocraticum*, Wiesbaden, 1956.

Lévêque, P., *Agathon*, Paris, 1955.

Levinson, R. B., *In Defense of Plato*, Cambridge, Mass., 1953.

Löwith, K., *Von Hegel zu Nietzsche*, Stuttgart, 1953.

Macdowell, D., *Andokides, On the Mysteries*, Oxford, 1962.

Machiavelli, N., *Il Principe e Discorsi*, Milan, 1960.

Maimonides, *The Guide of the Perplexed*, Chicago, 1963.

Malebranche, N., *Recherche de la vérité*, Paris, Flammarion, n.d.

Marcel, R., *Marsile Ficin: Commentaire sur le Banquet de Platon*, Paris, 1956.

Markus, R., "Love and the Will," in *Christian Faith and Philosophy*, by Armstrong and Markus, London, 1960.

Marrou, H. I., *A History of Education in Antiquity* (New York: 1964)

Marx, K., and F. Engels, *Die Deutsche Ideologie*, Berlin, 1960.

Merlan, P., "Form and Content in Plato's Philosophy," *Journal of the History of Ideas, 8* (1947).

Milton, J., "Areopagitica," in *Complete Poetry and Selected Prose of John Milton* New York, n.d.

Moravcsik, J., "Reason and Eros in the Ascent-Passage of the Symposium," unpublished lecture, 1961.

Morrison, J. S., "Four Notes on Plato's Symposium," *Classical Quarterly, 14* (May 1964).

Neumann, H., "Diotima's Concept of Love," *American Journal of Philology, 86* (1965).

Nietzsche, F., *Vom Nutzen und Nachteil der Historie*, in *Werke*, ed. K. Schlechta, 3 vols. Munich, 1954.

————, *Menschliches Allzumenschliches*, in *Werke*, ed. Schlecta.

————, *Also Sprach Zarathustra*, in *Werke*, ed. Schlecta.

————, *Jenseits von Gut und Böse*, in *Werke*, ed. Schlecta.

————, *Der Wille zur Macht*, ed. A. Baeumler, Stuttgart, 1959.

Nilsson, M., *A History of Greek Religion*, Oxford, 1949.

Oehler, K., *Die Lehre vom noetischen und dianoetischen Denken bei Platon und Aristoteles*, Munich, 1962.

————, "Neue Fragmente zum esoterische Platon," *Hermes 93* (4) (Oct. 1965).

————, "Die entmythologisierte Platon," in *Zeitschrift für Philosophische Forschung, 19* (1965).

O'Neill, W. J., *Proclus' Alcibiades I*, Hague, 1965.

Otto, W., *Dionysos*, Frankfurt-am-Main, 1960.

———, *Die Götter Griechenlands*, Frankfurt-am-Main, 1961.

Owen, G. E. L., "Plato and Parmenides on the Timeless Present," *The Monist, 50* (July 1966).

Pauly-Wissowa, *Pauly-Wissowa Realenzyclopädie*, 24 vols. Stuttgart, 1894–1962.

Pease, A. S., *Cicero's De Natura Deorum*, Cambridge, Mass., 1955.

Plochmann, G. K., "Hiccups and Hangovers in the Symposium," *Bucknell Review 11* (1963).

Reinhardt, K., *Aischylos*, Bern, 1949.

———, "Prometheus," in *Tradition und Geist*, Göttingen, 1960.

———, "Aristophanes und Athen," in *Tradition und Geist*, Göttingen, 1960.

———, "Platons Mythen," in *Vermaechtnis der Antike*, Göttingen, 1960.

Rettig, G. F. R., *Platons Symposion*, Halle, 1876.

Rieff, P., *Freud, the Mind of the Moralist*, New York, 1959.

Robin, L., *La théorie platonicienne de l'amour*, Paris, 1908.

———, *Platon, œuvres complètes, 4*, Paris, 1929.

———, *La théorie platonicienne des idées et des nombres d'après Aristote*, Hildesheim, 1963.

Robinson, R., *Plato's Earlier Dialectic*, Oxford, 1953.

Rose, H. J., *A Handbook of Greek Mythology*, New York, 1959.

Rosen, S. H., "Thought and Touch," *Phronesis, 6* (1961).

———, "Wisdom," *Review of Metaphysics, 16* (1962).

———, "Thales," *Essays in Philosophy*, University Park, Pa., 1962.

———, "Ideas," *Review of Metaphysics, 16* (1963).

———, "Herodotus Reconsidered," *Giornale di Metafisica, 18* (15 Marzo-Giugno 1963).

———, "The Role of Eros in Plato's *Republic*," *Review of Metaphysics, 18* (March 1965).

———, "The Irrational Choice," *Journal of General Education, 17* (April 1965).

———, "Heidegger's Interpretation of Plato" in *Journal of Existentialism* (1967).

Schleiermacher, *Introductions to the Dialogues of Plato*, Cambridge, 1836.

Schmid, W., "Das Sokratesbild der Wolken," *Philologus, 97* (1954).

Shorey, P., *The Unity of Plato's Thought*, Chicago, 1904.

Skemp, J. B., *The Theory of Motion in Plato's Later Dialogues*, Cambridge, 1942.

Souilhé, J., *La notion platonicienne d'intermédiaire dans la philosophie des dialogues*, Paris, 1919.

Stenzel, J., *Platon der Erzieher*, Leipzig, 1928.

———, "Über zwei Begriffe der platonischen Mystik . . . ," in *Kleine Schriften*, Darmstadt, 1957.

Stokes, M., "Hesiodic and Milesian Cosmogonies, Pt. II," *Phronesis*, 8 (1963).

Strauss, L., *Persecution and the Art of Writing*, Glencoe, Ill., 1952.

———, "How Farabi Read Plato's *Laws*," in *What is Political Philosophy?*, Glencoe, Ill., 1959.

———, *What Is Political Philosophy?*, Glencoe, Ill., 1959.

———, *On Tyranny*, New York, 1963.

———, *The City and Man*, Chicago, 1964.

———, *Socrates and Aristophanes*, New York, 1966.

Tait, M., "Spirit, Gentleness, and the Philosophic Nature in the Republic," in *American Philological Association, 80* (1949).

Taylor, A. E., *Plato*, New York, 1958.

Untersteiner, M., *The Sophists*, New York, 1954.

Vlastos, G., ΙΣΟΝΟΜΙΑ ΠΟΛΙΤΙΚΗ, in *Isonomia*, Berlin, 1964.

von Arnim, H., *Platos Jugenddialoge und die Entstehungszeit des Phaidros*, Berlin, 1960.

West, M. L., *Hesiod: Theogony*, Oxford, 1966.

Westerink, L. G., *Prolegomena to Platonic Philosophy*, Amsterdam, 1962.

Wieland, W., *Die aristotelische Physik*, Göttingen, 1962.

Wolfson, H., *Philo*, Cambridge, Mass., 1947.

Zimmern, A., *The Greek Commonwealth*, New York, 1956.

SUPPLEMENTAL BIBLIOGRAPHY

I list in chronological order some significant articles on the *Symposium* that either escaped my attention when preparing the first edition or that appeared after it was sent to the printer.

Bollack, J., "Eros und die Liebe," *Die neue Rundschau* 72 (1961).

Vretska, K., "Zu Form und Aufbau von Platons Symposion," *Serta Philologica Aenipontana, Innsbrücker Beiträge zur Kulturwissenschaft* 7/8 1962.

Wippern, J., "Eros und Unsterblichkeit in der Diotima-Rede des Symposions," in *Synusia. Festgabe für W. Schadewalt*, Pfullingen, 1965.

Vlastos, G., "The Individual as Object of Love in Plato's Dialogues," in *Platonic Studies*, Princeton, 1973; 2d ed. 1981.

Kosman, L. A., "Platonic Love," in *Facets of Plato's Philosophy*, ed. W. Werkmeister [*Phronesis*, supp. vol. 2 (1976)].

Diez, G., "Platons Symposion. Symbolbezüge und Symbolverständnis," in *Symbolon* 4 (n.s., 1978).

Sider, D. "Plato's *Symposium* as Dionysian Festival," in *Quadarni Urbinati di Cultura Classica*, no. 33 (1980).

Saxonhouse, A. W., "Eros and the Female in Greek Political Thought," *Political Theory* 12 (1984).

———. "The Net of Hephaestus: Aristophanes' Speech in Plato's *Symposium*," in *Interpretation* 13 (1985).

Nussbaum, M. C., "The Speech of Alcibiades: a reading of the *Symposium*," in *The Fragility of Goodness*, Cambridge, 1986.

INDEX

Achilles, 6, 41, 57, 257, 317 f.
Acumenus, 7, 202 n.
Admetus, 54
Aeschines, 64 n.
Aeschylus, 57, 65 ff., 170, 287
Agamemnon, 23
Agathon: general significance, xxxi,
xxxv, 3, 7 f., 12 f., 22 ff., 31 f., 91,
210 ff.; and Socrates, 15 f., 20, 26 ff.,
202 ff., 215–22, 224, 227, 232, 240 f.,
243, 247 f., 253, 261, 277; and Aristodemus, 17; and Phaedrus, 44, 56;
main teaching, 51, 159–96 passim,
198, 200, 236; and Pausanias, 60,
74; and Aristophanes, 120 f., 148 n.;
and Alcibiades, 283–89, 298–304,
308, 321–26
Agriculture, 108, 116 f.
Ajax, 309
Alcestis, 54 ff., 70, 257
Alcibiades: general significance, xix,
3–8, 15 n., 22, 24, 31 ff., 164 n.; main
teaching, xx, 19 f., 24 n., 198, 277–
327 passim; and Dionysus, 28 n.,
29, 34; and Agathon, 160–65; and
Socrates, 203, 232, 234
Alcibiades I, 280 ff., 284
Alcibiades II, 280
Alcidamas, 183 n.
Alcmaeon, 94, 277
Anaxagoras, 222, 224
Anonymous Commentator, xxix,
xxxix
Antenor, 317 f.
Anytus, 308
Aphrodite: and other gods, 38, 121,
152, 185 f.; and Pausanias, 48, 62 f.,
69 n., 73; and Eryximachus, 110;
birth of, 231 f., 302
Apollo: and Zeus, 3; and Apollodorus,
11 n.; and Socrates, 65 n., 297 f.; and

Apollo *(Cont.)*
medicine, 98, 191 ff., 226; and Aristophanes, 120 f., 141, 145 f.; and
Hermes, 153 n.; and Alcibiades, 324
Apollodorus: general significance, 7–
16, 38, 41, 264; and Pausanias,
90 n.; and Alcibiades, 290
Apology, xxxv, 11 n., 20 f., 29, 165 n.,
202 n., 222 n., 318
Ares, 141 n., 153, 185 f.
Aristodemus: general significance,
6 ff., 12 n., 16–25 passim, 30, 33, 198,
203 n., 234, 325 f.; and Agathon,
26 f., 202; and Alcibiades, 290, 304,
321
Aristophanes: main teaching, xxx,
2 ff., 120–58 passim, 198–202, 236;
general significance, 8 f., 12 n., 24 f.,
30 ff., 38, 118 n., 260; and Agathon,
159–65 passim, 169, 172 f., 178,
179 n., 185, 191 f.; and Socrates,
205, 210, 215, 229, 231, 244, 250,
325 f.; and Alcibiades, 281 n., 283–
87, 297, 307 n., 316
Aristotle: and Plato, xxi, xxvi, 3, 47,
134 n., 174 n., 198 n., 239, 247, 253;
Topics, xxi n., xxiv n.; *Metaphysics,*
4 n., 46 n., 111 n., 121 n., 138 n.,
217 n., 228 n.; *Rhetoric,* 16 n., 205 n.,
298 n.; *Nichomachean Ethics,* 21 n.,
216 n., 219 n.; *Politics,* 41 n., 69 n.,
75 n.; *Poetics,* 196 n.; *Physics,*
228 n.; *De Anima,* 228 n.
Asclepius, 94, 98, 104, 191 f.
Aspasia, 223 f.
Atē, 178 f.
Athena, 24, 36 n., 62, 67, 149 n., 191
Athenian Stranger, xiii, xviii f., 31,
71, 100, 108, 156 n.
Athens: general references to, 7, 13,
75–86 passim, 161; and Aristoph-

INDEX

Xanthippe, 204

Xenophanes, 110

Xenophon: *Memorabilia,* 17 f., 25 n., 42 n., 44 n., 60 n., 61 n., 128 n., 210 n., 236 n., 280–283 nn., 291 n., 311 n.; *Symposium,* 26 n., 69 n., 318 n.; *Cyropaideia,* 77 n.; *Anabasis,* 162 n.

Zeus: and the gods, 3, 62, 121, 123, 141, 149 n., 152, 192 f., 297; and Eros, 11 n., 69 n., 129 f., 231, 236, 255; and politics, 42, 65 ff., 117, 156, 191; and hybris, 124; and the circlemen, 142–48, 157, 163, 178 f.; and Aristophanes, 198; and Socrates, 227; and Alcibiades, 306, 321, 323 f.